The Evaluation
of Social Programs

THE EVALUATION OF SOCIAL PROGRAMS

Edited by Clark C. Abt

SAGE Publications   **Beverly Hills**   **London**

For information address:

SAGE Publications, Inc.
275 South Beverly Drive
Beverly Hills, California 90212

SAGE Publications Ltd.
St. George's House / 44 Hatton Garden
London EC1N 8ER

Printed in the United States of America

International Standard Book Number 0-8039-0735-4

Library of Congress Catalog Card No. 76-40712

FIRST PRINTING

CONTENTS

III

PAYOFFS OF EVALUATION RESEARCH

IV

RESEARCH VERSUS DECISION REQUIREMENTS AND BEST PRACTICES OF EVALUATION

V

EVALUATION OF HEALTH PROGRAMS

VI

EVALUATION OF EDUCATION PROGRAMS

VII

RESEARCH ALLOCATION STRATEGIES

PREFACE

This book consists of the formal and informal discussions at a conference on Social Programs Evaluation sponsored by and held at Abt Associates Inc. in Cambridge, Massachusetts on September 23 and 24 of 1974. I attempted to bring together some of the leading practitioners of evaluation research from universities and other independent research organizations with experienced government officials who are consumers of such research. There were about 100 participants,* representing much of the evaluation research community and all of its diverse institutional, disciplinary, and problem-oriented components.

The common concern we addressed was our desire to improve both the scientific quality and policy utility of social programs evaluation. We were aware of our responsibilities for providing government executives and legislators with valid, relevant, and timely information to assist them in making sensible social policy and social program decisions—decisions such as whether or not to start, modify, expand, contract, or terminate major social programs. As a community of applied social scientists devoted to improving government social policies and programs through scientific evaluation research, we wanted to learn from each other how we could improve our work.

It was the general concensus that we did learn something from each other at that conference. Our belief that there were some important evaluation issues ably analyzed at that conference motivated the preparation and publication of this book. We hope that other evaluation researchers and research users will obtain useful ideas and insights for their own work.

I want to express my gratitude and respect for the many distinguished social scientists and U.S. government officials who created the contents of the conference and this book. They contributed many days of their time and energies without pay. Their knowledge, skills, and informed opinions sometimes conflict but that may be taken as an

---

*For a complete list of participants, see p. 477.

indication of robust dedication to the search for truth, in a field where the intellectual tools are still being developed while their finished use is daily demanded in the muddy matrix of social policy analysis.

The conference that produced the contents of the book would not have been possible without the resourceful organizational skills and energetic charm of the conference coordinator, Ms. Perenna Fleming, and the devoted assistance of Ms. Lori Sullivan, Jackie Thomas, and Alice Madio. The book as well owes its existence to Ms. Fleming's continuing efforts, and to those of Ms. Marianne Rusk, Kathy Lewallen, Barbara Jaffe; proofreaders Michael Brannon, Len Andersen; production coordinator Karen Malmberg; and to Ruth Brannon and Alan Kornheiser for a careful and difficult job of copy editing. My thanks to the writers, speakers, organizers, and the publishers of Sage Publications, Sara and George McCune, for helping to create this book.

Clark C. Abt
Cambridge, Mass.
2 June 1976

INTRODUCTION

The contributors to this volume share (with the editor) one basic goal: to determine how social program evaluation can be made more effective and efficient in achieving policy relevance and scientific validity. In the following pages, many leading practitioners and users of social programs evaluation share their experience in the field, identify the major obstacles in doing this kind of evaluation, and exchange ideas on how to improve evaluation techniques and the policy relevance of evaluation findings.

Certain historical facts made the conference on which this volume was based particularly important. During the previous decade the federal government had expanded its social welfare programs. Recently, however, the expansion policy evolved into a policy of retrenchment. Social programs were being severely criticized for taking an ever-increasing share of the federal dollar. Therefore, automatic increase or even renewal of program funding was past. Programs had to be justified in terms of effectiveness, efficiency, and equity. The evaluation of the benefits and costs of these programs took on renewed importance.

The contributors to this volume include representatives of four of the sectors of society most directly involved in social programs evaluations: government, universities, charitable foundations, and independent research organizations. Some of the researchers involved began their careers by doing systems analysis for the Department of Defense; others began as university professors. As national priorities shifted to the developing field of social science research applied to education, employment, housing, health, criminal justice, and environmental protection, they were attracted to interdisciplinary programs in these areas.

The differences between social sciences research and physical sciences research are representative of the problems that make social programs evaluation so difficult. Evaluation research can depend very little upon proven theories. Opportunities to stimulate, observe, and test behaviors of social groups under carefully controlled conditions are limited. The nature of the data being collected usually requires a lengthy and costly survey. Political realities and decentralized decision-making processes, particularly in education, health and housing, often negate the impact of evaluation on policy decisions. These conditions of applied social research create challenging problems for its practitioners, evaluators, users, and funding agencies.

This volume is divided into seven parts—corresponding to the Conference's seven panel discussions: 1) *social experiments,* 2) *impacts* of evaluation research on policy decision, 3) *payoffs* of this research, 4) *best practices* of evaluation, 5) *health programs evaluation,* 6) *education programs evaluation,* and 7) better *research allocation strategies.* There were also several round table discussions, and two plenary sessions presenting the seven panel reports.

Part I is devoted to the "Evaluation of Social Experiments" (based on a panel chaired by the late Professor Paul Lazarsfeld of Columbia University). A survey of social experimentation as a research method for social program evaluation is offered, and examples of several major social experiments are described. Professor Henry Riecken of the University of Pennsylvania advocates the use of social experiments to evaluate social programs by identifying the weaknesses of the post hoc evaluations of the 1960's, primarily the evaluator's tendency to uncover only negative evidence. Professor Riecken also argues that demonstration programs have shortcomings as evaluation tools because they do not have randomly assigned participants as controls.

Dr. Ira Lowry of the Rand Corporation discusses HUD's Housing Assistance Supply Experiment being carried out in South Bend, Indiana and Green Bay, Wisconsin. This program is intended to test the effects of a full-scale housing allowance program on the housing market and on residential relocation. It represents unique pioneering in the field of social experimentation because it is long-term (10 years), enrolls everyone in the eligible population (local saturation), and examines the indirect effects of the treatment on other groups. A program of this scope encounters many difficulties, including survival in a politically sensitive arena, administration, pressure from the client for premature findings, and the danger that the program administrator will develop a personal stake in its outcome and thus bias the analysis.

Dr. Joseph Newhouse of the Rand Corporation discusses HEW's Health Insurance Experiment, in which 2,000 families are enrolled under 11 different treatments varying the amount a family must contribute toward coverage by a health plan.

Professor Kenneth J. Arrow of Harvard University feels no fear of the costs of social experiments, stating that the benefits are likely to heavily outweigh the costs. He does express concern over the limitations of extrapolating from one scale to another in both magnitude and time. He also urges experiments designed to reveal the underlying relationships in complex social systems. Professor Richard Light of Harvard University makes important distinctions between control and randomization. Although favoring randomized controlled evaluations as ideal, he defends the utility of observational studies by showing how they can offer checks to background variables. Professor Alexander Mood of the University of California urges awareness of sponsor interests and fuller exploitation of previous studies. Professor Adam Yarmolinsky of the University of Massachusetts suggests that the distinctions between new programs, experiments, and evaluations may vanish, particularly in the political context. Professor Lazarsfeld completes the discussion of social experiments with an example from a criminal justice experiment in which the experiment must be dissected into its components.

Part II on "Policy Research, Decisions, and Political Impacts of Evaluation Research" (based on a panel chaired by Professor Adam Yarmolinsky of the University of Massachusetts), expresses skepticism about the lack of real policy impact of much evaluation research. Dr. Joseph Wholey, of the Urban Institute, expresses two frustrations—that "of the evaluator trying to meet management needs," and that "of the manager trying to get some results from the evaluator." Three problems are said to impede effective evaluation—lack of defined objectives, lack of plausible processes leading to objectives, and lack of authority to implement a program that can reach objectives. Dr. Wholey offers a nine-step model to yield timely information on program intent and performance, stressing evaluation that provides sequential information that allows one to assess over time whether the effort will be productive.

Dr. Sylvain Lourie of UNESCO is also skeptical about the impact of educational research on decision making. Contributing to this lack of impact is the often coded language of research, which makes it of little use to the policy maker. Dr. Lourie also echoes the call for an ongoing evaluation process. Dr. Norman Beckman of the Congressional Reference Services discusses the provision of unbiased and non-partisan information to Congressmen and their staff in evaluation of proposals before Congress. Finally, Ms. Alair Townsend of the Joint Economic Committee considers the many legislative decisions that are made without the benefit of evaluation or analysis. She also stresses the need for research findings to be presented in a straightforward and understandable manner so that their usefulness to decision makers can be increased.

Dr. Joseph Cronin, State Superintendent of Education of Illinois, stresses the need for rapid feedback evaluation during the course of a program and the need for "autopsies" of obsolete governmental inputs. Norman Gold of the U.S. Office of Education, on the other hand, strongly attacks what he regards as the retreat of evaluators into self-criticism, when he sees the real problem in lack of evaluation application to policy decisions as a national withdrawal from commitment to social progress.

Part III, on "Payoffs of Evaluation Research," is based on a panel chaired by Dr. Eleanor Sheldon, President of the Social Science Research Council. The general theme of this discussion is that evaluation has to meet many different criteria to be useful. Dr. Constance Newman, Assistant Secretary at the U.S. Department of Housing and Urban Development, stresses the need for research to be valid, objective, and timely if it is to be useful to the policy maker. Her emphasis on the "real world" includes a conviction that social scientists should understand what policy decisions are feasible in terms of Congress, public opinion, and funds. In addition, researchers must be prepared to supply the policy makers with information before the end of a project because few policy decisions can wait until a research effort is completed and the final report submitted.

Dr. Lois-ellin Datta of the National Institute of Education traces the history and impacts of the Westinghouse/Ohio evaluation of the Head Start Program. She vividly tracks the controversy over the results of that evaluation, which indicated that Head Start was not having a long-term effect on the lower-income children who participated in it. Head Start survived the evaluation, although its growth was curtailed. What then was the impact of this evaluation? Some social scientists feel this study proves that social science research has little impact, but others point to the subsequent greater emphasis placed on evaluation and, in fact, the restriction of other social experiments as proof of the study's impact. Dr. Datta concludes that evaluators should take their tasks very seriously and realize the role that they play in deciding whether a program should be continued or whether program recommendations should be implemented.

Professor Michael Scriven of the University of California addresses the need to clarify the relationship between the policy maker and the researcher. His theme is "cost-free" evaluation, meaning that "evaluation has to pay its own way and has to be subject to evaluation in turn." Experimental evaluation should pay off in many areas: it should serve as a reliable guide to selection among program options, and it should provide immediate gains in quality or savings. Finally, Dr. Norman Zinberg of the Harvard University Medical School discusses how qualitative problems of evaluation are often neglected in analyzing evaluation research. In evaluating social science projects, it is necessary to consider more than whether or not certain specified goals are met. Psychological and social variables should be taken into account as well as objective standards in order to do justice to the project being evaluated.

Commenting on these views, Dr. Alice Rivlin (now Director of the Congressional Budget Office) expresses doubts concerning the usefulness of expensive social experiments and evaluations, and suggests that evaluation efforts be redirected towards a continuing collection of longitudinal cluster samples for panel studies in which people stay for some time. Professor William Capron of Harvard University's Kennedy School stresses the political context of evaluation. Dr. Clark Abt of Abt Associates suggests efforts to overcome the likely cognitive dissonances between evaluators and users, and several ways of estimating the worth of evaluations as a necessary preliminary step to designing an optimal mix of them under resource constraints.

Professor Edward Tufte of Princeton University chaired a panel on "Research Versus Decision Requirements, and Best Practices of Evaluation," on which Part IV is based. The principal concern of this discussion is why evaluations so often produce negative results. Evaluators are urged to seek new approaches and methodologies, but to remain realistic about the limitations of evaluation research and the probability that rapid social change will not occur as a result of such research. Dr. Irwin Deutscher discusses the "goal-trap," or the tendency to evaluate a program solely in terms of stated goals. An alternate approach is to examine process instead of the input-output model. Discussions with program administrators can be useful in determining relevant lines of inquiry and real program goals. Dr. James Fennessey of Johns Hopkins University deals with the appropriateness of Bayesian Inference in overcoming some of the deficiencies of present evaluation research methods. Bayesian theory would reveal rather than mask the sources of contradiction between different studies on the same topic; it would present the results in a meaningful way; and it would aid in accumulating disciplinary knowledge as well as public understanding.

Professor Richard Light of Harvard University focuses on the question of external validity, which he has used to identify volunteer effects in randomized studies. He questions whether or not the experience of the experimental subjects can be generalized to the population involved in a full-scale program. Keith Marvin of the General Accounting Office (GAO) describes that office's evaluation activities. The GAO is expected, under the new Budget Act, to assist Congressional committees in developing evaluation methods and goals. It is, accordingly, working to educate Congressmen on the significance of program evaluation and the art of technical review.

Professor John Tukey of Princeton University discusses some basic premises of social evaluation. He particularly stresses the need to document small effects as well as large ones, because most progress occurs as the result of the accumulation of many small gains. He also stresses the need for randomization of assignment as the only reliable measure of the difference between two natural groups offering scientifically confirmed knowledge. Professor Mancur Olson of the University of Maryland criticizes Professor Tukey's suggestion that program administrators are opposed to evaluation as too simple. He also feels that Professor Deutscher goes too far in finding evaluation attempts to relate goals to means and ends to means unproductive. Professor Michael Scriven of the University of California at Berkeley defends Professor Deutscher's avoidance of the "goal trap" and amusingly illustrates how it defends against the common biases of instant co-option risked in excessive evaluative attention to goals investigation. Professor Paul Wortman of Northwestern University describes some moving human obstacles to truly random assignments in biomedical evaluation research.

Part V is based on a panel chaired by Dr. Ralph Berry of Harvard

University School of Public Health, "Evaluation of Health Programs." Dr. Martha Blaxall of the National Academy of Sciences offers "A Budget Examiner's Perspective" on the questions of evaluation. She feels that policy makers have an obligation to think through experiments, decide what they want to find, work with evaluators in designing the effort, and make use of the results as they become available. In terms of health care, evaluation research has had limited value because of a lack of accepted criteria for measuring health status, difficulties of measuring the impact of non-health care factors on health status, and lack of knowledge of what impact health programs have on other social programs. Dr. George Nash praises the value of short-term demonstration projects and gives a detailed account of two such programs—one with positive findings and one without—which he had evaluated in New York City. Short-term projects have advantages of low cost, relevance to real events, and capacity for answering questions quickly. They are an alternative to most larger and longer social experiments and demonstration programs. John Sessler of the Drug Abuse Council, Inc. discusses the value of an in-house evaluation capability. His recommendations are based upon experience with the Operations Evaluation Group and other operations research and study groups within the Department of Defense, and a conviction that these kinds of groups could be very useful to the agencies funding social science research. Such organizations need to have qualities of independent funding, projects selection, and reports distribution; and a close working relationship with the client group. Dr. Jerry Cromwell of Abt Associates Inc. analyzes the measurement of hospital productivity trends in short-term, general hospitals. There has been a rapid rise in hospital costs since 1966, accentuating the need for research in hospital efficiency. Increased labor costs have more than eliminated savings achieved by technological advances. He feels that more theoretical and empirical work needs to be done and new ways devised to measure productivity in hospital departments, which are experiencing a significant rate of improvement in service quality.

Commenting on the health programs evaluations, Dr. Helen Nowlis of the U.S. Office of Education, worries about the feasibility of planning any long-range evaluations in the uncertain context of the annual federal funding cycle. Professor Henry Riecken of the University of Pennsylvania argues that, although impact studies are missing in many areas of health services, they do not need to be. Dr. Mildred

Shapiro of the New York State Department of Health comments on Dr.
Jerry Cromwell's discussion of hospital productivity decline by offering
some explanations for it, and urges that real measures of productivity
include all the inputs to production, pointing out that as laboratory
tests are doubling every five years, there is little reason to believe that
medical care is also doubling in quality every five years.

Part VI, "Evaluation of Education Programs," is based on a panel led
by Dr. Alexander Mood of the University of California. Dr. Michael
Timpane of the Rand Corporation offers an historical and political
analysis of the development of education evaluations and the impact
they have had on policy decisions by analyzing the evaluations of Title
I education projects. Dr. Timpane strikes the rather optimistic note that
early educational evaluations made significant contributions to the state
of the art of such evaluations, as well as contributing to program
improvements. For example, when early reports found that there was a
wide dispersion of compensatory education funds among pupils and
activities, guidelines were implemented to concentrate available funds
in adequate per pupil awards.

Dr. Marvin Cline of Abt Associates Inc. argues that many kinds of
social experiments can be evaluated in the sense of determining why
one treatment works better than another, rather than deciding that one
treatment does or does not work. He suggests that the most effective
way to provide the policy maker with a useful directory of effects is to
ascertain the reasons for the effects by testing the hypothesis of a
project. He concludes that it is past time "to bring research strategies
into the arena of public policy decisions."

Professor Anthony Boardman of the University of Pennsylvania
considers the education process as a simultaneous equation model, by
which variables can be jointly and interdependently determined. More
traditional approaches view the educational process as a single equation
production function in which pupil achievement depends linearly on a
number of pupil, teacher, and school variables. Estimated simultaneous
equation models provide more insight into the educational process and
strengthen the ability of policy makers to devise appropriate guidelines.

Dr. Mats Hultin of the World Bank discusses evaluation in education
projects funded there. He feels that evaluation of education projects
should be a comprehensive and continuous process and that therefore
the project objectives should be stated in a way that makes it possible
to evaluate them. In addition, there is a need for education researchers

to find quantitative correlations between education and development and to provide the tools to measure these correlations.

Commenting on Dr. Hultin's views, Dr. John Evans of the U.S. Office of Education cautions against built-in evaluation processes, because they cannot contain control groups for estimating the effects of non-treatment. He also disagrees with Dr. Alice Rivlin's conclusions that program evaluations be dropped in favor of panel studies. Dr. Andrew Porter of the National Institute of Education makes a case for small scale as opposed to large scale evaluations, unless the latter are essential to the kinds of questions to be answered. Dr. Marshall Smith, also of NIE, agrees with Dr. Porter in insisting large scale evaluations are outdated (although most conference participants did not), pointing out how much has been learned from repeated small studies of the three school variables of "coordinated purposefulness," "closeness," and "time on task." He also makes important points about the non-replicability of education research findings from one site to another, and the need to understand the underlying causes of educational differences by psychologically oriented research on cognitive states of development.

Part VII, on "Research Allocation Strategies," is based on a panel chaired by Dr. Mary Rowe of M.I.T. Dr. Clark Abt, President of Abt Associates Inc., discusses the need to evaluate evaluations to maximize their benefits to users. He describes several measures of information and utility for evaluating evaluation benefits. If a production function for alternative evaluations can be produced, it is possible to select the "optimum" mix of evaluations for a particular program. Evaluation objectives and information criteria should be elicited from the users of policy research to aid in the selection of a satisfactory design for the research. In addition, steps that research users could take to conserve their efforts and increase the efficiency of the procurement process include keeping performance records on bidders, so that quality of past work influences the selection process, motivating performance and reducing the needed length and quantity of proposals.

Dr. Harvey Averch of the National Science Foundation comments on the strategies of research and development funding from a funder's viewpoint. A principal concern of funders of social science research is how much they are getting for their money. In evaluating research proposals, funders look for a clear statement of the technical problem, the research procedure, and the potential use of the findings. Some government agencies are beginning to keep track of an evaluator's previous performance—this too is considered in funding a proposal. Dr. Richard Barnes of the National Institute for Law Enforcement and Criminal Justice presents an analysis of research allocation strategies of evaluations of criminal justice programs. He stresses the conflict between the need for basic research efforts and the need for immediate information to feed into the short-term decision making process. Finally, Dr. Bette Mahoney of HEW discusses the need for evaluations which ascertain the payoffs of different types of research. Policy analysis should be a part of the research process. It is neglected because of the difficulty of doing long-range strategy planning when the press of managing existing projects is great, and because there are not sufficient incentives for such analyses.

Commenting on the research allocation strategies presented, Professor Daniel Bell of Harvard University attacks Clark Abt's economics approach to evaluation as a rationalistic attempt to obtain production functions on research in the face of the overriding non-rational considerations of policy research. Professor Bell argues that semantics and symbols count more than literal fact, even in social programs evaluation, and that political realities dominate economic rationality. Dr. Joseph Newhouse of the Rand Corporation, however, insists that there are real issues to be faced in research allocation by government decision makers, and that although there are problems in evaluating evaluations for productivity, such measures of output as the citation index can be helpful. Dr. William Pollin of the National Institute of Drug Abuse then suggests the need for properly valuing negative findings of evaluation research, raises the issue of whether weak research is better or worse than none (as does Richard Light with different conclusions), and cautions against simplistic uses of citation indexes.

There are several concerns that are shared by the editor and contributors alike—regardless of their institutional background. Aspects of the relationship between users/sponsors and evaluators remain an area of ongoing concern. Government users clearly need to have research findings presented in an understandable way if these findings are to be useful. It is also clear that users as decision makers bear many political stresses, which they may pass on to evaluators. Evaluators, on the other hand, sometimes feel pressure from users/sponsors who have hidden agendas, for instance, support for continuation of a program.

This volume presents many thoughtful contributions to the ongoing discussion of what the real purposes of evaluation should be—whether it should solve problems or merely identify program successes and failures. Some contributors feel that clearer program goals are necessary before effective evaluation can be completed. Others are interested less in being able to measure end results (administrative or impact evaluation) and more in being able to describe the dynamics of an activity, i.e., what actually happened (formative or process evaluation). The need to develop standard research techniques and encourage their use is expressed by those who believe that randomized assignment and experimental design should be used more often in evaluation research. Another issue is whether or not evaluation should be built into a program from its inception. Although some contributors warn of the problems inherent in being both the administrator of a program and its evaluator, others feel that making evaluation an integral part of a program is an excellent way to keep the program on target and maximize information flow.

Many questions and issues are raised in the following pages. While there are few definitive answers, we are all agreed on the need for continued testing, research, and above all, closer communication among the various research and user groups concerned with the evaluation of social programs.

Clark C. Abt
Abt Associates Inc.

I

EVALUATION OF SOCIAL EXPERIMENTS

PART I □ CONTENTS

EVALUATION OF SOCIAL EXPERIMENTS

Chairperson: PAUL LAZARSFELD, Columbia University

THE HOUSING ASSISTANCE SUPPLY EXPERIMENT:
Tensions in Design and Implementation

Ira S. Lowry
The Rand Corporation

In a brief essay I cannot hope to explain the design of the Housing Assistance Supply Experiment (HASE) in persuasive detail; for that, I must refer you to our *General Design Report*. What I will attempt is to highlight the design features that make it unusual among social experiments and to discuss the implications of these features for the implementation of the experiment and the analysis of its results.

EXPERIMENTAL OBJECTIVES

The experiment is basically designed to test the effects of a full-scale housing allowance program on the housing market within which it operates. We want to find out how the suppliers of housing services and the market intermediaries respond to a substantial permanent increase in the effective demand for housing by low-income families; how the community is affected in terms of residential redistribution; how participants, nonparticipants, landlords, tenants, homeowners, and other definable interest groups are affected by the program, and how they perceive those effects.

DESIGN CHARACTERISTICS

As designed to fulfill these objectives, the experiment has several unusual features.

First, *it is a long-term saturation experiment.* Rather than offering housing allowances to a thin sample of poor people for a short time, we are attempting to enroll all eligibles in each of two metropolitan housing markets. If he remains eligible, a participant's housing allowance may continue for up to 10 years. The local housing market will be monitored for the first five years of this period.

Second, *the experimental treatment is unique.* All participants receive benefits on the same terms and conditions, not only within each site but at both sites.

Third, *while we are treating one group* (low-income renters and homeowners), *our monitoring program is aimed primarily at other groups* (landlords, market intermediaries, nonparticipating households) *who may be affected by the actions of program participants.*

These design features have powerful implications both for the implementation of the experimental allowance program and for our monitoring and analytical agenda.

PROGRAM IMPLEMENTATION

Because HASE is a long-term saturation experiment, it was necessary to design and staff a large, quasi-permanent institution to administer the experimental allowance program. If enrollment targets are met, participation in the program will reach 6,100 families in one site and 9,600 in the other.

Once created, such institutions tend to develop their own allegiances and agendas. A major problem for us has been to devise a system of institutional governance that simultaneously enables the HAO to conduct its own daily affairs, assures us of its fiduciary responsibility, assures us that the allowance program will continue to serve its experimental purposes, and gives the host community a sense of participation in decisions affecting its welfare.

The uniqueness of the experimental treatment is a corollary of experimental purpose and scale; I will return later to the reasons. Here, I want to comment on the terrible burden of judgment that is imposed on the designers of such a large-scale and visible experiment when dissenting opinion cannot be accommodated by adding another program variation.

The shared intent of HUD and Rand in program design was to anticipate the features of a national housing allowance program that would serve housing objectives efficiently and which would have a reasonable chance of Congressional approval. Everyone, of course, has his own ideas about the preferable features of a national program, the balance of objectives, the effectiveness of methods, and the Congressional reaction to possible program features. Several times over the past three years, we have come nearly to the parting of the ways with HUD over such questions.

Given reluctant agreement on program design, there is the further problem that, over time, we will surely recognize mistakes in that design or will think of changes that would be useful in one site but not in the other. Over the life of the experiment, we expect continual tension between the analytical neatness of a fixed experimental treatment, comparable between sites, and the programmatic value of adaptive response to changing national and local conditions.

MONITORING AND ANALYSIS

In most social experiments, those to whom the treatment is administered are also those whose responses are monitored. In HASE, the allowance program and the monitoring program are quite distinct. Although we will analyze administrative records of the allowance program, formal monitoring is accomplished mostly by an annual cycle of field surveys addressed to the owners and occupants of a sample of residential properties chosen from all sectors of the housing market. Among program participants, only those who happen to live on these properties will be interviewed.

One interesting consequence of this arrangement is that program costs and monitoring costs are independently fixed by quite different considerations, funded from different budgets; each cost is highly visible as a separate item. Program costs, I am happy to say, are protected by 10-year annual contribution contracts. Monitoring costs are not, and it would be quite possible for some future unsympathetic administration to starve the monitoring program, thus blocking the completion of the experimental agenda without abrogating benefits to program participants.

Combining this fact with HUD's sense of urgency about its legislative program and with the necessarily slow pace of research that entails primary data collection, we anticipate severe pressures for early, perhaps premature, reporting of experiment findings.

As I noted earlier, the uniqueness of the experimental treatment is a corollary of experimental purpose and scale. Running program variations within a single site would only confuse us in relating the program as *cause* to housing-market changes as *effects*. A saturation experiment is too expensive to replicate with variations in a statistically useful number of sites.

Because we have only two metropolitan housing markets to observe, their selection was an especially critical issue. While others may dispute our criteria of choice, I am pleased (and somewhat surprised) to report that at no time during the protracted process of site selection were political criteria imposed. The sites were chosen strictly because, among the available alternatives, they best fit experimental needs.

Having only two cases also forces analysis into a clinical mode. Because the two sites were chosen for the contrasts in their housing markets, we expect the allowance program to have different effects in each. Ascription of differential results to specific market characteristics will require a large element of analytical judgment, and we must therefore expect our conclusions to be debatable.

I should emphasize that the clinical mode does not imply any necessary absence of rigor in measuring market events that follow the introduction of the allowance program. The limitation there is a matter of resources. Survey research is expensive and housing markets are complicated. It remains to be seen whether we have properly balanced these considerations so that our data will be adequate to measure small as well as large market-wide changes.

Given the inherent limitations of the clinical approach and uncertainties about the adequacy of aggregate estimates from sample data, I find large comfort in the analytical possibilities of our survey records on individual properties and households. In fact, provided that we do not drop our IBM cards on the computing-room floor, I expect HASE to complete its five-year monitoring program with one of the nation's most versatile social science research files. Above all, it will serve research on housing-market dynamics far better than any existing data.

The versatility of this file reflects the third characteristic of our experimental design that I mentioned earlier. Rather than primarily monitoring program participants, we are surveying a cross-section of the metropolitan housing market. We will have longitudinal records on individual properties, their owners, and their occupants, with concurrent and linkable data from both landlords and their tenants.

It is only fair to add that building this file is in itself a risky undertaking. Each year, Rand will receive approximately one million bits of data (answers to individual survey questions) from each site—data that must be edited, formatted, stored in machine-readable form, audited, and made accessible to analysts with a variety of interests. Clearly, each year's wave of data must be mastered before the next arrives; it would be only too easy for HASE to drown in a sea of IBM cards, a prospect that has been forecast by some of our best friends. Over time, storage and retrieval will become increasingly complex as analytically important linkages among the records are attempted. As an institution, Rand is far from amateurish in the development of computer software, but this enterprise nonetheless strains our resources.

Our greatest challenge, however, is to serve the immediate needs of our client for timely but reliable analyses of the effects of the experimental housing allowance programs on their housing markets. How hard pressed we are in this respect will depend on a legislative time table over which we have no influence. My current judgment is that interim reports will be available on a schedule that will enable them to help shape legislation; but if I am wrong about the legislative time table, experimental findings will certainly be available to help shape program administration, which may be an even more important consideration.

In closing, I would like to make a general point about the nature of this experiment. Neither Rand nor (so far as I can judge) HUD undertook HASE with the purpose of proving that housing allowances are a good thing. We are committed to calling the shots as we see them. But it is necessary to worry about how well both institutions can maintain that posture over the term of the experiment.

In our thinking, we try very hard to distinguish the success of the program from the success of the experiment; we can properly hope for both results and will exert ourselves to achieve them. However, given Rand's double responsibility for program administration and experimental design, there is the nagging possibility that our vested interest in the success of the program will bias our experimental findings. In this regard, I can only assure you that we plan to document our findings in sufficient detail so that others could detect such a bias and to open our data files to independent analysis.

COMMENTS ON EVALUATION OF SOCIAL EXPERIMENTS

Joseph Newhouse
Rand Corporation

The design of the Health Insurance Experiment calls for enrolling around 2,000 families in 9 different health insurance plans. The plans cover all the same kinds of health services, but vary in the amount that the families must pay out of pocket, that is, in the coinsurance rate. The coinsurance rate varies from nothing—all care is free—to 95 percent—approximately a deductible. In addition, all of the plans have a feature that limits the family's maximum annual out-of-pocket payment to a certain fraction of their income. That fraction is either 5, 10, or 15 percent.

The experiment is scheduled to be run in four sites. The sites are selected so as to vary the amount of access to the medical care system, particularly the ambulatory system. We use measures such as the length of time to an appointment as indicating the ease of access. Even among the major metropolitan areas there is enormous variation in this measure, from about two days to about twenty days, and we will pick sites from all parts of that distribution. In order to induce families to participate and to assure ourselves that there is no adverse selection in our sample, we pay families a lump sum payment that is equal to their worst case. In other words, the families could never be worse off from participating in the experiment. That is a brief description of the experiment.

The objectives are several. First is to find out what difference out-of-pocket payments make to the family's utilization of health services, to the quality of care they receive and to their ultimate health status. That is to say, what are the costs of changing cost-sharing arrangements and what are the benefits? Second, we would like to know, holding the insurance plan constant, what difference access to the physician makes in terms of who is treated for what kind of problem? What difference does it make that a person has to wait 20 days for an appointment with an internist or pediatrician rather than two days? Third, we would like to say something about the rules of operation of plans that have income-related features; for example, if a plan says the family will not pay more than 5 percent of its income for medical payments during a year, what happens if the family splits up in the middle of the year? That turns out to be a very troublesome issue.

Those are some of the major objectives. I would like to put them into a broader context of the debate over health insurance and health planning. At a very general level, there is still to some degree an open question in this country about whether medical care, at least non-hospital care, will be delivered primarily through a market or primarily through some kind of central planning. If insurance pays the vast majority of medical bills, then usual market forces do not operate, and some kind of planning is inevitable. On the other hand, if insurance pays only large bills, then market forces will primarily govern resource allocation.

Choice between these two modes of organizing medical care is now being made in the political process. At the same time, there is relatively little evidence (as opposed to ideology) on which to make the choice. One of the points at issue is consumer ignorance. It is argued that the consumer does not know what he is doing and that therefore out-of-pocket payments are harmful to him. The experiment can shed some light on this by comparing the health status and quality of care received by individuals who obtain all their medical care free with those who must pay for their care. On the one hand, it may be the case that individuals do make poor decisions about when to seek care, and that this adversely affects their health status. Or, particular kinds of individuals such as the less well-educated may make poor decisions. On the other hand, individuals may make good decisions. This can be resolved by ascertaining what differences in health status, if any, exist after five years between those who receive their medical care free and those who pay for almost all of it.

It is probably naive, however, to think that the choice to which the market is used or not used can be much affected by the analyses that will be possible with these data. More likely is that, given a set of institutional arrangements, analysis can contribute to subsequent choices. For example, suppose that the national health insurance plan is a catastrophic type plan and that current tax incentives to purchase additional insurance privately are reduced or eliminated. The results of the experiment can then say something about the benefits and costs of relatively small changes in the cost-sharing arrangements. Alternatively, suppose that the national plan is a full coverage plan with the public sector controlling resource allocation. Questions will then arise about the effect of adding more physicians or more hospital beds on health status. Again the results of the experiment will be useful, by permitting comparisons of health status among individuals with similar demographic characteristics and with the same experimental insurance plan, but who live in areas with different resource endowments. Thus, under either set of institutional arrangements, the results from the experiment will be quite useful.

SOCIAL EXPERIMENTATION[1]

Henry W. Riecken
University of Pennsylvania

Program evaluation has become a very popular activity for social scientists in part because much recent social legislation includes a requirement for evaluation of the legislative program. The wave of domestic social reforms in the 1960s that led to compensatory education, community action programs, manpower training, and measures for diminishing racial segregation and sexual discrimination has been responsible for the creation of a mini-industry of evaluation. It is premature to judge how influential such evaluations have been in reshaping social policy, but experience to date suggests that there are certain difficulties associated with the usual and ordinary procedure of conducting post-hoc evaluations of national programs—that is, with the common administrative practice of waiting until the program has been put into full operation before giving appreciable attention to its evaluation.

One difficulty is that many, if not most, national programs are not designed so as to permit comparison of effectiveness among varying combinations of program elements or comparison with alternative treatments. Some programs, indeed, do not even permit comparison of outcomes from a treated population with those from an untreated or control group. Thus, for example, in a compensatory education program, it may be difficult or impossible to find adequate control groups or to find naturally occurring variations in intensity of treatment, in age of children to whom treatment is applied, duration of treatment, or in other characteristics of children or families that might help explain differential outcomes of the program. The national program is not designed to provide information about its effectiveness but rather to deliver a service—a service whose effectiveness or value is not known, but which also cannot be discovered unless an adequate basis of comparison can be devised. Most often, however, the naturally occurring variations do not provide an adequate basis. Furthermore, even when they do, the likelihood is that the persons or other units eligible for the program are not assigned randomly to systematic variations in the program treatment, but rather that population characteristics, motivational factors (such as volunteering) or accidental features of the situation are confounded with the treatment received. After-the-fact evaluation of a program's effect is intrinsically handicapped because the program was not designed in the first place to make available the systematic information needed to assess its effectiveness. Such conditions can be designed into the administration of the program at its outset, provided there is explicit recognition of the need for deliberate and designed variation of the treatment for program assessment purposes. Of course, such a recognition then fundamentally alters the evaluation process, and it is no longer a post-hoc evaluation. Recognition of the need for and the integral role of program evaluation also alters the orientation of program administrators, developers, and designers, as well as those responsible for program evaluation. The service delivery purpose is retained, but it is recognized from the very beginning that the service is of unknown or uncertain value (effectiveness) and there is frank acknowledgement that, besides delivering service, it is equally important to discover whether the service accomplished its purpose. The importance of this reorientation toward an innovative social intervention can hardly be over-emphasized. It not only opens the door for deliberately designed variations in treatment, but it begins to involve the evaluators in a collaborative relationship with the program operators. Furthermore, it casts the whole venture in a new light. The innovative program becomes an exploration in which all parties are committed to learning how to tailor their actions to achieve more fully the goals of social policy.

Such reorientation also removes another kind of handicap from which post-hoc evaluations suffer, namely, hostility and resistance to evaluation on the part of program operating personnel. It is a common experience, perhaps the most common, to find that those who are responsible for designing and implementing ameliorative social programs do not welcome evaluation of their efforts. Indeed, they are sometimes uncooperative and may even sabotage the evaluators' work. A moment's reflection will suggest why such attitudes are so common. Nearly every social program is difficult to start and requires a great deal of effort and commitment on the part of those charged with implementing it. Many unforeseen difficulties are encountered and must be resolved, often in too short a space of time and under pressure to "get moving." As the obstacles are overcome and as seemingly necessary compromises are made between the ideal goals of the program as it was conceived and the intractable social reality it confronts, those who are running the program become committed to their decisions, convinced that their efforts are worthwhile and that the program is achieving success. Often the program operators develop a high morale, an esprit de corps, a solidarity akin to that of pioneers in the wilderness or veterans of a battle. A program evaluator intrudes into this scene in a most unfortunate posture. Without having borne any of the burden of early beginnings, without any battle scars, he, nonetheless, presumes to sit in judgment of what has been accomplished. Is it any wonder that he is often viewed as an alien, a troublemaker, and above all, a Monday morning quarter-back whose keenness of perception is entirely attributable to hindsight? The situation is even worse when the program has been experiencing failures that are apparent to its operators. Under these conditions, hostility and resistance to evaluation can become staggering.

Furthermore, even if program operating personnel do not interfere with the evaluation process itself, it is common to find that the recommendations for program change issuing from such evaluations are ignored or rejected. Some of this resistance stems from the attitudinal and emotional factors mentioned above, but some of it also arises from the sheer inflexibility of commitment to established procedures in an ongoing program. Most people and most organizations arrive at some tolerable accommodation with task requirements and the social environment such that major changes in objectives, procedures, or requirements are, in fact, disruptive; and hence, resisted. The discomfort of such disruptions and resistance to them are reduced if the program is perceived from the outset as an exploratory and experimental one rather than something which is likely to continue as an activity for an indefinite period of time. The expectation of subsequent changes makes them more tolerable than the expectation of stability would.

For these reasons, post-hoc evaluation is handicapped from the outset in both a scientific and a managerial sense. Post-hoc evaluation comes too late in the line of program development, testing, and assessment.

Accordingly, it seems reasonable to reconceptualize the place of evaluation in a broadly experimental framework that takes as its frame of reference a cycle of program development, testing, and revision, leading to further development and revision, prior to installation on a large scale. The cycle begins with an idea, a notion about how to intervene in a social process, which must then be developed into a program or treatment, by working out details of procedure and operations. An experiment is designed around the developed program to measure the effectiveness of either variations in treatment or alternative treatments in achieving the social objective of the intervention. The program is viewed as a tentative one in which services are delivered both for their own sake and for the sake of learning their value. The results of analysis are fed back into program design so as to eliminate unintended and undesirable effects of treatment, worthless treatments, and to incorporate into a redesigned program those features of treatment which have demonstrated effectiveness. Only then is the full-scale program installed. Each of these steps deserves more detailed comment than can be presented here, but it is important to grasp the fundamental notion of a cycle of program development, experimental testing, and modification (or abandonment) based on the outcomes of the experiment. It is in this sense, as an integral part of the cycle, that the notion of social experimentation is put forward as an advantageous method of program development and evaluation.

To take a concrete case, the idea has been widely circulated in the medical and public health community that a protein-deficient diet of post-weaning children in many less-developed countries is responsible for an uncertain amount of intellectual deficiency at school age and in adulthood. This opinion has resulted in proposals to feed protein supplements from six months of age (or whenever the weaning process is completed) until a substantial amount of physical growth and development has taken place. In order to test this proposition in an experiment it is necessary to develop a feeding program. That is, one must work out a dietary supplement which is acceptable, palatable, and protein-nutritious. One must develop some sort of system for administering the supplement, for making sure that the children who need it get it, that it is not sold in the local market by the families to whom it is given, and that it is not consumed by the adults, but indeed gets to the children who need it. All of these features of a program sound simple once they have been worked out, but they all need to be invented and made a functioning part of the treatment. Incidentally, in the course of developing an experimental treatment from an idea into an operating scheme, a good deal can be learned about the potential problems and desirable administrative features of a full-scale program.

Besides the development of treatments, the experiment itself must be designed. A true experiment involves at least two treatments—perhaps one active treatment and a control treatment or two active treatments, together with randomized assignment of treatments to experimental units. (This definition is conventional in the statistical literature but quite different from common administrative or bureaucratic usage where "experiment" may mean simply a try-out, a preliminary version of a program that will later be conducted on a larger scale.) Methods of monitoring the delivery of treatments have to be worked out and methods of measuring (changes in) the factors that are supposed to be affected by the treatment (e.g., in physical and mental development) must be perfected. Competent, trained technicians are required for testing, and professional skills must be applied to problems of data collection and analysis. The final, crucial stage is to bring the results to bear upon program (treatment) revision and/or the development of social policy.

It might be objected that this randomized comparison design is too cumbersome and time consuming for social planning—why not try to simulate or model the treatment or use a procedure such as direct observation of a demonstration or pilot program?

In the first place, it appears that much social intervention has been misdirected because of the lack of knowledge rather than because of the absence of good intentions or restricted investment of resources and effort. Social planners are likely to be the victims of inadequate data, of conventional beliefs and folk wisdom, and of inadequate understanding of complex social processes. Most interventions are directed at social processes that are so complex that they cannot accurately and fully be modeled or simulated. Even where they can, there is often a dearth of information about important parameters, and it is clear that intuition and casual observation are not good substitutes for scientifically obtained knowledge, both factual and theoretical.

Furthermore, as pointed out above in connection with post-hoc evaluations, there is often a gap in knowledge that cannot be filled either from the study of existing social conditions or by simply launching a new social program without designing it to provide information about its effects. For example, the work disincentive effect of unearned income on low-income workers cannot be estimated from existing data or prior experience because very few, if any, low-income workers in the labor force have unearned income. Or again, in the case of the Health Insurance Experiment, existing data on the way people with health insurance make use of the health care system do not provide an adequate basis for forecasting how they might respond to conceivable national health insurance plans. There is little or no experience, for instance, with response to coinsurance rates about 20% nor to certain other features such as high payment limits, high deductibles or absolute limits on coinsurance. Existing health insurance written in the United States simply does not include certain ranges of variation in these dimensions. It would be extremely helpful to know, in designing a national health insurance plan, the effect of more extreme values of these variables upon the demand for health services. Finally, the evidence obtained from a randomized experiment will avoid a difficulty that besets all existing survey data and other records of behavior of those who currently have health insurance; namely, "adverse selection" effects—the tendency for those who are more at risk (think they will be sick) to buy insurance.

A second justification for experiments is that, in comparison with simple observational and retrospective studies, experiments are generally better able to eliminate "plausible alternative explanations" for social phenomena. An experiment virtually rules out the possibility of "causal displacement," whose operation is best illustrated by the way in which volunteering to participate affects the outcome. Because volunteers are likely to be more able, more highly motivated, or more suited to the program, the observed effects may seem to indicate that they benefitted more than those who did not participate. The true explanation, however, may be just the reverse—that those who were superior were those who volunteered. Furthermore, when two equally plausible types of treatments or programs are in competition for acceptance and have a prima facie equal claim to effectiveness, a carefully designed experimental comparison will yield a better relative measure of effectiveness than merely casual observation of each in operation. Still another advantage of experimental designs is that they make it easier to examine variations in intensity of treatment and in susceptibility of units treated. For example, a program to use money incentives to accelerate children's learning to read should probably include children from very poor families as well as a level of payment that may be well beyond practical limits for a nationwide program. Still, a presumably highly susceptible group and an extremely intensive treatment would show whether the treatment was at all effective, even under the most favorable circumstances. Extreme treatments and extremely susceptible units will not give an unbiased estimate of "average" treatment effect, but they may be useful in detecting completely ineffective treatments.

Finally, social experimentation is justifiable on the ground that it is both a humane and an efficient approach to the formulation of social policy and the development of social programs. It has been argued that social experimentation amounts to "playing with peoples' lives," a remark that carries the strong implication that experimentation is at least irresponsible and perhaps unethical. The same argument, of course, should apply to social planning and a fortiori to legislating and implementing untested ideas for social improvement. The history of social reform and amelioration is littered with examples of large-scale and costly catastrophes (e.g., public housing programs such as Pruitt-Igoe) as well as more modest mistakes (e.g., women-power training programs that inculcated tasks and attitudes which helped to alienate the trainees from their peer groups at home; or community action programs that appeared to have improved the bank accounts of a few entrepreneurs a lot but the welfare of the general community very little) and simply ineffective treatments that appear to have done neither good nor harm, but only expended public funds. None of these programs was undertaken in the spirit of playing with peoples' lives, yet they affected the lives of a larger number of people at a considerably greater cost than experimental programs would have done. Surely, there is something misguided about this criticism when it is applied to undertakings that are directed specifically toward the purpose of learning how well the intended effects of a planned intervention will be achieved and what unintended consequences may also occur. Since a well-designed experiment can ordinarily be conducted with a lesser risk to human well-being and a lower cost than a full-scale national program, it seems reasonable to believe that experiments are more humane and more efficient. They certainly fulfill the "service" purpose of a full-scale program, albeit for a smaller number of people in the experimental treatment groups and ordinarily do not deprive those in the control group (except in a relative and tenuous sense). Perhaps proposed social experiments should be subjected to the same sort of public scrutiny that is given to proposed social legislation—a step that could be easily incorporated into the legislative and budgetary review process for the experiment-performing agency.

Two remarks about the design of social experiments may be apropos. As mentioned earlier it may be prudent to add an extremely intensive, even an implausibly intensive treatment, to a design just in order to test whether any treatment at all of the character proposed, at any intensity of application, would be effective. Since many social interventions seem weak in comparison with spontaneous counter-forces, it seems worthwhile to inquire whether it is the character of the treatment or merely its intensity of application that produces null or negative results. This is an argument for including treatments that would not be programmatically feasible on a national scale since feasibility is of no consequence if even an unfeasibly strong treatment is shown to be ineffective. Secondly, one must face the question of representativeness in the choice of experimental units. It is important to ask: "representativeness for what?" Is the experiment being done for purposes of parameter estimation and generalization to some population, or is the experimenter simply looking for treatment effects? The answer will determine whether representative sampling of subjects is important.

Two or three further remarks may anticipate some common criticisms of experimentation.

Cost: Dependable information about the costs of social experimentation is hard to obtain. There is no commonly accepted method of accounting for costs; and, in most experiments, there are unrecognized institutional subsidies or shared costs. Costs vary greatly with the content or topic of the experiment and with its duration. The Negative Income Tax Experiment, for example, will cost about 10 million dollars over five-six years, including the outlays for income maintenance payments and analysis costs. The Manhattan Bail Bond Experiment cost about $200,000 for a three-year period, and the Taiwan experiment on acceptability of birth control devices reported spending only $20,000 for a full year of treatment and on-site measurement. In general, one can conclude that the principal difference in cost between experimental and non-experimental social research is the cost of treatment administration and the length of time for which the research staff must be employed.

Delay: On the matter of time delay, the same variability exists. During the six years of the New Jersey experiment there was a national debate about welfare reform which was not brought to any kind of conclusion, but this inconclusiveness cannot be attributed to a deliberate decision to wait for the outcome of the experimental results. In other words, it seems unreasonable to attribute the delay in welfare reform to the experiment, but it is more reasonable to point out that many reforms seem to require a long incubation time during which an experiment is possible and its results possibly useful in the resolution of the action. On the other hand, the Manhattan Bail Bond Experiment which lasted from 1961-1964 was incorporated in federal legislation enacted in 1966 to reform court procedures. It is probably reasonable to conclude that experiments should be undertaken only after strategic consideration has been given to the need for results and the likely costs of either taking no action in the interim or taking actions which are stop-gap and of uncertain effectiveness, but potentially enduring once they have been begun. Finally, it is clear that anticipation of social and political receptivity for an intervention can favor the success of social experimentation.

Hawthorne Effects: On the question of Hawthorne effects, the same murkiness surrounds social experiments as it does laboratory experiments or experiments in factories, schools, offices or other sites involving human beings. Under just what conditions Hawthorne effects will occur is unclear. How strong they will be is also unclear. But it seems likely that in many social experiments the Hawthorne effect is likely to be swamped by forces of everyday life. That is to say, if there is some response, evident in the dependent variable, to the sheer fact of being a subject in an experimental treatment, it seems intuitively plausible to believe that this response might well be temporary and would disappear in the course of an experiment lasting one-to-three years. The durability of "Hawthorne effects" is, however, unclear. Most reports of such effects have concerned short-term responses and there is little evidence either to support or to deny the belief that dependent variable behavior in social experiments is "artificially" or "unnaturally" inflated by the fact of being in an experimental group and being observed. In any case, it seems probable that personal and social responses to experiments would resemble personal and social responses to innovative social reforms or social interventions on a large scale. That is, there would be gradual adaptation to the intervention such that certain responses would not appear in the beginning, but only after a period of adaptive time; and certain responses that did appear at the beginning might become modified later. The point, however, is that the behavior in response to an experimental intervention should in principal resemble the behavior in response to the routine or institutionalized version of the intervention. The chief exception to this generalization should appear in the form of "context effects"—i.e., when the intervention is widespread or universal rather than being confined to an experimental group. Little is known about context effects.

Replicability: The replicability and generalizability of experimentally developed social interventions is a serious question. Like prototype emission control systems on automobile engines, which produce acceptably low levels of gaseous discharge on the test bench but malfunction when the production version is tended by the average car driver and mechanic, so too are experimentally developed social interventions likely to be somewhat less effective when institutionalized. The specially selected and trained staff of an experimental program are likely to be of higher quality than one would expect to find as the average in a national program. Facilities may be exceptional or unrepresentative. As a consequence, the results of such experimentally developed programs may not be replicated under ordinary operating conditions, when the program is installed in an average school or community, for example. Indeed, there may be a trade-off between the precision obtained in a highly controlled experimental development process and the generalizability of its results. It can be argued, on largely pragmatic grounds, that experiments ought to be conducted in more realistic settings even if that forces them to be less neat and precise.

Experiments are, perhaps, most likely to succeed when they are mounted in advance of the development of political pressures to a specific solution for a social problem. When there are several competing alternative solutions for a social problem and there is sufficient time between the undertaking of the experiment and the making of the political decision, then the conditions for experimentation are enhanced. In fact, when the experimental intervention is one to which only a relatively few people are willing to give serious consideration at the time it is proposed, then it may be possible to carry out an experiment without the intervention being captured by political forces and concretized into a total national program before adequate information is available about it. There are other favoring political conditions, but we cannot go into further detail here.

NOTES

1. This paper draws heavily upon a monograph entitled Social Experimentation prepared by a Social Science Research Council committee of which the author is chairman. The author hereby acknowledges his indebtedness to his colleagues on this committee (Robert Boruch, Donald T. Campbell, Nathan Caplan, Thomas K. Glennan Jr., John Pratt, Albert Rees and Walter Williams). The opinions and conclusions herein are, however, the responsibility of the author.

DISCUSSION: Evaluation of Social Experiments

Discussants: Kenneth Arrow, Harvard University
Richard Light, Harvard University
Alexander Mood, University of California
Adam Yarmolinsky, University of Massachusetts

ARROW: I would like to make a preliminary remark about the several references to the cost of these experiments and whether it could be justified. To put this in perspective, one has to consider what it costs to get knowledge, whether it be policy knowledge or research knowledge, in other fields. When a military airplane is designed, there is a prototype. There is a competition at the prototype level between two airplanes. The cost of getting to that stage, and therefore making the policy decision of choosing one, make all the costs we are talking about quite infinitesimal by comparison.

Even in the fields of pure research, the costs of certain kinds of scientific research, particularly high energy physics, can be staggering. One accelerator easily costs 30 to 40 million dollars a year to operate, and this is one among several. I am not in any way speaking against these; on the contrary, I think they are among the glories of our civilization. We do need a certain perspective when we talk about 8 or 10 million dollars for the administrative costs of some of these projects; it doesn't strike terror into my heart, and I don't think it should strike terror into the heart of any sensible taxpayer either. The benefits, if they are positive and measurable, are going to be much bigger than any cost of this kind.

Now, the values of experimentation are inherent in the very topic. It is obvious that you can really compare two policies, in a genuinely controlled way, and get an unequivocal result on a reasonably large random sample. You actually know something. And, therefore, the values which have been discussed in these papers, with an undue degree of modesty in some of the presentations, I think are obvious and probably do not need spelling out. There are a couple of limitations which have been alluded to one way or another. They have to do with scale, in the sense that you are picking out a small part from a large, interconnected system. The policies will be applied on a scale which is large relative to the system. In other words, there are repercussions in the system which cannot adequately be controlled in the experimental procedure. Now, that does not mean that experimental procedure is not useful; what it means is that the results have to be interpreted properly. If you take something like the health study, what you really expect to get information on is the possibility of an increased utilization of medical resources if insurance is high enough to make the price for the consumer very low. Now that does not tell us what is going to happen in the system; and indeed, Dr. Newhouse referred to this toward the end of his presentation. If you take 10% of the population of a city and increase their utilization by 20 or 30 or 40%, that is a 2 or 3 or 4% increase in the demand for medical services in that city. The supply will probably accommodate itself without terribly noticeable strain, although there may be problems locally in specific clinics. On the other hand, if this were used as a prototype for the country as a whole, if everybody had a 20 or 30 or 40% increase, then there would be a large strain on the supply of services.

In the housing supply study which Dr. Lowry reported on, presumably the emphasis there is just the opposite: the idea is to create a high demand by letting everybody relevant have additional housing support, and then find out what the effect is on the supply of housing. On the national housing market, it is going to have a relatively small impact. Of course, there is an empirical question—what is the mobility of housing resources, particularly talking about construction. Obviously, existing housing mobility cannot be very high, except to the extent that you are going to get mobile homes. But certainly, when you consider the effects on new construction, the obvious fact is that if the market gets good there is going to be entry.

Do not misunderstand, this does not mean you have not acquired useful information. That is a different question. For example, in the health study you learn that demand will go up and some strain will occur on the supply. I do not think you can predict very well just what the response of the supply mechanism is; of course, that is partly a matter of policy, not really a matter of prediction.

The other scale question is the temporal scale, which almost everybody did comment on. One difficulty in studying human beings is the fact that the observer lives approximately the same length of time as the observee. The fruit fly, a great subject of genetic experiments, has one very great virtue, maybe not from its point of view but from that of the experimenter, in that its whole life is on the order of fifteen days. You can have many generations in a short length of time. Most of our theories tend to suggest long-term effects of one form or another. In theory, if in an income-support experiment, the subject is told he is going to have that support for three years or five years, the effect will be different than if you have some expectation of its remaining in perpetuity. For example, Dr. Kershaw referred to the effect on schooling, a greater propensity to keep the youths off the labor market and in school. You do not know if this is a straight substitution effect or a liquidity effect; the fact that there is simply more cash in the household. The perfectly rational family or child should borrow because of the anticipated income, but in fact they cannot borrow, so we are just getting a greater ability to keep them in school.

These are the problems that you cannot disentangle in this kind of experiment. You might be able to disentangle some others. It is possible to observe lagged reactions in three to five years, and get, therefore, some evidence on the longer-term reactions. After all, longer-term reactions have to proceed by steps; it is not that something happens and then ten years later something pops up. Presumably, something is happening in the intervening period.

Let me cite some analogs. The real problem is not specific to social science. I do not think the problem is that we are dealing with human beings that have free will and are unpredictable. There may be some ultimate obstacle there, but I do not think we are anywhere near it. The problem is dealing with large, complex, interrelated systems. A strong analog to the social system or an economic system is the atmospheric system that gives rise to the weather. It is a large and complex system;

the forces involved are extremely large; experimental modification is therefore not easily accomplished. You can only introduce perturbations which are rather small compared to the real world in question. Predictability is notoriously modest. A policy issue has come up which I have a very modest knowledge of, so anything I say should be taken with a grain of salt. It is the very large study which is being made on the effects of the supersonic transport on climate and on health. I am not going to try to summarize, but it has to do essentially with the fact that there is a kind of pollution of the stratosphere which may give rise to certain effects on the ozone layer and possibly other effects. Now nobody in that study has suggested experimentation. The most obvious thing is that the conceivable scales are all wrong. The second problem, which is really very acute, is that there is a lot of natural variation to this phenomenon, some of it with a long time scale, roughly equivalent to business cycles, if I can draw an analog, except that some of the cycles are even longer. Therefore, it is very difficult to isolate or interpret any effects we get because they might have been due to other natural covariations. This does not only mean that experiments are not going to be useful, but even the actual operation of a fleet will have great difficulty being interpreted afterwards. And this, of course, is with reference to post hoc evaluations. We might go back in history and, as you know, there have been a lot of big reforms. We read about them in our history books—the progressive era, the New Deal era. It might be an interesting question. What effect did they have? Can we really find out now what difference it makes whether we had, for instance, regulation of railroads? Or now for social security, you might say it had one obvious effect; many people get checks. But are there more subtle things? What does it do to savings patterns, work patterns? Do they spend in different ways because they anticipate social security? Do they save less and, therefore, are they not as well off?

Someone a few years ago did a study of the Tennessee Valley Authority. The analysis was extremly crude, but he compared Southern states in the TVA area and those outside and found no difference whatsoever in economic growth. That was a pretty crude test, and I do not want to hold it up as a model. As Riecken said, it is very hard to find significant differences for anything. You wonder why. I am beginning to question the methodology; I cannot believe none of these things matters.

I would like to discuss briefly the difference between research orientation and policy orientation. The question of policy orientation can be compared to the airplane prototypes: people really want something which is going to work and either have one plane and fly it until it goes, or maybe have two competing ones and test the alternative systems. However, if the problem is, for example, building a better understanding of the economy, you can have a large experiment which provides an opportunity to interpret theoretical results. You can design the experiment to interpret them. It is very limiting; the overall nature of the experiment does prevent you from going into a lot of directions. Typically, you really have to take the theory as given and concentrate on estimating parameters in it. It is rather hard to confront two quite different theories. Now I do not know how it is ever going to be justifiable to Congress to do experiments of an economic kind, which take a relationship that you predict in theory and test it, even though that relationship by itself gives you no policy handle. It only will give you it in conjunction with a lot of other things. Even within these income experiments, for example, one might have thought of testing for pure income effects. Take theoretical decomposition of effects of the system on the work habits into an income effect and a substitution effect. One might have tried one experiment where you just give people money, and find out what happens to the effects. This is not a scheme which could possibly be a genuine policy, but one which will give you information on part of the policy results, or a totally different experiment in which you try to get substitution effects. The results of these experiments may in fact give you a deeper insight into a particular area than you could have gotten by actually using plans. What you really want to test are not the plans but their theoretical basis. If you have a plan that resembles something that you might possibly adopt in legislation, you have something quite complicated already, and to isolate what is in the plan that works becomes very difficult. One could manage, and I have not thought this through, experiments to test how an economic unit, say a firm, would behave if they anticipated the rate of inflation to be zero. I think I can construct a model, essentially guarantee the firm against price level fluctuation, and find out, would they behave differently than they will when they are also speculating on inflationary expectations, and more precisely, how. That by itself does not answer the question, what to do about inflation. But it does tell you something about what a change in expectations would do. I would hope that at some point it will be possible to do experiments designed to get at more underlying relationships in the system.

LIGHT: I would like to make three points about randomization. Are the papers here essentially optimistic or pessimistic about the increased use of social experimentation? Many people alluded to political difficulties, but on the other hand, we see that indeed there is a large and fairly well-funded group of experiments now underway. The need for randomization has also been commented on extensively in these papers. I certainly agree, in terms of ideal design.

Perhaps there are two steps in the development of an awareness among both the researchers and evaluators, and also, perhaps, among funders, say Congress or state legislators, as to what kinds of methodological steps are useful in conducting evaluations. Perhaps we can make a distinction between the idea of control and the idea of randomization. It seems clear that the ideal study or evaluation in social innovation involves both the idea of control and randomization. I mention this because there are some areas, in particular manpower training and preschool education, where there have been some very good control studies but very few good randomized studies. In preparation for this group of papers, I just noticed that in a recent National Academy of Sciences report which came out several months ago, the following sentences, "Manpower training programs have been in existence for a little over a decade, yet with the possible exception of the Manpower Development and Training Program, little is known about the educational or economic benefits of manpower training programs. This is troublesome, especially in light of the fact that about $180 million has been spent over the past ten years in an attempt to evaluate these programs. There are several reasons for the lack of clarity." The report then goes on to document the lack of randomized studies. I am sure some people know a lot more than I do about the details of manpower training studies. I might just mention the one good effort, a randomized study that was quoted by the National Academy of Sciences report, happened to be a study done in Cincinnati using the Neighborhood Youth Corps as an innovation in 1969. And what happened is, a group of older teenaged girls were randomly assigned into two groups; one was given a treatment and the other was not given a treatment, and indeed, a statistically significant difference was found between the two groups. The group given a treatment essentially performed *worse* than the group not given a treatment. It is very disturbing when this is the only randomized study. So to those of us who believe that more randomized studies should be done, perhaps this just provides an example.

Moving to another area, many are familiar with something called the Head Start Planned Variations study. This was an example, I believe, of a study where there was lots of control; that is, it was not just an observational study, where evaluators went and observed what was going on in certain Head Start centers. Rather specific models of Head Start curricula were assigned to different centers. Now, this was done in a very conscious and carefully planned way. However, there was again no randomization of either treatments to sites or children, to treatments versus controls. This makes good inference a little bit difficult. It is, therefore, quite important to make the distinction between control and randomization, realizing that a randomized control study is indeed the ideal study, where it can be carried out.

My second point again relates to randomization. Given that the value of a randomized experiment has been commented on, it strikes me that it would be very useful to see what the benefits of using randomized versus non-randomized studies actually are. How would one go about doing that? Perhaps one would have to take a certain problem where a treatment has been studied many times and compare those studies which are carefully randomized with those which were not. The results would be very interesting.

The last point I would like to make has to do with the need for one new methodological procedure. Suppose that for any particular social or medical innovation there are a couple of good randomized studies. If these two, well-controlled studies give a consistent result, does that mean we should essentially say stop? Should we throw away all the information that has been accumulated over the years in the literature, that comes from non-randomized, uncontrolled studies? I think it would be a shame if we did that, because there are certain kinds of information that come from uncontrolled, observational studies, presumably well-done ones, that really are not necessarily duplicated in a randomized study. Let me give you one example, and just propose that it might be a very worthwhile exercise to think of some others. I cannot offhand. Anyway, the example is the following:

Suppose we have a situation where the treatment we are looking at interacts in some important way with a background variable. Let me choose for this example A. Suppose it turns out that A is better than B for older people, and B is better than A for younger people. The idea being that, with a randomized study, the whole virtue of randomization is to somehow eliminate the importance of a lot of these background variables, so that we can get a sort of raw average comparison between A and B. Indeed A, on the average, may be a lot better than B, but suppose for very young patients, or particularly elderly patients, B is better than A. We will probably not pick that up in a randomized study unless, in advance, we have reason to think of looking at age, in which case indeed we can bring it into the design and see whether there is an age by treatment interaction. But if we do not suspect age, a randomized study will probably not help us very much in picking up the important interaction between age and treatment.

Now, on the other hand, what is the value of looking at observational studies in conjunction with a randomized study? Well, suppose we have 10 observational studies that have been done over the years in the literature and we plow through them. We realize that they are not methodologically pure, but what we find is that in five of the studies treatment A is better than treatment B—each one, say, refers to a particular hospital—whereas in the other five B is preferable to A. What that might tell us to do, assuming the studies were basically well done, is look and see what hospital-to-hospital differences exist which might explain these conflicting results. And we might or we might not pick up age differences. The point is that the conflicting results would give us a clue to look for background variables which explain them. What we might find then is that, for example, five of the hospitals where A is better than B had primarily younger patients, and the other five had primarily older patients. In conclusion I think that we would then want to do once again is stress the value of randomization in a well controlled randomized study bringing in both the treatment comparisons and age, stratifying on age, where we could indeed investigate quite carefully and rigorously the importance of the age by treatment interaction.

It strikes me it is a little bit too easy to just say, let's always do randomized studies. In the real world we will all have many data that come from uncontrolled, unrandomized studies, and it seems to me valuable to try to think of useful ways to use those data together with the data from randomized studies to come up with the conclusions that are as powerful as possible.

MOOD: In considering the problem of evaluating programs, the first example that came to my mind was the Elementary and Secondary Education Act, which has been evaluated sort of haphazardly and found to lack any significant effect. It is a tremendous program, a billion dollars a year, yet it does not seem to accomplish much. We certainly ought to be able to get rid of that one, because it is a Johnson program. Nowadays in Washington, people are not interested in Johnson programs. Here is something that does not work, but it has a life of its own. Suppose that one of us were asked to do an evaluation of it? We would have a very big problem because of the client's interest. It would be almost impossible to go in there and tell them the program is no good. In this business we have a limited number of customers. That particular customer would never look at us again after we evaluated the program, for sound reasons, as far as the customer could see. I know a lot of the people who are administering that program—able, responsible people—but they would not come back to us after that evaluation because we had not been imaginative enough in our evaluation; we had misinterpreted the data, we did not really understand what the program was trying to do, all kinds of legitimate reasons. There would be no likelihood of their calling on that contractor again.

So we in the contracting business have to be aware of the client's interest. They got the money out of Congress for the big experiment. They begin to develop an interest in this thing, its possibilities, its large-scale implementation. So, it is very difficult for us in the business in that situation in that kind of institutional structure. I would say that dealing with the client's self interest is the biggest problem in this budding evaluation business. If it falls backward, it is going to be pretty much on that account.

Irvine is doing an evaluation of a HUD program. HUD put a great deal of money into a half dozen cities to get an urban information system modernized and mechanized. All this information about the locality was in easily accessible form. Various local agencies could use it and generally improve the quality of their service. My colleague, Kenneth Cramer, is evaluating this program with NSF money. You cannot imagine what a comfortable position that puts us in. NSF really has no axe whatever to grind in this program. Government can evaluate its programs in a sensible way, it does not have to do it just through NSF; there are various agencies. I know GAO has proposed that it do evaluations of this sort, and certainly OMB would be a very satisfactory agency to do this sort of thing. One could feel very comfortable working with OMB in evaluating a Federal program.

The other point I would like to make concerns the utilization of existing information. The HUD evaluation I am doing has turned out to be a bigger evaluation of what all the other cities are doing to mechanize and automate their information systems. A lot of program money is being spent out there that did not have to be put out for this particular investigation. There is a tendency when we do experiments to think of using the data from the experiment alone to settle the issue in question. There is tremendous variety out there in the world. There is almost any experiment you could think of. There are other data that could be dug out; and, in some cases, hopefully, for less than the program cost in some of the experiments. They are unsatisfactory data—or we would not be doing experiments. But the question I would like to raise is whether the experimenter should forget about closely related naturally occurring experiments or should he put a little effort into building a bridge from that data to the question at issue.

Professor Lazarsfeld: I think his idea of using existing data, of the use of accumulated data, is undoubtedly very important and I think very often neglected because it is so much easier to experiment, rather than spend two months ingeniously finding existing sources of a secondary nature.

YARMOLINSKY: I would like to remark on bias in the experiment on the part of the experimenter. It reminds me of Niels Bohr's response when someone observed a horseshoe nailed up above the door of his laboratory. They said, "Surely you don't believe in that stuff." And he said, "Oh, no, but they tell me it works whether you believe it or not." The first point I want to make derives more from my experience in the defense establishment, and takes off from Clark Abt's argument about the difference between federal weapons systems evaluation and social experiments today, and I simply wanted to suggest that the difference is perhaps not as great as Clark for understandable purposes suggested it might be. If you look at the history of weapons systems evaluation, you find that practically all the problems that have been discussed here are present, perhaps not on as complicated a scale, but certainly on a larger one. If anything, the negative results of those problems are perhaps even more striking. One example is the problem of concurrency, of pursuing the separate pieces of an experiment; that is, the development of a new weapons system, while trying to get each one of them perfected to the maximum possible degree and then ending up with a set of pieces that do not fit all together into the system. The analogy is to the political investment in the dimensions and shapes of an experiment, when it is a large one, so that you end up with a considerable bias in favor of at least one of the sets of variables even though none of them checks out because you have spent so much money in getting up to that point and so many people have invested their jobs and their futures. Impartial observers like Niels Bohr might suggest that an experiment had not worked, but a lot of people are going to insist very loudly that it has worked because they want to go on staying in the same business.

Apart from that analogy I want to return to my own experience in helping to put together the OEO to ask whether every new social program that we see being launched is not in fact an experiment with or without plan. It may be a bad one, it may be a poorly designed one, but it is going to be an experiment because it is going to be tested in the political arena. We are not, over the next 10 or 20 years, likely to initiate new pieces of public activity in, broadly speaking, the social welfare field, which are either so simple or so obvious that they do not need to go through a very lengthy process of gestation even after they have been brought out into the public and reified by some form of legislation. We are not going to have another social security system or analogy to the social security system; whatever form of health insurance we get, we are likely to get it in pieces, and as new pieces arrive it is likely to change the deal. We may move two steps forward and one step back. The world is just more complicated and difficult and perilous than it was for the social programs of the 30's and even, perhaps, the social programs of the early 60's, and certainly than for the social programs of the 40's.

That being so, I suspect that the distinction between new programs not preceded by social experiments and social experiments is likely over time to erode, and perhaps to disappear. And if that is so, then I suggest that there is both a Scylla and a Charybdis here as there usually is in the real world. There is the danger of launching an insufficiently planned program; but there is also the danger of launching a social experiment that is so much geared to the professional interests of the experimenters that it is not sufficiently in tune with the policy needs of the people who eventually will make up its constituency, and it is not going to be politically viable. Even if what is launched goes under the name of an experiment, if it is big enough, and we are talking about big experiments, it is also, and I am almost inclined to suggest it is primarily, a program. That is to say, it lives or dies more in the world of politics, in the world of competing constituencies, than it does in the world of competing methodologies and experimentation. Therefore, I think that while we concern ourselves with questions of methodology, questions of objectivity, questions of technique, we need also to think about questions of politics and questions of constituency.

Professor Lazarsfeld's Comments: I am afraid that is rather optimistic. There is also a clinical approach. Far be it from me to be against controlled and randomized experiments; it is just like being against mother love or the American way of life. I hope at least the question will be raised as to whether something like quality control, as an official procedure, should not be built into any kind of large-scale social experiment.

I am, at the moment, the evaluator of one of those federally prescribed enterprises. The Federal Investigator Institute for Criminal Justice has taken over the whole probation system of Brooklyn, and has established their own new procedures of getting as many people as possible released on their own recognizance. After they have been arrested they are left alone until they come to the final court procedure. There are two obvious criteria for such an enterprise: (a) Can the Bureau machinery convince the judges to release more people on their own recognizance, and (b) Won't they come back the final time if they do not have to pay bail? The whole effort of the Bureau experiment in Brooklyn is to keep so continuously in contact with the RORs, which means Released on their Own Recognizance, that the final jump rate will be as small as possible. When the man gets arrested, you have to get the necessary information of where he lives, does he have a dog, his community rootedness, in order to decide whether you recommend him. Then the judge might or might not accept the recommendation. There is first a daily and then a weekly contact system by telephone by representatives with those defendants. Then they get various letters from the court which the Bureau machinery is supporting. And the question is, which part of this machinery really accounts for whatever the outcome is? Maybe the Bureau system has, as a matter of fact, decreased the jump rate. But, has it decreased it because they made a more careful inquiry so that the recommendation for release was more reliable?—because they had better telephone contact?—because they had a better local representative in the high arrest area who stayed in contact with those people?—etc.

Dissecting an experiment into its separate parts and trying to see how the possible outcomes (which you do not know in advance) might be improved is quite difficult to do. In this case, it is an interference with the procedure, because you do not wait until the year is over to see whether the jump rates have improved, you make little improvements at those different steps and then see whether month by month as an effect, the jump rate improves. I have to grope with conventional controls, of course. I have to compare this year with last year when there was no Bureau experiment. Those controls are really relatively useless because the record keeping is different and the arrest situation different and the employment situation different, so in the end this intrinsic concurrent quality control seems to me to be a much better service rendered.

This is of course the terminological question: Do you want to call this an experiment at all, and can you rule it out of court? I think there was enough of an element of that that you might keep it positively or negatively in mind. I would say that one advantage is that a lot of friction gets eliminated with this because this kind of concurrent quality evaluation keeps you in pretty steady contact with operating agencies—with the courts, with the probation office who runs the same thing in four other counties, and who has to be pacified if the Brooklyn experiment goes better.

I would like to think of such a sociological situation that has happened historically, that first every industry was run by their own workers. You had the famous managerial revolution and the managers took over, but we are still responsive to the old in one way or another. And now you have a kind of a fair trade, where the quality controllers are built into the whole machinery. They, so to speak, check on the management, but are they subject to management jurisdiction? But in industry, and I think also in public administration, this new function of the built-in quality control, with all the details which you can imagine very easily, operates and forms a part of the broader notion of the social experiment. I wanted to bring up the connection between concurrent quality control and controlled experimentation including randomization as a possible problem which might come up much more often.

II

POLICY RESEARCH AND DECISIONS AND POLITICAL IMPACTS OF EVALUATION RESEARCH

PART II □ CONTENTS

POLICY RESEARCH AND DECISIONS AND POLITICAL IMPACTS OF EVALUATION RESEARCH

Chairperson: ADAM YARMOLINSKY, University of Massachusetts

USE OF A STAFF AGENCY BY THE CONGRESS:
Implementation of The Legislative Reorganization Act of 1970 by the Congressional Research Service

Norman Beckman, Deputy Director
Congressional Research Service
Library of Congress

The mission of the Congressional Research Service is to provide the Congress, and only the Congress, with research and reference assistance on the complete spectrum of public policy issues that Congress must consider. The Service has no monopoly on this function—sharing it with a wide range of resources within the Congress; i.e., members' staffs, professional staffs of committees, policy committees and informal research groups, the General Accounting Office, the Office of Technology Assessment, and the new Congressional Budget Office and with such outside resources as the executive departments and agencies, the various interest group organizations located in Washington and elsewhere, and universities and private research organizations.

Following a very brief history and introduction to the Service, this paper will speak to four questions: What has been done to implement the specific new statutory mandates given the Service in 1970? What has been done to provide additional analytical support to the Congress? What are some of the new directions being considered by the Service? What are the implications for CRS of new proposals to improve Congress' research and information base?

To emphasize the priority to be given by the Service to public policy research, section 321 of the Legislative Reorganization Act of 1970 (Public Law 91-510) changed the institution's name from the Legislative Reference Service to the Congressional Research Service. The intent of this section of the Act was to expand and change the nature of CRS support to Congressional committees, emphasize the primary importance of assistance on legislative matters, promote analytical and original research, grant the Service greater autonomy within the Library of Congress and render it more directly responsive to the Congress. Several of the Act's provisions are directed to the Service's support of Congressional committees: an explicit mandate for policy analysis of legislative proposals, new anticipatory functions—the submission of subject and terminating program lists at the beginning of each new Congress, the preparation of purpose and effect memoranda on legislative measures for which forthcoming hearings have been announced—and a directive to maintain continuous liaison with all committees. The continuation of traditional CRS services was authorized as well, including the preparation of briefs and background reports, research and reference materials, digests of bills and other legislative compilations.

The general intent of the 1970 Act was not significantly different from that of the 1946 Legislative Reorganization Act, which emphasized committee support, appointment of senior specialists, and greater organizational independence for the Service. But this idealistic postwar Act, like the Employment Act of the same year, never achieved its potential. In the first four years after the 1946 Act, appropriations for the Service increased from $213,000 in 1945 to $514,700 in 1949, and its staff grew from 62 persons to 117 in 1949. In contrast, budget increases during the first four years after the 1970 Act raised the Service from a base of $5,653,000 and 363 positions in FY 1971 to $13,345,000 and 703 positions in FY 1975.

The Joint Committee on the Organization of the Congress, in proposing the Reorganization Act of 1946, had "endorsed the principles that (a) research can be most effectively supplied by a pool of independent experts, and (b) that the Congress should have direct access to its own separate research agency." In effect, Congress reendorsed those less than fully achieved principles in the Legislative Reorganization Act of 1970, with an added emphasis upon support for the functions of Congressional committees.

The House Committee on Rules, in its report on the Reorganization Act issued on June 17, 1970, emphasized the Service's new and expanded committee-related duties. "The complexity of committee responsibilities," the report said, "requires another supplementary staff to provide massive aid in policy analysis. For this purpose we propose that Congress expand the functions and facilities of the Legislative Reference Service."

Advance planning is essential if committees are to derive the maximum benefits from the resources to be made available by the Congressional Research Service.

A number of organizational options were available to the Congress in achieving better oversight over the administration of the laws and in getting policy analysis assistance in examining the new legislative proposals. The House Rules Committee rejected making additional staff available to each committee on the grounds that they would be absorbed in day-to-day work, could not do specialized in-depth work, nor provide for exchange of information. A pooled research staff offered a number of advantages:

> Supplementary research staffs, equally available to all committees and operating in a coordinated fashion, can provide better assistance to committees and their staffs not only in program review but also in policy analysis.
>
> Supplementary staffs would: Ensure the equal availability of information to both Houses of Congress; insulate the analytical phase of program review and policy analysis from political biases and therefore produce a more credible and objective product; and more easily develop common frames of reference and analytical techniques that would make such analyses more useful and meaningful to all committees. Finally, the pooling principle underlying supplementary staffs makes them inherently more economical and efficient than dispersed staffs, for they can more easily reallocate resources as changing conditions and Congressional needs warrant.
>
> A new agency for these purposes would face formidable problems of organization and acceptance in Congress. Fortunately, two suitable existing agencies are at hand: the General Accounting Office, and the Legislative Reference Service in the Library of Congress.
>
> Both are used extensively by, and are intimately familiar with the unique needs and problems of, the Congress. Both have personnel experienced in organizing, conducting, and administering research, a rare and valuable commodity. Both have excellent relationships with many committees, and well-earned reputations for objectivity, nonpartisanship, and confidentiality. Both are insulated from political and lobby pressures.

The Service is now the largest institution solely devoted to providing public policy research and information assistance to the Congress. It receives and responds to over 200,000 requests a year, which include over 400 assignments for in depth analytical assistance requiring a significant amount of manpower. CRS provides factual information, analysis of issues, alternatives to proposals, and evaluation of alternatives without either advocacy or partisan bias. It also observes strict confidentiality of both requests and responses. Its assignments are received from four primary sources—committee staffs, Members and their staffs, constituents (received through Congressional offices) and specific statutory requirements such as provision of lists of terminating programs and activities and preparation of the Digest of General Public Bills and Resolutions. The Service, a relatively autonomous entity within the Library of Congress, has subject matter specialists organizationally located in seven research divisions, which are essentially based on the concept of professional skills.

What kinds of public policy research and information, especially as they impact on evaluation of current public programs or proposals, are needed by elected officials at the national level? What are reasonable expectations on the part of the Member of Congress and what kinds of strategies or constraints are placed on a staff agency of the national legislature in providing information used to evaluate and make decisions on public policies?

The following statement by the director of the Service at oversight hearings on Congressional research support and information services by the Joint Committee on Congressional Operations in May, 1974 addresses itself to this issue.

> One of the difficulties in considering the information and research needs of Congress is the tendency to think of the legislature solely as a monolithic institution possessing unified, coherent, and consistent desires. Our experience indicates that it is quite misleading to pose the question only in terms of what "Congress" wants or needs because Congress is, in fact, an enormously complex pluralistic entity.
>
> Yes, Congress has its informational needs as an institution. But Congress also consists of a great many Members, all of whom may have different needs because of their differing backgrounds, interests, constituencies, and circumstances. It also consists of a large number of committees and subcommittees whose needs may parallel or differ greatly from those of individual Members.

Furthermore, every Member is himself a plural entity whose information needs often vary with each of his multiple roles. A Member may want one kind of informational support in a wide variety of formats for his role as a member of a committee, a different kind of support in other formats for dealing with legislative proposals before committees of which he is not a member, a third kind of informational support with respect to other measures and proposals upon which he must vote on the floor of his legislative body, and still a fourth kind to carry out his informational responsibilities to his constituents.

Finally, we face a situation in which Members, committees, and staffs of Congress often disagree with each other about the kinds of information support they want personally or think Congress should have generally. Some Members, for example, say Congress must have a think-tank type of support; others believe such a resource is totally unnecessary and a waste of money. And let me point out that despite the directives of the 1970 Act and its legislative history, there are a few committees that either do not need or do not want "massive aid in policy analysis," although obviously there are a great many more that do.

What, then, does Congress "really" want?

Our experience indicates that Congress as an institution and as a pluralistic entity wants a reasonable parity with the executive branch in access to information and expertise. It wants unbaised information, free from the taint of personal, group, or institutional self-interest. It wants meaningful and reliable information and research that will facilitate legislative decision-making. It wants analytical, interpretive, and consultative services.

It wants research that is relevant, authentic, compact, complete, objective, nonpartisan, and timely. It wants research that reflects communication with the past by reference to the relevant historical record, with the present in such forms as reference to contemporary views of authorities, including views not yet committed to writing, and with the future by way, for example, of anticipating and understanding social and technological change and the possibility that budget commitments may preempt future options.

It also wants policy analysis that will identify, define, and sharpen legislative issues, offer and explore alternative policy and legislative approaches and solutions, and recognize implications and consequences. It wants authoritative opinions and expert technical support. It wants resources that will help it anticipate public policy problems so they can be dealt with in a timely fashion.

It also wants literally hundreds of thousands of facts on an encyclopaedic and ever growing range of subject matter—legislative and non-legislative. It wants those facts arranged in dozens of different ways and embodied in a wide variety of formats— in summaries, in exhaustively detailed reports and analyses, in speeches, in publications, and, most recently, displayed on office television screens. It wants them tailored for dozens of different purposes and uses, written in technical or laymen's language as necessary. Sometimes it wants cursory treatments; sometimes it wants penetrating analyses. And it wants all this, and more, on time: this month, this week, this day, within the hour, at this minute over the telephone.

IMPLEMENTATION OF NEW STATUTORY RESPONSIBILITIES

The legislative history of Section 321 of the Legislative Reorganization Act of 1970 indicates that the Congress sought to achieve two principal goals in revising the basic statute of the Service. First, it was clearly intended that the Service's research and analytical support for the committees of Congress should be expanded. Second, while sanctioning CRS assistance to committees and Members in their representative functions and activities, it intended to make clear, as the House Report put it, that "the major function of the Congressional Research is to provide assistance to committees and individual Members of the Congress with respect to legislative matters."

The current operation goals of the Service are:

−To provide in-depth analytical and research assistance to the committees of the Congress to support them in their legislative and oversight responsibilities.

−To provide both Members and committees with other analytical and research assistance to support their legislative responsibilities.

−To assure that CRS assistance to the Congress is of the highest feasible quality and that it is responsive to the needs of the Congress.

−To provide information on the status and content of current legislative proposals.

−To provide both information and reference assistance to Members and committees to support their legislative and oversight responsibilities.

−To assist Members of Congress with their representative functions.

−To provide the necessary administrative support to ensure the optimal use of CRS resources in meeting Congressional information and research needs.

Stemming from these goals are four major new directives to the Service to be examined in more detail: (a) To provide policy analysis and research to assist committees in their legislative function; (b) Submission of lists of subjects and policy areas to committees at the opening of each new Congress; (c) Submission of a list of programs and activities scheduled to terminate to each appropriate committee at the beginning of each Congress; and (d) Maintenance of continuous liaison with all committees.

Policy Analysis for Committees. The statute (P.L. 91-510) directs that: "(a) Upon request, CRS is to advise and assist all committees and joint committees of Congress in the analysis, appraisal, and evaluation of legislative proposals in order to assist them (1) in determining the advisability of enacting such proposals, and of alternatives to them, and (2) in evaluating alternative methods for accomplishing the goals of such proposals."

This bold and idealistic directive to supply committees with objective, in-depth analysis and presentation of alternatives on any subject matter raised a number of questions for CRS. Is it necessary to set up a separate research staff to provide these in-depth services? What is the relationship between the jurisdictions of the Congressional committees involved and the subject specializations of each of the existing CRS divisions? What gaps exist in subject coverage and competence within CRS? What kinds of methodology would constitute sound policy analysis research and what new analytical techniques and resources should be implemented by the Service? Can policy analysis leading to "determining the advisability of enacting each proposal" be provided without violating CRS policies of non-advocacy? How rapidly can the Service expect to meet the large volume of unanticipated needs without compromising standards of quality and timeliness? How are priority research efforts to be determined? How can the possible fears on the part of professional committee staff about the impact of the Service's new duties be allayed? Should the Service concentrate on committees already receiving considerable research support or on those committees receiving little or no assistance at the present time? Should contacts be made at the subcommittee level or channeled through the full committee? While the Service has explored each of these questions in depth, most will remain unanswered until further experience has been gained.

As part of its evaluation and planning effort, the Service now identifies and monitors major committee projects that require analysis, have a direct connection to legislation, and require a significant investment of CRS manpower. During FY 1973, 220 such projects were initiated. These projects involved work with 36 committees and subcommittees of the Senate, 40 of the House, and 1 joint committee—a total of 77 committees and subcommittees. By the end of March 1974, an additional 261 major committee projects had been initiated and the number of committees and subcommittees served had increased to 46 in the Senate, 48 in the House, and 4 joint committees—a total of 98 committees and subcommittees.

A current analysis of CRS research for committees highlights a number of variables affecting the amount and type of work CRS provides Congressional committees. ("Recent Development of CRS Research and Analytical Work for Committees," In U.S. Congress. Joint Committee on Congressional Operations. Congressional Research Support and Information Services: a compendium of materials. (Joint Committee print). Washington, Govt. Print. Off., 1974.) This analysis notes that even with its new mandate, CRS progress is conditioned by factors over which it has little or no control. The basic decisions that determine both the volume and the type of work are made by the committees. A committee's workload may vary from Congress to Congress, session to session, and even week to week, and its need for research and analytical support may fluctuate correspondingly. In addition, the basic character of a committee's jurisdiction may require little, or only sporadic, research support, as is the case of the House Committee on Rules and the Committees on Rules and Administration and Standards and Conduct in the Senate. Furthermore, some committees prefer to employ other research resources—their own staff or an executive agency, for example—as in the case of the Joint Committee on Atomic Energy.

In spite of these variables, the overall pattern was one of more time spent for more committees. A significant number of committees moved from the category of minimal support in FY 1971 to categories of larger time expenditures in FY 1973. Thirteen committees to which CRS devoted fewer than 1,000 research hours in 1971 received more than 1,000 hours in 1973, and in several cases considerably more.

Lists of Subjects and Policy Areas for Committees. One of the major new responsibilities assigned to the Congressional Research Service by the Legislative Reorganization Act of 1970 was designed to assist committees with their advance planning. CRS was thus directed to make "available to each committee of the Senate and House of Representatives and each joint committee of the two Houses, at the opening of a new Congress, a list of subjects and policy areas which the committee might profitably analyze in depth . . ."

Here too a range of problems and options confronted the Service. Should a comprehensive list be prepared for each committee or should the lists be limited to subjects on which CRS could offer assistance? Should only lists be provided or should additional analytical materials be provided? Should lists be provided to committee chairmen only, all members of a committee, or to Congress as a whole? What methodological procedures should be used in identifying and tracking policy areas in each major subject field? What if a committee does not desire the submission of such a list?

For the pilot implementation of this new responsibility, the following procedures were developed and carried out. Late in 1972, in preparation for the 93rd Congress, appropriate CRS staff met with committee staffs and, in some cases, Members. Ad hoc teams consisting of some 30% (144 persons) of the total research staff were formed to work with each Congressional committee. Individual teams were composed of individuals knowledgeable in most aspects of a committee's jurisdiction and in many cases included staff from several divisions. The committee was encouraged to discuss their plans and needs for research with the appropriate team and in turn CRS staff suggested additional promising subject areas for the committee to consider. It was also an opportunity to describe CRS capability in the committee's fields of interest. The resulting lists of subjects and policy areas thus incorporated contributions by both CRS and the committee.

Each committee was given the option of receiving a selected list consisting only of subjects on which the Service could provide assistance, or a comprehensive list, which included but was not limited to those subjects on the selected list. The final product, unless specifically requested otherwise by a committee, included a summary list of agreed-upon subjects and policy areas, a one-page description of each subject to explain the reasons for its inclusion and provide additional sources of information, and, to the extent feasible and desired by the committee, additional materials to supplement and illustrate the one-page treatment.

To obtain systematic data about the impact of the lists on committee activities, the Service compared the subjects that appeared on each committee's list with those the committee actually took up in one way or another during the first session of the 93rd Congress. Without exception, every committee to which a list was submitted—standing, special, select, and joint—took up at least one of the subjects submitted to them. Overall, House committees took up a fraction less than one-half the subjects on their lists, Senate committees took up almost

5% more than half, and committees as a whole dealt in one way or another with 48.3% of their subjects. This reflects the Service's attempt to make the lists realistic working documents rather than esoteric or academic products. Committee participation in evolving the lists also contributed to this characteristic.

Terminating Programs. Documentation and current status of legislation has always been a concern of the Congress. The Reorganization Act inaugurated new documentation responsibilities by directing the CRS prepare for each Congressional committee a list of programs and activities, within its jurisdiction, scheduled to terminate during each Congress. CRS, in developing its guidelines, assumed that the principal purpose of preparing the lists was to assist further the committees in their advance planning efforts. This section examines the Service's progress in implementing this new responsibility.

Beginning in late 1971, the American Law Division of the Service examined over 4,000 statutes enacted during the preceding decade and by December 1972 had identified some 730 programs and activities scheduled to terminate during the 93rd and subsequent Congresses. Over half of these programs related to authorization of appropriations, and an additional 23% provided general authority for programs operated by executive branch agencies. Other categories included termination of commissions, loan authority, tax authority, reservations of land, pensions, and reporting requirements.

Following identification of terminating programs, the Service prepared summary lists of the 458 programs and activities scheduled to expire during the 93rd Congress and transmitted these, with supplementary descriptive materials, to 32 House, Senate and joint committees of Congress. Each committee packet included basic identifying information and a legislative history on each terminating program within the committee's jurisdiction. for 319 programs terminating during the first session of the 93rd Congress, the Service, insofar as resources permitted, also sent to each committee a more detailed report to aid the committee in reviewing the program.

The issues involved in implementing the terminating program responsibility were largely internal in nature. What should be the relative division of labor between the legal staff of the Service and the substantive researchers in other divisions? How much more than a mere list of program activities would prove useful to committees? Should additional background material be provided only on important legislation or only to clearly receptive committees? To what extent should the substantive report on the expiring programs evaluate performance? If evaluative material is presented, can advocacy with respect to possible extension or modification of the program be avoided? Can individual programs and activities or even individual pieces of legislation be discussed independently of other related programs?

CRS Liaison with Committees. The Legislative Reorganization Act requires CRS to maintain continuous liaison with all committees so that they may better understand and utilize the Service's multidisciplinary research resources and facilitate advance planning. Although separately stated in the 1970 Act, several of the Service's new duties concerning Congressional committees are closely related in overall purpose. Because preparation of lists of subjects and policy areas and terminating programs for committees was not required until late 1972, the Service early turned its attention to the general liaison function.

The objective of the new liaison effort to be undertaken was described in a memorandum from the Director (contained in the 1971 Annual Report) stating in part:

> Because each committee is unique to one degree or another, liaison efforts should be applied with the flexibility necessary to accommodate the unique circumstances of each committee, the present state of our relationship with the committee, the degree of liaison the committee will tolerate, the degree of liaison suitable to that committee, and, of course, the available resources of the Service.
>
> Overall, our goal is to establish closer and more continuous contact between the Service and all committees so that we may more effectively assist them in every suitable way and most particularly in the area of policy analysis.
>
> Our liaison efforts with committees should be directed toward: (a) keeping them informed about our present and potential resources for assisting them; (b) acquainting them with Service reports, already prepared or in preparation, of interest to them; (c) informing them about other, non-Service materials of use to them and of techniques by which the Service can keep them regularly informed about such materials; (d) the preparation and submission of those lists of subjects and policy areas the committees might profitably analyze in depth that we are obligated to supply them, including subjects of emerging interest to them; and (e) preparing and submitting the lists of expiring legislation also required by the Reorganization Act.

Perhaps the major options facing the Service in implementing the liaison function were those of internal organization and rate of implementation. A recent internal memorandum describes the basic organizational issues:

One of the first questions the Service examined after passage of the 1970 Act was whether it should establish a staff exclusively devoted to committee liaison—that is personnel whose sole function it would be to maintain communication and contact with committees. After careful consideration, and at the urging of virtually every senior CRS staff member with experience in working closely with committees, the Service decided not to adopt this approach, at least during the first few years of operations under the 1970 Act. Until circumstances indicated another course, therefore, we decided to rely upon our senior subject people, those who actually do substantive work for committees, for the liaison function.

The Service is aware that other agencies, including the General Accounting Office, employ the exclusive liaison group system, and we know something about their experience with it. We realize that such a system is more amenable to direct control by top management, that liaison with committees requires special talents, and that placing the liaison function upon subject staff inevitably erodes some of their time.

On the other hand, several factors have persuaded us to adopt the course we have taken. Ours was and remains a relatively small organization; we do not feel we can afford to devote positions to this exclusive function, positions better devoted to research. We are not like other agencies in our dealings with Congress and its committees. Ours is a supplementary staff function; we are often an extension of committee staff. This involves a close, day-to-day working relationship between our people and committee staff and Members. Our people sometimes participate in the full range of committee work, from the first ideas about hearings through floor proceedings and conferences between the two houses on bills. We believe that a bureaucratic layer of professional liaison staff inserted between our subject experts and the committees for whom they work might disrupt these necessarily close relationships. We also feel it would introduce a communication barrier distorting the nuances and subtleties of committee research and analytical needs which are often so important and which only close personal relationships can convey. Finally, our experience indicates that, by and large, members and staff of committees much prefer to deal directly with subject experts than with professional liaison people.

While a more formalized network might have been expected to be established by this time, the process to date has been an evolving one. This, in large part, is due to the number of committees and subcommittees involved, approximately 350. The goal continues to be an evolutionary approach designed to build working relationships based upon subject expertise.

OTHER INNOVATIVE SERVICES

The Service's response to Congressional needs goes beyond the very ambitious and explicit statutory provisions of the Legislative Reorganization Act. The House Rules Committee report on the Reorganization Act directed CRS to experiment with additional ways of providing assistance to Congress:

> Staffs should become proficient in existing analytical techniques and develop new ones as necessary. Both agencies (CRS and GAO) should be encouraged to experiment and to be innovative in carrying out their new as well as their older functions.

The Director of the Congressional Research Service, in recent testimony before the Joint Committee on Congressional Operations, identified certain new services not explicitly required by the 1970 Act:

> ... We sponsor several series of seminars at which outside experts discuss major public policy issues with Members or staff. We have steadily expanded our automation facilities and sought new and promising applications. One of these, for example, provides us, and therefore the Congress, with one of the largest and most up-to-date economic data bases currently available and includes programs for analyzing the economic impact of alternative fiscal and monetary policies. With the encouragement of the Senate Committee on Rules and Administration, CRS is developing an issues briefing system through which we will be able to provide concise updated information about current legislative issues by video screens located in the offices of Members.

The public policy seminars for Members and staff, and the automated information services, are described in more detail below.

Public Policy Seminars. The Service has expanded cooperative arrangements with outside organizations to permit Members and their staffs to meet informally with experts on national issues. With the Advanced Study Program of the Brookings Institution, CRS initiated in the fall of 1972 a series of seminars for Members of Congress and a separate series for the senior staffs of Member and committee offices. In the past two years, 12 seminars for Members have included discussion of such topics as: U.S. relations with China, crime prevention and law enforcement, energy and the environment, national housing programs, consumer protection, media and the government, and the multinational corporation. Eight seminars have been held for Congressional staff on: legislative implications of the 1972 election results, budget reform and control, legislation affecting the status of women, and new trends in strategic weapons policy in the national defense budget. The series has attracted an overall attendance of 277 Members and 677 staff.

Additional seminar activities have included a continuing series on national urban growth policy, four seminars exploring basic tax issues, held for Congressional staff in 1973, and presentations by CRS and the Office of Management and Budget in February 1974 to House, Senate, and CRS staff on use of the 1975 budget documents.

Automated Information Services. The Service has identified a number of procedures with potential for the storage and delivery of information through the application of data processing techniques. Thus, in recent years, the Service has gained access to or has internally developed a number of data files. The legislative Information Data Base includes the contents of the Service's Bill Digest and additional information on all public bills and resolutions of the current Congress. Each bill is monitored for 22 data elements (for example, bill co-sponsor, committee action, identical bills) and information is retrievable via video tube in several formats (for example, a run of all bills assigned to a particular committee and a listing of all bills relating to a specific subject).

Most recently, at the initiative of the Chairman of the Senate Committee on Rules and Administration, the Service has been developing an automated Issues Briefing System. This experimental new service is being made available on a pilot basis, pending its further development and refinement. The system is designed to serve the current information needs of Members, committees, and their staffs by maintaining general, easily accessible summaries of many key issues of public policy. The summaries, or Issue Briefs, are provided by means of a computer information storage and retrieval system that can be accessed by videotube terminal. Copies of individual Issues Briefs are also available to both the Senate and House in printed form. Each Issue Brief (currently on 130 topics) contains current information on background facts, legislation, Congressional hearings, reports, and chronological developments, and provides useful references.

In addition to these programs maintained by CRS personnel and stored in the Library's computer, the Service currently has rental access to five outside data banks. The *New York Times* Information Bank is accessed by a video-tube and associated high-speed printer and queries are transmitted by direct telephone line to the data files. These files contain indexes and abstracts of all news articles published in the *New*

York Times since 1969 and abstracts from selected additional magazines and newspapers. MEDLINE contains over 400,000 entries from some 1,200 journals in the medical research and public health fields. Its bibliographic data are retrievable by author or subject. JURIS (Justice Retrieval and Inquiry System) maintains the text of six information files, including the U.S. Code. Additionally, CRS has access to programs that provide the program grants and expenditures of the Department of Health, Education and Welfare; that can project the costs of federal support to education and other programs; and that provide an econometric model of the national economy, which enables extensive analytical review of the federal budget.

THE PAST IS PROLOGUE

In the past four years, CRS appropriations requests have placed the highest priority on implementation of new and expanded responsibilities under the 1970 Act. Although the rate of growth has been slower than anticipated, the Service has acquired significant new staff resources, and assistance to committees has grown correspondingly. Now that the Service is moving toward completion of its five-year implementation program, new approaches are being explored to satisfy the research needs of the Congress.

A statement by the Director of the Service at the May, 1974 hearings of the Joint Committee on Congressional Operations on research and information support for the Congress sketches certain of these exploratory efforts:

> The Service has already asked for funds that will permit us to explore the addition of another dimension to our support for Congress: futures research. This relatively new discipline might help us to do a more penetrating job of identifying and analyzing emerging public policy issues, especially of the type suitable for the team approach I mentioned a moment ago. The potential of futures research was endorsed by the House Select Committee on Committees, which recommended that each House Committee establish a subcommittee devoted to this area and to oversight functions.
>
> ... We also hope to establish closer liaison with the scholarly community, perhaps by a program of temporary assignment of scholars to the Service who could provide tangible assistance on specific projects and who would bring fresh insights to the staff of CRS and the Congress. With this in mind, we have held preliminary discussions with the Woodrow Wilson International Center for Scholars at the Smithsonian Institution, exploring

the possibility of having their scholars spend some time with us on mutually agreed-upon assignments. I particularly want to examine how CRS might take advantage of the Civil Service Commission's new Government Affairs Faculty Fellowship Program, which is intended to encourage faculty fellowships in government agencies.

Many Members and committees show increasing interest in the use of public opinion surveys to supplement their informational resources. Although it is probably inappropriate for CRS to conduct such surveys, there are a number of ways in which we might assist Congress in this area. We are going to be examining the availability of survey research information, its values and techniques and its applicability to legislative research.

I have already mentioned our interest in establishing programs that would permit us to attach some of our staff to committees for limited periods so they can learn more about the needs of those organizations.

The recommendations of the House Select Committee on Committees, as contained in House Resolution 988, would also have a number of impacts on CRS, as well as on the delivery of research and information services to the Congress generally. Of major long-term significance, the resolution would create a House Commission on Information to study and make recommendations on "the information problems of the House of Representatives against the background of the existing institutions and the services available to the House . . .' The study is to include, but not be limited to CRS, the General Accounting Office, and the Office of Technology Assessment and the organizational framework that makes them effective or ineffective.

Other proposals contained in the resolution of the Select Committee on Committees called for creation of a legislative classification office, preparation of summary descriptions of House bills, expansion of standing committee staff, and revision of committee jurisdiction. Each of these proposals, if enacted, would have a significant impact on CRS responsibilities and relationships with committees.

Other legislation introduced in the 93rd Congress to establish new offices and commissions in the legislative branch would also impact on CRS and its plans for further implementation of the 1970 Legislative Reorganization Act. These proposals include the establishment of:

Office of Goals and Priorities Analysis (S. 5, Sen. Mondale)

Congressional Office of Policy and Planning (S. 3050, Sen. Humphrey)

Congressional Center for the Study of Domestic and International Policy (H.R. 2144, Rep. Reid)

Office of Consumer Counselor (S. 1409, Sen. McIntyre and H.R. 6879, Rep. Stephens)

Office of the General Counsel (S. 1726, Sen. Gravel; S. 2615, Sen. Hartke; S. 2569, Sen. Mondale; S. 2992, Sen. Humphrey; H.R. 1101, Rep. Abzug; and H.R. 13018, Rep. Owens)

Office of Constituent Assistance (S. 2500, Sen. Hartke)

Office of Congressional Communications (S. 2992, Sen. Humphrey and H.R. 13018, Rep. Owens)

Office of Congressional Ombudsman (H.R. 7680, Rep. Owens)

Citizen's Committee to Study Congress (S. 2992, Sen. Humphrey).

Implicit in certain of the proposals for improved Congressional decision-making is a search for a "philosopher's stone," a device that will produce the right answers; a *deus ex machina* that will recommend legislation that best achieves the public interest.

The Service, as a staff arm of a policy-mediated and partisan power structure, operates on an entirely different premise. It has no official views as to which is a better solution to a legislative problem. It attempts to identify choices and to forecast the apparent implications of the alternatives, but it is the Member and then the Congress that makes the decisions.

Hairline distinctions must be observed by a CRS staff member on the one hand to avoid either advocacy or sterility and on the other maintain a reputation as a leading specialist in his subject field. The rules of the game are described in a recent Praeger volume on U.S. Government agencies, *The Library of Congress:*

> In order for the CRS to survive, the congressional inquirer must never be able to guess where the researcher himself stands on any particular issue. The result is that if someone believes deeply that a particular solution is the only answer, that person is inappropriate for the CRS ... But the person who believes deeply in the importance of his subject field and who is eager for the Congress to have as many solutions available to it as possible and to have as great a knowledge of the impact of these alternatives, together with a sensitivity to what these solutions will cost this generation and five generations to come, and who yet recognizes that, for the democratic system to survive, the choice of a solution must be left to the elected representatives—that is the person the CRS seeks for its staff.

These and other proposals will continue to involve CRS and the Congress in carrying out the spirit of the Legislative Reorganization Act of 1970. The CRS mission remains to respond to the research, analytical, and informational demands of Congress. To do so will mean constantly seeking and implementing new and improved ways of fulfilling that mission within the ground rules of confidentiality, non-advocacy, and non-partisanship.

POLICY RESEARCH AND DECISION MAKING
IN EDUCATION

Sylvain Lourie
UNESCO

In spite of the many statements and resolutions at national or international gatherings promoting innovations in education, the results showing up quantitative or structural changes have yet to be related to objectives originally defined by researchers and interpreted by planners. Changes in education are not generally initiated through a recognition of the dysfunctions of the system as these may have been detected, analysed, or classified by researchers. In reality, they are set in motion by "extrinsic" factors. They are not only alien to research in education but, more often than not, to phenomena affecting directly the structures or operation of the educational system.

Thus, a decision-maker[1] may move towards a new policy in education (nine years compulsory education, rural-based school, looser admission criteria to universities, qualification of work performance to be equated to academic standards, within the concept of life-long education) more because of his "sense of timing" of an opportunity-target such as increase of popular support, potential gains within the power structure or improvement of relations with trade unions, particularly with teachers. He may also be obliged to react to national policies which may affect his domain; such as, income and wage policies to the extent these may change incentives or motivations for career choices at the secondary or university level and dependency on traditional agricultural exports and its consequences such as stagnancy of the land structure and utilization of a cheap and illiterate labor force, etc.

This does not imply that when decision-making "time" comes, the stock of past research on alternative strategies will be forgotten. Many analyses, studies, simulation models and exercises will have piled up in universities, private institutions, and international organizations. Some of it may have even trickled down—or up—to the administration entrusted with the preparation of the decision and, ultimately, with its implementation. Often the very same administration will have asked—and paid—for the studies, which, elegantly bound and printed, filled its storage rooms and corridors but no one's mind . . . until somehow a signal for some action is initiated from the "front-office." Then, gradually, some of the material is filtered to the decision-maker in a form which its authors would hardly recognize or condone.

Thus, for example, a reform of education was launched some years ago in a small Latin republic on the premise that television would revolutionize the schools. This was more the result of a minister having been convinced, by skillful commercial salesmanship, of the merits of educational television, than the outcome of deliberate preliminary analyses. Researchers, little fond of lock-step "reforms" but rather more attracted by a permanent process of "change," had hoped for a decision to start studies, experiments, and analyses on the software (curriculum, course content, teaching guides) as a prerequisite to any commitments on the hardware.

In this particular example some of the preparatory research work was not entirely wasted since the educational television programs did take into consideration some of the substantive suggestions made by the policy researchers concerned with new course content or programs. Generally speaking, however, the television did not reform the system at all. It added costs, helped create a small reserve of local technicians, and—on the whole—did improve the qualifications of the teachers. It had, however, become the battle horse of an aggressive education minister and had set in motion a process which may one day lead to questioning the existing unchanged forms of school education. A far cry from the proclaimed "reform."

The contact between policy research and decision-making seems then to occur when the decision-maker, either prompted from inside or eroded from outside, seeks ammunition with which to bombard his political targets. Within his power is the selection of existing research results. In so doing he may reject the whole for some of its parts, simply because they appeal to him in terms of their potential short-term spectacular effects.

What conclusions can one draw from such a working hypothesis? First, is that the decision-maker should be offered, almost on a permanent basis, ideas of possible changes which researchers have either proven or experimented with so that he may become aware of "vehicles" for his motivations. Conversely, researchers should be alerted and grow accustomed to the "extrinsic" preoccupations of the decision-maker. In short, channels of communication should be left continually opened between research and policymaking to foster mutual contamination. This is rather obvious and "banale" for it begs the real issue: how to open and maintain these communications' channels? This paper in no way proposes to set down formulae but simply suggests that the involvement of decision-makers at the earliest stages of any research program is almost an unconditional prerequisite for reasonably efficient action. It may entail establishing structures, either formal (committees) or informal (week-end seminars), or it may limit itself to inviting decision-makers to participate in research planning processes. Solutions must fit special situations and cannot be prefabricated in universal or general terms.

Let us take another example to clarify what should be a second lesson for the partners in the research-decision-venture: Ivan Illich's "deschooling of society" concept. In the mind of a minister, this motto means, "We have to do away with schools." The impact of Illich's idea is totally nil as no minister, politician, or average citizen for that matter would entertain a possibility which smacks of irresponsibility or of anarchy. Let us however de-escalate the proposal and explain that "de-schooling" means freeing society from a traditional mold cast by the school (selection, elitism, discipline, fear, social stratification, etc.). The minister, upon hearing this, might at least raise an interested eyebrow and show some comprehension. If he is truly alert he might even see in this proposal a socially-charged political message (whether it be compatible or not with his or his party's ambition . . .). Let us be more concrete still and clarify the statement further: de-schooling really means shifting the school from academic, conventional, traditional subjects inculcated by rote learning to problem-solving activities centered on community and local issues. Our same minister might then find no threat in such an idea and could see in it the terms of a reform suitable to his requirements.

In this imaginary scenario we tried to show the need to "decode" research-based language[2] in political terms. Thus, using the binary responses "yes-no" of our minister to different levels of disaggregation of the same idea, we selected in fact a practical path leading from a research product to an input into his power game.

Too often policy research rests on models taken from reality but so lifted from the world of decisions to that of reflection, experimentation, and analysis that they are frozen and then used as bases for testing assumptions. The independent variable turns out to be indeed the most volatile one. While it may appear formalistic, the situation might be different if the language used in research were constantly related to that of decision-making. For example, in education research, the concept of school-enrollment ratio is hardly ever used seriously as it disguises phenomena such as repeaters and school leavers which in turn reflect the selectivity or irrelevance of the educational system. Yet, it took more than 20 years of international conferences to shift the attention of decision-makers from the short-term payoff of enrollment growth to the medium and long-term damages of low productivity of schools and the irrelevance of their content to the demands of contemporary society and of the employment market.

This is attributable of course to the inevitable pressure in favor of more schools for more children or more universities for more students, but also, to a larger extent than suspected, to the dichotomy of criteria and consequent duality of language, between analysis of the educational scene and its main actors. Had researchers understood the importance of devoting their energy to explaining the quality problems instead of building increasingly complex supply models of education, some years of irresponsible and meaningless target-setting for school enrollment might have been saved. Researchers could have studied and publically presented the results of financial analyses pointing up the high cost of low productivity and offered targets of output instead of letting decision-makers propose growth targets. This might have wielded some influence in slowing down the rush towards "more of the same."

The second consequence, therefore, of our hypotheses, and, perhaps more fundamental, is the need to define research needs and results in *terms* of their policy implications.[3] The implication is that if research is to serve or influence decision-making, it must express the objectives and motivations of those on which research seeks to create an impact. We are suggesting, therefore, that a common language be developed. This implies:

1. That policy researchers not divorce themselves from semantics of decision-makers and accept well-known "bottles" in order to fill them with enriched contents; that they find out how to "translate" their premises and findings in a manner readily understandable by the decision-maker.

2. That decision-makers gradually learn to "decode" the messages of the researchers.

In summation, the two requirements for making research more *relevant* and decision-making more informed are:

1. The opening up and preservation of permanent channels of communications, and

2. The establishment of a common language between researchers and decision-makers.

Before reflecting on the applicability of these criteria to social researchers producing evaluations and decision-makers applying evaluation of government social programs, two reminders seem appropriate: the realm of choice of decision is considerably more reduced in reality than the decision-maker would like it to be or than the researcher seems to assume it is. Decisions are not the product of a free choice in an infinite array of possibilities. They are in fact conditioned by previous and collateral decisions or events which limit the choice of the decision-makers to a minute range of possibilities. Hence, both decision-makers and researchers should do well in their future permanent relations in a "common language" to restrict the orbit of their prospective flights into the world of decisions by preselecting those unchartered routes which may in fact be assumed to be opened.

The other caveat which might be worth introducing at this stage is that decisions are never really global, certainly not in education. One more change—or a "reform" as some structuralists may christen it—affects only a small portion of the educational edifice. The sum of these changes, provided they be strategically consistent, does lead to a global change. So it is with the decisions concerning the changes. The gradual accumulation of coherent decisions taken in the same direction lead to a modification of functions and institutions. A single decision however is rarely "monumental," but here again, both decision-makers and researchers—for different and sometimes opposing reasons—behave as if one decision will "do the trick." Institutions are as "good as the men and women running them"; and, in social programs, human beings will ultimately determine, by their behavior or their reactions, whether a decision is to be viable and affect their lives, or whether one more sweeping decision is to be added to the collection of non-starters which politicians quickly forget but which historians or ethnologists unearth to justify their Ph.D. theses.

Looking now on the more specific issue of *evaluation* one might venture some thoughts based on the experience obtained in the realm of policy and oversimplified in the preceding paragraphs. The first suggestion is that the relationship should be considerably simpler although it does not appear that way from what has happened and is still happening.

It should be simpler because evaluation is an integral part of an action which itself is the product of a decision. Here, the chicken-egg dilemma does not exist, as the start of an operation signifies the start of the evaluation process. An operation which can be defined in terms of "its terminal performances specifications" and of defined methods and means has already established the conceptual framework of the evaluation operation. Only later, when evaluation has yielded its results, can one speak of the role of evaluation as subject and no longer object of a social program. This will occur as evaluation proposes:

a) Feedback to the decision-maker, and

b) A "loop" to action-based research to be fed back, in turn at a subsequent sequence, to the decision-maker.

Unfortunately, it is not so simple. Evaluation researchers generally must use as a framework a "frozen" model. More serious still, they assume that it will offer an alternative for the decision-maker which in fact is beyond his reach and will permit a global change which is unrealistic. Hence, to the extent that the techniques of the researchers find their way to the decision-maker, he does not recognize the model as it no longer fits his needs.

If, however, he is attracted by the far-reaching proposal for change involved, he will soon be faced with the harsh reality of the two "caveats." The proposals of the evaluation researchers will then lose most of their credibility.

Here again the remedy lies in the existence of communication channels and in a common language. But in the case of evaluation, it should be considerably more natural to achieve both than in the case of policy. Let us take the case of the educational television already mentioned. A recent evaluation based on excellent research covering the techniques, the programs, and the audience did yield results which were immediately translatable into decisions. Why was it so? Simply because the evaluation accompanied the operation and consequently both communications channels and language were common to the evaluators and the decision-makers. The evaluators had to translate and sometimes promote research work so as to buttress their own analysis. But they were able to keep their use of the research perfectly attuned to the decision-maker's motivation.

The cycle was: decision-maker (develop rapidly national education television) → operation (program development, construction of production, transmission and reception facilities) → evaluation (of the operation as defined by the decision-maker) → evaluation research (loop) → evaluation (improved techniques) → decision-maker. By definition, the evaluation report was expressed in terms (chapters and sections) each of which had been an element of the original decision as reflected in the operation. Thus, the evaluation was couched in the "language" of the decision-maker and readily recognized by him as an instrument for possible action.

Another lesson we may draw in this case is that just as evaluation was an integral part of the decision-operation nexus so was evaluation research part and parcel of the evaluation process. It was fed by the first results of the evaluation; and, as it helped develop new criteria for measurement or assessments, it was fed back into further evaluation. Hence, the original reference to a "loop" operation.

One is tempted to suggest an apparently unfair and certainly debatable conclusion in the form of a question rephrasing the objective of our exercise. Can a "production" of evaluation by social researchers be organically separated from the application of evaluation by decision-makers? My view (profoundly marked by extended propinquity with decision-makers . . .) is that such a separation would threaten the very meaning of evaluation and therefore of evaluation research.

To be sure, a body of experience must be built up and wide circulation of results among practitioners must be fostered so as to achieve rational use of efforts and time. In that sense, some "evaluation research" is necessary. But then, would not a more appropriate name for it be "compilation" of action-based and oriented evaluation research?

NOTES

1. For the sake of illustration and in order to "caricature" the constraints—and contradictions—between policy research and decision-making, the latter function will be attributed in this paper to a political agent, say the minister, and not to a professional—although this is often the case.

2. Illich's highly intuitive and emotionally charged messages are nonetheless products of research.

3. This is not to say that research must limit itself to the short-term spectacular payoff sought by the decision-maker as this would cut the very lifeline of research which feeds on unfettered and creative imagination.

POLICY ANALYSIS AND EVALUATION RESEARCH IN CONGRESS[1]

Alair A. Townsend
Research Director
Subcommittee on Fiscal Policy
Joint Economic Committee

When I was asked to give my views on how Congress uses evaluation research and policy analysis and how such research could be made more useful to Members of Congress, I found I had more questions than answers. My Congressional experience has been with a non-legislative study committee, not with a Member's office or a legislative committee. The mandate of the Subcommittee on Fiscal Policy of the Joint Economic Committee for the last three years has been to produce broadly conceived studies about the public welfare system. My job has been to conduct and disseminate analysis and evaluation on a day-to-day basis. Since our office has thus been rather insulated from the overwhelming daily legislative pressures, my views must be acknowledged for what they are—namely, not those of a Congressional insider.

As in the Executive Branch, many, perhaps the bulk, of decisions in Congress are made without extensive analysis or evaluation. Much legislative action is simply the extension of actions taken before and hence does not seem to require thorough-going review. Yet, on certain issues, research and analysis do have an impact. This seems especially likely if there are to be major shifts in domestic policy. Policy analysis and evaluation research can provide the rationale for change and can make the change more acceptable and the probable outcomes somewhat more predictable. This is one of the values of the income maintenance experiments, for example.

Many of the day-to-day voting decisions in Congress do not involve major shifts in policy. Instead they are small steps that, cumulatively, take us farther down one road or another. For example, when a social security bill is considered in the Senate, floor amendments are possible, unlike in the House. Each time this happens, Senators offer a flood of amendments to broaden medicare and social security coverage and benefits. Are such amendments desirable? Should an unmarried, aged, dependent sister be allowed to draw social security benefits on the account of the dead brother who formerly supported her? Should medicare premiums be held constant rather than increased slightly? If I were asked to judge these amendments as an analyst concerned with the social security system, I could only say that the desirability of such actions depends on where and how you want the social security system to evolve. It is very clear that taking these legislative steps would make social security more social and less insurance. It is less obvious what, if anything, should be proposed instead, or how likely Congress is to consider the fundamental question of what goals the social security system ought to try to achieve and how it should achieve them. This would require the broadest kind of program review, taking several years. Meanwhile the Member would have to vote, and it is hard to vote no to such popular measures without being able to offer better reasons than one's desire for overhaul of the system and greater reliance on income-tested programs.

Since so much legislation consists of such small versus big policy shifts, the role of research and evaluation is limited. What is important in such cases, it seems to me, is to understand and promote the need for analyses that do look at the broad choices, even though such studies cannot be expected to have immediate impact. It is in these areas—very technical, requiring access to data and heavy use of computers—that Congress has acceded to the Executive Branch. But the Executive Branch is not always anxious to review highly popular programs. That branch has its own defenses. That is why I expect Congress increasingly to undertake or commission more of its own broad analyses. Incidentally, it is clear to me that a debate over directions for social security financing and benefit structure is very likely, if for no other reason than widespread worry about the system caused by a flurry of newspaper articles about whether social security is going broke.

Newspapers also have contributed more than analysis to policy change in the area of social services furnished to welfare receipients and other groups among the poor under the Social Security Act. Several articles in the *Washington Post* suggest that social service funds were being used to refinance state and local governments. As a result, Congress quickly moved to put a ceiling on these appropriations. The fact that some evaluations had shown certain of the services to be ineffective may have helped, but the threat of a treasury raid and the lack of accountability for spending these funds made more of a difference in the final outcome.

One area in which evaluation seems to have changed policy slightly is manpower training programs. Evaluation after evaluation suggested that programs overall were having little impact. In this case, the result was to turn over more discretion and authority to states and localities. There seemed to be a general willingness to accept the results of program evaluation, but a difficulty in knowing how they should be translated into legislation. The course was changed slightly, as I noted, but the commitment to training programs precluded simply scrapping them.

This same response is seen in many compensatory education and pre-school programs. Evaluation has shown them not to be wonder cures and perhaps has slowed substantially their expansion. But, again, getting rid of the programs would mean loss of substantial funds for states and localities, and hence they are more likely to be slowed in growth than to be scrapped. Moreover, many feel that since dollars for domestic programs are hard to come by, we should not lightly eliminate programs unless we can be assured of substituting something better in their place.

All in all, I would say that for a variety of reasons policy analysis and evaluation research do not have a significant impact on the bulk of legislative activity. I think Alice Rivlin, in her book *Systematic Thinking For Social Action,* puts her finger on the key issue—which is that we have tried a variety of programs to solve some social ills and they have not done so. Yet, no one has demonstrated clearly how to do better, so the old programs get changed at their fringes.

I believe that the major potential pay-off for policy analysis and evaluation research in the next few years will be in the area of helping to bring about big policy changes in certain areas. One of these is income maintenance program reform. All the necessary elements, I believe, are there, especially disenchantment with current programs, documented very thoroughly by many, including the subcommittee with which I am associated. The Subcommittee on Fiscal Policy is highly visible, its findings are widely circulated, and it is a creature of Congress. Moreover, broad new proposals have been analyzed in some depth, and the income maintenance experiments have shown that at least a certain group of such programs can be administered and have put to rest some of the worst fears about the impact on work. There has been so much analysis and research and evaluation over the last decade in this area that the basic concepts will not be foreign to Members of Congress and the public. This slow growth of knowledge and experience over the last decade should lead to change of some sort.

One specific charge to me was to consider how program research could be made more useful to Congress. I have nothing magic to offer, only a few rather obvious suggestions. First, if the audience is policymakers and their aides, findings must be digested and translated into common English. Policymakers and their top aides, who are generalists with broad concerns rather than technicians, will not struggle through complex equations and arcane terminology. Too often, I think, we write for each other in our own jargon and then wonder why we are ignored.

Not only is it essential to present material as simply as possible, it is also important to give a good idea of what the evaluation or research process involved. There is much armchair evaluation of programs such as child-feeding programs or manpower training programs. The idea that mere delivery of services is a sign of success must constantly be challenged. When the subcommittee published a study that raised grave doubts about the overall effectiveness of training programs, for example, we received many letters from the public citing specific and small programs in particular locations which, we were told, had been highly effective. After all, some graduates had been placed in jobs! There tends to be a great reluctance to trust evaluators, perhaps because what we do seems so complicated. For this reason, the methodology itself must be part of the translation process to the extent possible.

I want to make one last comment about the substance of the analysis or evaluation. Most programs have competing goals, in the sense that maximizing one means giving relatively less emphasis to another. These goal trade-offs in public welfare programs, for example, have been quite well explored in print, but they can never be over-emphasized. Often decisions are made in which the nature of the trade-offs involved is never made explicit. In my view, the analyst-evaluator can make one of his biggest contributions by clarifying and making explicit the competing goals and trade-offs inherent in programs and policies. What was given up or deemphasized to reach what hoped-for objective? We cannot determine the appropriate weights to be assigned to the various criteria for judging policies and programs, but we can help assure that policymakers assign a weight greater than zero to each important factor and that the terms of the trade-off are dealt with explicitly.

To do this well, researchers must seek to understand the political context in which programs are enacted or changed. There is no sub-stitute for reading transcripts of hearings, Committee reports on bills, learning the legislative histories, poring over the bills in their various forms as they slowly were transformed into law, and reading the floor debates. This allows researchers to learn more about the salient issues, the sought-for goals, the information on which decisions were based, and the trade-offs that went into the final decisions. This learning process can lead to casting evaluation research and policy analysis in quite different terms than might otherwise be the case. And it alerts the evaluator to the fact that if evaluations are negative, goals can be changed. If, for example, early childhood education programs are found to be ineffective in producing long-term educational gains, goals can be changed to providing high quality day care and public employment. If anticipated, the evaluator can have something to say about, for example, the cost and likely success of reaching these goals.

I would guess that at this point politicians have ambivalent feelings about researchers. First, they know that a lot of money has been wasted on complex trash. Second, they feel that researchers are reluc-tant to leave their language and complicated technology behind when they approach policymakers. Third, they are aware that analysis cannot help them in most of the routine voting decisions they make. And fourth, of course, they do not always like the results of the evaluations. But this is tight budget time, and a period when the Administration has grown more reliant on policy analysts, computer models, and evalu-ators. The desire to compete is one of the strong forces behind the new House and Senate budget committees and Congressional Budget Office, and the expansion of analytic staffs both in the Congressional Research

Service and the General Accounting Office. In short, the door is open wider than ever before. Especially with the new institutional arrangements in Congress referred to above, analysts will have greater entree. Our effectiveness will depend on whether we are willing to work with the Congress within its frame of reference.

NOTES

1. Views are those of the author only and do not necessarily reflect those of the Chairman, members, or staff of the subcommittee.

IF YOU DON'T CARE WHERE YOU GET TO, THEN IT DOESN'T MATTER WHICH WAY YOU GO

Joe N. Nay, John W. Scanlon,
Richard E. Schmidt, Joseph S. Wholey
Urban Institute

Presented by Joseph S. Wholey

DIAGNOSIS: THE TYPICAL
FEDERAL PROGRAM IS UNMANAGEABLE

We define *management* as the purposeful application of resources to tasks in order to achieve specified objectives. The term "manage" implies the need to obtain information on progress toward achieving objectives in order to know whether it is necessary to modify the tasks or the application of resources. Typically, program objectives are stated quite ambiguously in authorizing legislation or program plans. From the perspective of the manager, an objective has reality only when its achievement or progress toward its achievement can be verified, or "measured," in quantitative or qualitative terms. Moreover, management is possible only in the context of assumed causal relationships linking possible program activities to program objectives.

In order to allow a program to be managed to achieve objectives, the program must satisfy three criteria:

(a) measurable objectives have been specified (i.e., those in charge of the program, such as policymakers, program managers, have agreed on measurable objectives for the program, including any necessary measures of program costs, program activities, intended program outcomes, and intended impact on the problem addressed by the program), and

(b) there exist plausible, testable assumptions linking application of resources to program activities, linking program activities to intended program outcomes, and linking program outcomes to program objectives,[1] and

(c) those in charge of the program have the motivation, ability, and authority to manage.

It is recognized that programs may be more or less manageable, according to the extent to which these three criteria are or are not satisfied.

Our research reveals that the typical federal social program is *unmanageable* because it fails to meet one or more of these criteria:[2]

The typical federal program cannot be managed to achieve its stated objectives (as implied, for example, in the authorizing legislation) because:

- the program lacks specific, measurable objectives related to program goals,
- the program lacks plausible, testable assumptions linking program activities to the achievement of program objectives, or
- managers lack the motivation, ability, or authority to manage.

Though every federal program has a number of objectives, the objectives are generally not defined by those in charge (policymakers and program managers) in such a way that progress toward objectives can be measured or important underlying program assumptions tested. The programs are sufficiently well defined to be funded, but are not sufficiently well defined to be managed to achieve specific objectives related to the goals implied in the authorizing legislation. In such programs, whatever activities are carried out tend to become synonymous with objectives; i.e., from a "management" perspective, the intended effect is achieved when the program activities are carried out, regardless of program outcome or subsequent impact on the problem addressed by the program.

During a recent study of programs in one major federal agency, The Urban Institute assessed seven programs to determine the extent to which they could be managed to achieve program objectives.[3] We were seeking to determine in each program the extent to which the type of relationship illustrated in Figure I-A existed: a management function (M) allocating resources to a set of program activities (A-1) that are assumed to result in achievement of one or more objectives (0-1). (Evaluation could then be used to test the validity of the linking assumption (H-1), providing an empirical basis for modifying the program activities if necessary).

What we found, in most cases, was the program model illustrated in Figure I-B; that is, a management function allocating resources to a set of program activities *without* measurable objectives. The implementation of the program activities was the apparent objective of the management process.

Because most federal programs follow the model in Figure I-B, most federal evaluation tends to resemble the research model in Figure I-C. Within this evaluation model, the manager and researcher often agree on a general definition of the program activity and a general research question: what is the impact of the program activity? The objectives of the resulting studies are to discover the nature and extent of the problem addressed or the effects caused by the program activities (*not* to determine whether pre-stated program assumptions are satisfied in order to assist specific management decisions.) During the resulting research studies, the researcher usually has to exercise his judgment in specifying measures of program activities and effects and in deciding what constitutes an adequate test of cause and effect. Typically, great variation is found in the program activities making findings inconclusive, the research hypotheses are not relevant to the manager's real needs, or the research methodology is not accepted by the manager. This approach to evaluation has generally proven expensive and time consuming (one-to-three years to obtain results) and has produced a paucity of reliable findings.

Assessment of program evaluability is an apparently promising modeling technique which Urban Institute evaluators have developed and used to determine and to communicate to managers whether and to what extent program activities and program objectives have been defined in measurable terms and whether there exist plausible, testable assumptions linking expenditure of resources to program activities, program activities to program outcomes, and program outcomes to program objectives.[4] In an assessment of program evaluability, the evaluator (in one-to-three months of work based on examination of

FIGURE 1: THREE MODELS OF A MANAGEMENT AND EVALUATION CYCLE

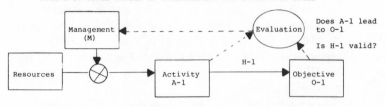

I-A. HYPOTHESIZED FEDERAL PROGRAM

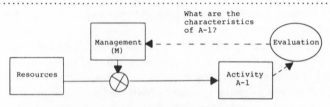

I-B. TYPICAL FEDERAL PROGRAM

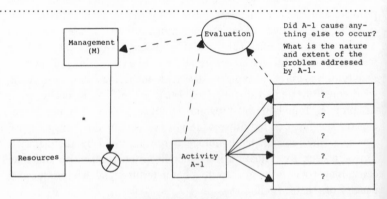

I-C. TYPICAL FEDERAL EVALUATION

program documentation and interviews with management staff) develops program models that capture the program activities and objectives and the links that reflect the assumed cause-and-effect relationships. The evaluability assessment:

(a) produces a *"rhetorical program model,"* which describes the program in terms of stated goals and objectives, program activities, assumed causal links between program activities and objectives, and administrative processes used to direct the agency and the program.

FIGURE II: COMUNITY MENTAL HEALTH CENTERS RHETORICAL PROGRAM DESIGN

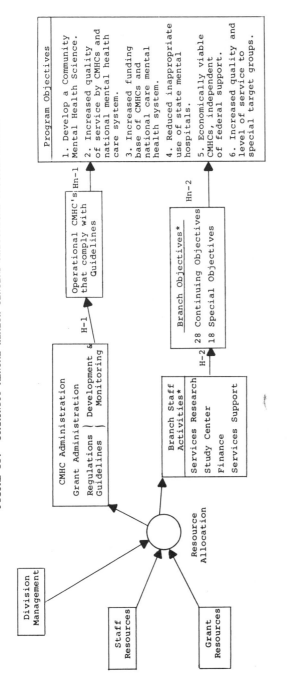

FIGURE III: COMMUNITY MENTAL HEALTH CENTERS EVALUABLE PROGRAM DESIGN

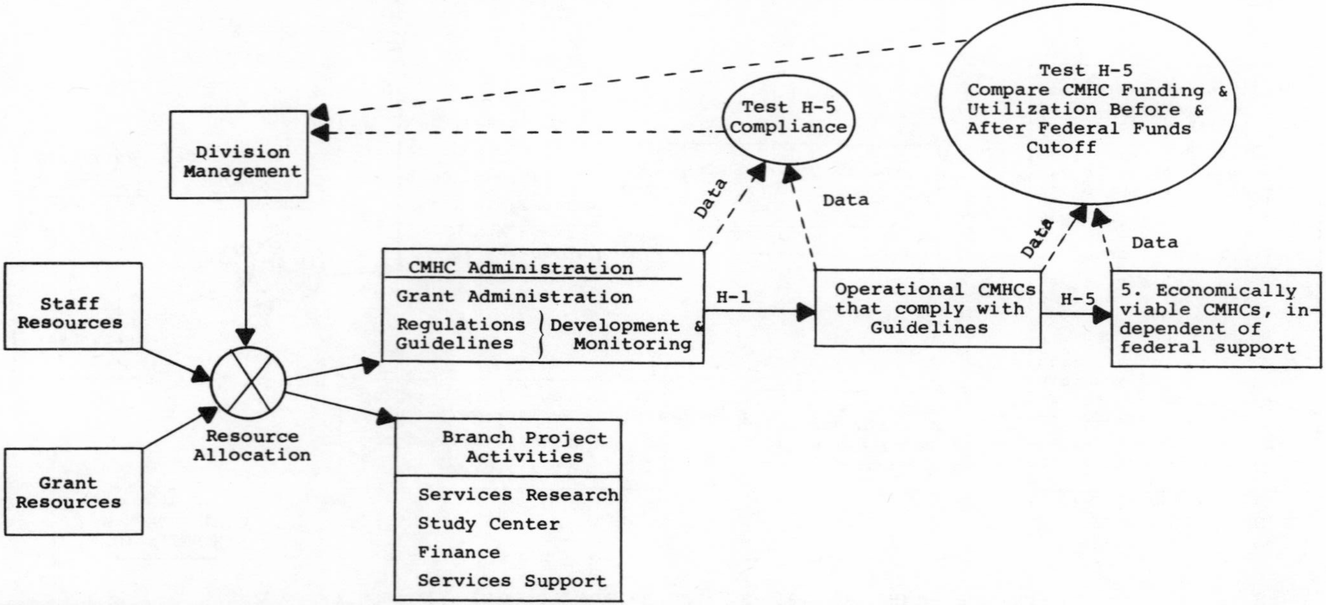

(b) produces an *"evaluable program model"* which describes the program in terms of measurable objectives, measurable program activities, and plausible, testable assumptions linking program activities to objectives,

(c) contrasts the rhetorical program model with the evaluable program model, and

(d) establishes whether there is a management use for the information defined in the evaluable program model.

Analysis of the Community Mental Health Centers program of the National Institute of Mental Health, for example, yielded the following program models: Figure II (the "rhetorical" Community Mental Health Centers program model, as revealed by program documentation and meetings with program personnel) and Figure III (the "evaluable/ manageable" Community Mental Health Center program model, omitting all objectives that could not be stated by the program staff in measurable terms). The "evaluable" program model that resulted from our assessment excludes all of the special and continuing objectives of the four branches and all but one of the program objectives, because they were not stated in measurable terms.[5] One set of program activities—intended outcomes, objectives, and program objectives—*did* appear to satisfy the evaluability/manageability criteria: those intended to result in "economically viable CMHCs, independent of federal support." These activities and objectives appear to be measurable, and the assumed causal links to be testable. (Note that over three dozen objectives vanished during the evaluability assessment.)

The typical outcome of an assessment of program evaluability is an apparent gap between the rhetorical program defined by the policy statements and the evaluable/manageable program. The gap exists because many of the objectives are not defined (or definable) in measurable terms and many of the assumed causal links are missing, are only vaguely defined, or are not verifiable or testable as the program is presently structured and operated.

We consider, in Section II, some likely causes of this situation; in Section III we discuss four evaluation tools that deal with some, but not all, of these problems.

HYPOTHESES: POSSIBLE CAUSES

In summary, then, though every federal program has goals, the program typically cannot be managed to achieve measurable objectives related to these goals. A condition so common—and so far-reaching in its implication—invites inquiry into its potential causes. To explore these questions systematically, the Evaluation Staff of The Urban Institute has recently begun to conduct a case study of these government management questions in conjunction with each of our recent evaluation systems' design projects. The following possible causes of the problems above are offered as a set of hypotheses growing out of our own past experience and the experience of other evaluators.

The first problem was stated as follows:

(a) *Program managers have no measurable statements of program objectives related to stated program goals.*

Our hypotheses regarding the major causes for the typical lack of measurable program objectives are that:

- Governing legislation is generally vague regarding program objectives;

- There exists no formal mechanism within (or outside) the typical federal agency for defining program objectives in measurable terms;

- Managers cannot find the time necessary to define carefully program objectives in measurable terms;[6] and

- There is generally no reward from either the bureaucracy or Congress for defining measurable program objectives. In some cases, systems for specifying measurable objectives exist or have been introduced, but they have rarely been workable or received priority from top management. Management by Objectives (as presently practiced) is probably not suited to management of large federal programs. Approaches such as Planning-Programming-Budgeting Systems have fallen of their own weight. Managers who have watched this process see no evidence that measurable program objectives are regarded as a vital component of the agency or department management style. Defining measurable objectives is hard work, increases the risks, and promises no obvious professional reward for success. In addition, managers often perceive that unmeasurable objectives are an asset in order to retain flexibility and ensure survival.

  Unmeasurable objectives, which are either vague or intuitively known to be orders of magnitude larger than can be achieved with given resources, sometimes permit managers to shift emphasis and approach to meet new priorities without seriously damaging their programs.

In order to manage; i.e., take purposeful action to improve the probability of success, it is necessary to begin to understand the relationship between the actions taken (program activities or tasks) and the desired objectives. In this regard, our second major observation about the inability to manage typical federal programs was that:

(b) *Program managers have no plausible, testable assumptions linking program activity to the achievement of objectives.*

Our hypotheses regarding the major causes for lack of plausible, testable program assumptions are that:

- Undefined objectives preclude definition of testable assumptions. A clearly defined objective is a necessary precondition to determining, at least hypothetically, a plausible, testable strategy to accomplish the objective.

- There is insufficient knowledge available on what program activities would lead to achievement of the objective. Social programs are replete with examples in which either current knowledge is inadequate, or the only known solutions are politically unacceptable.

- Programs are not viewed as opportunities to manage in order to achieve objectives, but rather as sets of administrative activities to be carried out.

- Agency managers cannot find the time necessary to state testable assumptions underlying program activities. The administrative activities (e.g., preparing budgets and paper objectives, the details of making grants, preparation of program regulations, meetings and task forces) tend to pre-empt the time and attention that would be necessary to think through key program assumptions in the detail necessary for them to be tested.

Finally, we noted the problem that:

(c) *Program managers often lack the motivation, authority, or ability to manage.*

Our hypotheses regarding the major causes for management unwillingness or inability to manage are that:

- The success of most federal officials does not depend on achieving measurable program objectives (and they are aware of that),[7]

- Many federal managers do not have the authority to manage programs or do not think that they have the authority because clear definitions of authority and responsibility are not documented,[8]

- In many federal programs, knowledge is not available that would allow managers to manage to improve their programs and to achieve program objectives.

Experience demonstrates that there is probably no general solution to many of these problems that result in unmanageable programs. We believe that our research indicates the disabling effects of these conditions on effective evaluation and, more fundamentally, on performance-oriented management. If our hypotheses are correct, then systematic agency-wide or government-wide approaches to solutions may generally be expected to fail. Having said that, however, we still believe that in many situations managers have the opportunity to adopt well-defined objectives and to manage to achieve those objectives.

One of the most important distinctions is between those cases where there is a desire on the part of the managers to manage (where application of some simple evaluation "tools" or procedures may produce helpful feedback information) and those cases where the managers lack the sense of direction, ability, or authority to manage. For the former case, we present in the next section tools that allow the sequential purchase of increasing amounts of information about a program until the needs of the program managers are determined and met (or found impossible to meet at a reasonable cost). For the latter case, it does not much matter. Until someone in a position of management authority defines measurable objectives and indicates a willingness to manage to achieve these objectives, little real help can be provided.

SOME APPROACHES WORTH TESTING

Given program managers who intend to manage to achieve specific objectives, we believe that substantial progress can be made using available evaluation tools. Four evaluation approaches are available which make it possible for managers to obtain, relatively quickly and inexpensively, increasing levels of useful information about progress toward well-defined program objectives, while retaining the ability to stop the information collection at a point where their information needs have been met within the constraints of available time and resources. These techniques *("assessment of program evaluability," "program monitoring," "evaluation design," and "quick assessment"),* help clarify to what extent a testable program approach exists and what evaluation information may be obtained and used. They are particularly useful in existing programs but a number of them are applicable to new programs as well. (The Evaluation Staff of The Urban Institute has developed methods of applying these approaches to social programs, found them promising, and is in the process of testing these new approaches as opportunities arise.)

Paradoxically, the techniques produce results much more quickly than managers expect results from evaluators (useful results appear in months rather than years) but generally require managers to invest large amounts of their own time in the process over periods of from one-to-six months. Evaluators can help present and structure the issues, but the decisions on policy questions such as definitions of program objectives, measures of progress toward objectives, and important program assumptions should be made by the managers, not by the evaluators.

1. *Assessment of Program Evaluability* (see above). The evaluability assessment, which can be completed in one-to-three months depending on the complexity of the program, results in a clarification of the program design, revealing which objectives are measurable, which assumed causal links are plausible and testable, and what information might be used by the managers. We believe, and have some experience which suggests, that evaluability assessment, if it involves real interaction between a manager and an evaluator, can also assist the manager in developing a program strategy that is plausible and testable.

As we saw above, typically there will be an apparent gap between the program as defined by policy statements and the evaluable/manageable program, resulting from a lack of defined, measurable objectives and/or lack of testable assumptions underlying the program.

Assessment of program evaluability/manageability is a useful method for determining and communicating to policymakers and program managers whether the program already has agreed-on measurable objectives and explicitly stated testable assumptions linking program expenditures, program activities, intended program outcomes, and intended impact on the problem—or whether *"program design"* work would be required to reshape the program into one that would meet these prerequisites for an evaluable/manageable program.

If managers see the gap between the rhetorical program model and the evaluable program model as a problem and desire that their program should be managed to achieve specific, measurable objectives, then they can embark on a *"program design"* effort to define measurable objectives and explicit, testable assumptions linking expenditures, program activities, intended outcomes, and intended impact on the problem addressed by the program. If we start with the premise that a manager has objectives and is committed to achieving them, the objectives can first be tested to determine to what extent they are measurable. The process will take time, most importantly the time of the manager. Involved is a joint determination by the manager and the evaluator as to what evidence will satisfy the manager that his objectives have been achieved, using the evaluator's estimates of the feasibility and cost of obtaining such evidence. No "cook book" exists for program design work.[9] While the evaluator can play an important role in a program design effort (e.g., helping secure and document agreement on program objectives and appropriate measures of progress, and clarifying the feasibility and costs of measuring progress and testing assumptions), the program design effort will also require extensive input from managers to select appropriate feedback systems that would produce evaluation information needed for program management.

The definition/selection of objectives, etc., are policy matters, not matters that can be entirely delegated to evaluators. Issues concerning program design and management needs for information can only be clarified and resolved within the organizational context of the manager. To ensure that the program design work is relevant to management needs, it is extremely important to have the support and participation of agency management.

(*Note:* It is quite likely that program (re)design will be strongly resisted for at least the following reasons:

(a) it would minimize freedom of action at several levels within the bureaucracy,

(b) it would require substantially more accountability than most bureaucracies are willing to accept,

(c) it could well reduce the objectives to more realistic objectives, although this result may be politically unsatisfactory).

(*Note:* In many federal programs, since most of the program is beyond the control of the federal "program manager" (the program has no measurable objectives, there are no constraints on the types of program activities, the program manager has little authority over the initiation or continuation of local projects), the only program that a federal manager can or could manage is that represented by the internal resources he controls: federal staff, R&D funds, and evaluation funds. In such cases, the likeliest possibility of producing an evaluable/ manageable program relates to use of federal staffs to achieve defined objectives.)

2. *Program Monitoring.* This process obtains, and makes available to the manager in easily digestible form, information on measures that describe program results (expenditures, activities, outcomes, and/or progress toward objectives) and compares actual results with planned results.[10] (Program monitoring does *not* test assumed causal links relating program activities to program objectives.) Often monitoring systems can be developed and implemented in two-to-four months.

Monitoring provides current information to management on the resources expended, activities implemented, output produced, or objectives achieved by a program while the program is in process. When these are judged inadequate, management can take corrective action to increase the chances that the program will meet its objectives.

The Urban Institute has developed and tried out a number of potentially useful monitoring tools including:

- relatively inexpensive, systematic (telephone) surveys of random samples of all relevant federal/state/local program staffs and recipients of program services, from which surveys one can generalize with known confidence to obtain objective and subjective data on (a) what services are actually being delivered by the program and (b) what are staff members' and recipients' attitudes toward those services;[11]

- signaling systems which present information to program managers on which projects are performing "extremely well" or "extremely poorly," where relative project results are calculated for projects which are comparable from the managers' perspective;[12]

- comparisons of planned versus actual project outputs based on site visits,[13] project reporting systems,[14] anonymous surveys,[15] and comparisons using photographic techniques.[16]

The major tasks in developing an appropriate monitoring system are:

(a) to establish agreement with program management on what monitoring information is needed and is satisfactorily measurable (helping the manager articulate specific information requirements).

(b) to establish agreement with program staffs and grantees on what specific activities and results will be monitored,

(c) to develop procedures to produce the type and quality of information required, and

(d) to assure utilization of the monitoring information produced.

The Urban Institute has developed and tried a number of monitoring systems, found it feasible to produce potentially useful information relatively simply and inexpensively in a form understandable to management, but has often found management unable or unwilling to act on the basis of monitoring reports because, for example, the appropriate corrective management actions are often not obvious—or the monitoring information, or the changes indicated by it, threatened the established bureaucratic system.

One of the main problems with evaluation as a solution to managers' information needs is that, in the real world, definitive evaluation (i.e., tests of assumptions that program activities cause progress toward program objectives) is often not feasible at a reasonable cost. Either plausible assumptions cannot be formulated given present knowledge (how do you teach disadvantaged children? stop child abuse? reduce crime?) or the actual program design does not lend itself to definitive tests of program assumptions (sufficient replications are not available to yield convincing evidence on whether treatment A is better than treatment B, or no treatment at all, under condition C). Under these circumstances, however, all too often evaluators are hired to carry out costly, usually fruitless efforts to "address" unanswerable questions on the effects caused by program activities (questions that *cannot* be answered definitively given the actual program and the actual time that the manager has available for evaluation). In our judgment, program monitoring is often much less costly and much more useful to managers under these real-world conditions.

3. *Evaluation Design.*[17] If a program passes the tests of manageability/evaluability, then there exist measurable objectives; plausible, testable assumptions linking expenditures, program activities, intended outcomes, and program objectives; and management needs for evaluation information testing key program assumptions. Before extensive investments in evaluation, which attempts to test the assumed cause-and-effect relationships, the Institute recommends an *evaluation design* process that generally takes from three-to-six months. The evaluation design process should nearly always be coupled with a quick assessment, described below. The evaluation design process:

(a) identifies potentially useful evaluation information (measures of progress toward program objectives and feasible tests of program assumptions) and documents management's requirements for evaluation information.

(b) examines the cost and feasibility[18] of obtaining the required evaluation information (including estimates of the cost and feasibility of specific evaluation designs),

(c) examines the potential value of such evaluation information in alternative management processes directed toward achieving program objectives, and

(d) specifies data collection and analysis plans for the most appropriate evaluation alternatives.

The Urban Institute approach to evaluation design is based on a five-step planning process:

STEP I. MODELING OF THE DECISION-MAKING SYSTEM

Questions of how far to go in developing data, what size samples are necessary, etc., are heavily conditioned by the needs of the intended users. The first step is carried out to specify the evaluation information required by the relevant decision-making processes. This step provides the criteria necessary to determine how much information and what type of information should be purchased.

STEP II. MODELING OF THE PROGRAM ACTIVITIES

This step (which documents measures of program activities, program outcomes, and the progress toward objectives and makes explicit the choice of assumptions linking expenditures of resources, program activities, intended immediate outcomes, and intended impact on the problem addressed) is carried out to provide a measurement and analytical framework for evaluation design work. This groundwork must be explicitly worked out to give the manager and the evaluators a common basis for discussing program objectives, program activities, and evaluation designs.

In this step, the evaluator documents agreement among relevant managers on measurable objectives and testable assumptions.

The Institute then calculates first-cut estimates and bounds on the likely program costs and impact, based on order-of-magnitude calculations on the effects of exogenous factors. The purposes are to bracket the likely range of uncertainty using simple calculations, to highlight key assumptions and get estimates of the cost and feasibility of testing those key assumptions, bound the effects of likely exogenous variables, and to suggest what data are needed to estimate program impact.

STEP III. DEVELOPMENT OF EVALUATION DESIGNS

With the information developed in Steps I and II, it is a straightforward matter to start developing alternative evaluation designs for testing hypotheses. The results of this step are described as: (a) specification of measurements and comparisons to be made to test hypotheses and (b) specification of the estimated cost and expected value of each proposed evaluation design. (At this point it often develops that, given the present program design, there is no way to make a definitive test of program assumptions. If the program manager really needs to test the program assumptions, it may be necessary to conduct controlled experiments to test the assumptions; i.e., to change the program design rather dramatically.)

STEP IV. SELECTION OF APPROPRIATE EVALUATION DESIGN(S)

This step represents the process of deciding which information to buy based on the criteria established in Step I, the models of Step II, and the designs of Step III.

STEP V. SCHEDULING OF DATA COLLECTION AND ANALYSES

This step develops the operational plan for the scheduling of data collection and analyses.

As can now be seen, the evaluability assessment is simply a set of tools for performing the evaluation design work in a limited way, in a manner directly comprehensible to agency managers. Evaluability assessments are feasibility studies to determine whether an evaluation design is possible and to gather much of the information needed for evaluation design.

This approach has evolved through a number of Urban Institute efforts involving the design of specific evaluation studies and the design of evaluation systems (i.e., procedures and methods for planning, managing and utilizing evaluation information). It has been used by The Urban Institute to plan evaluations and to critique proposed evaluation plans and designs for federal agencies. When it is based on evaluability assessment and evaluation design work, program evaluation then represents purchase of the full set of information that will be sufficiently useful to justify its collection.

4. *Quick Assessment.*[19] Our experience demonstrates that, while going through the effort necessary to design an appropriate evaluation, it may be worthwhile to conduct simultaneously a relatively inexpensive "quick assessment" (preliminary evaluation) of the program and its effects. Based on the results of the evaluability assessment, evaluation design work on the costs and feasibility of evaluations that are potentially useful to policymakers and program managers, and synthesis of readily available evidence on the extent to which program objectives have been achieved, the Institute produces a quick assessment of the degree to which program assumptions are satisfied, i.e., a preliminary evaluation of the program. Within six months, it is generally possible to produce both an appropriate evaluation design and a quick assessment of the program.

The quick assessment assembles what is known about the program activities, outcomes, and effectiveness of the program in terms of the evaluable/manageable program model; the evaluation design(s) specifies whether and how needed additional information could be obtained and at what cost.

When coupled with an analysis of managements decision needs, the quick assessment may well obviate the need for the more expensive, time-consuming evaluation, that is, it may produce an adequate information base to satisfy management decision needs. The key factor here is time. Some management decisions generally will not be deferred for the one-to-three years it may take to complete an in-depth evaluation study or the research or experimental demonstration program needed to reduce or eliminate knowledge gaps. The quick assessment will provide a structured synthesis of what is known already. Should this satisfy the decision requirements, there would be no need to proceed with the full evaluation. On the other hand, from the related evaluation design work, evaluation design(s) would be available if management decides that more information is necessary and will be timely.

To the extent that information is available, the quick assessment provides what is known about the program and an estimate of the precision of that knowledge, including:

(a) statements of the key assumptions that link program expenditures to program activities, program activities to intended program outcomes, and program outcomes to intended impact on the problem addressed by the program,

(b) quantitative estimates of the relationships that relate these factors,

(c) estimates of ranges of performance and effectiveness of projects,

(d) estimates of the reliability of the above estimates,

(e) identification of any factors seen likely to lead to program success/failure, and

(f) clear gaps in present knowledge.

The quick assessment assembles what is known about the program activities, outcomes, and effectiveness of the program in terms of the evaluable program model; the evaluation design(s) specifies whether and how needed additional information could be obtained and at what cost. The evaluation design/quick assessment approach is now being tested on a broad scale, in the Law Enforcement Assistance Administration's National Evaluation Program.

The successive steps of evaluability assessment, evaluation design, quick assessment, and evaluation represent a suggested process of buying worthwhile information, allowing managers to spend big money only on big, answerable, questions (i.e., evaluations that test *testable* hypotheses). Evaluability assessment, evaluation design, and quick assessment often reveal that proposed expensive, time-consuming evaluation is impossible, infeasible and/or unnecessary. These approaches can be used to identify knowledge gaps that both need to be filled and can, at reasonable cost, be filled. The results of the quick assessment will generally be incomplete in a broad sense, but they will represent what is presently known about the program, its design, its effectiveness, and the reliability of that knowledge.

A good deal of input is required from agency/program management to make this work useful, since the definition/selection of objectives, etc., is a policy matter (not one that can be delegated to evaluators.) Issues concerning program design, program evaluability and management intent can only be clarified and resolved within the organizational context of the agency. A contractor working independently—or a contractor and a staff office working independently of the agency decision processes—cannot expect to have much impact. It is necessary to have the support and participation of agency management.

Earlier, it was stated that most federal programs are not sufficiently well defined to permit them to be managed to achieve performance objectives or to be satisfactorily evaluated. We have now presented a series of approaches or tools which, for managers who wish to manage, can be used to obtain feedback information through evaluation approaches tailored to fit management needs. In addition, by following a set of sequential steps of buying partial information, these approaches help to protect both the manager and the evaluator from entering initially into large evaluation commitments that may turn out to have been unneeded, impossible to accomplish, or not suited to the actual needs of management.

As can be seen from the discussion above, the proposed tools and approaches are aimed at properly evaluating those programs which management desires to manage. (Here a serious test of intent is that a manager wants information that can be used directly to alter things that are truly under his control, such as the activities of his own federal staff or the commitment of his discretionary funds.)

As all of us know, many evaluation contracts are let with intended uses of "informing a broad national audience" or "assisting local and state officials." In many of these cases, evaluability assessment will show little evidence of intent to manage or of plausible links from the manager to the program in question. In these cases the evaluator will always have to make a series of judgments and guesses on most of the questions reserved for management throughout this paper (since it is impossible to design and evaluate without measures, linking assumptions, and desired degrees of accuracy.) In these cases, furthermore, the evaluator can expect that no one in particular will be eager for his results when and if they emerge.[20]

The members of the Evaluation Staff of The Urban Institute hold a wide range of views about the propriety and usefulness of performing large evaluations on programs that no one intends to manage. No one disagrees that it can often be a frustrating and difficult task. As mentioned earlier, we have begun to study three problems more closely in a search for the root causes of this lack of management on many programs. In the meantime, the approaches above are offered to evaluators and managers alike so that they can more fairly assess the evaluation possibilities for their own programs.

SUMMARY

Many of the older federal government programs involve program activities whose nature has been clearly defined and agreed upon and which have been described in detail in a body of law or regulation (e.g., Social Security). The implementation of such a program is largely an act of administration of the laws and regulations. Evaluation of success or failure of the act of implementation is primarily a matter of assessing compliance with the guiding laws and regulations. Management discretion is at a minimum (at least over the short term.)

In contrast, many new missions that the federal government has been called upon to undertake (e.g., lowering hard-core unemployment; reducing crime, poverty, or inflation) involve problems in which the proper program intervention mechanism is not well understood, or defined, or in some cases even known. Since in these cases no one knows exactly what detailed program intervention will be of value, greater management discretion is allowed and exercised.

The newer program areas are characterized by *uncertainty* and *discretion:* uncertainty as to the nature of the problem and what constitutes effective strategies of intervention, and discretion in how the problem and the intervention are defined and how the intervention is implemented.

This paper, very much a progress report, is born out of the frustrations of the evaluator in seeking to meet management needs—and the frustrations of the manager in trying to get useful progress reports on program results. It is a relatively untested assumption in public administration theory that providing managers in large governmental organizations empirical evidence on program performance leads to more efficient and effective public programs.

Based on six years of trial—and a good deal of error—The Urban Institute has identified a number of problems inhibiting management of public programs to meet program objectives, hypothesized some of the underlying causes, and suggested promising approaches that still require much testing. This paper:

- outlines a set of conditions that must be met to allow a public agency or public program to be managed to achieve performance objectives,

- notes that, given the characteristics of typical federal programs, these conditions are not met in many federal agencies and programs,

- presents a set of approaches that can be used by policymakers, program managers, and their staffs to assess the manageability/evaluability of their programs and to obtain feedback information on progress toward program objectives, and

- arrays the approaches to show how they can provide useful information matched to the needs of those managers who have the willingness, authority, and ability to manage their programs. The options range from buying nothing to full-scale evaluations, and criteria are developed at each stage to assess the value of going forward.

The approaches can allow managers who desire to manage programs to pick their way through the myriad of pitfalls that may otherwise disable their most well-intentioned efforts. They also bring into sharp relief, at an early state of investigation, cases where attempts at management *and* evaluation will likely be fruitless unless considerable rethinking of program objectives, program assumptions, and program activities is accomplished.

At this point we are relatively confident that evaluability assessment and evaluation design work can prevent the waste of large sums of money on irrelevant or infeasible evaluations; we are hopeful that rather simple performance monitoring systems can help managers who know where they want to get to; and we believe that the quick assessment technique may produce useful, timely preliminary program evaluation of by-products of careful evaluation design work.

If a manager wants to manage his program to achieve specific, measurable objectives, two of the tools we have tried appear useful:

- *evaluability assessment,* to help the manager clarify objectives, define measures of program expenditure, program activities, program outcomes, and progress toward program objectives, and

- *program monitoring,* to compare actual program results (resources expended, activities carried out, outputs produced, and/or progress toward objectives) with planned results.

In those cases in which managers want evaluation to test key program assumptions,

- evaluability assessment and
- evaluation design

can identify appropriate measures and feasible comparisons before large sums are invested in evaluation, and

- quick assessment

can produce preliminary evaluation information as a by-product of the evaluation design effort.

Finally, in the cases where the entire sequence of steps can be accomplished successfully,

- program evaluation

can be attempted with reasonable expectations and a high chance of success.

We believe that these techniques are promising. Further demonstrations are needed to test the value of these evaluation tools, and, to the extent that they are successful, build the willingness of managers to invest the time needed to get relevant feedback on program performance. When managers are unable or unwilling to give their programs a clear sense of direction, neither these nor other techniques are likely to be helpful.

NOTES

1. The *plausibility* of program assumptions is really subject to the test of reason; i.e., is it reasonable to expect that doing x will cause y? The *testability* of program assumptions relates to the feasibility of obtaining sufficient evidence to attribute y to x, rather than to the influences of other independent variables.

2. See Pamela Horst et al. (5); Joe Nay, John Scanlon and Joseph Wholey (7); and John Scanlon et al. (8). (Numbers in parentheses refer to bibliographical entires at the end of this paper.) Many local programs are also unmanageable according to these criteria: See Bayla White et al. (16).

3. See Pamela Horst et al. (5)

4. In the context of this paper, the technique should strictly speaking be called "assessment of program manageability." We follow the terminology of Pamela Horst et al. (6). Horst and her colleagues concluded that a major reason for the frequent lack of utility of program evaluation is the fact that programs fail to meet one or more of the three evaluability/manageability criteria. They recommended the conduct of assessments of program evaluability to discover what the cost and utility of evaluation will be *before* large sums are spent on program evaluation.

5. The following examples illustrate some of the objectives that were omitted because they were not stated in measurable terms:

- "Reduced inappropriate use of state mental hospitals," excluded because of the lack of an explicit definition of "appropriate" use and assumptions linking activities to the reductions.

- "Increased quality and level of service to special target groups," excluded because of the lack of explicit definitions of "quality of care" and of the specific requirements of "special target groups."

- "Improve the quality of technical assistance and expand the capability of the branches to provide appropriate assistance to responsible authorities that will assist in strengthening programs and operations in the field commensurate with national program goals," excluded because of the lack of known or hypothesized effects of technical assistance in relation to program goals.

- "Promote on-going improvement in technology and practices of planning for delivery of mental health services," excluded because of the lack of measures of the state of technology and of the extent and effectiveness of planning practices.

This and similar examples are discussed in more detail in Pamela Horst et al. (5).

6. In particular, in many federal agencies policymakers come and go with astonishing speed.

7. For example, the relatively high turnover rate among key managers may make program changes or new starts more important than demonstrated performance in achieving objectives. In many cases, promotion depends more on responsiveness, rhetorical program success, or political considerations than on achieving program objectives.

8. Often there is no "management contract" that makes clear both the performance expectations and the limits of authority given to the manager. There are so many offices that are involved in planning and control of federal programs that it is unclear what a manager can and cannot do. The decision process itself is diffuse, with many contributors and few identifiable "decision makers."

9. See Joseph Wholey (17), for the description of an interactive process that might help managers define measurable objectives and testable assumptions linking program activities to objectives.

For some programs (e.g., programs directed at improving education, improving community mental health, reducing crime and delinquency at reasonable costs) not enough may be known to allow production of plausible assumptions on how program objectives can be achieved.

10. See John Waller et al. (13); Bayla White et al. (16); Louis Blair and Alfred Schwartz (1); Alfred Schwartz and Sumner Clarren (9); Hugh Duffy et al. (4); Leona Vogt et al. (10); and Richard Zamoff et al. (18).

11. Richard Zamoff et al. (18).

12. Bayla White et al. (16).

13. Hugh Duffy et al. (4).

14. Leona Vogt et al. (10).

15. Peter Bloch and Deborah Anderson (2); Harriet Connolly and Judith Greenwald (3); and Alfred Schwartz and Sumner Clarren (9).

16. Louis Blair and Alfred Schwartz (1).

17. See John Waller and John Scanlon (13); John Waller, John Scanlon and Joseph Wholey (12); Leona Vogt et al. (11); Donald Weidman, Francine Tolson and Joseph Wholey (15); and John Scanlon et al. (8).

18. The testing of a program assumption ideally excludes, or severely limits, alternative explanations of causation. This ideal is extremely difficult to achieve outside of the laboratory because of the many intervening variables that exist. The more detailed is the specification of assumptions, the easier is the task of eliminating alternative explanations of the effects observed.

19. See Donald Weidman et al. (15).

20. See Pamela Horst et al. (6).

REFERENCES

(1)   Louis Blair and Alfred Schwartz, *Measuring the Effectiveness of D.C. Solid Waste Solid Waste Collection Activities,* The Urban Institute (Working Paper), September 1971.

(2)   Peter Bloch and Deborah Anderson, *Policewomen on Patrol: Final Report,* to be published by the Police Foundation, Fall 1974.

(3)   Harriet Connolly and Judith Greenwald, *Policewomen on Patrol: New York City,* to be published by the Police Foundation, Fall 1974.

(4)   Hugh Duffy et al., *Design of an On-Site Evaluation System for the Office of Legal Services,* The Urban Institute, June 1971.

(5)   Pamela Horst et al., *Evaluation Planning at the National Institute of Mental Health: A Case History,* The Urban Institute, April 1974.

(6)   Pamela Horst et al., "Program Management and the Federal Evaluator," in *Public Administration Review,* Vol. 34, No. 6, July/August 1974, pp. 300-308.

(7)   Joe Nay, John Scanlon and Joseph Wholey, "Benefits and Costs of Manpower Training Programs: A Synthesis of Previous Studies with Reservations and Recommendations," in *Benefit-Cost Analyses of Federal Programs,* Joint Economic Committee, 92d Congress, 2d Session, January 1973.

(8)   John Scanlon et al., *An Evaluation Strategy and Plan for the Department of Labor*, The Urban Institute, January 1973.

(9)   Alfred Schwartz and Sumner Clarren, *Evaluation of Cincinnati's Community Sector Team Policing Program; A Progress Report: The First Six Months Summary of Major Findings*, The Urban Institute (Working Paper), July 1974.

(10)   Leona Vogt et al., *Health Start: Final Report of the Evaluation of the Second Year Program*, The Urban Institute, December 1973.

(11)   Leona Vogt et al., *Development of Evaluation Designs for Assessment of Alternative Legal Services Delivery Programs*, The Urban Institute, March 1974.

(12)   John Waller, John Scanlon and Joseph Wholey, *Critique of the National Level Evaluation Plan for the High Impact Anti-Crime Program*, The Urban Institute, March 1973.

(13)   John Waller et al., *Monitoring for Criminal Justice Planning Agencies*, The Urban Institute, August 1974.

(14)   John Waller and John Scanlon, *Urban Institute Plan for the Design of an Evaluation*, The Urban Institute (Working Paper), March 1973.

(15)   Donald Weidman, Francine Tolson and Joseph Wholey, *Summary of Initial Assessment and Evaluation Study Design for Operation Breakthrough*, The Urban Institute, December 1973; revised May 1974.

(16)   Bayla White et al., *The Atlanta Project: How One Large School System Responded to Performance Information*, The Urban Institute, March 1974.

(17)   Joseph Wholey, *Proposal for Contract Extension: Implementation of a Performance Management System in a Large Urban School District*, The Urban Institute, February 1974.

(18)   Richard Zamoff et al., *Evaluation of Head Start Experience with "Healthy, That's Me" in the Second Year*, The Urban Institute, September 1973.

CRONIN: After three years I have my job description down to one sentence. I advise the Governor on budgets, education, colleges and universities, libraries, television, and the arts and humanities. This is what the Secretary of Education does. There are only four of us in the nation, in four states.

I am really here as a consumer of research—policy research and evaluations on social programs. Someone said that Massachusetts does not have any major social experiments. Now, does it? Well, it is a matter of opinion. In South Boston, this month, they would say the busing of some 20,000 students might be under that category, whereas those from South Newton or the academics from North Lexington or the revolutionary town where I live, would say, "No, it is just proper social policy." Meanwhile, we are deinstitutionalizing simultaneously our reform schools and our mental hospitals and our big institutions for mentally retarded and handicapped children and mainstreaming the children into local school systems. At the same time, we are experimenting with how to cope with the building of sufficient new schools and colleges for the great population bulge for the 1970's without overbuilding for the 1980's when the experts say there will be a 25 to 30 percent decline in the number of children using these facilities. At the same time we are trying to inform people about the impact of that and the over supply of teachers, while coping with the unbelievable pressures of all informed young people to get into medical and health specialities in our colleges and universities. There are a variety of other challenges, more so than experiments, because they really need so many of them. Very few of the criteria are for experimentation. Some are planned, some are intended, some are evaluated; all of them are thrust upon a government and all of them are political realities.

The comments of the panelists were illustrative on a number of our problems as policymakers at the state level. I was particularly taken by the recommendation that, in addition to long-term research or perhaps even as part of long-term research or in-depth studies, there be some quick or early assessment. Somehow that has gotten kind of a bad name—quick and dirty research. I think the more euphonious description is a rapid feedback evaluation—that is going to sell. I have one federal program that my staff is administering. It is an outreach and referral program for people who might want to think about higher education for job skills for working class poor people, and enormously helpful was the evaluation about three months into it, telling me which of the six centers were actually doing it the way it was intended and which ones had done it entirely differently. Probably with a one-year or three-year evaluation you would never have known the appropriate activities specified.

It is bad enough to ask the bureaucrats and policymakers if they know what they are doing. An equally important question is whether anyone in an executive agency has thought much about how you would measure the outcomes if you knew what you were doing and have the right people in the right places. It is a useful function of researchers, even though they might want to shy away from it, to render some assistance to decision-makers and bureaucrats making earlier decisions about measurability. The work of the Congressional Reference Service on terminations fascinated me because I did not understand what it was on the first reading, but I caught it later. I could not believe that there were 730 federal programs that would terminate during one session, until you explained about expiration, the usual practice of a two- or three- or five-year term for all laws. One of the decision points where those engaged in social program policy evaluations potentially have the most to offer and the greatest possibility of having some impact is the decision of expiration versus continuation of programs as commented on by two of the speakers. One of my assignments on leaving the university and going into state government was to identify first the programs which had been carried on for years and years without much thinking about the benefits and overruns. Just to provide some rather evocative examples, the Boston school system in 1906 launched a revolutionary (at the time) innovative program of having an M.D. visit each school each day to inspect the children and evaluate health care. That program in 1974 is still going on. Doctors visit each school for an average of 90 seconds, they ring a bell, the sick and mobile children can get down to the doctor in time, but if they have a broken leg or something, they miss their chance that day. While this program and the back-up of school nurses now costs a million dollars per year, it is probably a very poor alternative to the notion of community-based family health type centers with all the back-up of neurology, serology, and all the things they can identify—all the other things which probably do interfere with student learning in urban school systems. But we continue that program with very little review.

At the state level we have discovered a state agency dedicated to Americanization and immigration, established in 1914, to serve the great wave of European immigrants with all kinds of literacy programs rendered by this bureau. We are no longer trying to homogenize and Americanize people in the old sense of making them white, middle-class Americans. There is another agency with bilingual and bicultural unit which is designed to help people retain their native language. We have another agency that is still Americanizing which costs about a quarter of a million dollars a year. Its function is pretty much to help people fill out their federal forms. The federal government people are delighted with this service. Since they do not have to do it, they refer people to the state agency to fill out the federal forms. We do not get a federal subsidy for having this agency. It just continues and spins on, presumably, forever. Plans to terminate it failed; that is why I am so interested. What we need is some research in getting government programs terminated because we really do not know much about how to do it. Clark Abt has promoted the notion of a social audit for corporations and for governmental agencies. What we need is some kind of analogous agency autopsy. Why not? Medicine has pathology units and all good hospitals certainly have a medical examiner who does post-mortems when the operation does not work out. It seems to me we need that government specialty in education.

GOLD: Right now, social scientists in general stand in disrepute. After all, in OEO they have had at least four years to diagnose the incipient problems of poverty in the nation, discuss them, and develop programs for solving them. What really happened was that the commitment was pulled back just about as fast as it was developed, because people were frightened of what the legislation meant in terms of equal opportunity and in terms of constituencies. We heard today about social experimentation. I did 35 studies in five years. I really took seriously the fact that people wanted evaluation, that they wanted to know what it was that these programs could do for the people. The evaluations that were done were not earthshaking landmark studies, but they were rational procedures to try and understand what people were doing, to try and understand what effects had occurred in a short period of time. And we looked at the programs during a time of great innovation, when some people were thinking about social change and social power-sharing, how to really do something about problems of declining cities. So anyway we did 35 studies and I am proud to tell you today that not one policy relevant decision was made on the basis of those 35 studies. And I really tried. I mean, I did summaries. I did beautiful summaries. I even got policymakers to sit in a room to hear evaluation findings. I knew that the policy decisions had already been made, that the dye had been cast and that the programs were going to be terminated. Now the response, as far as good evaluators were concerned, is to say we are doing something wrong here, we do not have good control groups, or we really need randomization. And I feel that is sad. I mean it is sad to me after spending ten years of my life doing this sort of thing. It is sad to me to see that kind of defensive action. In a sense, social scientists took this hook, and that is what it was. They took the bait, there was supposed to be bait on the hook, but it was just a hook, with the saying that, look we have a commitment to do something about problems of poverty, declining cities, problems of disenfranchisement of the country. We want you to come forward and share your ideas, test some things, and see if we can really do something. Use the federal auspices to really do some social experimentation once more, social problem solving.

Perhaps what we lacked was a national policy that had some stability. The lack of such a policy made most of the difference in terms of the retrenchment from dealing with the problem. I think that we did make progress. Some of the things, such as the income maintenance experiment, I do not think ever had a chance of really being implemented because I think it is just basically antagonistic to the kind of acceptable social policy which would work in this country at the present time. The housing allowance experiment was mentioned today and I do not think that that has a prayer because I do not think that people are really going to pay a housing allowance. But more than that, there is no social welfare policy that would allow there to be a housing allowance program, and I think that is where we have to start. Unless there is national commitment, unless there is national support to solve problems, not to keep programs, but to solve problems, social problems, I do not think that we are going to go very far. Everybody is saying that what we are doing is irrelevant. I have an idea of how we might go about averting that in the future. It is true that we develop income maintenance experiments, housing allowances and so on, out of the fabric of a very small group of people. The constituency for these in terms of the interest groups has never been very large. If you have a powerful senator, a powerful congressman, or if you have some set of people that you could build up around the program, you might get it to work. I do not think that we can really generate programs in the way that we have done before, but that we must use a participatory process where various interest groups who are concerned about certain kinds of problems would come together and try to develop alternatives that they would like to see tested in some kind of controlled environment. Again, this cannot be done without some kind of national commitment. But if there was a serious process developed for participatory problem-solving, where the government involved various interest groups in making decisions about where it should act, perhaps this would overcome some of the problems which snared the social scientists. Finally, I would just like to say that social experimentation is a very serious business. We are fooling around with people's lives. The kinds of experiments we talked about this morning require a great deal of cooperation, a great deal of faith, and hope on the part of the people involved. In a sense, we have really played a dirty trick on people because we have built up their hope in the area of experimentation.

III

PAYOFFS OF
EVALUATION RESEARCH

PART III □ CONTENTS

PAYOFFS OF EVALUATION RESEARCH

Chairperson: ELEANOR SHELDON, Social Science Research Council

THE IMPACT OF THE WESTINGHOUSE/OHIO EVALUATION ON THE DEVELOPMENT OF PROJECT HEAD START:
An Examination of the Immediate and Longer-Term Effects and How They Came About

Lois-ellin Datta
National Institute of Education[1]

HOW THE STUDY BEGAN

The Westinghouse/Ohio evaluation began in 1967. The Office of Economic Opportunity (OEO) was then three years old, having started in 1964 with a FY1965 appropriation of $800 million, initially allocated among eight programs: Job Corps, Neighborhood Youth Corps, Work-experience, Community Action, Migrant, Rural Area, VISTA, and Adult Literacy.

In the summer of 1964, Sargent Shriver, then Director of OEO, asked Dr. Robert Cooke, a pediatrician, to form a planning committee to suggest ways in which projects for children might contribute to the overall OEO goal of reducing poverty. The committee, chaired by Cooke, met in November 1964 and recommended a comprehensive program for preschool children. These recommendations became the official OEO statement of rationale, goals and objectives of a new program to be funded under Title II of the Economic Opportunity Act of 1964. Title II authorized special programs for educating the poor to be located outside regular public education. The program, as described in the Cooke recommendations, would meet the health and nutritional needs of children from low-income families, would involve their parents and the community in helping foster the children's development and would provide a happy transition from the home to a group setting. Emphasis was placed on the children's personal and social development: curiosity, motivation, trust in others, and independence. The seven major objectives [16] of the program were:

1. Improving the child's physical health and abilities

2. Fostering the emotional and social development of the child by encouraging self-confidence, spontaneity, curiosity and self-discipline

3. Improving the child's mental processes and skills, with particular attention to conceptual and verbal skills

4. Establishing patterns of expectations of success for the child that will create a climate of confidence for his future learning efforts

5. Increasing the child's capacity to relate positively to family members and others while strengthening the family's ability to relate positively to the child and his problems

6. Developing in the child and his family a responsible attitude toward society and fostering constructive opportunities for society to work together with the poor in solving their problems

7. Increasing the sense of dignity and self-worth within the child and his family.

Head Start, as the program was titled, was to supplement OEO's adult-oriented programs. Like these programs, Head Start was expected to contribute to the institutional changes believed necessary for more durable effects.

To the concern of Head Start planners who preferred slower growth, the program expanded from the 50,000 to 100,000 children anticipated by the committee to 560,000 children in the first summer (1965). In FY1965 and 1966, funds for Head Start were included within the Community Action budget. In FY1967, Head Start appeared as a line item program in the OEO budget. Head Start was then serving 681,400 children at a cost of $349.2 million, about 20% of the total FY1967 OEO budget.

The other Community Action programs had been authorized earlier than Head Start but were slower to expand. By 1967, they wanted additional funds. Toward the close of the Johnson administration, however, OEO's growth slowed and competition among OEO programs increased. In addition, pressure from Congress and the Bureau of the Budget for accountability added to the desires of the changing OEO leadership to know what they were getting for the $349 million investment in Head Start.

Rivlin observes:

> Ironically, the new human service programs might have been judged a great success if their enactment had not quite accidentally coincided with another development; a new demand for "accountability" for demonstrable "outputs," and measurable results of government spending. [60, p. 10]

As Williams and Evans [82] note, in the early 1960s Secretary of Defense Robert McNamara brought planning, programming and budgeting systems (PPBS) to the Pentagon. Soon, PPBS was installed in most federal agencies. The OEO version of the PPBS, Research, Plans, Programs and Evaluation, was among the original staff offices. Robert Levine, Director of RPPE, in 1967 recruited John Evans as the first head of the new OEO Evaluation Division. Until Evans joined OEO, most impact evaluations were conducted by each program. Head Start, like other OEO programs, had both summative and formative ongoing evaluations as well as a number of experimental and research studies intended to find possibly better ways of serving low-income children and their families.[2] The Head Start research and evaluation budget was about $6 million in FY1967.

With the autumn 1967 formation of an OEO Evaluation Division, a distinction was made among Type I (summative), Type II (program improvement), and Type III (program monitoring) evaluations. Type I was the responsibility of the central office and Types II and III of the program offices.[3] Evans swung rapidly into action, organizing simultaneously national evaluations of Head Start, Upward Bound, and the OEO manpower training programs.

Opinion varies as to why Head Start was selected for these first evaluations and why the design attempted the quickest possible statement of average long-term effect.

From one point of view,

> "The real purpose of the evaluation, in my judgment, was to find a way to kill Head Start or to mutilate it."

From another perspective:

> "There was a commitment to the notion of rigorous evaluation of all OEO programs. There was the view that OEO's mission was to devise new programs. A big chunk of money was going to Head Start, and there were honest convinctions that Head Start should be appraised so the arguments against the Westinghouse methodology were seen as self-serving, from people protecting the turf."

And from still another view:

> "The Head Start evaluation was not part of an effort to kill Head Start within OEO. It was one of a series of evaluations systematically identified as part of a larger plan. This 'devil thing' simply isn't so."

The Director of Head Start, Julius Richmond, his Deputy, Jule Sugarman and the Head Start Research Advisory Council agreed with the idea of learning what each program was getting for the money. Their quarrel was with the design for the study proposed in late 1967 and developed rapidly thereafter.

Under Evan's leadership, the OEO Evaluation Division began with the program's assumption that children from low-income families would be less disadvantaged when they began school if they had some of the preschool experiences and comprehensive health, nutritional and social supports enjoyed by more advantaged children. This was taken one step further than anything the program proposed, however, to mean that children would *remain* less disadvantaged ever after. No one responsible for Head Start ever stated that as a goal. According to the Evaluation Division, one legitimate way to determine if Head Start was getting its money's worth was to see how much better Head Start children did on standardized tests one, two and three years after entering public school in comparison to children who had not attended Head Start.[4, 5.]

The Head Start Research Council battled the design of the study up through Bertrand Harding, Acting Director (May 1968 to June 1969) of OEO. Their arguments and the Evaluation Division's replies then were much the same as the extensive criticisms and equally extensive rebuttals that appeared later.

The Research Council pointed out the insensitivity of a design without true controls; the difficulties of finding comparable children who had not attended the program and of controlling for selection biases statistically; the almost complete lack of adequate measures of personal-social development and social competence; and the probable inelasticity of basic cognitive functioning; the diversity among Head Start programs and children; the probable consequences of testing the concept of Head Start on children who attended the earliest programs with their operational rough edges; lack of information on both the Head Start and public school curricula experienced by the children; problems of inference about program effectiveness with the children attending diverse and probably inadequate public schools; and the lack of developmental sense in testing a comprehensive, community action-related early childhood program that lasted for a few weeks or a few months as if it were an academically oriented long-term intervention. In the Council's judgment, these and other problems added up to a study designed only to give a go/no go decision rather than information to help redirect or improve the program, or to give a fair test of Head Start's value.

None of the arguments was regarded by the OEO Evaluation Division as new or convincing. They offered as counter-arguments the urgent need for summative information about the long-term effects of Head Start, and the expectations presumably held by Congress and the public that Head Start would help lower-income children catch up academically to children from higher-income families, thus contributing to reducing inequality of educational and later economic outcomes. In addition, Evaluation Division staff were convinced that the selection biases would be random; that other bias would cancel out, and that the study, while imperfect, would improve decision-making substantially in comparison to evidence then available on the effects of Head Start.[6]

These debates influenced the Westinghouse study by (a) expanding the range of measures from academic achievement to parental satisfaction and affective/motivational variables, and (b) establishing an advisory board of experts.[7] The design of the impact study was unaltered.

The RFP for a Head Start national evaluation was announced on April 22, 1968. On June 20, a $247,000 contract (later increased to $387,000) was awarded to the Westinghouse Learning Corporation and Ohio University. Work began June 24th, with a hastily assembled staff. None of the senior researchers had visited a Head Start program and none had previously studied early childhood education.

According to the terms of the RFP, the instruments were to be chosen by August, field staff selected and trained by September, data collection begun in October and completed by November, a draft report completed in March, and the final report delivered by April 1969.

The main findings of the report are given in Appendix A. To summarize: Children who participated in Head Start summer programs did not score higher at the beginning of first, second, and third grades in such programs on all measures of academic achievement, linguistic development, and personal/social development than children who had not participated. Children who had attended the full-year programs and were tested in the first grade achieved higher scores on the Metropolitan Reading tests and some subtests of the Illinois Test of Psycholinguistic Abilities. Scores of children who had attended full-year programs and were tested in the second and third grade were not different from the scores of comparison children.

Parental opinion for summer and full-year programs was highly favorable; the consumers could not have been more satisfied. Subgroup analyses showed that children tested immediately after Head Start, Black children, children from the South, and children from inner-city areas scored higher than comparison children on a variety of measures. These findings were soon confirmed by Smith and Bissell [69] who used alternative statistical methods in an attempt to correct for the higher socioeconomic status of non-Head Start children. Smith and Bissell interpreted this finding as demonstrating the effectiveness of Head Start for children most likely to need it, and the importance of asking for whom Head Start is effective, rather than reaching conclusions based on averaging the children and programs.

The Westinghouse interpretation of the findings is less charitable:

> ... although this study indicates that full-year Head Start appears to be a more effective compensatory education program than summer Head Start, its benefits cannot be described as satisfactory. [11, p. 11]

Westinghouse recommended phasing out summer programs. They also recommended improving full-year programs by beginning earlier and continuing longer; individualizing curricula; parent education; remediating specific deficiencies; devoting substantial resources to experimentation; and, organizationally, making experimentation a major part of Head Start's mission.

A GO/NO GO STUDY BY DESIGN:
A PROGRAM MODIFICATION STUDY BY RECOMMENDATION

Except for phasing out summer programs, none of the recommendations are based directly on the findings, which would not have been possible, given the lack of program data. They are rather extrapolations from other sources, and from consideration of alternative interpretations of the findings. The recommendations do not directly address the go/no go decisions implied in the design, except for the recommendation to phase out summer programs. Thus, the design only informs a go/no go *policy* decision while three of the four recommendations are directed to the *program* decisions.

The source of the Westinghouse recommendations is not always made clear in analyses of what has been learned from the war on poverty [23,31,32]. Tyler, for example, writes:

> In an effort to identify successful programs and to discover major problems, the Westinghouse Learning Corporation and Ohio University were commissioned in 1968 to conduct an extensive evaluation of the impact of Head Start on children's cognitive and affective development. It identified four types of programs that seemed to have more impact . . . One involves parents in the training of their children; a second uses immediate incentives and rewards to reinforce the children's learning of language and numerical exercises; a third focuses on perceptual training of the Montessori type; and the fourth engages the children in seeking answers to the questions they raise, thus emphasizing inquiry learning. [173, pp. 171-172]

The four programs are not directly mentioned in the Westinghouse Report; they were, however, among the ones recommended to Head Start for nationwide adoption in an internal OEO memorandum.

While evaluation design, data collection and data analysis were debated within OEO, and concern increased about the consequence of what the Head Start Research Council regarded as inevitably "unsatisfactory" findings, other events set the stage for the utilization of the report in a way not entirely foreseen in 1967.

In a period of a few years several reports challenged assumptions regarding the federal service delivery strategy, the reasons for social problems, and the value of compensatory education. In early 1969, one of the most influential authors of this period, Daniel Patrick Moynihan, became advisor to the new President, Richard Nixon.

Moynihan [40] concluded that many of the problems faced by Blacks in the United States are related to patterns of belief and behavior fostered in the typically matriarchal Black family.

Coleman [15] found that individual differences in academic achievement are not strongly related to variations in several indicators of school quality.

Mosteller and Moynihan [39], reanalyzing the Coleman data to examine criticisms of Coleman's methodology and analysis, reported that Coleman's conclusions stood. More of the individual differences in tested academic achievement seemed explained by home background (parental education and economic status) than by variations in school quality.

The General Electric/TEMPO evaluation [36] of Title I of the Elementary and Secondary Education Act of 1965 did not show benefits for children in Title I school districts.

Jensen [29,30] concluded that the hereditability of the IQ is so high that educational interventions are unlikely to affect the correlations among social class, ethnicity, scholastic achievement and IQ.

Moynihan [41] stated that the War on Poverty as a whole was misconceived and based on invalid assumptions about community action, the nature of the problems of economic inequality, and the appropriate role of the government.

These reports splashed across the headlines, commanding attention in Washington and the academic policy community. The effect has been described as an energizing one:

> The Westinghouse and Jensen reports have to be looked at together. The impact from the Westinghouse was that Head Start wasn't working, and from Jensen, here's why it wasn't working, and won't ever. That's very persuasive to researchers: here is an effect or lack of it, and here is why—the explanation for the results. So the two together had a very powerful effect.

Between 1965 and 1969, national priorities had shifted from social action to the war in Vietnam. Doubts about the benefits of compensatory education and social action programs, and the federal strategy of financing individual services and encouraging community action were gathering to disillusionment.[8]

A new President was inaugurated in January 1969, Moynihan was in the White House as advisor to the President, and the time for a new approach to old problems seemed at hand.

What happened next, according to Williams and Evans was:

> The study proceeded in relative quiet but as it neared completion, hints came out of its negative findings. Because President Nixon was preparing to make a major address on the poverty program, including a discussion of Head Start, the White House inquired about the study and was alerted to the preliminary negative results. In his Economic Opportunity message to the Congress on February 19, 1969, President Nixon alluded to the study and noted that "the long term effect of Head Start appears to be extremely weak." [82, p. 124]

According to Moynihan in his February 18, 1971, testimony before the House Select Subcommittee on Education,

> One of the Nation's leading newspapers repeatedly suggested in its editorial columns, not only at the time but as much as a year later, that the White House had somehow deliberately called attention to this . . . document. The facts are quite simple. The White House was not even aware of the existence of the evaluation which had been commissioned under the previous administration. The preliminary findings were brought to our attention by a professional employee of OEO who thought we ought to know. [p. 12]

Moynihan states that as a direct consequence of these findings, Head Start was changed in the Presidential message of February 17, 1971, on the problems of poverty from an operational program to an experimental program in describing the organization categories of the Head Start delegation from OEO to DHEW. One implication of the distinction is that operational programs usually serve all eligible persons while experimental programs may serve only a small proportion; Head Start in 1969 served about 12% of the eligible children.

The Presidential message added fuel to controversies already smoldering about the location of Head Start, the fate of OEO, the War on Poverty, and the service provision strategy.

On February 4th, the *New York Times* reported that a study team headed by Richard Nathan had proposed a spin-off of OEO national emphasis programs to other agencies and had called for a transfer of Head Start to the Department of Health, Education and Welfare. The intended transfer was mentioned five days later in a speech by Vice-President Agnew.

On March 3rd, the *Times* noted that a plan backed by Presidential

Aide Moynihan would set up an umbrella agency to operate Head Start and other early childhood education programs. The plan was said to be opposed by Acting Children's Bureau Chief Jule Sugarman and by Education and Labor Committee Chairman Representative Carl Perkins.

In hearings before the House Education and Labor Committee, reported on March 23rd, Dr. Robert Mendelsohn, then American Academy of Pediatrics' Director of the Head Start Medical Consultation Service defended the program, stating that children face a "deadening atmosphere and loss of educational achievement when they enter public school," a conclusion that was challenged by Representative Edith Green.

On April 4th, Secretary of Health, Education and Welfare Robert Finch announced Administration plans to increase the number of children in year-round Head Start programs while decreasing the number in summer programs. The President simultaneously announced the transfer of Head Start to a new Office of Child Development to be located within DHEW.

On April 14th, a draft report of the Westinghouse results was released.

Robert B. Semple, Jr. [66] reported in the *Times:*

> The most comprehensive study ever made of the Government's widely admired Head Start programs asserts that poor children who participated in them were not appreciably better off than equally disadvantaged children who did not. Accordingly, the authors of the study have told the Nixon Administration that the preschool program for disadvantaged children is not worth the cost in its present form and should be radically revised. (The report) had already made a great impact on Mr. Nixon's domestic policy-makers at the White House—indeed, it directly influenced some of his recent recommendations on Head Start.
>
> "One of the principal implications of this report is that we really do not know as much as we thought we knew about improving the lives and the minds of poor children," one ranking White House aide declared last week, "thus the question is whether we proceed down the same old path, which might soothe our egos but will certainly damage the children, or whether we take a new look and surround this thing with some science."

Semple noted that the follow-up message to the February 19th statement included expansion of the Head Start operated Parent Child Centers to $12 million and "a substantial expansion" of the Follow Through program.

On April 15th, Richard Orton, then Director of Head Start, commented on the study, emphasizing the need to continue to search for better ways to help children. [46]

On April 25th, Secretary Finch criticized the Westinghouse Report before the House Education and Labor committee. Finch is quoted [49] as saying,

> I challenge the basis for the report. It was not broad enough . . . Some people in our department feel the data were sloppy. The only thing we got out of the preliminary report was that the summer programs are not as effective as full year programs and we knew this from other studies.

Two days later, on April 27th, the *Times* reported, "White House and advisor stand by report critical of Head Start program." According to Robert B. Semple, Jr.: [67]

> Despite criticism within the academic community and even its own ranks, the White House and its chief antipoverty advisors remain convinced that the controversial Westinghouse Head Start report is a reliable guide to policy planning . . . (The report) has touched off a major and occasionally bitter debate here and in the education community, which has criticized its design and its statistical soundness . . . These criticisms at first threw the White House on the defensive but it is now beginning to retaliate, in part because the report is crucial to several policy decisions Mr. Nixon has already made.
>
> The defenders of the report believe that failure to understand the modesty of their objectives will ultimately discredit the document, which most of them regard as the most comprehensive study of the program ever done. As one put it in an interview, "Accusing the report of failing to do something it was not intended to do may tend to undermine the credibility of what it did; namely, suggest that summer Head Start has no effect and that year-round Head Start programs by themselves do not do much for children."
>
> This point is given particular emphasis in the White House. Mr. Nixon has based many of his first initiatives in the education field on the Westinghouse report, which was available to him and his aides two months ago.
>
> Mr. Nixon has said nothing disparaging about Head Start and indeed appears to have decided to have another go at making it work. But, because of the report, he had said he will treat it as an 'experimental' program rather than as an established program or final answer."

On May 13, the *New York Time's* editorial, "Discrediting Head Start," stated,

It is a dangerous snap judgment to suggest now that compensatory education, which has barely been tried and only with a halting influx of funds
and talent, is just another dead end street . . . Divisions created by political
utilization of the Westinghouse Report are harmful, not only to Head
Start, but to the administration's own promising proposals. Secretary
Finch has helped to put the report back into proper focus. [50]

Until mid-summer 1969 the study was unavailable to the public.
Although the findings were made known in February to the White
House, draft copies of the interim report were not given to Head Start
or the advisory group of experts until late March. Some copies circulated under the table to a few other researchers, providing lead time for
the methodological comments appearing in summer and fall of 1969.

The experts' reaction was mixed. Sheldon White, while agreeing that
there were some methodological deficiencies, concluded that the findings were probably accurate, a position elaborated in his article [78]
"The National Impact Study of Head Start." William Madow repu-
diated the analyses so completely that he requested his name be taken
off the title page of acknowledgements, for reasons he presented in the
Britannica Review of American Education [34] . Barbara Biber did not
agree with the methodology or the conclusions. An internal Head Start
critique ran to 40 single-spaced pages.

In response to these criticisms and others, some additional analyses
(e.g., analyses using individual children rather than class data, non-
parametric analyses, different covariate analyses) were completed.
Caveats, like those regarding untested effects such as the health and
nutritional benefits emphasized by Finch on April 4th, that temper the
final report were inserted. The major conclusions and recommendations
were unchanged.

The final report was released on June 12, 1969. Copies were scarce.
Comments, particularly those stimulated by the Campbell and Erlebacher analyses of regression artifacts which appeared in 1970 [10] and
the 1969 Williams and Evans article on the politics of evaluation [82]
seem to have been read more widely than the report itself.

In 1973, the journal *Evaluation* included an article, review, and
featured quote which assessed the impact of the Westinghouse Report.
All concluded that there was little impact and considered this lack of
effect as a failure of evaluation to influence program decisions or public
policy. Mushkin [43] considered this was probably to the good since
she believed the report was not a methodologically sound basis for

decisions, but was concerned about the impact of evaluations on other projects.

> Not withstanding President Nixon's support of Head Start after evaluations of that program issued generally negative findings, programs are being felled or coming under reassessment because of critical evaluation reports.

The other writers concluded that this reassessment was probably to the bad, maintaining that the report offered the best and most comprehensive information available on Head Start.

According to Levine,

> There is little evidence that Head Start has either changed or been cut back as result of this largely negative evaluation . . . Use of the evaluation by the Office of Economic Opportunity of its Head Start program provides a case history of the difficulties of making evaluative conclusions stick politically in the face of determined technical and political attack. [33, p. 91]

and Moynihan,

> The difficulty here is that the expert turned advocate too rarely reverted to being an expert when the experiments failed to produce the hypothesized results, as seemed in 1969, to be the case with Head Start. If evaluations were disappointing, the sponsors (of the program) would too often content themselves with denouncing the evaluator and redefining the putative objectives of the program. [42, p. 25]

None of these articles or others making similar statements present evidence of lack of impact other than the fact that Head Start has survived.

A STUDY WITH LITTLE IMPACT OR INFLUENCE?

What happened between June 12, 1969 and February 1974? What impact did the report have on program decisions, on policy relating to young children, and on evaluation and how did these effects come about? Or are the *Evaluation* citations correct and is the fate of the Westinghouse evaluation an instance of throwing water on the Prometheus bearing the fire of more rational decisions? But if so, who turned on the faucet?

The answers are incomplete, since some lines of inquiry were only partially followed. Also, there are many views on what constitutes a substantial change, when a change can be ascribed to the report, or whether a change necessarily is an improvement.

To one person, for example,

> One would have to assume that the report said Head Start was bad and should be cut. I don't agree that is what the report said . . . and the evaluation, to justify a cutback, would have to show that the program was actually harmful to children.

To another:

> Effects go into people's head and change directions. You get tidal movements. No one in Washington is dumb enough to say on the basis of research, I'll do thus and so. You won't ever find a direct linkage. People in Washington—decision-makers—sense changes in the wind. And when it's right, out come the axes for the old programs and the ideas for the new programs.

Despite these, and other limitations, four conclusions seem justified:

1. Specific recommendations in the report accelerated the shift from summer to full-year programs, transformed Head Start Planned Variation from a demonstration project into a national experiment, and strengthened the hand of the first director of the Office of Child Development in calling for an experimental approach to Head Start. Together with the less well-known General Accounting Office 1968 evaluation of Head Start, the report stimulated an intensive effort to improve program quality through national and regional monitoring and technical assistance.

The content of the program is not, however, greatly different from the general development approach to which many program directors aspired in 1969. The report's call for an emphasis on remediation of specific deficiencies in language, spelling and arithmetic has had little influence on Head Start goals or content. Today Head Start may be a better program for children, providing highly regarded national leadership in developing alternate ways to serve children of low-income families from infancy through early primary school. It is not, however, the academically oriented preschool emphasized in discussions of the Westinghouse Report and in the preoccupation with changing IQ that dominated many of the debates of 1969 and 1970.

2. General effects of the program include a diversification of objectives and approaches, particularly the shift in emphasis from a comprehensive preschool program serving three- to six-year olds to a more experimentally oriented program broadly concerned with the well-being of young children from low-income families.

In addition, the report is regarded as influential in restraining the expansion of Head Start (which serves about 12% of the eligible population), and in reducing support for early childhood education in the Office of Education. Some observers conclude the Westinghouse Report is avoided like a shoal when new legislation is offered at national and state levels. In both testimony and in proposed bills, the language of early preschool intervention to prevent later academic problems is rarely heard today.

Effects on childhood education as it is practiced at the state and local level are few. The growth internationally of enthusiasm for early childhood education also seems undiminished by the report.

3. Specific effects on evaluation methodology include a growing literature on regression artifacts in quasi-experimental designs, much of which has centered around and gained visibility from the Westinghouse data. This literature is incorporated in some newer statistical texts and in the work of a narrow band of evaluators, policy analysts, and high-level consultants; but not, apparently, in the evaluation studies conducted at the state and local levels or in federal agencies outside of the Division of Education, the Office of Economic Opportunity, and the Office of Child Development.

A second influence is seen in generations of evaluative research designs, moving rapidly from the design of the Westinghouse Report, through longitudinal studies, the planned variation designs, and social experiments. While these designs can be traced to other sources, there seems to be a reasonably clear Westinghouse influence. Researchers involved in one study have applied their recent experiences to the next series of evaluations, cross-pollinating education and social action studies.

Thirdly, the debate on whether or not the Westinghouse study measured too few outcomes, and those poorly, stimulated review of measures available for preschool and primary school evaluations and efforts to improve the reliability, validity, and sensitivity of tests and observational techniques. While improved measures of affective and motivational variables received earliest attention, cognitive, perceptual-motor, and achievement measures have been revised as well.

4. More broadly, the Westinghouse Report contributed to two trends. The first is an emphasis on experimentation before initiation of new strategies or programs. Experimentation has become something of a by-word since 1969. Enthusiasm for experiments is seen as related to the chastening effect of the negative evaluations of social action and education programs and, according to some observers, to a decline in federal willingness to initiate large-scale new social reform programs.

The second trend is a climate of skepticism about the contribution of evaluation, social research and educational research to improved decisions. This climate in turn has influenced support for evaluation, which some believe may decrease in Congress and also in the National Institute of Education.

The response of the social policy and planning community to experiences with evaluation are strikingly similar to the response of early childhood educators to the Westinghouse Report. Some are confident that the assumptions underlying evaluation are valid and expect the present generation of studies to demonstrate that evaluation is more than an income transfer program for some social scientists. Others foresee the evolution of evaluation into a more exploratory research mode, with more modest expectations for its potential contributions. And some would not encourage further public investment in evaluation.

SPECIFIC EFFECTS ON HEAD START:

"RECOMMENDATION 1: Summer programs should be phased out as early as possible and converted into full-year or extended-year programs." [11, p. 10]

Evidence suggesting that summer programs were less developmentally effective than full-year programs and that the academic gains of Head Start were not sustained had been available almost since the beginning of Head Start. In 1966, for example, Max Wolff was scheduled to speak at the American Psychological Association meeting in Miami. Inadvertently, he left the scheduled paper behind and brought with him the still incomplete manuscript of a follow-up study on children who had participated in the 1965 summer Head Start programs. The study showed that gains documented during the program were not sustained after children entered regular public schools. [84] A reporter sitting in on the session picked up the story and the press gave it a great play.

Shriver, scheduled for a major speech, demanded a response. The response was "Follow Through," an extension of the Head Start comprehensive program to the first three grades of primary school. The OEO staff argued that the Wolff-Stein data confirmed what developmental psychologists had advised: further support would be needed to ensure that the Head Start gains would be maintained in regular public schools.

The 1969 *Summary of Head Start Research* by Edith Grotberg [26], then National Head Start Research Coordinator, referred to the Wolff-Stein report and to over 30 other follow-up studies. Most showed immediate benefits of the program but gave little evidence of large, durable effects after the children entered public schools. A pattern, called the "catch up effect" emerged from these studies. During the first one, two or three years after leaving the preschool program, the *rate of gain* of preschooled children leveled off, then slowly declined. On entering public school, the non-participating or control children showed a growth spurt. Their rate of gain was less steep than the gain of the participants *during* preschool, but it was sharp enough to reduce the once highly reliable gap between the two groups, eventually to non-significant levels, both educationally and statistically. While a cross-over or complete loss of advantage is not found, (a) the final levels of both groups suggest poor academic performance and (b) the controls, for most practical purposes, have caught up.

Recent studies, with better programs and better designs, are now showing important changes from this picture. In 1967-68, however, the "catch-up effect" fairly described most of the follow-up findings.[9]

James Miller, in his 1968 review of intervention research with young children [37] concluded: "It's no trick to raise a child's IQ 10 to 15 points. The trick is to keep it there."

Miller, Grotberg, Gray, and others recognized both the immediate benefits of preschool programs and the need to find ways in which these benefits could be sustained. The hypothesis that the "catch-up" indicated family income-related hereditary limits to educability apparently was not regarded as a likely explanation of much of the variance until the Jensen [29] article. There was, however, concern that the reports such as Wolff's would discredit the compensatory education strategy and the importance of early childhood intervention before evidence was available on alternative hypotheses such as the need for developmental continuity.[10]

Three ways to maintain the higher absolute levels of achievement and the accelerated rate of gain were recommended in these studies: start earlier, continue longer, and involve parents. Head Start responded rapidly to these findings, which were consistent with the recommendations of groups such as the President's Commission on the Mental Health of Children. The Parent Child Centers were funded by Head Start in 1967 to demonstrate the effects of beginning earlier. Follow Through originally was intended as a service program for all Head Start graduates. After Martin Luther King's assassination the Head Start parent component was strengthened, primarily by increasing the power of parents as decision-makers and by support for parent education research.

The greater benefits of full-year versus summer programs were evident also in the 1965-to-1969 data. Within Head Start, the trend was to increase full-year authorization rather than expand the summer programs.

The summer programs were, however, an area of conflict. They reached almost every community in the country. Although some people felt these were little more than an employment program for teachers, employment for adults has been among the attractions of Head Start, particularly for some members of Congress. Also the summer programs have been viewed as essential in building grass roots support for Head Start and for increasing competence in managing programs and in organizing political power.[11]

By these criteria, the summer programs might be as good in investment as the full-year programs. As for benefits to the children, Head Start advisors reaffirmed that a six-to-eight week program could help youngsters adjust to group situations, have other socialization benefits, and might be an excellent way to identify and treat the many medical and dental problems found in the first health screening efforts. But most advisors before 1969 cautioned that brief programs would have limited effects on language, cognition, or other aspects of intellectual development.[12]

The Westinghouse Report moved thinking into action with respect to the summer programs. Opinion varies on whether the report legitimized this interest within Head Start and influenced a reluctant White House to switch, or whether the White House used the report to justify its own desires. At any rate, the funds were redistributed. By 1970, summer programs largely were phased out, and, wherever possible (that is, wherever summer funds were sufficient to permit a full-year program), the full-year programs were begun.

As one observer noted: "People hadn't made up their minds about taking the flak from the shifts. Westinghouse helped them make up their minds."

This decision has reverberated in the training of Head Start staff and in the evolution of the Child Development Associate project. The full-year programs did not have access to school facilities unused in summer and to kindergarten or first grade teachers. They had to locate other buildings and to recruit and train new staff. Trained early childhood specialists willing to work at Head Start salaries, with Head Start uncertainties, and in the hundreds of rural Head Start communities, simply were not available to staff all the new full-year programs; neither were there training or supervision infrastructures. Paraprofessionals and community aides had to assume greater prominence; career development ladders became increasingly important, and the emphasis on staff training and technical assistance that was relatively minor for summer programs became a large operation within the full year programs.

Without Westinghouse, these changes might have occurred but probably more gradually.[13]

"*RECOMMENDATION 2:* Full-year programs should be continued but every effort should be made to make them more effective. Some specific suggestions are:

a. Making them part of an intervention strategy of longer duration, perhaps extending them down toward infancy and up to the primary grades.
b. Varying teaching strategies with characteristics of the children.
c. Concentrating on the remediation of specific deficiencies as suggested by the study; e.g., language deficiencies, deficiencies in spelling or arithmetic.
d. Training parents to become more effective teachers of their children." [11, p. 10]

"*RECOMMENDATION 3:* In view of the limited state of knowledge about what would constitute a more effective program, some of the full-year programs should be set up as experimental programs (strategically placed on a regional basis) to permit the implementation of new procedures and techniques, and provide for adequate assessment of the results . . . ." [11, p. 10]

The Bureau of the Budget had urged Head Start to become more experimental and Head Start management had responded to both the Bureau of the Budget and the advice of its own consultants and staff. As noted earlier, the Parent Child Centers and Follow Through programs were influenced by earlier studies such as the Wolff-Stein report (Follow Through) and the 1968 Report of the Child Development Task Force of the President's Commission on the Mental Health of Children (PCC).

In 1968, before Westinghouse, Head Start was preparing for a Planned Variation study. When the cut in the expected Follow Through budget prohibited expansion as a service program, Follow Through evolved, by an internal management decision rather than by an Act of Congress, into an experimental program testing the relative merits of different approaches to kindergarten through third grade education. Since 1967, Head Start and Follow Through leadership had talked about a demonstration study linking Head Start and Follow Through under the same curriculum and program sponsorship. The Westinghouse Report, which led to renewed prodding for Head Start to become more experimental, was influential in transforming Planned Variation from a demonstration program to an experimental test of the effectiveness of the different curricula and of the hypothesis that continuity of program experiences would be associated with continuity of development.[14]

As an experimental effort Head Start Planned Variation can be traced to the influence of Westinghouse. The evolution of other experimental and innovative efforts such as Home Start and Health Start, while on a longer time and more indirect, are also related.

YES, BUT HOW DID HEAD START SURVIVE THE WESTINGHOUSE REPORT?

The Westinghouse Report arrived when the Office of Economic Opportunity was being reorganized and when leadership was shifting. Bertrand Harding, Acting Director of OEO when the Westinghouse contract was awarded, was succeeded by Donald Rumsfeld as Director of OEO from June 1969 to December 1970.

With the inauguration of President Nixon, and Moynihan's arrival as Presidential Aide, the transformation of OEO into an agency testing out social action ideas and the spin-off of many service-like programs such as Job Corps and Head Start to other agencies accelerated.

The Westinghouse findings arrived when there was a changing of the guard at OEO, and the report was received largely by people who had not asked for it. Also, there were no organizational precedents for using findings from such a national impact evaluation, and a means of making recommendations approved by OEO top management binding on the program had not been developed. In addition, the FY1970 budget already had been approved, and the most salient question about Head Start was not if, but where. Within DHEW, the Westinghouse Report is recalled as having almost no relevance to the discussion of where to put Head Start.

One person recalls:

> There were several things happening at once. There were the methodological issues and the public debate. And the loss of OEO impetus generally: people leaving, no leadership, no managerial continuity. And no formal decision was ever made in OEO about the implications of the findings that would be an action plan to be carried out and followed up.

And another:

> Within DHEW there was no aura of failure about Head Start. The issue was where to put it. Everybody thought Head Start was good and should be protected from disaster.

And a third view of the situation at the time:

> The Westinghouse Report was used by one side or another depending on what the side wanted. We wanted to keep poverty an emphasis and concern in the Government. Head Start was one way of doing this, and we didn't want Head Start to sink in the sands of the Office of Education. The concern was not with outcomes for kids, but how Head Start was used as a focus for black political awareness, for the political awareness of the poor.

The Office of Child Development (OCD) was created in March 1969. The new agency was formed of all of Head Start—except oddly enough for a program intended to be experimental, the $3 million per year in Head Start research money and six experimental Parent Child Development Centers—and from the Childrens' Bureau research program.[15]

Thus in June 1970 when Dr. Edward Zigler, the first Director, arrived at OCD, he found still uncertain relationships with OEO regarding budget authority, and uncertainty regarding the future of the Head Start program and its nature: experimental, demonstration, or service.

In the period between June 1970 and January 1971, however, issues raised by the Westinghouse Report gained in importance. The Office of Management and Budget (OMB) sent forward to Congress a FY1971 budget substantially below that requested by the program. Anticipating this cut when Congress acted, a 10% cut in all Head Start budgets authorized under a continuing resolution was announced. The new Director saw that the Westinghouse Report coupled with the Jensen findings was now assuming greater influence among decision-makers. Within OEO, the move to phase out Head Start—a biennial battle—had grown much stronger. Anxiety about the future of Head Start grew in communities. One autumn day the new Secretary of DHEW, Elliott Richardson, found over 500 people in the auditorium of the Department, insisting on a statement regarding Head Start. The demonstrators, mostly Head Start parents, some of whom had come great distances and made personal sacrifices to present their views, left little doubt as to their enthusiasm for the program.

As a staff member in the Secretary's office recalls the situation:

> There was a lot of talk about the report, and a great deal of talk about Head Start being dead, cut out of the budget, over. Richardson decided explicitly against this, however, and he had to fight all levels of OMB against the decision to cut out Head Start before he won. For the 1971 budget, OMB had their long knives out for Head Start.

Zigler's course was tri-fold. First, a strong believer in the importance of the early years of life and the needs of young children, he reasserted in public and in private the urgency of learning how to meet these needs and to serve the nation's children. Second, he emphasized that the purpose of Head Start was not and never had been to raise IQ but to attend to the child's medical, nutritional and developmental needs, particularly motivation and social competency. Throughout the nation, Zigler warned, "Don't crucify children on the cross of IQ." And third, Zigler did not perceive Head Start as a new orthodoxy of five day a week center-based programs. He urged that Head Starts become centers of innovation, trying out new ways, and seeking many alternatives.

The strategy of defending the concept but not the five day a week orthodoxy influenced events.[16] In November 1970, Richardson assured the parents that he supported Head Start and that the program would not be cut back.

The path was open to move in directions which have turned out to be consistent with the Westinghouse recommendations. In summer

1971, the first Health Start program was opened and a new curriculum "Healthy, That's Me" got underway. In fall 1971, awards were made for the first national Home Start projects. In winter 1971, through the Child Development Associate effort, plans to upgrade the competence of care-givers in Head Start and day care were announced. In fall 1973, the individualized Child and Family Resources Program was initiated; and planning and design grants for the Developmental Continuity Program and a national longitudinal study were awarded.

As OCD leadership perceives this history, the Westinghouse Report was used constructively, not defensively. The selection of specific projects and the time-lines are seen as internal: choices made by Head Start leadership based on their beliefs regarding the experimental programs.

As some note:

> "We used Westinghouse and other studies constructively to reaffirm the Head Start focus on the whole child; the concerns about the summer projects were reasserted and the short-term innoculation notion was shown to be fallacious; the notion of a single magic year was also shown to be limited; and the folly of selecting as criteria stable measures of development was emphasized."

> "Westinghouse is just the only book on the shelf about Head Start and so people point to it. But the issues being debated about Head Start and early childhood education are issues we'd have been debating anyhow."

> "Westinghouse helped justify what we wanted as early as 1966: continuity, earlier involvement, greater concern about parent involvement. And we used Westinghouse to legitimize these."

As seen by others, the experimental strategy was not unrelated to perhaps the best path to Head Start stability: adopting an experimental posture while maintaining and strengthening field operations and grass-roots support.

Most people agree that the program now is relatively secure: the administration has recommended a three-year extension for Head Start, and the budget has increased.

> The budget situation has been very positive since the transfer to DHEW. The discussions haven't been on eradicating Head Start but on what the budget should be. We have had a $100 million increase since moving to DHEW; the budget has held constant or increased.

The reasons for this relatively secure position vary. According to one DHEW official, the political uproar of cutting out Head Start is not worth the relatively small gains. It is a popular program with support in Congress by those committed to both community action and child development.

The future directions of Head Start may depend on the child care bills pending in Congress and on the leadership a new Director and new administration may give. The Westinghouse Report may have subsided into the background. "What's new since the Westinghouse Report" continues to be asked by the public, however, and some policy analysts are uncomfortable with a $400 million investment which has yet to demonstrate a long-term impact on academic achievement.

BUT NOT AN ACADEMIC REMEDIATION PROGRAM: AND PERHAPS NOT EXPERIMENTAL ENOUGH?

As noted, most changes are consistent with Westinghouse recommendations although only the shift from summer to full year is seen as a direct effect. There is one exception: concentration on remediating academic deficiencies. The OEO evaluation stressed achievement in the primary grades as the criterion of Head Start success. This is a position the program has never accepted. [52] It may remain as both the initial and final point of divergence.

> The times were exclusively cognitive, the field was all wrapped up in arguing about cognitive gains. And the Westinghouse Report came from this time, and influenced it.

There are at least five reasons why this one recommendation has not been programmatically absorbed.

The Director of OCD did not believe the idea was a good one. Zigler, on the basis of his extensive research and that of others he respected, concluded that basic intelligence is probably not very elastic, that motivational and social competence interact with learning ability to produce achievement, and that preschool programs can best influence learning opportunities, physical and nutritional health, parental support for child development, motivation, and social competence. [85]

Key Head Start staff and educational advisors were opposed to academically oriented or remedial preschool training. Most had studied under Dr. James Hymes, whose approach to early childhood stresses free play. Attempts to accelerate the child's cognitive growth, to help the child learn to read, or otherwise to make early childhood experiences preschooling are regarded, in this approach, as harmful to the child. The greatest benefits are believed to come from a happy, healthy, safe environment where children can interact freely with each other, with well-organized materials such as the doll and the block corners, and with adults who care about children, listen to them, know how to respond individually to them. The more academically oriented or directive approaches to early childhood education were distrusted by these key staff.

The Planned Variation studies reduced the need to select immediately one curriculum approach for national emphasis. Since evidence of longitudinal benefits for academically oriented preschools was scanty, a good case could be made for waiting for the Planned Variation results.

Head Start's strongest supporters in Congress did not regard Head Start's raison d'etre as increased academic achievement.

By 1971-1972, the Jensen article, Title I evaluations, and reanalyses of the Coleman data [28, 39] created a climate of opinion which did not expect lasting academic gains from a preschool intervention. It would not have been entirely consistent in this climate to press for a pre-academic emphasis in Head Start.

Thus, although some conditions favored an academic emphasis, this recommendation, unlike the others, ran counter to trends within Head Start and failed to arouse significant external support. Paradoxically, the search for evidence of durable cognitive effects through interventions in which early childhood education plays a substantial role continues among those with the strongest theoretical objections to the Westinghouse Report. The interventions being studied are not, however, remediation of specific academic deficiencies.

The scale of experimentation is another point of divergence. Those who originated the report thought a substantial portion of funds should be allocated to experimental tests of different approaches. Those who operated the program had to consider capability for mounting and responsibly managing experimental programs as well as the problems of reallocating funds.

Since 1969, Head Start has begun five major experimental projects: Planned Variation, Home Start, Health Start, the Family and Child Research Program, and Developmental Continuity as well as developing a new health-oriented curriculum, "Healthy, That's Me," and the Child Development Associate program. Each experimental project has its own evaluation, usually including an assessment of program compliance with the experimental guidelines, studies of program process and implementation, individual case histories, and cost analyses as well as evaluations of the immediate and longer-term effects on the focal children, their parents and younger brothers and sisters, and the community. The present experimental program allocation is $6 million for project operation, plus about $1.5 million of evaluation funds. This is about 1% of the Head Start total budget.

Opinion is divided as to whether Head Start has devoted "large-scale and substantial resources to the search for finding more effective programs, procedures and techniques for remediating the effects of poverty on disadvantaged children." [11, p. 10] Those within the program point to the increase in funds reallocated to experimentation from $3 million to $6 million, the assignment of scarce full-time positions to manage the projects, the variety of ideas being explored, the calibre of staff recruited to lead the projects, and the prominence given to experimental activities.

On the other hand, these experimental programs all modify or add to existing Head Start projects. The research designs do not involve true controls or design features such as random assignment of treatments to sites and participants that permit strong inference about program effects and that may be necessary for adequate sensitivity to program benefits. Project leaders have several responsibilities in addition to the experimental projects, and staffing has been a problem. There are few plans for utilizing the findings, although in two instances (the Home Start and Family and Child Research Program), the project leader is trying to create the institutional changes needed for the Head Start programs themselves to benefit from the studies. Those who have urged more extensive experimentation feel that the experimental effort falls short of what is needed and of what was recommended in the Westinghouse Report.

Unresolved too is the nature of Head Start: experiment, demonstration, or service program. Too small to be a service program, it is too large and institutionalized to be regarded as an experimental program. It is currently termed a "mature demonstration program."

GENERAL EFFECTS ON THE PROGRAM:

At least two general effects may be traced. First is the stabilizing of Head Start funds at levels close to the 1970 budget (in 1970 dollars), and the second is the continuing search for program effectiveness and its documentation.

Table I presents the Head Start requested and received budgets from 1965 through 1974: Head Start was not growing rapidly after 1967, and since 1970, has held at about the same purchasing level.

Head Start expanded between FY1965 and 1966 ($105 million increment, 100% increase) and between FY1966 and 1967 ($150 million increment, 75% increase). In 1967, an enthusiastic Congress even added $45 million to the $324 million request.

Between FY1967 and 1968, the appropriation *decreased* by $23 million, and was $74 million *less* than requested. The disparity between request and appropriation was $88 million less in FY1969, $55 million less in FY1970, and $58 million less in FY1971.

The influence of the Westinghouse Report on the "hold steady" pattern is suggested by several sources. While the report may not have swayed those in Congress committed to the concept of early childhood programs, justifying program expansion was difficult.

"I think it restrained the growth and exuberance of the program. In the Executive Branch, people expected to see measurable cognitive gains from Head Start. The report didn't show cognitive gains and so a shift in allocations to Head Start or early childhood became a less attractive notion."

"In the absence of the report, there might have been a quick turn-around of belief about Head Start. Under the Johnson Administration, the

Table 1

PROJECT HEAD START: BUDGET IN MILLIONS AND CHILDREN ENROLLED
1965 through 1977

Fiscal Year	Children Enrolled	Requested Budget	Actual Budget
1965	561,000	---	$ 96.4
1966	733,000	---	198.9
1967	681,400	$324.0	349.2
1968	693,400	389.8	316.2
1969	663,600	472.7	333.9
1970	434,800	380.0	325.7
1971	415,800	398.0	360.0
1972	379,000	408.0	376.3
1973	379,000	---	400.7
1974	379,000	---	400.7
1975	379,000	430.0	---

decision had been made to hold down on the Office of Economic Opportunity. Without the Westinghouse Report, under a new administration, the program might have expanded."

"The report was a very serious problem for the program. It undermined Congressional confidence to a great degree. Congress voted to continue the program. Without the Westinghouse Report, they might have voted to expand it."

"There was definitely an impact on the federal bureaucracy. The Bureau of the Budget examiner for Head Start at that time had doubts about the value of preschool to begin with and the Westinghouse Report clearly documented his doubts."

"The evaluations slowed things down. If they never had been done, Head Start and other compensatory education programs might well have gone on to greater budget increases and wider applications. Everyone loved Head Start: Congress, the press, academics. Without the evaluation, Head Start and the others might have increased substantially."

The relationship between the Westinghouse Report and a hold steady posture is suggested by the *New York Times'* August 7, 196! report, "Farmer asks delay on Head Start plan."

Assistant Secretary of Health, Education and Welfare James Farmer told the Senate Labor and Public Welfare Subcommittee that more detailed study was needed before he could take a position on legislation calling for expansion of Head Start. Senator Walter F. Mondale said that "The Administration was substituting study for action and rhetoric for substance." Mondale's bill would provide $15.3 billion for Head Start expansion over the next five years, increasing enrollment to 1,000,000 children. [51]

One person commented, however:

The report doesn't deserve ascription for keeping Head Start at the same level of funding. The report was used to rationalize something that would have happened anyway. Look at all the other social action programs: they didn't have evaluations and they're gone. Head Start survived because of grass-roots support.

A second theme is the continuing search for evidence of program effectiveness [1,27,38]. The Westinghouse Report was criticized for not measuring the right variables as well as for limitations in design This search had begun before the Westinghouse Report, as the evalua tion studies described in footnote 1 suggest. The evaluations mentioned below are of how well the regular Head Start program is working, rather than the experimental variations improvements. The evaluation funds ($3 million per year, approximately) and staff (four full-time researchers with shared responsibility also for about $7 million of Children's Bureau research grants in early childhood) had to stretch fairly thin, however, in designing and managing these national studies and the evaluations of the Head Start experimental programs. Four large evaluation studies were continued or begun after 1969.

- The Educational Testing Service comprehensive longitudinal study of the development of 2,000 low-income children before, during, and after Head Start, begun in 1968, was continued, despite competing pressures to release the funds for this fairly expensive and long-term study for other evaluations. Over 15 reports from the study are available; final reports on the immediate and longer-term effects should be completed by 1976. Early findings indicate that Head Start children come from the most disadvantaged sectors of the community and that they begin the program with more handicaps in health and nutrition as well as in psychological variables than do non-Head Start children from low-income families. This finding is consistent with one of the key assumptions (selection bias favoring non-Head Start controls) in the controversy regarding regression corrections in the Westinghouse analysis.

- The Kirschner Community Impact study begun in 1968 was completed in 1970. Head Start programs influenced changes in community institutions in ways benefitting low-income children. Changes included the development of food purchasing cooperatives, increasing hours and varieties of service in child health clinics, and increasing the quality and quantity of parent involvement in the primary schools. Control communities without Head Start programs showed few such changes, and the greater the Head Start commitment to institutional reform, the more long-lasting and substantial the change.

- The MIDCO parent involvement evaluation begun in 1971 and completed in 1972 showed that parents' involvement in their child's development increased when the children entered Head Start and that the greater the parent involvement—as teacher aides or other paid staff, as educators for the children at home, or as decision-makers regarding program policy and practice—the more the parents' own sense of competence and self-worth changed, and the greater the growth in their children's abilities and scholastic motivation.

- In 1973, the Office of Child Development awarded a grant to the Rand Corporation to design a longitudinal study of social competence. The origin of the study was the perceived need to demonstrate (or have underway a study that gave promise of testing) that Head Start *does* work on its own terms, if not the terms of the Westinghouse Report. Social competency has been defined to include virtually all aspects of child development, from nutritional well-being to metalinguistic skills. The terms of the design are uncertain as yet, but the thesis seems to be that a longitudinal effect of substantial magnitude is expected from Head Start alone, if the appropriate measures and design are used.

The questions of whether long-term effects are an essential criterion of Head Start's value and what are the theoretical bases for expecting such effects from one-year, center-based programs do not appear to have been resolved. The messages seem inconsistent. On the one hand, those close to the program emphasize that expecting long-term effects from a fairly brief experience is developmental nonsense, and that most developmental psychologists would recognize this as such. On the other hand, considerable effort has been invested in designing a study which makes sense only if one believes that demonstrating long-term benefits of some kind from a short-term heterogeneous program is either necessary for the program's survival, or possible.[17]

MORE GENERAL EFFECTS ON EARLY CHILDHOOD EDUCATION

Practitioners seem unlikely to have heard of the Westinghouse Report, and when they have, unlikely to take it seriously except as another reason for distrusting researchers. The convention programs of local and national groups concerned with early childhood education focus on improved practice, finance, management, parent involvement, and staff training. The study is not emphasized in training programs for early childhood educators or in the texts they use. The direct effects on practitioners are probably negligible.

As one person noted:

Practitioners basically discount the Westinghouse Report. It isn't that they have better evidence; it's their gut feeling about Head Start and their programs, an emotional feeling.

And another:

The report just isn't discussed with an average group of child care workers. Westinghouse is certainly not alive as an issue with the front-line worker. And there is a whole new generation of students who haven't even read it. It's just not an issue, except for just a few people.

One practitioner noted, however,

> With regard to impact: well, the first impact on all of us was a scramble for an interpretation, how to explain and rationalize the findings. I don't mean the conventional design stuff about controls and so on, but program stuff. One big interpretation was that the Head Start teachers were not adequately trained. Our concern with training teachers, that eventually influenced the Child Development Associate project, was bolstered by the report. The notion that people who teach young children don't need training could be answered in part by, "Well, look at the Westinghouse-Ohio report."

The effects of the report on the desires of rich and poor among the general public for quality preschool education for their children also appear to be slight, although the access to such programs is unequal. The number of children in day care has increased since 1970, with most of the increase coming from low-income families. Federal support for child care also has increased mostly through Title IVA of the social security legislation. Enrollment in early childhood education programs, however, has increased disproportionately among middle and upper-income families.[18]

One observer commented:

> With regard to national policy concerning preschool, I'm absolutely fascinated by the persistence of interest in preschool. And there is world-wide interest in preschool education. A few years ago people in Great Britain had a massive child development bill in the works and they said, "Keep your Head Start data in America. We don't want the data coming across the Atlantic." And today, 95% of all British kids are in nursery school. It's happening all around the world. People tell me, "The parents want it. They think it's good for their children."[19]

Middle- and upper-class parents seem willing to pay for their children's preschools. Some commercial operators report that parents are taking out preschool education loans, so anxious are they for their children not to miss out on anything.

The scholarly community seems as eager as any other. As Tanner [72] and Rothman [63] note, the public decisions denying investments in preschools or educational quality are made in terms of other people's children.

One person remarked:

> There are differences in the tests you make for deciding how to spend your own money and the tests for a public taxing body. The issues of early childhood education and private schools are going to be decided one way by decision-makers when they are acting as parents, and another way by parents when they are acting as public taxing decision-makers. People are willing to tax themselves to pay for better schools for the poor; they are standing still for all that money for Title I, year after year. But they won't tax themselves to pay for preschools for the poor. Before they will be willing to pay for Head Start for all kids, the public will have to be shown a difference as a result of Head Start that affects regular school performance.

THE REPORT AND PUBLIC POLICY FROM 1969 TO 1974

The Congressional supporters of day care, Head Start, and programs on behalf of children are said to care little and believe less in the findings of the Westinghouse Report, but since there is little to refute it, they avoid the issues of long-term benefits for children or closing the developmental gap. In recent years, there appears to be little administration enthusiasm for early childhood education or day care except as an accessory to welfare reform. While opinion on the adequacy of the Westinghouse Report varies, policymakers seem to believe that nothing has come along to reveal such substantial benefits that a new national emphasis would gain greater support.

The impact of the Westinghouse Report on these trends is frequently mentioned.

> "There was an inherent flaw in the way programs such as Head Start were presented to the nation. They were oversold. And that bred over-optimism among the bureaucrats and the man in the street. And over-optimism always gives way to over-pessimism because you've got to fail. So sooner or later since Head Start was oversold, the balloon would have had to deflate. But the Westinghouse Report was like a pinprick to the balloon. It exploded. It let people feel righteous about their pessimism."

> "The Westinghouse Report consistently came up in conversations with members of Congress and with their Administrative Assistants, who are very influential. When it came to support for Head Start and child development, some potential friends said, 'What about this Westinghouse Report? We can't go out for this thing, given that kind of data.' And as far as our real friends went, they saw the Westinghouse Report as an obstacle. They couldn't push Head Start or child development as effectively. It was a thing that had to be explained."

"Westinghouse gave a signal to all of us—not to be euphoric. It dampened a lot of enthusiasm, not a total wipe-out, but a soft dampening, all over the country. Yet, most people still seemed to feel that working with young, poor kids was a good thing to do."

The Westinghouse Report came along at a convenient time to shake confidence in OEO's ability to manage successful programs and to dampen public hope in family or child educational interventions as an effective way to reduce poverty. It is said that the day the findings from the preliminary Westinghouse analyses were reported, Moynihan pulled the negative income tax proposal and Family Assistance Plan from his desk drawer and brought them, and the news of the findings, to President Nixon.

The Administration position on Head Start and on OEO was lukewarm. The Westinghouse Report confirmed Moynihan's own conclusions. His book, *Maximum Feasible Misunderstanding,* came out just a few weeks before he came to Washington, and he concludes in it that OEO was doing all the wrong things. The President didn't think OEO was worth very much either, and the Westinghouse Report was proof that it wasn't.

The Westinghouse evaluation had the McNamara charisma. Cost/benefits analyses and impact evaluations and PPBS were all riding high. The Westinghouse Report became the cannon to replace the toy pistol of the Wolff report, and so it became a very important political affair.

Rivlin notes that:

Jencks and his associates dismiss the whole preschool child development movement in a few skeptical paragraphs, citing the Westinghouse-Ohio study's findings that, on the average, Head Start children showed no long-term cognitive gains over non-Head Start children. [58, p. 69]

Few articles on early childhood education written for social policy fail to mention the report as reasonably conclusive evidence that, if long-term effects on school achievement are the goal, Head Start alone is not the way to achieve it. In this sense, it seems likely that Westinghouse has been as influential as any single report of the past decade on policy relating to early childhood education. It is widely cited, and its conclusions form part of the belief system of many in positions of national influence. The report has become an item to be avoided in the language of Congressional testimony and pending legislation. The new child care bills contain little or none of the language of the 1960s concerning cognitive, intellectual, or personal social gains for children. The focus is more on the need for child care for working mothers.

One person said:

> The academics who testified in the 1970 hearings on the Child Development Act weren't grinding an ax against Head Start or interventions. They were grinding an ax that interventions have to start earlier. Congress was protected essentially from that study. The academic community really played the Westinghouse Report down in that testimony, or used it as a lever to get more funds for younger kids.

Steiner, in analyzing the impact of lessons from the War on Poverty on welfare reform, concludes, however;

> Both groups (welfare reform and early childhood education groups) lost enthusiasm for day care as an element of reform as the absence of safe and sanitary facilities became apparent, and as a study by Westinghouse cast doubt on the permanence of gains . . ." [71, pp. 61-62]

Thus, the recommendations of the report apparently have had a catalytic effect on several program changes, such as the phasing out of summer Head Start, that were already being considered. The go/no go decision implicit in the design, on the other hand, seems to have had a fixative impact on public policy. The Westinghouse report is virtually the only study cited in policy analyses, almost as if the many other research reports had never been written. And it has "fixed" a fairly widespread belief that, "Universal comprehensive preschools for low-income children won't work."

The increasing demand for day care and the interest in using empty schools and employing teachers threatened with loss of their jobs as primary school enrollment decreases may combine to create new patterns of publicly-supported early childhood care. Already, pathfinder projects such as Burton White's are underway in which the public schools are the central agents for developmental care from prenatal through primary years. Commissioner of Education, Terrel Bell [2], Assistant Commissioner of Education for the Handicapped, Edward Martin; and President of the American Federation of Teachers, Albert Shanker [68], among others, have proposed new roles for public schools in providing child care and coordinating children's services in the community and are urging that the schools must become the custodians of the vital preschool years through universally available preschool education. According to Shanker,

> Universal early childhood education is a must—the responsibility for the enlarged program should be borne by the public schools.

While some involved in early childhood programs are skeptical about universal preschooling or the schools as the primary agent for the young children, the weight of the education community may create an "if you can't lick 'em, join 'em" movement to consolidate support for widely expanded early childhood education.

In addition, the pendulum is swinging back from extreme pessimism regarding early interventions. Recent reports emphasize the conditions under which durable benefits are found [6,64], the relationships between what happens in a classroom and outcomes for children [70], and assert that indicators of educational quality do account for substantial variance in socially important outcomes.

EFFECTS ON EVALUATION

One of the more controversial aspects of the report was the use of regression analysis to adjust for inequalities of economic background between Head Start and non-Head Start children. If social class is correlated with the outcome measures (scholastic achievement, motivation, and self-esteem), and the non-Head Start children come from more advantaged families, Head Start might have a substantial effect relative to true controls but appear less effective relative to more advantaged comparison children. Since information on the psychological status of the children before Head Start was unavailable, regression analyses controlling for social class were used to estimate true program effects.

Several major articles have appeared on the statistical analyses of the Westinghouse study. Perhaps the most widely known is the Campbell and Erlebacher [10] series on evaluation artifacts in quasi-experimental designs. A second series, also on regression artifacts, has been published by the Institute for Poverty Analysis at the University of Wisconsin [74]. And the third series, which influenced the analyses of the Follow Through/Head Start Planned Variation Study, began with the Smith/

Bissell article in the 1969 *Harvard Educational Review*. A fourth influential criticism was prepared by William Madow for the Britannica Review in 1969.

In its simplest form the debate has two main parts. The first part is which of several possible regression analyses are most appropriate, if one believes that Head Start children were selected initially from among the most disadvantaged versus if one believes that selection biases either were not operating or that the comparison children were the initially least able group. The second part is whether, assuming the worst, the selection bias created such artifacts that even the best regression analyses currently possible are likely to yield results substantially different from the true effects of Head Start. Campbell and others conclude the results of true experiments show such designs are substantially more sensitive to treatment effects than quasi-experimental designs under Westinghouse conditions. [7,9,10,57] Evans and others do not believe the findings would have been much different even with a true experimental design and other methodological improvements. [12,13,20,22, 35, 61,62]

The Campbell/Evans controversy of 1969 and 1970 stimulated methodological interest in the properties and feasibility of true experiments, in expanding knowledge about quasi-experimental designs and in developing new algebras to grapple with regression artifact problems in such quasi-experimental studies. The debate on regression analysis is regarded by social scientists as a contribution of Westinghouse to improved evaluation and decision making. Campbell previously had pointed out the limiting assumptions of regression analysis and encouraged his students to develop improved analytic techniques and algebras. The technical issues gained visibility and significance in the politically charged context of the Westinghouse Report. While opinion is not unanimous on whether the statistical problems mean the Westinghouse findings are unreliable guides to policy, there is considerable agreement that the issues raised by Campbell, Watts, Evans and others must be taken into account by any serious statistician.

Other methodological criticisms also have been responded to by Evans, Cicarelli, Williams, and Schiller, all of whom were closely involved with the report. [12,13,20,21,82]

Methodologically, there are at least five points in the controversy:

1. Who decides what are the proper objectives of a program? Evans et al. claim it is reasonable to evaluate Head Start's success by its long-term effects on scholastic achievement, academic motivation, self-esteem and parental attitude. Others believe Head Start should be evaluated by immediate impact on these and other outcomes including child well-being, health, and nutritional status or on grounds such as consumer satisfaction, increased political awareness, income distributive effects and managerial efficiency. The argument is not easily answerable in terms of legislation or Head Start documents.

The problem was not lack of goals, but the multiplicity of goals and expectations within Congress, DHEW, OEO and Head Start itself. As a policy analyst recalls,

> I've talked with people on the Hill, the Congressional staffers. When I came to DHEW, I did a survey of what people thought the objectives of Head Start were. Some people saw Head Start as an employment program that also took care of kids. Others saw Head Start as a way to keep the community action agencies going. Most Congressional staffers saw it in these terms—in terms other than as a child development program.

None of these goals are seen as "putative" or after-the-fact avoidance of the harsh realities of the report by those who hold them, and the record of speeches, presentations, guidelines etc., appears to back this up. However, the 1965-1969 materials do not include clear statements of the magnitude or durability of effects expected or of the priorities among possibly conflicting goals.

One consequence of the glorious goalfulness of Head Start is that the Westinghouse evaluation has defined for many people what the implicit goal "really" was. One observer comments:

> The evaluation helped to define Head Start as a program whose effects were primarily cognitive. That is now the definition in the public mind. Actually Head Start was presented as a comprehensive program. The Westinghouse report changed the public image. Head Start became, in the public mind, a program to get kids' scores up. The public was told that Head Start hadn't done it and that it wasn't very much of a success. Westinghouse was not an appropriate assessment of Head Start. But the tail has wagged the dog and the evaluation wound up defining the purpose of the program. And that's the biggest effect of the Westinghouse.

If we believe Congress, with the approval of the President, decides what are the proper objectives for a program such as Head Start, perhaps who defines the objectives in terms sufficiently precise that the

Congressionally required evaluations can be fairly completed should return to Congress as an issue. The likelihood of increasing Congressional specificity and analyzing evaluation implications of the possible conflicting agenda is not seen as very great by one researcher, who remarked,

> You need to collect under one umbrella many constituencies to support a program. Some will see Head Start as a way of raising a child's IQ. Others see it as a means of income redistribution and providing service to poor families. Others see it as a focus of community organization. The diverse aims embedded in Head Start make it salable to Congress and you cannot expect a program to pass without diverse aims.

2. How adequate were the measures? Evans et al. point to the considerable efforts made to select the best possible measures and the extensive discussion in the report of the psychometric characteristics of all the tests. Others note that the reliabilities cited were for different populations than the children tested, and question both the sensitivity and reliability of the instruments, particularly those assessing self-esteem and scholastic motivation. The Research Council has argued that lack of reliable, valid measures of affective and motivational variables made the Westinghouse study premature. Thus the report was caught between the unwillingness of OEO to delay an evaluation until better measures of affect and motivation could be developed and the reluctance of Head Start to have only achievement on standardized tests represent the impact of the program. At least three reviews of preschool measures are now available. According to these reviews the achievement and reading measures used by Westinghouse are reasonable guides to child performance, but there is still no satisfactory way to assess motivational variables, which increasingly are regarded as of great significance for children from low-income families.

3. Was the sample sufficiently large and representative? Of the 104 sites, 75 were summer programs and 29 full year. The sample seems large enough for the summer programs but not the full year. Also 121 out of 225 of the sites originally selected refused to participate, raising the question of how the sample of cooperative sites may have been biased. A third question is "representative of *what?*" The dimensions of Head Start program heterogeneity were largely unknown, and what difference variance in processes made to variation in outcomes was even less certain.

4. Were the data reasonably free of tester error? The Westinghouse report and later papers by Evans et al. describe efforts made to ensure clean field work: how the field supervisors were selected, training of field supervisors by test originators themselves; selection and supervision of interviewers and testers, and the quality control procedures for scoring and coding. The intent of obtaining data as free as possible from tester errors and the logistical snafus is clear. The extent to which intent was achieved, and whether the Westinghouse data are worth analyzing from the point of view of quality control is less certain.

First, subsequent experience with large-scale studies of young children has shown that, even with great effort to anticipate field error, it happens often enough where it is detected to raise a certain suspicion of the remaining data. Even with good measures, field problems are such that one can get bad data.

One researcher with extensive experience in such efforts said,

> People spend years on data analysis, like on the Coleman study and the Westinghouse, and have no idea of the quality of the data on which they're spending so much time and don't seem to care about it. As far as I'm concerned, I'm amazed that in spite of all our problems with instrumentation and data collection and everything we get any results at all. So I believe in every positive result we get and expect that the real result is even larger. It has to be, if it can survive these evaluations and show up.

A second reason for caution regarding the quality of the data are comments about field work. For example:

> You ought to talk to _____. He worked for Westinghouse and has horror stories about how the instruments got written in three days and how supervisors were selected. They went to New York City and were just bringing them in off the streets. One person talked all day and didn't hire anyone and the other recruiter liked everyone. There is a lot of discussion about the analysis, but people have no idea about the quality—or lack of it—of the data and instrumentation.

Considering the effort that went into keeping the field work clean, it seems probable that the horror stories are atypical. On the other hand, in some comparisons the samples are very small, and data error, which typically decreases sensitivity of statistical tests to true differences, could disproportionately reduce confidence in the findings.

5. At what point is something better than nothing for policy and when is something worse than nothing? Evans [21] concludes that even imperfect evaluations are better guides to policy decisions than a parade of witnesses or the purely political considerations that otherwise might have the field to themselves. He argues equally strongly that we should strive for the best designs and methodology possible, and indeed, the evaluations conducted under his leadership at the Office of Education are creating some of the most sophisticated designs to date [53]. To many methodologists, Evans' position seems supported after five years of discussions. One statistician summed up his perspective:

> Of course there's been a lot of methodological disagreement about the analysis and the study. But the methodological issues don't really change the conclusions of the report.

Others conclude that the Westinghouse study is too flawed to have the influence it does on the climate of opinion; and, that in this instance, nothing would have been a better guide to policy than the something available. Another statistician sums up his views:

> I've been amazed at how Cicarelli and Evans defend the evaluation. The OEO group seems to have been extremely defensive about the study. I can't buy the conclusions.

To a third observer, whether the Westinghouse study was better than nothing should be answered in the context of its time:

> The report was a major attempt. It did many things for the first time. The report ought to be recognized as the groundbreaking effort it was, the first large national evaluation, even if we know how to do things better than when the report was prepared.

Some observers have reservations about large scale national evaluations, however improved, as guides to policy.

> Despite the inevitable limitations of its ideas and data, the large-scale study normally carries an authority which is politically attractive to its sponsors. Small studies can be readily repeated (with one or another decisive modifications) by intellectual and political rivals whose arguments are then as strongly based in fact as the original investigators. By its scale a very large study becomes historically unique, so that its data can only be challenged

by internal weaknesses which cannot be concealed or are voluntarily disclosed. Even should a rival study of comparable magnitude subsequently be mounted, it can neither erase nor exactly reproduce the original which is, to that extent, invulnerable. [54, p. 590-591]

The effect of the Westinghouse Report on subsequent evaluations can also be traced. If the findings of the report burst a balloon of expectations about preschool education, the debate about methodology may have popped a bubble of expectations about evaluating social action programs.

> Westinghouse certainly gave us an impetus to do a broader job of evaluating than Westinghouse itself. The other evaluations which we subsequently initiated would have come along eventually, but they would not have come as quickly.

Change has been perhaps too rapid, because until the data are collected, analyzed and the reports sufficiently considered, the apparent lessons of one innovation may be too swiftly applied to the next evaluation.

In general, the younger generations of evaluation differ from the Westinghouse Report by:

- Beginning with programs that have more limited and explicit statements of objectives and of the magnitude and durability of expected effects;

- Creating designs that permit generalization to the desired population through replication and sample selection;

- Spending more time on measurement development, with greater efforts to measure a wide variety of outcomes through various approaches;

- Giving greater attention to field logistics and collecting reliable data;

- Studying program implementation, and independently measuring whether the treatment to be evaluated has occurred;

- Allowing more time for effects to be shown, with longitudinal designs rather than cross-sectional studies;

- Using true experimental designs with randomly assigned experimental and control groups;

- Using multiple contrast groups in addition to true controls;

- Adopting multiple perspectives on the program including standardized tests, observations, anthropological and ethnographic assessments, and individual case studies;

- Focusing greater attention on the social matrix of the treatment, including the effects of parents, teachers, community support and the setting in which the innovation is occurring;

- Placing greater emphasis on consumer satisfaction, managerial, and distributive aspects of the innovation as well as individual outcomes;

- Using multiple techniques for analyzing the same data, more extensive secondary analyses, and adversarial analyses;

- Layering evaluations, including local or self-evaluations as well as national, comparative, and summative evaluations;

- Providing more attention to process questions, and not separating summative and formative aspects of the evaluation as much;

- Testing the relative effectiveness of alternate ways of achieving similar objectives, as well as designs involving the no-treatment condition;

- Establishing closer relations among program developers, operators, and evaluators from the initiation of the program;

- Evaluating smaller scale projects that treat heterogeneous larger populations as a series of mini-evaluations of local activities serving population sub-groups; and

- Extending front-end conceptual analysis and evaluation planning, anticipating the strengths and limitation of alternate ways of stating evaluation questions, and establishing alternate designs and measurement strategies.

It seems fairer to describe these as changes rather than improvements. They shift evaluation further from the selection among relatively few alternatives of the classic policy realm to the exploratory realm of research. Some people urge that evaluation not be used to describe more recent studies, in part to avoid association of policy decisions of a go/no go kind with the findings from a study. Others point out that policy analysis itself is evolving to a greater search for alternative strategies and approaches, and a more exhaustive consideration of options. Appreciation of the long-term consequences of actions has grown, along with the development of planning heuristics requiring consideration of many more variables, of the degrees of uncertainty in data and of more complex tradeoffs. [14,19,24,55,76,77]

Shortly after the Westinghouse Report was released, in August 1969, the first national meeting of Head Start and Follow Through Planned Variation sponsors, evaluators, and consultants was held in Menlo Park. The Westinghouse Report heightened the sense of urgency at that meeting in trying to solve the problems of how to assess outcomes and classroom processes with the often inadequate measures and how much money could be diverted from collecting only moderately satisfactory data to developing better measures. A fear that the Planned Variation curricula would be "failed" in the same way that many sponsors believed that the Westinghouse "failed" Head Start—by impact evaluation before a reasonable time for implementation and by weak or narrow measurement—was evident.

Investment in measurement development was extensive in earlier Head Start evaluations [18]; after Westinghouse, Follow Through and Head Start joined forces to improve measurement of program implementation and of affective-motivational outcomes.

Comparison of the Johnson's 1970 review of preschool tests, the 1973 U.C.L.A. compendium, Walker's 1974 critical analysis and the Rand 1974 [56] survey of measures for a comprehensive evaluation of Head Start show: (1) progress in the variety and number of measures in various stages of development, with much fuller coverage of the many areas of child growth; (2) mixed, but still considerable success in preparing improved measures of achievement and skills; (3) encouraging results in the development of observational techniques; but (4) still inadequate assessment of how children feel about themselves and others, and how hard they are willing to work for approval from friends and family, for academic success or other goals.

While the Westinghouse Report thus stimulated great concern for the adequacy of measures, and the investment of several hundred thousand dollars in measurement development, a comprehensive evaluation of Head Start would be only somewhat less premature in 1974 than in 1968, insofar as measurement is concerned. Some believe that with more time, or more resources, measures could be substantially improved. Others suspect that the intransigence of the affective-motivational domain goes deeper, into an inherent instability of this area because the moods and emotions of the child are so responsive to the changing social environment or because the theory on which measurement should be based is itself too primitive.

One difference, however, between 1968 and 1974 is the reluctance of researchers and evaluators to analyze measures which fail statistical tests of internal reliability or to recommend program evaluation without fairly extensive prior work or improved measures [56]. If psychometricians have not created the better measure, evaluators, in part sensitized by the Westinghouse controversy [56] are less likely to risk challenges to either the study or the program due to measurement problems.

EFFECTS ON EVALUATION POLICY

The Westinghouse Report was among a series of "negative evaluations"—national studies in which a social intervention was not found to yield a substantial effect.

These evaluations, broken primarily by the more favorable reports on *Sesame Street*, have raised questions about the value of evaluation itself. As some observers note:

> "I don't think evaluation as such really exists, that you can tell if a program is good or bad. Most of the issues that create government programs are too subtle and complex, and no evaluation is going to tell if the program works."

> "Westinghouse and other skeptical studies have influenced the re-direction of research interest toward families, and it has contributed to more skeptical research on the efficacy of schooling and early intervention. In turn, this has contributed to general skepticism about research and evaluation: the Greek messenger problem. Researchers kept turning out gloomy studies about the value of early childhood programs and schooling and people begin to think that researchers and evaluators are gloomy people who are not worth supporting."

> "The major lasting effect was viewing the Westinghouse Report as a case study of what evaluation could and could not do; the difficulty of having objectives for a program which were not measurable, and being faced with the issues of how to evaluate on the basis of measures which may or may not be good criteria for a program. It was a real learning experience for program managers looking to evaluation to help them to realize that program evaluation was a much more complex issue than we thought."

> "Any evaluation in the foreseeable future is going to be imperfect. People who don't like the findings are going to be able to argue that it's not valid. You can usually do some kind of job on almost any evaluation."

This consequence was anticipated as early as 1969 when evaluators in DHEW received calls from the White House urging that the criticism of the Westinghouse Report not damage the developing interest in social science research as a tool of public policy.

> This is the first time since the Coleman study that we've tried to have an evaluation by social scientists of the goodness of on-going programs. A lot

of people are trying to discredit the evaluation because it shows no cognitive advances. The defenders at Head Start are disappointed and are trying to knock out all social science evaluation. Be sure this isn't used to discredit all large attempts at social science evaluation.

Again, there is a sense of irony. Social scientists were becoming intrigued with their potential role in increasing rationality through the use of research in decisions affecting social welfare. Policy analysis was moving into favor. But it was hard to have it both ways. Some social researchers believed in the negative findings, and did indeed use them to recommend policy. However, the negative findings, as foreseen, aroused considerable and public controversy. Evans notes that had the Westinghouse findings been favorable, the methodological controversy might have been muted.

The extent to which this has affected public and Congressional trust in education research and social science research more generally is uncertain. [18] Some predict that before long, Congress will start cutting evaluation offices and budgets.

People are concerned with how research and evaluation might be more useful. They try to explain what their problems have been in the past as a prelude to improving the value of research and evaluation in the future. I'd believe, though, that evaluation will be cut out sooner than I'd believe Head Start will be cut out. I wouldn't be surprised if evaluations started being cut by Congress.

In 1974, this comment came true in at least one instance: the Office of Education planning, budgeting, programming and evaluation budget was cut.

There are at least three points of view regarding evaluation and social policy.

Forget It For Policy Decisions. The first point of view is that inevitably, people will use findings to suit their purposes, regardless of methodology, and that evaluation and evaluative research should be de-emphasized. [8,76,77,81] From this perspective, Congress and decision-makers would do well to back off from expecting that evaluations will contribute directly to improved decision-making, if indeed such expectations have been widely held.

As one person said:

Evaluation data will not change basic ideologies. If the Westinghouse report had come out in 1964, the same data could have been used entirely

differently. As researchers, all we can do is work hard to give honest data.
There is no way we can prevent evaluation being used by people who have
various positions.

And another:

Evaluations can influence fine-grain program decisions, and that's about it.
For any of the big policy decisions, research is marginal. These yea/nay
decisions are made on the basis of political tea leaves. The value of
evaluation in child development should be seen more as influencing fine-
grain program design, and this is the big lesson we have learned from
Westinghouse.

Modify Its Purpose. Another view is that the state of the art of
evaluation is too limited for policy making, and research to inform
policy rather than evaluation to influence policy should be cultivated.
This position seems to be an evolving middle ground:

"Perhaps evaluation has been unreasonably burdened with the guidance of
policy, and it is time to realize that evaluation, like other research, can
provide the facts that are one of the bases on which policy decisions should
rest, but should not be expected to make the value judgments."

"The scientific evaluations trying to measure changes in kids as a function
of interventions are of questionable value. Evaluations of process are
showing how the programs get started, the effects of good and bad
planning, and showing how an idea gets from start to operation—these
evaluations can be effective."

"We are redefining what evaluation and policy research is about. A lot is
now discussed in different terms. For example, there is a lot more attention to what is the program, to variations in program characteristics and to
predicting what will be the effect of these variations. You can't run out
and gather all citations and weigh the evidence; people are more aware of
what has to be known to make a decision of a particular kind and how to
design an evaluation. This is a very complex view of the relation between
research and practice. This newer approach means that the task of evaluation can become hopelessly complicated but interesting as hell. It means
you have to learn to ask basic questions about everything you do."

"Today people accept the macro-negative effect. Most evaluations show
non-significant differences and this result is not diabolic or manipulative.
The force of this macro-negative argument delivers some ex post facto
validity of its own to the Westinghouse evaluation. There *are* two usable
criteria: *management*—is the program well run and efficient, and *distributive*—does the program get money where we want it to go. This approach is

understood and accepted by most program officers and Congress. Most don't really care about effectiveness evaluations. The rule is, 'If it's legislated, and it occurs, it's a success.' Only scandalous failures in effectiveness terms can upset that paradigm."

Improve It. There is a third point of view, which is that evaluations can and should contribute directly to policy, and that if the lessons of experience are applied, evaluation can have a beneficial influence that is only beginning to be realized. [21]

> There is no sense in doing a study that can't influence or improve decision-making and policy. Timpane, in his *Harvard Education Review* article, says that where interest in a program is too great, people won't wait for evaluations and where there is so little interest, there is no support for an experiment. So either way, no experiment and the evaluator can't win. This may be true if one adopts the standard social science research approach to an obstacle to the use of research for social policy. I believe you don't give up. It *is* possible to do studies even if they are not ideal and this will improve decision-making. We have to recognize that longitudinal and true experimental designs are superior, and we do these when we can. But the alternative, if these are not possible, is to act on nothing and to go back to the parade of witnesses and the most effective argue-ers. And this is what we are trying to correct.

> The compromises we may have to make shouldn't cause us to say that evaluations are a waste of time. They can, and do provide good information for decisions. Evaluation isn't all weak and it isn't all powerful. Evaluations contribute information and that information is going to have to compete with everything else in a pluralistic society. We can't give up as long as we succeed some of the time.

In summary: Has the Westinghouse Report had an impact? Or is it indeed an example of how little evaluations influence practice and policy?

There are at least two parts to this question: was there a change, and is it likely that the Westinghouse Report had something to do with this change?

Both questions are difficult to answer.

First, what impact people expected from the Westinghouse evaluation and how much of a change would be regarded as durable and substantial was not stated in advance nor afterward. The tone of some articles suggests that nothing short of abolishing Head Start would be considered a sufficient change, although this was not a recommendation of the report.

Recommendations in the report were limited to some aspects of the program and mostly urged an expansion of experimentation leading to more effective ways of helping young children from low income families. There were never any official recommendations for Head Start policy, compensatory education or evaluation that developed as a result of the report. Consequently, there are many opinions on whether the report was implemented.

Second, many of the changes in the program, in attitudes toward early childhood education, toward compensatory education, and toward evaluation policy and practice are viewed as consistent with other, often earlier influences. Without extensive analyses of memos and fugitive documents, and possibly not even then, it is difficult to separate the external pressure of the report from other events, and from present and past convictions.

Third, some of the impacts are non-events, and the reasons for these non-events are often not well documented. One such non-event was the failure to phase out Head Start. The question of whether the threat was a biennial problem or one made desperately serious by the convenient arrival of Westinghouse at a time when the new administration wanted to cut out the program is viewed differently even by the people close to the action.

Thus some people may regard these points as evidence of greater impact than expected. Others may regard the effects as minor, and conclude that the Westinghouse Report is a case history of the political forces constraining the use of evaluation for public policy.

McLaughlin, studying the relation between evaluation and reform in Title I of the Elementary and Secondary Act of 1965, concludes:

> An important lesson of the Title I experience is that the logic of inquiry should be perceived as relative, not absolute, and that a realistic and useful evaluation policy should acknowledge the constraints of the policy system and the behavior of bureaucracies. Evaluation efforts based on expectations for reform by means of a social report, or better information on program accomplishments, certainly find justification in theory. But in practice they may turn out to be little more than empty ritual. [36, p. 111]

An important lesson of the Westinghouse experience suggests something different: that evaluators would do well to act as if they believe their findings and recommendations had substantial, far-reaching social consequences. Evaluations, as seen from the perspective of the report, tend to be perceived as absolute, not relative, and realistic and useful evaluation policy should acknowledge the often terrible responsibility for understanding the program and policy alternatives, for helping formulate statements of these options if necessary, for dealing with the value-laden question of what a better decision would be, and for anticipating in the design, conduct, interpretation and reporting of evaluative studies, the possible consequences of the findings for actions that can affect millions of children.

The weakest link in evaluation, from this perspective as from McLaughlin's, is not in strengthening design, measures, data collection and analysis although dispute may focus on these and strengthening is often needed. It is rather in anticipating the range of decisions within the power of the many decision-makers who may apply what is learned from evaluations. Small though this range may be for a single person, through the effects of many decisions or actions—how one tilts at a meeting or receives a program idea—evaluations relevant to the decisions may have long-term application, cumulating knowledge and social reform. Without such a change in the decision and action analyses when such studies begin, evaluations may continue to have large and durable effects without yielding the improved program and policy decisions which are the hoped-for payoffs.

NOTES

1. The opinions expressed in this paper are those of the author who was National Coordinator of Evaluation for Project Head Start from 1968 to 1972. Endorsement or approval by the National Institute of Education should in no way be inferred.

2. Head Start had initiated a number of evaluations, mostly of the immediate impact type [17,18]. One of the beliefs in the literature is that Head Start has been so reluctant to evaluate its programs that OEO had to create an Office of Planning, Research and Evaluation to get honest answers. The issue of what is an honest answer in evaluation and how to get it is another paper. Briefly, however, Head Start funded a national, random sample post only evaluation using cognitive, linguistic and affective measures in summer 1965 (Planning Research Corporation). Another national, random sample evaluation using a pre/post design and a program characteristics model of analysis with cognitive, affective and linguistic measures was completed for the 1966 full-year programs (Planning Research Corporation, 1967). Still a third national evaluation, with extensive observational measures of what was happening in the classrooms, correlations of

classroom variance with outcomes for the children, and a pre/post design was conducted in summer 1966 (Educational Testing Service, 1966, three volumes). In addition, national evaluations of a pre/post design with extensive, diverse measures and classroom observations were supported for full year 1967, 1968 and 1969 programs. Small studies of immediate impact, experimental studies of a planned variation nature and follow-up studies were begun between 1965 and 1969. The Kirschner evaluation of the impact of Head Start on community institutions started before the Westinghouse study. There was considerable evaluation activity, much of it innovative in the sense of studying implementation and the effort to match measurement to program objectives. Missing, however, was a true experimental test on a national scale of the immediate impacts and a national longitudinal study. These are, if one believes them important, still missing although a fairly large number of smaller scale, well-designed, immediate impact and longitudinal studies are now available [6,64].

3. The Research Advisory Council included Edward Zigler, Urie Bronfenbrenner, Boyd McCandless, Edward Suchman, and Edmund Gordon. The Council urged more evaluation and research for Head Start and initiated in 1967 such evaluations as the Educational Testing Service longitudinal study and the community impact study. The Council believed that adequate evaluations would be longitudinal, comprehensive, involve a priori multiple comparison groups, and require a great deal of information about the families' and children's experiences before, during and after Head Start. Dr. Gordon directed the Head Start research and evaluation program until August 1967. Dr. John McDavid, the first full-time director (August 1967 to August 1968), in addition to his other duties, was the often embattled Head Start liaison with RPPE during the planning and design phases of the Westinghouse study.

4. The comparison children were selected at random in 1968 from youngsters who had not attended Head Start. Age and sex were matched; everything else such as parental SES and teacher at time of testing was left to vary as it might. Eight such children were chosen at grade levels one, two and three in schools at the focal site. The Report and much other discussion refers to these children as "controls." "Comparison" seems a more accurate description.

5. Effects four, five or six years later weren't tested because the earliest Head Start programs began in summer 1965, so the longest possible follow-up in fall 1968 was in third grade for children who entered first grade immediately after their 1965 Head Start program. The Westinghouse design reflects an eternal benefits criterion for Head Start success, although no year-by-year expectations of durability of magnitude were anticipated as guides to program or policy decisions. From the 1968 literature, it would have been possible to state, for example, magnitude and durability of expected Head Start effects relative to those reported (or more accurately those not found) for early interventions with substantial immediate impact. A 1969 headline might have read, "Head Start Nationally Found As Effective As Many Experimental Programs."

6. See Williams and Evans [83] and Evans [20] for one perspective and Grotberg [26] and Datta [18] for another.

7. There was also a modification in analysis plans. Originally, data from children who had participated in summer and full-year programs were to be

pooled. At the Council's urging, analyses were run separately for full-year and summer participants.

Another aspect is that for some children Head Start was a kindergarten program and for some, nursery. Thus, children tested in the first grade in fall 1968 may have been followed up after three months *or* after 15 months. The analyses disaggregating these groups showed substantial gains for children tested about three months after Head Start. Most Westinghouse analyses pooled these groups, however, as the disaggregated Ns were quite small.

8. See Rivlin [58,59,60] In emphasizing climates of opinion, it is important to remember that there were many whose convictions regarding the potential of early (and continuing) intervention on behalf of children did not waver. Throughout this period, for example, Bronfenbrenner, Caldwell and Zigler have warned against over-optimism and have continued to develop in theory and practice programs demonstrating what can be accomplished for young children.

9. These studies were based on three-to-four hour a day, group programs that vary from six weeks in length through about 10 months, with no follow-up or continued program after the child enters regular public schools. Under other conditions such as parent education and continuity between preschool and primary school special programs, both immediate and sustained gains have been reported. See for example, Ryan [64] and Bronfenbrenner [6].

10. As Tukey has pointed out, improvements in areas such as medicine and education tend to be incremental rather than cataclysmic. The importance of documenting fully these incremental improvements from relatively small changes, and examining the reasons why some programs are effective and others do not yield some of the benefits anticipated was of concern to observers such as Kagan who commented in 1969 that the strategies had barely been tried before they were pronounced failures. In 1968, an internal OEO paper by Richard Armstrong gave five interpretations of why the gains from Head Start leveled off after the children entered primary school while the non-Head Start children showed a spurt in their development. One interpretation is that any fairly large change in a child's environment produces a spurt in growth and that Head Start merely advanced in time what occurs anyhow in first grade. Another interpretation stressed the continuity of development, by analogy to nutrition: if you give a child proper nutrition up to age six, you cannot expect to have a healthy 18 year old if the child is starved for the next 12 years. The alternative hypotheses have yet to be tested systematically although at least two have been or are being tested individually: continuity of curriculum (Planned Variation) and continuity of teacher inservice training.

11. Some indication of the strengths of these agenda is found in the 1971 Congressional Record. In one interchange, Dr. Zigler recommends discontinuing the summer programs entirely; Representative Perkins states they will be continued.

12. See White [79]. A study of foresight and hindsight in expert advice on policy and practice might be instructive, since one belief about Head Start was that the experts were both rash and wrong. A brief review of Congressional testimony, some of the articles in scientific and popular magazines and of books of readings between 1964 and 1969 yields very few claims for the value of early

childhood programs that would seem exaggerated in 1974, and many more cautions about the complexity of the task, the time required and the resources needed, although there are stronger statements about the urgency of some action on behalf of children.

13. Before June 1969, many educators discussed the importance of training child care workers. Training programs at the college level for Head Start personnel had already begun, and bachelor's level and advanced courses in early childhood education were expanding. The shift to full-year programs without the lead time required to train large numbers of early childhood educators forced Head Start to rely on staff whose qualifications had been obtained in nontraditional ways, and spurred by the findings from the GAO monitoring study and national staff visits to sites, to move as rapidly as possible to develop a monitoring, training, and credentialling system. The anticipated passage of the Family Assistance Plan which would have increased the demand for day care several fold also played an important role getting the Child Development Associate project underway.

14. A report on the origins and consequences of the Head Start/Follow Through Planned Variation studies edited by Alice Rivlin and Michael Timpane is now available as a Brookings Institute publication.

15. Three million dollars of Head Start research funds plus research staff were retained in 1969 by the Office of Economic Opportunity. Delegated to the Department of Health, Education and Welfare were $3 million of Head Start evaluation funds plus two evaluation staff and authorization to conduct Type II and III evaluations only. OEO retained six Parent Child Centers designated as Parent Child Development Centers (PCDCs) for research purposes; the 22 remaining PCCs were delegated to the Office of Child Development. In 1974, with new spin-offs from OEO, the six PCDCs "came home" and are now part of OCD's responsibility along with a major day care experiment which had evolved during the 1970-1973 period from the Head Start research funds retained by OEO. Such can be the Government.

16. The fragility of Head Start's situation in fall 1970 and the influence of the Westinghouse Report upon this situation is probably not too well known; Zigler's private discussions within DHEW and the strength of his presentations to Congress and to OMB are seen by those close to the situation as pivotal in encouraging Richardson to fight OMB for Head Start's survival.

17. The scope of work called for the design of a longitudinal study of social competence in Head Start children and the first chapter of the Rand report [56] traces the lineage of this issue from the Westinghouse study. OCD has apparently decided not to initiate another massive longitudinal study at present.

18. In 1972, experts from the United Kingdom visited the United States under a grant from the Ford Foundation to examine U.S. policy and practice with regard to early childhood care. The "possible lessons for policy in the United Kingdom" are described in Blackstone [25]. Blackstone refers to a United Kingdom proposal for expansion of programs to provide nearly universal part-time nursery education by 1981 and recommends adopting from the American experience comprehensive programming for health, care of nutritional as well as education needs, the principle of positive discrimination, central control, parent education such as Home Start, a wider choice of alternatives such as family day

care, greater variety in conditions of child care provision, parental involvement, and research evaluation. She warns, however, that, "Policies of early childhood intervention should not be defined primarily in terms of operating to eliminate personal deficiencies on the part of children, but in operating on environmental factors or burdens which limit some families' opportunities." [5, p. 63]. Similar recommendations were suggested in the 1972 international seminar on early childhood education sponsored by the Bernard Van Beer Foundation; in addition, the symposium urged greater teacher participation in curriculum development, individualized teacher training, and greater use of paraprofessionals. The symposium report noted, "The tendency to interpret preschool programmes as a panacea for social ills should be tempered by the comparative absence of demonstrated educational success of such programmes for the disadvantaged so far. This might suggest a more modest goal for preschooling. Rather than being aimed at long-term scholastic and thereby social success . . . programmes seem to improve the quality of life for the child and the family at the time of preschooling and better equip him to make the entry into primary school." [3, p. 4]

19. A recent report on education program evaluation by Foskett and Young cites confusion between evaluation and program failure as a pitfall to be avoided, recalling the Westinghouse report "in which the Head Start program was labeled a failure" as one instance of such confusion. See, *Search for Success,* National Advisory Council on Education Professions Development, June 1974, p. 27; the Westinghouse is the only evaluation cited in this report, as in many others.

WESTINGHOUSE SUMMARY

"The impact of Head Start" an evaluation of the effects of Head Start on children's cognitive and affective development. Volume I; Text and appendices A-E."

Victor Cicarelli et al.

Westinghouse Learning Corporation–Ohio University June 12, 1969

Contract: Office of Economic Opportunity, B89-4536

Project operative June 24, 1968

PURPOSE

"In a relatively short period of time to provide an answer to a limited question concerning Head Start's impact; namely: Taking the program as a whole as it has operated to date, to what degree has it had psychological and intellectual impact on children that has persisted into the primary grades."[1]

FINDINGS

1. "In the overall analysis for the Metropolitan Readiness Tests (MRT), a generalized measure of learning readiness containing subtests on word meaning, listening, matching, alphabet, numbers and copying, the Head Start children who had attended full-year programs and who were beginning grade one were superior to the controls by a small but statistically significant margin on both "Total Readiness" and the "Listening" subscore. However, the Head Start children who had

attended summer programs did not score significantly higher than the controls." (p. 3)

2. "In the overall analysis for the Stanford Achievement Test (SAT), a general measure of children's academic achievement, containing subtests on word reading, paragraph meaning, arithmetic and so on, used to measure achievement at grades two and three, the Head Start children from both the summer and the full-year programs did not score significantly higher than the controls at the grade two level. While the children from the summer programs failed to score higher than the controls at grade three, an adequate evaluation of the effect of the full-year program at this grade level was limited by the small number of programs." (p. 3-4)

3. On the Illinois Test of Psycholinguistic Abilities, Head Start children did not score significantly higher than the controls at any of the three grade levels for the summer programs. For the full-year programs, two differences favoring the Head Start children were found: Visual Sequential Memory and Manual Expression.

4. On the Children's Self-Concept Index (projective measure of the extent to which the child has a positive self-concept), Head Start children from full-year and summer programs did not score significantly higher than the controls at any of the three grade levels.

5. On the Classroom Behavior Inventory, a teacher rate assessment of the children's desire for achievement in school, Head Start children from the summer and full-year programs did not score significantly higher than controls at any of three grade levels.

6. On the Children's Attitude Range Indicator, a picture-story projective measure of the child's attitudes toward school, home, peers and society, Head Start children did not score significantly higher than controls. One isolated difference for summer programs was found on "home" subtests at grade one.

7. Summer subgroup analysis by geographic regions, city-size groups, and racial/ethnic composition categories did not show differences between Head Start children and controls.

8. "Analysis of the full-year programs by the same subgroups revealed a number of statistically significant differences in which, on some measures (mostly subtests of cognitive measures) and at one or another grade level, the Head Start children scored significantly higher than their controls. There were consistent favorable patterns for certain subgroups: where centers were in the southeastern geographic region, in core cities, or of mainly Negro composition." (p. 6)

9. Scores of Head Start children on cognitive measures fall consistently below national norms on standardized tests. "While the former Head Start enrollees approach the national level on school readiness at first grade, their relative standing is considerably less favorable for tests of language development and scholastic achievement. On the SAT they trail about six-tenths of a year at second grade and close to a full year at grade three. They lag from seven to nine months and eight to eleven months respectively on the ITPA at first and second grades." (p. 6)

10. Parents of Head Start children expressed strong approval of the program and its effect on their children. They reported substantial participation in the activities of the centers.

RECOMMENDATIONS

1. Summer programs should be phased out as early as feasible and converted into full-year or extended year programs.

2. Full-year programs should be continued but every effort should be made to make them more effective. Some specific suggestions are:

   a. Making them part of an intervention strategy of longer duration, perhaps extending downward toward infancy and upward into the primary grades;

   b. Varying teaching strategies with the characteristics of the children;

   c. Concentrating on the remediation of specific deficiencies as suggested by the study, e.g., language deficiencies, deficiencies in spelling or arithmetic;

   d. Training parents to become more effective teachers of their children.

3. "In view of the limited state of knowledge about what would constitute a more effective program, some of the full-year programs should be set up as experimental programs (strategically placed on a regional basis) to permit the implementation of new procedures and techniques, and provide for adequate assessment of results. Innovations which prove to be successful could then be instituted on a large scale within the structure of present full-year programs. Within the experimental context, such innovations as longer periods of intervention, or total family intervention might be tried." (p. 10)

4. "Regardless of where and how it is articulated into the structure of the Federal government, the agency attempts the dual research and teaching missions presently assigned Head Start, should be granted the focal organization, an identity and organizational unity necessary to such complex and critical experimental programs. Their basis of fund-

ing should take cognizance of both the social significance of these missions and the present state of the art of programs attempting to carry them out." (p. 10)

In conclusion, although this study indicates that full-year Head Start appears to be a more effective compensatory educational program than summer Head Start, its benefits cannot be described as satisfactory. Therefore we strongly recommend that large scale efforts and substantial resources continue to be devoted to the search for finding more effective programs, procedures, and techniques for remediating the effects of poverty on disadvantaged children." (p. 11)

REFERENCES

1.   Averch, Harvey A., Carroll, Stephen J., Donaldson, Theodore S., Kiesling, Herbert H. and Pincus, John. *How Effective is Schooling? A Critical Review and Synthesis of Research Findings.* Rand Corporation. Santa Monica, California, 1972.

2.   Bell, Terrel H. "The family, the young child, and the school." Presentation to the 10th Annual Conference of South Carolina School Officials, Myrtle Beach, July 12, 1974.

3.   Bernard Van Leer Foundation. *Summary Report and Conclusions: Seminar in Curriculum in Compensatory Early Childhood Education.* (Jerusalem, 15-25 November 1972).

4.   Bissell, Joan S. *The Effects of Preschool Programs for Disadvantaged Children.* Doctoral dissertation, Harvard University, 1970.

5.   Blackstone, Tessa. *Education and Day Care for Young Children in Need: The American Experience.* England: Centre for Studies in Social Policy, Doughty Street Paper No. 1, 1973.

6.   Bronfenbrenner, Urie. *Is Early Intervention Effective? Vol. II: A Report on Longitudinal Evaluations of Preschool Programs.* Office of Child Development, 1974. DHEW Publication No. (OHD) 74-75.

7.   Boruch, Robert. "Bibliography: Illustrative randomized field experiments for program planning and evaluation." Prepared for the Social Science Research Council. February 1974.

8.   Buchanan, Garth N. and Wholey, Joseph S. "Federal level evaluation." In *Evaluation,* No. 1, Vol. 1, Fall 1972, pp. 7-22.

9.   Campbell, Donald T. "Reforms as experiments," *American Psychologist,* Vol. 24, No. 4, April 1969, 409-428. Revised version in Caro, Francis G. (ed.) *Readings in Evaluation.* Russell Sage Foundation, New York, 1971, pp. 233-261.

10. Campbell, D.T. and Erlebacher, A. "How regression artifacts in quasiexperimental evaluations can mistakenly make compensatory education look harmful." In J. Hellmuth (Ed.), *Compensatory Education: A National Debate.* New York: Brunner/Mazel, 1970.

11.   Cicarelli, Victor G., Cooper, William H. and Granger, Robert L. *The Impact of Head Start: An Evaluation of the Effects of Head Start on Children's Cognitive and Affective Development.* Westinghouse Learning Corporation, June 12, 1969, OEO Contract No. B89-4536.

12.   Cicarelli, Victor G. et al. "The impact of Head Start: A reply to the report analysis." *Harvard Educational Review.* 1970, *40,* pp. 105-129.

13.   Cicarelli, Victor G. "The relevance of the regression artifact problem to the Westinghouse–Ohio evaluation of Head Start: Reply to Campbell and Erlebacher." In J. Hellmuth (Ed.), *Compensatory Education: A National Debáte.* New York: Brunner/Mazel, 1970.

14.   Cohen, David K. "Politics and research: Evaluation of social action programs in education." *Review of Educational Research,* Vol. 40, No. 2, April 1970, pp. 213-238.

15.   Coleman, James et al. *Equality of Educational Opportunity.* Washington, D.C.: U.S. Government Printing Office, 1966.

16.   Cooke, Robert. *Recommendations for a Head Start Program by a Panel of Experts.* Office of Economic Opportunity, 1965.

17.   Coulson, J.E. *Effects of Different Head Start Program Approaches on Children of Different Characteristics: Report on Analysis of Data from the 1966-67 and 1967-68 National Evaluations.* Santa Monica: System Development Corporation, Technical Memorandum, June 1972.

18.   Datta, Lois-ellin. "A report on evaluation studies of Project Head Start." Paper presented at the American Psychological Association meeting, Washington, D.C., September 1969.

19.   Elmore, Richard. "Planned Variation experiments in policy analysis." Paper presented at the American Educational Research Association meeting, Chicago, Illinois, April 1974.

20.   Evans, John W. "Head Start: Comments on the criticisms." *Britannica Review of American Education,* Chapter 15, pp. 253-260, 1969.

21.   Evans, John W. "Evaluating education programs—are we getting anywhere?" Invitational address, American Educational Research Association, Chicago, Illinois, April 1974.

22.   Evans, John W. and Schiller, J. "How preoccupations with possible regression artifacts can lead to a faulty strategy for the evaluation of social action programs: a reply to Campbell and Erlebacher." In J. Hellmuth (Ed.), *Compensatory Education: A National Debate.* New York: Brunner/Mazel, 1970.

23.   Ginzberg, Eli and Solow, Robert H. (Eds.), "The Great Society: Lessons for the future." Special Issue, *The Public Interest.* No. 34. Winter, 1974.

24.   Glennan, Thomas K., Jr. *Evaluating Federal Manpower Programs: Notes and Observations.* Rand Corporation Memorandum, RM-5743-OEO, Santa Monica, California, 1969.

25.   Government White Paper. *Education: A Framework for Expansion.* Cmnd 5174, HMSO, 1972.

26.   Grotberg, Edith, *Review of Head Start Research: 1965 to 1969.* OEO Pamphlet 1608: 13, 1969.

27. Hunt, J. McV. "Has compensatory education failed?" *In Environment, Heredity and Intelligence.* Compiled from the *Harvard Educational Review,* Reprint Series No. 2.

28. Jencks, Christopher et al. *Inequality: A Reassessment of the Effect of Family and Schooling in America* New York: Basic Books, 1972.

29. Jensen, Arthur R. "How much can we boost IQ and scholastic achievement?" *Harvard Educational Review,* 1969, 39, 1-123.

30. Jensen, Arthur R. *Genetics and Education.* New York: Harper and Row, 1973.

31. Levine, Robert A. *The Poor Ye Need Not Have With You: Lessons from the War on Poverty.* Cambridge: The MIT Press, 1970.

32. Levine, Robert A. *Public Planning: Failure and Redirection.* New York: Basic Books, Inc., 1972.

33. Levine, Robert A. Review of Rossi and Williams, Evaluating Social Programs: Theory, Practice and Politics. *Evaluation,* Vol. 1, No. 2, 1973, p. 91.

34. Madow, William G. "Head Start: Methodological critique," *Britannica Review of American Education,* Chapter 14, pp. 245-252. 1969.

35. McDill, Edward L., McDill, Mary S., and Sprehe, J. Timothy. "Evaluation in practice: Compensatory education." In Peter H. Rossi and Walter J. Williams (Eds.), *Evaluating Social Programs: Theory, Practice and Politics.* New York: Seminar Press, 1972. Chapter 8, pp. 141-183.

36. McLaughlin, Milbrey Wallin, *Evaluation and Reform: The Elementary and Secondary Education Act of 1965, Title I.* Rand Corporation, Santa Monica, California. R-1291-RC, January 1974.

37. Miller, James O. *Review of Selected Intervention Research with Young Children.* ERIC Occasional Paper, 1968.

38. Mendelsohn, Robert. "Is Head Start a success or failure?" In J. Hellmuth (Ed.), Vol. 3, *Disadvantaged Child: Compensatory Education:* A National Debate. New York: Brunner/Mazel, Inc., 1970. Chapter 20, p. 445-454.

39. Mosteller, Frederick and Moynihan, Daniel P. *On Equality of Educational Opportunity: Papers Deriving from the Harvard University Faculty Seminar on the Coleman Report.* New York: Random House, 1972.

40. Moynihan, Daniel P. *The Negro Family: The Case for National Action.* Washington: U.S. Government Printing Office, 1966.

41. Moynihan, Daniel P. *Maximum Feasible Misunderstanding.* New York: The Free Press, 1970.

42. Moynihan, Daniel P. *The Politics of a Guaranteed Income.* Random House, 1973. Cited in *Evaluation,* Vol. 1, No. 2, 1973, p. 25.

43. Mushkin, Selma. *Evaluation,* Vol., 1, No. 2, 1973.

44. *New Republic.* "How head a Head Start?" April 26, 1969, pp. 8-9.

45. *New York Times.* Nixon administration plans to shift Job Corps training to slums. April 10, 1969.

46. *New York Times.* Director defends Head Start's work; says it aids pupils. April 15, 1969.

47. *New York Times.* Two educators here assert Head Start helps youngsters. April 16, 1969.

48. *New York Times*. Dispute over value of Head Start. April 20, 1969.
49. *New York Times*. Finch criticizes Head Start study. April 25, 1969.
50. *New York Times*. Editorial. Discrediting Head Start. May 13, 1969.
51. *New York Times*. Farmer asks delay on Head Start plan. August 7, 1969.
52. *OCD-Head Start Policy Manual*. Department of Health, Education and Welfare, January 1973.
53. Office of Planning, Budgeting and Evaluation. *Work Statements from Requests for Proposals (RFPs) for Evaluations of Emergency School Aid Act (ESAA), Pilot and Basic Programs*. RFP-73-6 (November 1, 1972) and RFT 73-29 (April 11, 1973). U.S. Office of Education, March 1974.
54. Orlans, Harold. *Social Science Research*. Washington, D.C.: The Brookings Institution. Reprint 259. 1973.
55. Porter, Andrew C. "Comments on some current strategies to evaluate the effectiveness of compensatory education programs." Paper presented at the American Psychological Association Convention, Washington, D.C., September 1969.
56. Raizen, Senta A., Bobrow, Sue B. et al. *Plan for an Evaluation of Social Competence in Head Start Children*. Rand Corporation, Washington, D.C., 1974.
57. Riecken, Henry W. et al. *Social Experimentation: Method for Planning and Evaluating Social Programs*. New York: Seminar Press, forthcoming 1974.
58. Rivlin, Alice. *Systematic Thinking for Social Action*. The Brookings Institution, Washington, D.C., 1971.
59. Rivlin, Alice M. "Forensic social science." *Harvard Educational Review*, Vol. 43, No. 1, February 1973, 61-75.
60. Rivlin, Alice M. *Social Policy: Alternate Strategies for the Federal Government*. Washington, D.C. The Brookings Institution. General Series Reprint 288. 1974.
61. Rossi, Peter H. "Testing for success and failure in social action." Chapter 2, in Rossi, Peter H. and Williams, Walter (Eds.), *Evaluating Social Programs: Theory, Practice, and Politics*. New York: Seminar Press, 1972.
62. Rossi, Peter H. and Williams, Walter. (Eds.), *Evaluating Social Programs: Theory, Practice and Politics*. New York: Seminar Press, 1972.
63. Rothman, Sheila M. "Other people's children: The day care experience in America." *The Public Interest*, Winter 1973, No. 30.
64. Ryan, Sally (Ed.), *Longitudinal Evaluations. Vol. 1: A Report on Longitudinal Evaluations of Preschool Programs*. Office of Child Development 1974. DHEW Publication No. (OHD) 74-24.
65. Schorr, Alvin. *Poor Kids: A Report on Children in Poverty*. New York: Basic Books, 1966.
66. Semple, Robert B. Jr. "Head Start pupils found no better off than others." *New York Times*, April 14, 1969.
67. Semple, Robert B. Jr. "White House and advisors stand by report critical of Head Start program." *New York Times*, April 27, 1969.
68. Shanker, Albert. "Early childhood education is a job for the public schools." *Where We Stand. New York Times*, September 8, 1974. E-11.

69. Smith, Marshall S. and Bissell, Joan. "Report Analysis: The Impact of Head Start." *Harvard Educational Review*. Vol. 40, No. 1, Winter 1970, pp. 51-104.

70. Stallings, Jane. "What teachers do does make a difference: A study of seven Follow Through Models." Presentation to the Early Childhood Conference on Evaluation. Anaheim, California, August 6, 1974.

71. Steiner, Golbert Y. "Reform follows reality: The growth of welfare." *The Public Interest*, No. 34, Winter 1974, pp. 47-65.

72. Tanner, Daniel. "The retreat from education—for other people's children." *Intellect*, January 1974, pp. 222-225.

73. Tyler, Ralph. "The Federal role in education," *The Public Interest*, No. 34, Winter, 1974, pp. 164-187.

74. Watts, H.W. and Horner, D.L. *The Educational Benefits of Head Start: A Quantitative Analysis*. Institute for Research on Poverty. University of Wisconsin, Madison. 19DP

75. Weber, Evelyn. *Early Childhood Education: Perspectives on Change*. Worthington, Ohio: Charles A. Jones Publishing Co., 1970.

76. Weiss, Carol H. (Ed.), *Evaluating Action Programs: Readings in Social Action and Education*. Boston: Allyn and Bacon, Inc., 1972, pp. 250-266.

77. Weiss, Carol H. "Where politics and evaluation research meet." *Evaluation*, Vol. 1, No. 3, 1973, pp. 37-45.

78. White, Sheldon, H. "The national impact study of Head Start." In J. Hellmuth (Ed.), Vol. 3, *Disadvantaged Child. Compensatory Education: A National Debate*. New York: Brunner/Mazel, Inc. 1970. Chapter 9, p. 163-184.

79. White, Sheldon H. et al. *Federal Programs for Young Children*. Huron Institute, Cambridge, Mass. 1973. (Prepared for the Department of Health, Education and Welfare, Contract No. OS-71-170).

80. Wholey, Joseph S. et al. *Federal Evaluation Policy: Analyzing the Effects of Public Programs*. The Urban Institute, Washington, D.C., 1970.

81. Wholey, Joseph S. and White, Bayla F. "Evaluation's impact on Title I elementary and secondary education program management, federal level evaluation," *Evaluation*. Vol. 1, No. 3, 1973, pp. 73-76.

82. Williams, Walter. *Social Policy Research and Analysis: The Federal Agencies*. New York: American Elsevier, 1971, pp. 103-104.

83. Williams, Walter and Evans, John W. "The politics of evaluation: The case of Head Start." *Annals of the American Academy of Political and Social Sciences*. 385, 1969, 118-132.

84. Wolff, Max and Stein, Annie. *Study 1: Six Months Later. A Comparison of Children who had Head Start Summer 1965 with Their Classmates in Kindergarten (Case Study of Kindergartens in Four Public Elementary Schools*, New York City), 1966. Mimeograph.

85. Zigler, Edward. "Project Head Start: Success or Failure," *Learning*, Vol. 1, No. 7, 1973, pp. 43-47.

ACKNOWLEDGEMENTS

I am deeply indebted to Nancy Hunt who located many documents and references, to Dr. David Falk for his suggestions on the questions to be examined, and to the following persons who graciously made available their time and their knowledge about the Westinghouse study and its effects:

Robert Boruch
Urie Bronfenbrenner
Lew Butler
Donald Campbell
David Cohen
Raymond Collins
Richard Elmore
John Evans
James Fennessy
Thomas Glennan
Edith Grotberg
Lilian Katz
Ester Kresh
Gary McDaniels
Richard E. Orton
Andrew Porter
Senta Raizen
Alice Rivlin
Saul Rosoff
Florence Sequein
Jeffrey Schiller
Jule Sugarman
Michael Timpane
Deborah Walker

Michael Wargo
Sheldon White
Suzanne Woolsey
Edward Zigler

RESEARCH AND POLICY MAKING
UNDER UNCERTAINTY
A Case Study: Spray Adhesives

Constance B. Newman
Commissioner
Consumer Product Safety Commission

RESEARCH WILL BE USED BY POLICYMAKERS WHEN THEY
ARE OPERATING IN AREAS OF UNCERTAINTY IF THE RE-
SEARCH FINDINGS MAKE SENSE AND ARE ON TIME.

Newman's Rule on Research

Newman's Rule on Research continues as follows: From a policymaker's point of view, research, including evaluative research, has value
only if the research is:

- Relevant
- Reliable and valid
- Objective
- Understandable
- Timely

Few would argue with the general principles underlying the Rule on
Research. The arguments begin when the definitions begin. The arguments begin when the examples begin. What a policymaker means by

"objective" and "relevant" often is 180 degrees different from a researcher's meaning of those terms. A research report deemed understandable by the researcher may be unintelligible to the policymaker.

This paper will deal from a policymaker's[1] point of view with: a discussion of the criteria for research useful to policymakers; and an analysis of the role that research played in affecting policy decisions concerning certain spray adhesives. Further, the paper will include recommendations for policymakers and researchers interested in improving policy decisions through the use of research.

Hopefully the paper will stimulate meaningful discussion of the relationship between research and policymaking. Hopefully, the paper will stimulate actual improvements in the relationship between researchers and policymakers.

CRITERIA FOR RESEARCH USEFUL TO POLICYMAKERS OPERATING IN AREAS OF UNCERTAINTY

Let me first state the obvious: The hard decisions for policymakers are those where the impact of the decisions or even the nature of the problem itself exists in an area of uncertainty. Responsible policymakers are interested in developing effective methods for decision-making under uncertainty because:

> "... there appears to be a tendency for uncertainty to produce a bias toward overconservatism, toward routine ways to solve problems, toward doing nothing."[2]

The problem of most policymakers especially in the area of social public policy is that they are operating in areas of uncertainty a large percentage of the time. A few examples:

Issue: Should the Consumer Product Safety Commission initiate the development of mandatory safety standards covering the flammability of general apparel.

Uncertainties: The extend to which the public is sufficiently protected by existing flammability standards.

The realism of expecting technology and materials to track standard setting.

Public attitudes and desires regarding added protection if it also means added costs.

The extent to which other public needs require a higher allocation of public funds.

Issue: Should the Consumer Product Safety Commission allow staff members to participate in the activities of voluntary standards development organizations.

Uncertainties: The extent to which the mission of the agency will best be accomplished.

Options: By Commission activities only? By voluntary standards activities? By some combination?

Public attitudes concerning the appearance of the conflict of interest where voluntary activities are in areas where the Commission could and should regulate.

One basic tool for assisting policymakers operating in areas of uncertainty could be research which consists of systematic, diligent inquiry into some field of knowledge, undertaken to establish facts or principles. It is my contention, however, that research will be valuable only to the extent that it meets certain criteria. Below is a discussion of the criteria.

Research Must Be Relevant. The over-used word "relevant" correctly identifies an important feature of evaluative research. That is to say that it had a "bearing upon or relating to the matter at hand; to the point; pertinent, and/or applicable."[3]

Research to be useful must be conducted in response to a particular problem where some solution is required *or* where the research has identified areas perceived to be important to the policymaker. It is not crucial to the concept of relevance that the research be short term. Long-term research can have bearing upon a matter at hand, can be pertinent, and so forth. What is important is that the research be tied to an issue perceived or which could be perceived to be important to the policymaker. Note that it is rare when the policymaker can afford the luxury of requesting research to satisfy a scientific or intellectual interest. It is even rarer when the policymaker is interested in the results of research which satisfied the scientific or intellectual interest of the researchers.

Relevancy of the issue researched is important. Relevancy of the findings is equally important. The research conclusions must be responsive to the policy concerns of the decision-maker and, at the very least, must suggest actions which are not only feasible but practicable.

The Consumer Product Safety Commission has as its mandate to protect the public against unreasonable risks of injury associated with consumer products. For the Commission the following research topics would have varying degrees of relevancy to the mission of the agency from none to a great deal.

Study I.   Impact of Head Start on providing mathematical skills to 5-year old children.

Study II.   The relationship between mathematical skills and logic skills in 5-year old Head Start graduates.

Study III. The relationship between logic skills and safety sensitivity of 5-year old Head Start graduates.

Study IV.   Impact of Head Start on providing to 5-year olds a sensitivity toward safety issues.

A researcher bringing Study I to the Commission irrespective of its validity, reliability, objectivity and so forth has misdirected time and effort. Study IV on the other hand may well assist the Commission in developing education strategies, given the fact that a "sensitive-to-safety" public can be better protected against unreasonable risks of injury associated with consumer products.

Research Must Be Reliable and Valid. Before basing a decision on research findings, the policymaker wants to know that the research is "solid." What the policymaker really wants to know is: Will others studying the same issue, using the same methods come out with the same *conclusions.* In other words the policymaker wants to know if the research is *reliable.* Suchman indicates that reliability means that a measure "can be depended upon to secure consistent results upon repeated application."[4] As a matter of fact, the need for reliability in research is well-known to researchers. Psychologists require that ability and intelligence test scores be reliable, meaning to them that the scores are dependable and reproducible, that they measure consistently whatever it is they measure.[5] What may not be well known to researchers is that policymakers are also interested in research findings being reliable. Their concern is less in legitimatizing the study and more in being certain before making decisions which affect the lives of others. Public officials, as agents of the public, cannot take too many risks with the public's business. Bross' following observation accurately reflects the attitude of policymakers towards research.

"In scientific research an experiment which leads to remarkable new results will be accepted only if those results can be duplicated by other research workers who repeat the original experiment. This rule has avoided many scientific wild goose chases ... On a few occasions this rule has resulted in some delay in the recognition of important new research, but the net effect of the rule has been favorable."[6]

Validity refers to the "degree to which any measure of procedure succeeds in doing what it purports to do."[7]* A policymaker will be skeptical of using research findings if there is no indication that there were different types of tests conducted to support the research conclusions. This is in fact a requirement of research generally. Psychologists are concerned that intelligence test scores represent what they are supposed to represent and will often require two scores for those whose intelligence is being measured—one the test score; the other some measure of what the test is supposed to be measuring.[8]

Let me give a hypothetical example of how a policymaker might view the validity of research. Suppose a researcher concluded that according to machine tests certain child resistant safety caps will withstand attempts of children under 5 years of age to open the container. The policymaker will not act on this conclusion even if 100 other researchers indicated that the machine tests resulted in the same conclusion unless there is some evidence that the machine in fact is representative of the strength of children under 5 years of age. The validity criteria is not an esoteric requirement but a necessity and policymakers will not act without its presence.

It is true that both reliability and validity are difficult for a decision-maker to check. Possible checks available to policymakers are:

- Confidence in the reputation of the researcher for reliable and valid research using, where possible, past experience;
- Confidence in staff or external reviewers of the research;
- Expertise of the policymaker; and
- Common sense of the policymaker

When these elements are not present, the policymakers feel they are holding on to a weak reed. Policymakers do not like weak reeds and generally will not take chances; hence it is the obligation of the researcher to provide reliable and valid findings and the proof thereof. It is further the responsibility of the links between the policymaker and researcher, if there are any, to analyze the research in terms of validity and reliability.

Research Must be Objective. When policymakers are seeking an analysis of public opinion on the use of sampling plans in mandatory standards, for instance, they are seeking just that, not the researcher's subjective bias about sampling plans or what the public ought to think about sampling plans. When policymakers ask for the results of a scientific test on the use of wiring devices with aluminum and copper wiring, the policymaker does not want what the researcher thinks about banning aluminum wiring to be implicit in the report of the test result, but rather the policymaker wants to know exactly what were the results of the test. Objective research and objective reporting of research is required. Public policy issues can be decided properly only if decision-makers have the facts. This is not to say that biases of one kind or another do not or will not affect decisions. We all know that is not true. What is required, however, is that a policymaker know when and how decisions are biased. This is possible only if the research findings are objective.

It is true that objective technical advice on policy issues is hard to come by, but Margolis argues that "policy relevent disagreements among technical experts only occasionally derive from differences of technical judgment on what can be considered basic technical questions."[9] According to Margolis the objectivity of technical advice comes into question when differences arise as to: (a) extrapolation—where judgments differ as to the future of a decision; (b) context—where technical advisors reflecting different policy views will differ on what narrowly defined technical questions are really important, on how the technical questions ought to be formulated ... and how the answers to such questions would fit into a policy context; and (c) condensation—where the summary and translation of the research for policymakers alters in some way the thrust of the findings. One observation: the context and condensation of research studies could also affect the reliability and validity of those studies.

Research Must Be Understandable. Assume a policymaker with a combined MBA/Law/Chemistry degree with a side interest in gardening and two major policy decisions to make within the hour. Read along with that policymaker two reports presented to assist in the decision-making.

Report I: While queueing models have provided the framework for the analysis of congestion effects, the analysis of nontime measures of the deterioration of service quality as a result of congestion at a given facility has not been thoroughly undertaken.

Report II: It is imperative that there be conducted research on mutagenesis with specific biological systems. Current mammalian methods; i.e., cytogenetic and somatic cell genetics, host-mediated assay, dominant lethal and veritable translocation tests should be studied.

Several guesses as to what happens in the hour of decision, given that most policymakers are pressed for time because of the weight and volume of their responsibilities. The hypothetical policymaker concerned with these issues will probably have two or three issues to deal with in the next hour which must be decided. As to what the policymaker does about the information provided in Reports I and II, the options to consider are: (a) the policymaker goes to the technical dictionaries, research books and reference material for an understanding; (b) the policymaker calls the researcher or other staff persons for translation; (c) the policymaker ignores the research and uses conventional wisdom. Freeman gives his view about what often happens with evaluative research by observing that there is often a problem of policymakers understanding reports. He asks: what is the value of evaluation when only about 10,000 persons in the country know how to interpret a factor analysis, or what covariance is, or what a path analysis is about? Freeman goes on to say "the communication of relevant policy research findings so that attention is paid to them remains a neglected area of concern."[10] Researchers should not take the chance that their research would be ignored, researchers must make their research understandable.

Research Must Be Timely. Decisions on serious issues generally will not wait for research to be completed. It is therefore incumbent upon the researcher to provide information before the decision is to be made. This seemingly facetious statement represents the real world. Policy decisions which will wait for research to be completed are rare and often fall into one of four categories.

- Decisions where the force of law requires research,
- Decisions where public opinion demands research,
- Decisions where the policymakers are buying time, and
- Decisions where the policymakers are looking for support for what has already been decided.

If a researcher is working on an issue where the decision does not fall into one of the above categories, the effort had better be revved up. It is important, however, that timeliness not be substituted for quality; therefore, the researcher will have to be skilled in making the trade-offs between quality and thoroughness of the research versus the requirements for decision-making.

A CASE STUDY:
THE ROLE RESEARCH PLAYED IN AFFECTING POLICY DECISIONS CONCERNING CERTAIN SPRAY ADHESIVES[11]

Section 2(q) (2) of the Federal Hazardous Substances Act as amended, provides that if the Consumer Product Safety Commission finds that the distribution for household use of a substance presents an imminent hazard to the public health, the Commission may give notice in the *Federal Register* that the substance shall be deemed to be a "banned hazardous substance" pending the completion of proceedings relating to the issuance of regulations pursuant to Section 2(q) (I) (B).

In my view this provision of the Act contemplates the following:

1. *Two levels of decision-making*

● The initial decision, pending the completion of proceedings which could deem a product a banned hazardous substance

● The final decision after the completion of proceedings which could result in retaining or lifting the ban on a product

2. *The possible use of research at the two levels of decision-making*

● Research findings prior to the initial decision could be the foundation of Commission determination that the distribution of a hazardous substance presents an imminent hazard sufficient to deem a product banned pending further proceedings.

● Research findings prior to the final decision could be the foundation for the proceedings required before issuance of a final regulation.

In 1973 the Consumer Product Safety Commission was faced with two levels of decisions regarding whether certain spray adhesives presented an imminent hazard to the public health. Below is my analysis of the role research played at both levels of the decision-making. (Detailed information on the spray adhesive's issue is in chronological form in Appendix B.)

Level I Decision: To Deem Certain Spray Adhesives Banned Hazardous Substances Pending the Completion of the Proceedings. Dr. Rodman Seely, Director of Clinical Research Center,[12] presented to the Commission the results of his research which indicated the possibility that certain spray adhesives were capable of producing chromosome damage and potential mutagenic effects. Dr. Seely's preliminary data from 10 subjects, including two dysmorphic infants, suggested that transmissible genetic damage (mutagenic and teratogenic) may occur to individuals exposed to some commercial spray adhesives from their use in the hobby of foil art.

There is no question that the research was *relevant.* The Consumer Product Safety Commission has as its mandate to reduce unreasonable risks of injury associated with consumer products, in addition to the mandate under the Hazardous Substances Act referenced above. The Seely research was relevant because it identified a problem area perceived to be important to the policymakers responsible for implementing the Consumer Product Safety Act and Hazardous Substances Act.

(Note: To this point I have referred to the Commission and Commission decisions. For fear of misrepresenting the other Commissioners, I will continue the decision-making process primarily in terms of my considerations).

In order to decide the role Seely's findings should play in my decision to vote one way or another on an issue, I had to determine how to make the necessary *reliability* and *validity* checks. The rules discussed in the previous part had to apply here because I am not an expert in chromosome analysis. The steps taken were as follows:

1. To agree with the other Commissioners that the Consumer Product Safety Commission staff in the Bureau of Biomedical Sciences should go to Oklahoma for the purpose of interviewing and questioning Dr. Seely in order to get some understanding of the reliability and validity of the report.
2. To question the staff about the reputation of the researcher and about the reliability and validity of his studies.
3. To make my own commonsense analysis of his research which resulted in the following conclusions:
   a. Dr. Seely did make *reliability* tests on his research by having his slides read not only by himself but also by assistants. Further, Dr. Seely studied a minimum of 100 cells on both the control and test reading, in one case 613 cells, which meant he was interested in getting a large sample read as a check on his conclusions.

b. The *validity* of research was indicated based on the following observations: (1) the known common denominator of the parents of the dysmorphic children was the use of spray adhesives; and (2) the common denominator of the users of spray adhesives was chromosome breaks and gaps. Acceptance of this last point, however, depends upon acceptance of the reliability of the study.

Were the research findings *objective?* Actually, there was little disagreement between the researcher and Commission technical staff on what constituted the proper context of the policy issues to be resolved; hence, objectivity should not have been lost in the definition of the issues. It was agreed that the two basic issues were: (1) Do spray adhesives cause chromosome breaks and gaps and; (2) Do breaks and gaps result in dysmorphic children? I did not believe further that the objectivity of Seely's work was destroyed in its condensation. There was, therefore, no evidence that Seely's work lacked in objectivity. In fact, there appeared to have been no rationale for a lack of objectivity in this particular study. The one possible problem for both the scientist and the Commission was extrapolation of the data which led to a conclusion that there was indicated possible problems for the public health.

The research was both *understandable* and *timely*. The Consumer Product Safety Commission staff headed by Dr. Robert Hehir, Director, Bureau of Biomedical Science, briefed the Commissioners both in writing and orally on the research report. The actual report and the briefings were presented in plain English plus a few terms easy to find in a medical dictionary. Although this was not a case where a decision was awaiting the completion of research, a reference to the timing is noteworthy. It must be indicated that in the instant case, Dr. Seely presented his findings to the Commission soon after the completion of study, thereby underscoring the urgency felt by the expert. Where an imminent hazard is a possibility, this type of timely reporting to government is required.

Conclusion as to the Level I Decision. Presented to the Commission was sufficiently reliable, valid and objective data based on human experience indicating a possible link between the use of certain spray adhesives and birth defects. The risk of more defective children being born combined with the force of law requiring a ban where there is imminent danger to public health led to the conclusion that the research findings were sufficient to require a ban to halt the production, distribution, and sale of certain spray adhesives pending further proceedings. Furthermore, the research data were based on human experience. Under Sec. 1500-4 FAS Regs—reliable human experience data with any substance are significant; and, if different from animal data, the human experience takes precedence.

The Hazardous Substances Act requires after a Level I Decision that the Commission conduct further proceedings prior to the issuance of a final regulation. Below is a summary of the content of the further proceedings of the Commission (see Appendix C for the details).

1. Independent analysis by other experts of the clinical data developed by Dr. Seely.

2. Independent cytogenetic studies of industrially exposed populations by the University of Minnesota, the Mayo Clinic and the Canadian Government.

3. Analysis of epidemiological data gathered by the Center for Disease Control of the U.S. Public Health Service (Atlanta, Georgia.)

4. Exposure of laboratory animals to high concentrations of the suspect spray adhesives.

5. Commission review of the independent corroborative studies.

6. Publication of Commission final decision for comment.

Below is an analysis of the role research played in the Level II decision.

Level II Decision: To Lift the Ban on Those Spray Adhesives Banned in August 1973. A decision to issue final regulations to ban or to lift the ban on hazardous substances requires more stringent tests of the initial research. At this stage, the policymaker must be more certain of the reliability, validity, and objectivity of the data and conclusions in the research. Further, the conclusions of those reviewing the initial report must be checked for reliability, validity, and objectivity. In other words at this stage, the Commission had to decide whether to issue a final regulation lifting or retaining the ban on certain spray adhesives. At this stage, there must be a full analysis of Dr. Seely's work by determining if:

a. Other experts reading the original study slides or different slides of the same test and control subjects would reach the conclusion that there was a significant difference between the chromosome gaps and breaks in the exposed as compared to non-exposed group. (Reliability Check).

b. Others reading slides of a new group of persons exposed to spray adhesives would find significant difference in breaks and gaps as compared to a new control group (Reliability Check).

c. Epidemiologic studies will show an increase in birth defects tracking an increase in sale of spray adhesives (Validity Check).

d. Animal tests indicating that exposure to spray adhesives induced chromosome damage and/or significant increase in birth defects in the next generation (Validity Check).

e. The original researcher when reading the slides blind would come to the same conclusion (Objectivity Check).

Among the several *reliability* and *validity* checks made on Dr. Seely's study were those made by Drs. H. Lubs and F. Hecht, who reviewed the slides of 12 of the 22 in Seely's original group. Their comparison of the exposed and non-exposed did not indicate a significant difference between the two groups, therefore, providing a question about the reliability of Seely's data. The Lubs and Hecht conclusion may have also resulted in questioning the *objectivity* of Seely by suggesting a possibility of subjective bias since he knew the subjects. Dr. Robert Summit, in testing the hypothesis, re-cultured peripheral lymphocytes from individuals from the original study group (6 test and 4 control) and concluded that Dr. Seely's earlier observations could not be confirmed.

For a policymaker, the findings of these three scientists could support a decision that there may not be sufficiently reliable and valid information from the original study to conclude that there should be a final determination to retain the ban on spray adhesives. What was also available to us, deciding whether in the final determination to retain or lift the ban, was the following additional information:

- A manufacturer-sponsored Mayo Clinic study questioned the reliability and validity of Seely's original study because in a group of 14 patients (10 test and 4 control) with none too heavy exposure to spray adhesives, there was little deviation from "normal limits" for the breaks and gaps. Furthermore, this study indicated that a total of 7 children was born to the group using spray adhesives and none had birth defects.

- A University of Minnesota cytogenetic study of 14 industrially exposed (6 months to 4 years) and 5 controls failed to corroborate Seely's findings. Dr. David W. Smith's Department of Pediatrics/Dysmorphology Unit, University of Washington, Seattle, report of six pregnant spray users and the infant (male) of one of them were referred to study. Exposure period for the women varied from 6 months to 2 years. None of the spray adhesive users showed an increased frequency of either chromosomal gaps or breaks. (Report by personal communication.)

- Testing the products and individual chemical constituents for their potential mutagenic effect utilizing microbial screening assays failed to show mutagenic activity in the Ames test strains (Salmonellatyohimurium) which further questioned the extent to which Seely's study did what it purported to do. Dr. Seymour Abrahamson's (University of Wisconsin) report—Drosophila Screening Test for Evaluating Mutagenicity of a Spray Adhesive—concluded that systems for detecting gene mutation and chromosome breakage in Drosophila germ cells failed to show any effect of a single acute treatment with aerosol spray adhesives. (Report by personal communication.)

- A series of CPSC/FDA studies produced the following conclusions about the validity of Seely's conclusions: a mutagenic screening study with rats indicated that the spray adhesives produced no significant changes in bone marrow chromosomes; a teratological investigation wherein hamsters were exposed to spray adhesives resulted in no abnormal development or congenital malformation.

- Studies conducted by Dr. E. Hook from the Birth Defects Institute, State of New York, suggested that there was no causal link between adhesives and chromosome abnormalities.

- The staff concluded from Seely's rereading of his slides in a blind test that there was less difference between the test and control groups, hence the original study might be questioned for reliability and objectivity since the original slide readings were not blind (subject known to researcher).

- A Committee formed to determine if there was epidemiologic evidence available to support the validity of Seely's findings concluded that their study did not support nor refute any of the hypotheses concerning spray adhesives.

The Committee study highlights again the responsibilities of the policymaker in using research in decision-making. There was now the responsibility to question the reviewers of Seely for the reliability, validity, objectivity of their work.

See Appendix D for the series of questions the Commissioners asked after receiving the reports from those researchers assigned the task of corroborating Seely's work. A sampling of my concerns at this stage in the decision-making were as follows: In the Lubs and Hecht studies was a review of the slides of only 12 out of 22 persons in the original study sufficient? In other words, could this study actually be a sufficient reliability check? Did Summit's study lose something in objectivity in that the control group were laboratory workers? Seely's second readings of the slides, blind, still showed a significant difference between the exposed and unexposed groups. Does not this mean that his first study was sufficiently reliable to retain the ban? How relevant was the study of the Committee organized to analyze epidemiologic evidence to support or refute Seely's original hypothesis by determining if there was an unusually high proportion of spray users in a group of malformed children, since the Committee itself failed to answer clearly the very question it was formed to answer?

Note: An ad hoc group of experts reviewed all of the basic material and answered to my satisfaction the remaining questions as to the reliability, validity, and objectivity of both the original study and the follow-up studies commissioned to test Seely's findings.

Conclusion As to the Role of Research in Affecting the Spray Adhesive Decisions. Research brought the issue of the possible link between certain spray adhesives and birth defects to the Commission's attention. That research had value and complied with my rule on research in the context of the mandate of the Hazardous Substances Act. As indicated earlier, the research effort of Dr. Seely was sufficiently reliable, valid and objective to direct my vote to deem certain spray adhesives as banned hazardous substances pending completion of proceedings.

Research played a crucial role in the proceedings to determine if a final regulation should be issued banning or lifting the ban on the spray adhesives. Here it was important to test in various ways the hypothesis presented to the Commission by Dr. Seely. This was done by using research methods. Most of the research effort at this stage complied with my rule that it must be reliable, valid, objective and so forth. The staff and ad hoc group of experts assisted in making the necessary checks. Here was an instance where the decision to be made was not in an area of expertise of the policymaker, hence the checks had to be and were:

- Confidence in the reputation of the researchers for reliable and valid research,
- Confidence in the staff and ad hoc reviewers of the material, and
- Common sense.

Had the research not been understandable, had the research been biased possibly, had there been no evidence one way or another regarding the spray adhesives, research would not have played a role in this decision.

RECOMMENDATION FOR IMPROVING THE RELATIONSHIP BETWEEN RESEARCH AND POLICYMAKING

Although this paper has not specifically discussed evaluative research, the principles discussed, the problems noted, and the recommendations discussed below apply irrespective of the type of research. The evaluations of social programs bring to the policymaker valuable information upon which to make decisions concerning continuing programs, altering them, or discontinuing them. The information provided to the policymaker through evaluations *must* meet the criteria discussed in Part I. Those evaluations must be:

- Relevant,
- Reliable and valid,
- Objective,
- Understandable, and
- Timely.

As to research in general, and evaluative research in particular: *How do we get there from here?* Consider a simple four-point program, outlined below.

Point 1: Researchers and policymakers must communicate. Conferences, similar to the National Social Programs Evaluation Conference, where both researchers and policymakers attend, should be held regularly for the purpose of exchanging information about the use of research in policymaking—the problems and successes.

More reference material on the subject should be developed. Both researchers and policymakers would be receptive to *good* reference material on the subject.

Organizations should be structured to do business in such a manner as to allow policymakers to talk to researchers every now and then and vice versa.

Point 2: Researchers and policymakers should not take themselves too seriously. Both groups should recognize that their concerns and observations can be understood by others, if they are willing to admit the extent to which they are human. A researcher will have difficulty relating to a policymaker if the entire contact is made with words which must be translated to be understood. Policymakers will continue to have difficulty relating to researchers if they appear to indicate it is only they (the policymakers) who will save the world.

Point 3: Policymakers and researchers must understand each other's problems. Policymakers must understand the legitimate concern of the researcher regarding early release of research conclusions, forced completion of research, unreal condensation of research findings. These actions, often forced by policymakers, may seriously threaten the quality of the research. This threat to the quality of the research is of benefit to no one.

Researchers must understand that policymakers are forced by law, events, and the public to make many decisions in a short time frame. In most circumstances any information is better than none, therefore, researchers will become more valuable to policymakers when they are willing to become more flexible in providing research results. It is not always necessary that the study be in a bound volume, with completed charts for it to be useful to the policymaker.

Point 4: Policymakers should consider developing better intermediaries between themselves and researchers. Policy analysts should be available to the policymaker for the following purposes:

  a. to frame the issues to be researched,

  b. to work with the researcher in outlining the scope of work and timetable for the research, given the demands of the policymaker, and

  c. to place the research findings in the context of the issues to be decided.

NOTES

1. "Policymakers" as used in this paper refers to a decision-maker involved in the conduct of public affairs.

2. Ruth P. Mack, *Planning on Uncertainty* (New York: Wiley–Interscience, 1971), p. 5.

3. *Webster's New World Dictionary–Second Edition.*

4. Edward A. Suchman, *Evaluative Research: Principles and Practice in Public Service and Social Action Programs* (New York: Russell Sage Foundation, 1967), p. 116.

5. Ernest R. Hilgard, *Introduction to Psychology* (New York: Harcourt, Brace and World, Inc., 1961) p. 397.

6. Irwin D. J. Bross, *Design for Decision* (New York: The Free Press, 1953) p. 148.

7. Suchman, op. cit., p. 120.

*One reviewer of this paper asked the question: "How does the policymaker establish this criteria for validity?" Further the reviewer noted that "statistical validity for hard and soft sciences may be an esoteric requirement. That is to say it is designed for the initiated alone."

8. Hilgard, op. cit., p. 397.

9. Howard Margolis, *Technical Advice on Policy Issues* (Beverly Hills: Sage Publications, 1973) p. 14.

10. Howard E. Freeman, "Evaluation Research: A Growth Industry," *Social Experiments and Social Program Evaluation.* Cambridge, Massachusetts: Ballinger Publishing Company, 1974, p. 18.

11. A Glossary of Terms in Appendix A.

12. University of Oklahoma Medical Center.

APPENDIX A

GLOSSARY

Break (Chromatid or Isochromatid)—An apparent discontinuity in the substance of a chromatid, the portions of the chromatid on either side of the break being out of alignment.

Chromosome—One of several small dark-staining and more or less rod-shaped bodies which appear in the nucleus of a cell at the time of cell division. They contain the genes, or hereditary factors, and are constant in number in each species.

Chromatid—One of the two spiral filaments making up a chromosome, which separate in cell division, each going to a different pole of a dividing cell.

Dysmorphic—malformed.

Gap (Chromatid or Isochromatid)—An apparent discontinuity in the substance of the chromatid, the portions of the chromatid on either side of the gap remaining in alignment.

Interchange (Chromatid)— The result of interaction of broken ends at two or more breakage sites in chromatids.

Lymphocytes—The variety of white blood corpuscle that arises in the reticular tissue of the lymph glands.

Mutagenic—Causing change. Inducing genetic mutation.

Teratogenic—Tending to produce anomalies of formation, or teratism.

APPENDIX B

AN ANNOTATED CHRONOLOGY

1971-1972　Subjects of research by Dr. Rodman Seely began using certain spray adhesives in conjunction with the hobby of foil art.

3-1-73ff　Seely initiated chromosome analysis of: infant with multiple birth defects; parents of infant who had used certain spray adhesives.

Findings: incidence of comparable chromosome damage in infant and parents.

6-22-73ff　Seely initiated chromosome analysis of person engaged in hobby of foil art seven months pregnant.

Findings: incidence of chromosome damage; infant normal; father not engaged in use of spray adhesives.

7-20-73ff　Seely initiated chromosome analysis of user of spray adhesives.

Findings: increased incidence of chromosome damage.

*　　*

Seely initiated chromosome analysis of second infant with multiple birth defects. Both parents of that infant participated extensively in hobby of foil art.

Findings: increased incidence of chromosome damage in infant and parents.

7-27-73　Seely initiated chromosome analysis of parents of infant analyzed 7-20-73. As indicated above both parents participated in foil art.

[213]

Findings: increased incidence of chromosome damage.

7-25-73   Seely notified HEW and CPSC of the following:

7-27-73

8-13-73   "I think it is safe to say that there is growing concern by geneticists, physicians, regulatory agencies, and society as a whole over the possible inadvertent or careless widespread introduction into the population of mutagens or teratogens. Our preliminary data from ten subjects, including two dysmorphic infants, suggest that transmissible genetic damage (mutagenic and teratogenic) may occur to individuals exposed to some commercial spray adhesives from their use in the hobby of foil art (foiling). Foil art has been popularized in this region by a television program, and presumably there are a significant number of participants in the hobby." Specifically:

1. Using the criteria for measurement of chromosome damage (gaps and breaks) the mean incidence of breaks and or gaps in the control group was 1.65 ± 0.28 compared with 8.99 ± 0.89 in the study group. This difference is statistically highly significant.

2. There is probably an etiologic relationship with exposure to spray adhesives. The concern is greatly magnified by the persistence of the chromosomal findings for prolonged periods after exposure to the spray adhesives has ceased.

3. There are a number of possible explanations for these observations, but two stand out in my view. One is that the offending material(s) persists in the body for extended periods, directly exerting its influence and having access to a developing fetus via the placenta. A second and more likely possibility is that the material(s) is mutagenic and one of the consequences of this mutagenesis is a disturbance in the normal chromosomal repair mechanism(s). The result of this would be an increased incidence of chromosomal breakage, as was found. The presence of this phenomenon early in embryogenesis could explain readily the teratogenic influence. The phenotype of the malformed infants would be variable. If the disturbance in the repair mechanism was at the enzyme level, it is not un-

likely that a homozygous state would be required to be teratogenic (i.e., both parents would have to carry the mutation). Thus, we may be dealing with a mutagen-produced (commercially distributed) new teratogenic recessive disease(s), in which a given segment of the society (those exposed to the mutagen) could have a high incidence of individuals whose germ cells could be mosaic-homozygous normal, heterozygous mutated and homozygous mutated. For these individuals the risk of having involved offspring would be significant.

4. Because of the nature of the findings from chromosome analysis, one has to have the additional concern that there may be an oncogenic influence in involved individuals.

5. Further study will be necessary to define the gravity and magnitude of the problem, but their potential is alarming.

8-5-73   FDA and CPSC representatives met with Seely in Oklahoma to discuss research findings.

8-7-73   CPSC requested written information from manufacturer.

8-15-73   CPSC receives confidential information regarding the formulation for the products in question. CPSC received written report from Seely highlighting findings.

8-16-73   Commission representatives, Dr. Seely and industry representatives met in Oklahoma City to discuss Dr. Seely's research.

8-17-73   CPSC moved to halt the production, distribution, and sale of aerosol adhesives.

Manufacturer cooperated fully with the Commission by suspending all production, distribution and marketing of the product in question. One manufacturer indicated that "without minimizing the seriousness of the situation, the evidence on which this action is taken is limited and inconclusive; And: (the Company) is continuing its own investigation of the products involved."

8-21-73   Manufacturer met with CPSC and indicated products had been removed from market and had distributed 30,000 pieces of mail. CPSC indicated plan to develop advice for consumers contacts with AMA and NII. Manufacturer outlined its research program.

8-27-73   Commission had a panel of medical experts develop recommendations for three possible affected groups: adults who have been exposed to the sprays, families in early or late stages of pregnancy and have had one or both parents exposed; children.

10-15-73   Review of Dr. Seely's work by scientists at the Universities of Frankfurt, Bonn, and Heidelberg.

11-15-73   Commissioners receive a staff status report on the human cytogenetic studies, animal studies, and epidemiology.

11-29-73   Commissioners' questions indicating areas of uncertainty were compiled for purposes of submission to an ad hoc review group.

Establishment of an ad hoc review group of nine experts identified by CPSC and various medical societies to review data and answer Commissioners' questions.

1-18-74   A Commission decision to publish a FR notice announcing the Commission's intention to lift the ban on 30th day following publication unless comments led Commission to other action.

1-28-74   Actual publication date.

1-28-74   Three letters received by the Commission on issue of lifting the ban: two in support of lifting the ban; one letter expressing general concern about aerosols.

PAYOFFS FROM EVALUATION

Michael Scriven
University of California, Berkeley

It is one thing to list the many actual and possible advantages of effective evaluation. It is another to mention its political problems of disruption, threat, etc. It is something else, no more important but perhaps just *as* important, to propose a principle for determining when evaluation should be done and what it should achieve.

To put the matter very simply, I believe that evaluations, like programs and products and personnel, are themselves subject to evaluation and should meet the standard of providing a positive cost-benefit balance, as nearly as this can be determined. Naturally, they must also meet certain ethical standards, such as the avoidance of inaccuracy. On this occasion, however, I wish to concentrate on the requirement of cost-effectivness.

There are two qualifications to this requirement. The first is that there are some special circumstances—for example, those involving legal action or political accountability or historical research—when the evaluation serves only as an investigative tool in the cause of truth and cannot be expected to pay for itself. The rule I am proposing is intended to provide a standard for the usual evaluations of social action programs including, of course, educational programs.

The second qualification is one that applies to all kinds of empirical research and not just to evaluation research; namely, that one cannot expect to be right on every occasion in predicting the costs and benefits of an evaluation. One can only require that the best estimates show a positive balance and hence that in the long run there will be a positive balance.

This doctrine was christened the doctrine of cost-free evaluation by Dan Stufflebeam when he first heard me propound it at an AERA Workshop we co-directed, no doubt by analogy with the concept of goal-free evaluation which I had introduced somewhat earlier. I rather like the term, but one needs to apply it with some caution if one is to avoid a life of poverty and consequent inefficacy. Let me explain the sense in which I am proposing that evaluation should be cost-free. To begin with, we have to understand clearly the significance of the truism that the concept of cost is not a simple predicate of entities—like, for example, mass, energy, or chemical composition—but a relational predicate which expresses a property of the ordered pair consisting of the entity and a specific individual or group of individuals like, for example, the relation of "being to the left of." Costs are always costs of something *to* someone; when we use the language of the marketplace, as when we say that "sugar now costs twice what it did a year ago," this must be understood as an elision for the complete expression which would have to involve some reference to the typical consumer. The cost of sugar for the producer has not doubled in that time; the cost of sugar to the manufacturer or the refiner or the distributor or the grower has not doubled—except perhaps coincidentally. It may seem attractive to say that in each of these cases we are talking about a different substance: sugar cane, sugar syrup, bulk sugar, etc., and that we have no need to relativize the concept of costs. But manufacturers, distributors, and retailers all handle the same product in the same package, so the point is unsound. Common parlance here permits the elision because we are all retail consumers of sugar and hence we all assume that framework when no other is specified.

Hence it is clear that the doctrine of cost-free evaluation (or CFE, for short) is not completely specified unless we identify the population whose cost we are talking about.

For openers, then, let me suggest that the doctrine refers to the ultimate purchaser of whatever it is that is being evaluated. That is not always the same as the ultimate consumer or user or beneficiary; those who pay for research on radical mastectomy or optimal diets for astronauts, i.e., all of us, do not all expect to use the results of the research. Nor can those results be said to provide a benefit to al taxpayers in the sense of providing something which they value, per-haps because of direct pay-off for a relative or for the society as a whole. There are a good many taxpayers who value neither relatives nor the common good.

Nevertheless, the correct formulation of CFE does refer to the benefits for all purchasers (e.g., taxpayers), because it is incorrect to identify benefits with what is valued. Benefit or value is an objective notion and goes well beyond the "subjective" notion of recognized or accepted or perceived value. Not all benefits to some members of society are benefits to society, but a good many are, even if very few people recognize them as such. (Note that this is not a moral but a scientific point, though it is a point which provides a key part of the foundation for ethics.) A useful elaboration of this point can be found in the discussions of what constitutes ideal "fringe benefits" in a pay package.

Apart from the ultimate purchaser, there may be a number of other parties involved with an evaluation in one way or another who should or do obtain positive cost-benefits from it—these may include project managers and funding agencies. One needs to look in slightly greater detail at the circumstances of a particular evaluation in order to determine when the CFE criterion should be met. In general, it will apply to the manager and agency involved in the usual tax-supported social programs.

To illustrate the meaning of the doctrine, some examples may help. When someone asks a friend what the various services provided by a travel agency in issuing tickets and making reservations cost, it is perfectly correct (within the usual framework) to reply that they "cost nothing." This simply means that there is no extra charge for these services over what the tickets, etc., would cost if purchased from the airlines. The doctrine of CFE is in the same way a no-extra-charge-to-purchasers' doctrine. It does not imply that the travel agent (or the evaluator) works for free. It implies that there is no net charge to the ultimate purchaser for the services. Now it might be pointed out that there is a hidden charge in the price of the ticket which pays for the travel agent's fees. Here we get into the opportunity cost problem. If we could perfectly well dispense with travel agents and reduce the cost of tickets, this comment would make good sense (as it does with regard to traffic expediters and customs agents in many ports). But if the travel agents would have to be replaced by retail outlets paid for by the airlines, and/or if they generate enough extra business to produce economies of scale, then one cannot argue for a hidden charge, and one can say they are cost-free.

Business executives ought to be cost-free; management consultants ought to be cost-free; textbook salespersons ought to be cost-free; but few of them are.

Why ought they to be cost-free? There are both moral and pragmatic grounds for the claim, but neither is purely instrumentalist. The ultimate foundation for the claim is simply that it is irrational to spend something for nothing, and this applies just as well to spending the taxpayers' money as it does to spending one's own. CFE is the economic dimension of what one might call "public interest evaluation," analogous to public interest law and science. It is not a particularly strong doctrine—there are supervening obligations that will require the evaluator not only to save the public money (compared with the situation where no evaluator was used) but also to avoid the unnecessary expenditure of money even when the CFE standard has been met. This point can be handled by adding an optimization clause to the doctrine, which of course expresses an absolute criterion.

How can I be sure that the absolute standard expressed by CFE can be met? Very simply, if it is not met, the evaluation should not be done (a few special circumstances apart). In short, the crucial and proper justification of evaluation is that it improves the efficiency or yield of programs and projects. It is not or should not be seen as primarily a moral agency, for in the name of morality all costs are too easily justified. It should be seen as a pragmatic requirement of effective management or R&D work. Then we can look at it critically in the process which I call metaevaluation, the evaluation of evaluation— instead of reacting against it as intrusive, alien, threatening. Evaluation has to pay its way and has to be subject to evaluation in its turn.

It is very important that when the evaluator walks in through the door, the evaluee have a sense that the metaevaluation system is strong enough so that no careless or superficial criticism is going to lead to job loss, job disruption, or unreasonable load increase. In particular, this has to mean that preliminary recommendations from the evaluator are going to be circulated to all affected for response, that (company) time will be arranged for discussion by those affected with each other and then—with their counter-recommendations, if any—there will be appropriate arrangements for a convergence meeting. Preferably there should be a neutral party present at that meeting whose recommendations will be attached unedited to the evaluation if it is to have external circulation or is being done for an external client such as a funding agency. (Of course, the counter-recommendations of the affected parties should also be attached unedited to any such report.) This kind of arrangement makes managers very nervous—it sounds too much like (and will sometimes in fact become) the next round of union negotiations. That is just one of the burdens management has to bear; there is no escape from either the moral or the pragmatic advantages of feedback arrangements of this kind. Management might like to be able to implement whatever recommendations it liked from the evaluator's report, but management is not omniscient about the probable effects of doing so and the evaluator likewise; the safeguard feedback procedures described are almost certain to improve the yield from the evaluation considerably. It should also be a clear part of the arrangements for an evaluator of the kind we are discussing (typically formative and personnel-affecting) that useful suggestions from the employees/staff will be recompensed as evaluation-consultant contributions and/or from the savings they engender, and that any overall gains from the evaluation will be used in part to improve working conditions, where this is desirable. The combination of incentives to contribute and safeguards against unjustified harmful consequences can not only provide better evaluation input as such, but also provide so much better a climate for the evaluation that data-gathering by the evaluator(s) will be much improved, with consequent improvements in the reliability and range of recommendations.

I hope it can be seen that the cost-free approach is not a mere penny-pinching operation, but involves a major reorientation of thinking about the nature and formulation of evaluation.

This may be a good moment at which to remind the reader of the source which we are tapping in order to pay for these improvements in working conditions for project staff, etc.—and the fees/salaries for the evaluators, for that matter. And it should be stressed that few evaluators are going to be covering the whole range of management consulting that can yield gains of the kind we are discussing, including time-and-motion analysis, purchasing procedures, office machine evaluation, etc. Typically, too, management does not want that area reviewed, or does not want it done by the same evaluators, or knows it will not be done as well by these evaluators. But one source of the savings is exactly the same whether educational evaluators or management consultants are involved, namely shedding unproductive efforts or reshaping them.

When a soft-ware consulting firm comes in to provide what is (misleadingly) called an evaluation program for the computer installation in a large business, they do a cost-benefit analysis in advance which shows exactly how and where the savings will result from their services. For example, they can often show a way to reschedule or reintegrate or reprogram the hardware in order to increase efficiency with regard to a given workload to the point where the purchase of new peripherals or CPs can be postponed by at least a year. That may provide a savings of some tens of thousands of dollars, partly by avoiding a temporary rehousing move. In the same way, the educational evaluator can often identify non-optimal practices in a field-test cycle that is yielding negligible improvements in the materials. This leads to *internal* savings, i.e., releases contract dollars for better use. On the other hand, the evaluator may see a loophole in the field-trial procedures that needs to be blocked, e.g., failure to gather data on probable cognitive side-effects, which is going to cost the project dollars to fix. Here the savings that can yield a positive cost-benefit balance are *external,* i.e., the ultimate purchaser gets a better product for the same money, or a good product instead of a product of unknown or slight worth for lightly more money, depending on where the squeeze goes for providing the recommended improvements.

In the examples given, the internal savings were in money and the external in benefits, but the reverse could equally well be the case. It should also be noted from these examples that the evaluator's services are likely to be more valuable and certainly will be more appreciated, if he/she/they can make recommendations as to what is to be sacrificed if a new cost is to be incurred internally (externally, too). There are definite limits on the extent to which the ultimate purchaser or intermediate purchasers can provide supplementary funds even if they are getting a real bargain for them. These limitations may be legal or political (e.g., fixed-fee contract) or they may be absolute (no more money available for this project). And there is the basic fact that the marginal value of improvements to the purchaser varies considerably with the absolute cost to which they are incremental and with the press of other demands, so one cannot make confident claims about the value if very large sums or very long periods are involved. Nevertheless, there is nothing dubious about the claim that a 1% improvement in the efficiency of teaching reading would represent a very large benefit to the taxpayer either in reduced costs to present criterion or in reduced social costs due to over-criterion performance. And the use of good evaluation in the reading area should have no difficulty in yielding considerably more than 1% *net* gains without any dehumanization. So the CFE requirement is not a dream on large-scale projects; and on smaller ones, it is still feasible as a minimum. Normally, evaluation should perform well above that level.

It is a separate and empirical question exactly what savings or benefits are and can be provided by good, cost-conscious evaluation. I can think of many evaluations which have produced no gains whatsoever, and a very substantial cost. On the other hand, I can think of many that have paid off—not accidentally, but just as intended—by a factor of 100 times the cash outlay for the evaluation, or 1,000 times. I would think that we can reasonably expect that incisive evaluations by the best evaluation teams of 90% of current HEW-type programs should pay off at between 10 and 100 times their cost to the intermediate purchaser, e.g., a funding agency. They are, in my view, one of the best possible investments of program money and well ahead of those standbys of the cost benefit enthusiast—electric typewriters, copiers, and dictating equipment. Of course, the total effect of these rich lodes of pay-off is somewhat lessened by the qualification that not more than two or three such teams could, in my view, be assembled from the evaluators available today. The training of evaluators, both pre- and in-service, is terribly narrow; and narrow evaluations are exactly the ones that do not hit the big pay-offs. Nevertheless, at the *meta*-level, I would suggest that the net contribution of the evaluation methodologists in pushing for the experimental approach has been and will be huge. And Kenneth Arrow's argument that the pay-off from evaluation research experiments, if positive and measurable, must be many times repaid when the experiments are translated to full-scale seems to me inescapable at the practical end.

There are many other aspects of this topic that need investigation and discussion, and some of them I have covered elsewhere, e.g., the impact of this heavy commitment to metaevaluation on the design of evaluations. We have covered this to some extent in the special arrangements for a metaevaluation team in the Title VII evaluation which SDC is doing. It is obvious, for example, that metaevaluation is no more to be done by the evaluator than the evaluation itself is to be done (entirely) by the program people. It is obvious that the measurement of benefits and costs of the evaluation requires a kind of instrumentation that is quite different from that required for the basic evaluation. It requires a different contractual arrangement from the present one, since there has to be an option for cancelling the evaluation on cost-effectiveness grounds, not just incompetence or unfavorable content—and *that* requires some ingenious insulation. Again, one must discuss the limitations of traditional cost-benefit analysis (well expressed by Dr. Rivlin in her 1970 Rowan Gaither lecture, *Systematic Thinking for Social Action)* and the ways to get around this, using cost-utility analysis and qualitative cousins of it. But perhaps enough has been said to provide a target of interest.

THE QUALITATIVE ELEMENT IN EVALUATION RESEARCH[1]

Norman E. Zinberg, M.D.
Associate Clinical Professor of Psychiatry
Harvard Medical School

In many discussions of evaluation research the qualitative problems of evaluation are neglected; that is, in an effort to find out if the research has attained its goal, the project is treated as if it, in fact, started at point A and did or did not go to its intended destination, point D. I will describe the problems of a research project which indeed did begin at point A, but made unscheduled stops at points B and C, ending up at point E rather than point D, its intended destination. This research project was evaluated, and I will discuss the cognitive dissonance that arose between the well-meaning evaluator and the well-meaning research team.

My approach is intended to show that evaluation of social science research projects, which are part and parcel of their ongoing social milieu, must take into account factors other than the extent to which the projects reached their intended goals. I believe that evaluation is always basically subjective. For example, much has been made by Professor Richard Light of work that shows that those researchers who do evaluate their work quantifiably are less enthusiastic about it than those who do not. He does not go on to tell us whether their lowered enthusiasm stems from the failure to quantify or from their feeling that the work itself failed. It could, and I believe in some cases would, prove to be either. If one takes Light's figures to mean that enthusiasts are so only because they permit their positive biases to blind them, then this is a subjective decision to ignore the possible bitterness that develops in those to whom numbers are important, when the numbers fail to come out "right."

In my view, evaluation of research requires a complex awareness of the impact of the research on the research team, the research subjects, and the social milieu in which the research takes place. Obviously this is not, nor should it be, true of all research evaluation, but it should be true of some projects. To accept responsibility for taking the psychological and social variables into account does not abandon standards or objectivity. It merely demands considerable clarity from the evaluator about his points of view as he approaches the material and firm statements about what he took into account. Admittedly this makes appropriate evaluations of research roughly analogous to clinical case studies from which "discipline," heretofore despised by "objective" evaluators, could be learned.

The project whose evaluation problems are to be described here was conceived in early 1968 during the maelstrom of public and media preoccupation with the changing mores about sex and drug use among the young and in Boston with the busing of inner-city children to suburban school systems, sponsored by the Metropolitan Council for Education Opportunity (METCO). Harold N. Boris, a psychologist experienced in both social research and group work, joined me as co-project director. The project was designed in two parts and funded by The Ford Foundation. One part, the Group Consultation Program for Teachers, gathered together teachers from the inner-city schools and the suburban schools. Changing values and mores of their pupils assaulted the teachers, on the one hand, while administrative decisions clearly affecting the classroom were being made by superintendents, school committees, and town meetings, on the other. Teachers were seen as having been forgotten in all that was going on. Their emotional responses to the decisions on both sides as well as their methods of coping with all this—including the vast publicity—became the object of this study.

The other part of the project established a course in Arlington, Massachusetts, a carefully selected suburb of Boston. This course labeled Social Education, was eventually offered on a volunteer basis to both junior and senior high school students in that suburb, and meet ings were conducted more or less as dynamic groups. Since many more students and teachers volunteered than could be accommodated, a control group was available. The course was intended to give the students a chance to talk freely about sex, drugs, prejudice, and the like without a formal curriculum. A survey by the research team, preliminary to the start of the project, stimulated considerable doubt as to the wisdom of standard courses in sex or drug education as well as the new efforts to combat bigotry and racism by intellectual presentations of black history or prejudice in America.

In his original memorandum recommending the grant for our project, Mitchell Sviridoff of The Ford Foundation listed the following "research objectives" for the Group Consultation Program for Teachers: "to measure (1) the extent of attitude change within the groups; (2) the dynamics of that change; (3) the degree of individual internalization; and (4) the effect on the children." He indicated that the research on the Arlington youngsters' program might tell something about (1) the transfer of attitudes into and out of the group; (2) the value of the course in shaping adolescents' personal growth and at what ages that might best be done; (3) the transfer of group leader behavior of the teachers and their consciousness of group process into the classroom; and (4) incorporating all the above, research might produce a "how to" procedure for other school systems, professional psychologists, and psychiatrists.

These large aims as presented by Sviridoff accurately represented the original position of the applicants. However, even then we had begun to have considerable concern about our capacity to achieve even the rough quantifications Sviridoff suggested. In the end any efforts at quantification began to seem an interference with the social process we wanted to learn about, so that our viewpoint and Ford's grew ever further apart. What was probably more to the point was that, from the time the project had actually gotten underway, we had begun to see many pitfalls because our objectives were so varied. The project would be working with people who themselves had high hopes that their social conflicts might be resolved. We were to work within social institutions—METCO, the town and school systems of Arlington, Ford—which hoped that the project would offer a means of resolving conflicts within society at large. We were expected, we feared, to weigh, measure, and evaluate these hopes and what came of them. All this needed to be done, although we were increasingly convinced that for group leaders to anticipate some change, just because all of us were going around looking for it, was the equivalent of wanting something for and from the participants which led toward social engineering.

Doubts grew, but it was only very slowly that we relinquished the idea that we should be able to do a project emphasizing an interest in process and at the same time do a kind of formal research on that project which deeply affected the process itself. Our preoccupation by this time was with relative neutrality. This showed itself as a concern about not wanting things from people or for people. We found ourselves insisting that participants have a chance to think about what kept them from thinking about what they wanted for themselves, and this great care about not interfering with this process began to sound so damn pure, even to us. Was there something the matter with us? Each time we discussed our goals and someone like Ford's first research consultant talked about measuring variables like prejudice, hostility, openmindedness, tolerance for ambiguity, even greater awareness of motivation, we found ourselves muttering darkly in our beards about form and substance, and how would we know it if we found it. Were we sinking into research misanthropy?

Ford's request for an evaluation of the project was simply pro forma. Whatever concern they may have felt about the research aspect of the project, Ford's interest and support continued throughout, and anything they could do to assist in the success of the project was forthcoming. As an evaluator Ford chose someone with experience and a deserved reputation for objectivity and competence. He was interested in the area to be studied, yet he had no axe to grind. Our regard for the research evaluator (and there is evidence of mutuality) as well as for the program and administrative staff at Ford has never waivered. But our positive bias toward Ford, which took the form of wanting to do what they wanted, seems important to report. The urge to come up with "findings," so as to supply what Ford wanted out of the project, our fear that the nonquantification portion of the research represented inadequacy, obstinacy, or simply foolishness plagued us throughout. One should keep that knowledge in mind as he/she traverses this paper. (Erik Erikson found it important for his readers to know that a bias existed in his report on Gandhi. He wrote a letter to Gandhi mid-book acknowledging that they might not have liked each other, and, unques tionably, Gandhi would have resented this scrutiny of his life; bu Erikson, armed by knowledge of his bias, said he would maintain a objective stance.) Also, despite the evaluator's clear misgivings about the research and evaluation arm of the project, he recommended that Ford continue and even extend its support.

The program officers at Ford asked the evaluator to assess, first, the general approach "as a theory for social change or social conflict resolution." More specifically, the evaluator was asked in regard to the Group Consultation Program for Teachers to think about the following questions: "(1) Is the approach effective in changing, or helping teachers to deal with, their racial attitudes, especially for white teachers, as they affect black students newly integrated into their classrooms? (2) Would such changes favorably affect the performances of their students, particularly the METCO students? (3) Does the approach affect the teachers' views of themselves in teaching in a positive way?" And about Arlington: "Does the approach make a significant difference (1) in the participants' self-confidence? (2) in their ability to resolve social conflict within themselves? (3) in their ability to live with ambiguity? (4) in their ability to perceive more clearly myth versus reality?"

These questions are somewhat different from those in the original memorandum from Sviridoff, which probably reflects the program officer's sensitive reading of the research team's position. We were beginning to shift our point of view from "What happened?", which implies "What changed?", to "How is the group experienced?" Hence, the questions the evaluator was asked to report on were intended to fit more closely with what we had in mind. In the Arlington project, we were concerned with what happened inside the psyche of the participants and less interested in what the individuals did with it, such as using more or less drugs. The third question pertaining to the teachers' project also reflects this approach, although two questions resolutely hoped that these teachers would do "better" by their black students as a result of the group experience. That is, Ford (and hence the evaluator) assumed that there was something "wrong" with teachers, especially with white teachers' attitudes toward their new black pupils. They assumed that these attitudes should be changed for the better, that the groups would do it, and that when such changes occurred the students would "benefit" from this, and their school and human performances would improve. These assumptions amounted to a firm statement that we could get a hold of these attitudes, that they could be shifted toward what we knew to be better, and that, as a result, specific behavioral changes would come about not only in the teachers but also in the children.

From the vantage point of the present, the implicit assumptions outlined above seem untestable, particularly in the complex social and personal milieus of a school which was itself in the midst of social and educational upheaval. How does one *define,* let alone test, an ability to differentiate myth from reality? In what areas? At what times? For what reasons? To what degree? The same questions arose about living with ambiguity, resolving social conflict, or acquiring self-confidence. What about changing racial attitudes? At what level of personality does one change attitudes, and how is this reflected in behavior? Certainly when people leave a situation in which there has been great social pressure, they can be heard spouting a new line. They are sometimes even "convinced" consciously. But, if these persons still experience certain conflicts, less consciously, won't the conflicts emerge anyhow, appearing, though perhaps subtly, in the individual's "changed" behavior?

At the time, however, both the evaluator and the project team took the evaluation questions seriously. It was as if we agreed on something like the following: "Yes, the groups can't resolve any personal conflicts in depth; the groups are not a thorough-going psychoanalysis, you know. And just to let them have the experience and study that, why, where will that get anyone? No, let us researchers set a goal of less prejudice on the conscious level and accept that at face value. If the individual retains a complex conflict about prejudice, let him take it out on someone else, let him kick his kids more often or what have you, just so long as he behaves better in school. That would be a desirable social change, and it could be measured." This, of course, is an argument for social engineering, and it indicates a belief that some control of individuals' responses is consistently possible and their responses in a complex social situation directable. We do not share that belief now, and in retrospect realize that we really did not share it then.

In any case, whatever one thinks now of the mandate, the evaluator accepted it; and there was no protest from the project team (we were still laboring under the concern that we were delinquent by reason of our lack of faith in quantification). A full-scale evaluation of the project thus got underway.

On the Group Consultation Program for Teachers, there were four final suggestions from the evaluator in April of 1970. (1) Recruit, orient, and train group leaders who would be more knowledgeable and oriented to content questions, particularly black leaders. In turn they could better orient the groups away from studying process and toward achieving substantive change in racial bias. (2) Do a systematic comparison of all-white groups with mixed groups. (3) Get the program built into the school curriculum rather than after school; meet in homes and lounges not classrooms, in black areas. Try for broader involvement of administrators in preparatory work and evaluation. (4) Develop a more specific focus on white racism and problems of white children.

As to the first suggestion, it must be abundantly clear by now that the project team was moving ever farther away from content to an ever greater emphasis on process. The team pointed out to the evaluator that, except during the pilot program, black leaders had found it very difficult to remain neutral and had tended to exhort and lecture group members. Ruth Batson, the METCO director at that time, had specifically reported feedback on this as a problem for group members. She had been active in asking the project team not to rehire such leaders. Further, with reference to the evaluator's second suggestion, Batson had explicitly requested that we stop the practice of trying to arrange group member representation in the groups. When one deliberately arranged to have black leaders or black members in the group, she argued, then the group simply used them as resource people to tell about the black experience, which was no good for anyone. She strongly suggested natural groups, that is, take members as they came, either numerically or geographically, and let that *modus operandi* be clear to everyone. But in his final evaluation report the evaluator argued that "lack of *factual* data on race and racism and the (project team's) unwillingness to make direct data statements will allow the groups to proceed with false assumptions" on race and racial prejudice.

In all four of those suggestions, the evaluator did not recognize two cardinal principles of the whole project. One, the issue was *not* the acquisition of factual knowledge but rather the process by which people selectively perceive, misperceive, repress, and generally inhibit the acquisition of accurate information and maintain this process in themselves. Two, the project team did not conceive of working with prejudice in the usual direct sense. That is, a teacher who had a hostile response to blacks would bring up that prejudice in the group, be persuaded to recognize it as irrational, and would then change. Rather, the team thought that in the groups participants might come to recognize the extent to which people insisted on being prejudiced. If the members used this special opportunity where no one was likely to be hurt by the prejudice to study how it worked, we thought this indirect approach might be, somehow, more useful. No one who looked at the project ever bought this argument (sad to relate), despite our pointing out how in the pilot project our search for symmetry was used by the group members as a means of avoiding any more affectful response to prejudice.

Everyone agreed completely on the value of the evaluator's third suggestion (that the groups be built into the curriculum), but no school superintendent was willing to accept the scheduling hassle this would require.

The evaluator's suggestions for the Arlington project were similar. He thought the project should more actively recruit and select teacher/ leaders, circulate news about the project to various other schools so that they might know of its existence and perhaps build it into their curricula, and specifically "shift the focus from process to goals. The project should establish prior criteria for evaluation of solutions . . . to problems to be encountered in a social education approach."

Again, the evaluator clearly disagreed with the process-oriented approach and asked for goals and solutions without defining what they might be. He did not consider whether, if we aimed for "less prejudice," for example, anyone knew what that really was. Also—and this is the nub of our discussion of the difference between a social change project and a research project—in his interest in getting "better" leaders in both projects and getting the projects more securely fixed in more schools, the evaluator saw the project as a tool for social change. It was the impression of the project team that what Ford wanted was more and better (i.e., more quantifiable) research, and, at the same time, more and better use of the project to bring about social change as quickly as possible. Our conviction was that the groups were not crisis intervention techniques, that they could not be hurried into a particular direction, and that *how* they worked ought to be thought about and even studied. These convictions were pretty much at odds with the evaluator's recommendations.

These differences can also be seen in another area. The evaluator strongly supported the hiring of a research director. In the evaluator's words, this director would not be concerned with the groups and their processes, but only "with data to be collected and analyzed in a systematic fashion which will lead to some useful answers about the research questions posed by The Ford Foundation. Zinberg and Boris are not trained in, oriented toward, nor sympathetic toward scientific research as it relates to the kind of groups they are running in these projects. As is common with psychiatrists and psychologists, they view groups in a process-oriented rather than a goal-oriented context. Without established goals, it is impossible to evaluate output, for there is nothing to measure against."

The evaluator's two misperceptions of cardinal principles of the project become important here. For he goes on to state the need for testing the attitudes of participants before and after, in order to know what happens within the groups. He states that Zinberg and Boris resist such measures because of their fear that the groups might not be as "free" in their behavior as they would have been without a researcher present. And, indeed, this problem was mentioned and discussed both with the evaluator during his evaluation and then with the Ford program officer. But the team, with our self-conscious concern that it was our inadequacy at research that got in the way, allowed that to resist testing of the groups on such grounds was too precious. The evaluator neglected anywhere to mention a basic argument advanced by the project team about the extent to which group members reach for what they believe they are supposed to be doing.

There are actually two issues here. The first is the influence of the fact that the participants were being tested, and the second is the influence of the content of the tests on the subsequent behavior of people in the groups. The second issue reflects the first, because the willingness to test indicates that the testers will ask things that they fear they could not otherwise trust themselves to know. If a group member felt that group membership was a good idea for him/her because he/she was, let us say, too hostile a person, which of the following would be true or false?

(a) His/her test score would reflect the actuality of his/her hostility;

(b) It would reflect the severity of his/her conscience;

(c) It would reflect his/her docility in the face of his/her expectation that the group (leader) would change him/her;

(d) It would reflect an extreme in order to secure a big change;

(e) It would reflect the disguise that person makes for his/her hostility, because he/she feels hostility is bad;

(f) All of the above;

(g) None of the above.

One is hard put to find the correct answer. Chances are there is no one correct answer. Rather, different people would respond to the same test in different ways. We would have to know each person in order to know what individual test scores reflect. When we do not figure out in what spirit an individual takes the test, we do not know what the test score says about that individual. Totaling everyone's scores compounds the confusion and magnifies the uncertainty.

The next step in a testing procedure is to garner "after" scores to compare with the "before" ones. Assuming each person takes the test afterward in the same spirit in which he/she took it previously, we would still not know what the scores say about him/her, but we would, at least, know how much he/she has changed (or not) on a certain item. That is, we would not know for a certainty his/her Hostility Quotient, since we may not, in fact, be measuring that; but we would know his/her X Quotient. But what if the spirit in which she/he takes the test changes? This will possibly be reflected in his/her score; but how will we know what has changed? If he/she was docile at first and then became bold, yet his/her level of hostility remained the same, his/her test score would change; yet what would we know?

We would have to delude ourselves rather insistently in order finally to imagine that the tests measure anything we can know about. If, on the other hand, we do not delude ourselves, then what we have is a group of numbers which, with whatever statistical craft they are maneuvered, might as well have been taken at random from a telephone directory.

No responsible research scientist would knowingly delude the larger community with whom he/she shares his/her findings. He/she would not fudge his/her figures or statistical treatments. But self-delusion is quite another matter. Is there not every reason to suspect that test-taking behavior is so variable among people that to take a score as responsive only to the test items and not to the meaning the test holds for the subject in his/her larger context is to share the tester's unrealized delusion?

Our position is probably obvious. We have to regard the taking of a test as an act of communication from subject to tester; to make such a communication the subject will fortify him/herself with certain assumptions about the tester. These will likely be based partly on what she/he can learn of the tester from the circumstances of the testing, from the tester's person and manner, and from the tester him/herself. Then the subject may well consider to what use and by whom his/her communication will be put. Where there are unknowns or ambiguities, the testing situation itself will be like a projective test. The subject will read in some mixture of hope and previous experience to fill in the gaps. If, moreover, she/he takes the test in a group situation, she/he will be influenced by what she/he can make of the attitudes of his/her cohorts. When, finally, the subject checks an item, all of this will have gone into it. The specific issue posed in the item will have only partial weight in this assembly of factors.

The tester, then, cannot be reviewed as an antiseptic person in the halls of science. What she/he is doing has its parallels in the behavior of the members of our groups. She/he too, for example, is hoping to split off pure cultures from the admixtures. She/he hopes, also, to know only that which does not jeopardize other hopes, whose preservation actually depends on his/her *not* knowing. His/her faith in numbers is akin to the group member's preoccupation with the numbers present or absent, the number of sessions, or the number of times the leader spoke or used a given work. From our perspective, then, we must suffer the loss of an illusion in return for what the perspective enables us to know. We must sacrifice one form of knowing—of knowing through testing—for another—of knowing what one cannot know through testing. To know one cannot know seems scant consolation for the illusion of feeling one can, but have we really a choice?

The other of the evaluator's essential misperceptions is not quite as clearcut, but it is equally important. He sums up what he sees as the Zinberg-Boris approach by saying that the project "assumes that if they (group participants) can be freed up to clearly see themselves and the seas of value ambiguity in which they live, positive behavioral consequences will follow—*but it does not insist on this as a test*" (emphasis his). To the degree that we allowed that we had no negative responses should a teacher feel that the groups alleviated his/her direct feelings of racial bias by allowing that teacher to recognize their irrationality, the evaluator is correct. But he is not correct in implying that we believe behavioral consequences follow from the groups and insist only that they not be used as a test. He goes on in his report to quote Allan Winker, who found that fewer than 10 percent of groups tested showed "behavioral counterparts of changes in attitudes." The evaluator, then, was saying that if Zinberg and Boris believed that their groups would change the participants' attitudes, which in turn would change their behavior, Zinberg and Boris would jolly well have to prove it, for there was evidence against it.

One other phenomenon deserves mention. Zinberg and Boris, going along with the evaluator's suggestion, hired a research director who prepared forms of all sorts for the participants and group observer to fill out. These forms were considered positively splendid by the evaluator, who saw them as a breakthrough in the research and the first collection of data considered "hard" and appropriate for systematization and analysis. Data were collected and collected; and nothing could be made from any of it. Every attempt to analyze it fell afoul of what has been pointed out again and again: How could one *really*—really, mind you, not going by just what a person says—once find out if someone is "less prejudiced?" The Research Director played with it and played with it, then discreeetly folded his tent, moved to London with all the data so as to continue searching for a coherent scheme of analysis, and, despite written entreaty after written entreaty, has not been heard from since.

DISCUSSION: Payoffs of Evaluation Research

Discussants: Clark Abt, Abt Associates Inc.
William Capron, Kennedy School of Government
Alice Rivlin, Brookings Institution

RIVLIN: I am assuming that since we are talking about the payoff to evaluation research that we are really talking about how to increase that payoff, and it has occurred to me that maybe the whole evaluation movement started off on a couple of false premises which we are now realizing. One is that there is such a thing as a social program in the sense of a treatment which applies to people which can then be evaluated to see if it works or not. Most of the evaluations we have been talking about, at the federal level anyway, assumed that we were providing something to people, could say what it was, could define some sort of output, and could measure whether it took place or not. Well, most of the sorrow of evaluation, it seems to me stems from that basic lack of realism, as well as the uninterpretable results that the typical study has produced. Head Start was not a treatment, as Lois-ellin Datta pointed out very well, and as the Westinghouse study shows. There was not very much you could say about whether it worked or not, and nobody cared anyway about whether it worked or not. They were going to go on doing something about little children, no matter how that report came out. The interesting questions are what really works and for whom? The study was not designed to answer that. In general, evaluators tried to make sensible recommendations that somebody would listen to. When one gets into that sort of situation, one immediately finds several things. No one knows enough about the specific inputs to say very much at the end of the evaluation about what really happened. Enough is not known about the clients. One does know that this supposed program is only a small part of what is impacting on their lives. One doesn't know very much about the rest of their lives, and one ends up with the usual moan of "If we'd only had longitudinal data over a longer period" and "if we'd only known something more detailed about family background, or about the community, or about the other resources that were coming into the program, we could have done a better job."

At this point, the usual reaction is to call for experimentation, and that is even what the Westinghouse people did—to say, okay, we cannot do it this way—let's go ahead and do a clean experimental design and actually try things out and measure exactly what we are putting in and collect data over a period of years and see what happens. Although this approach can be useful, it is a terribly expensive strategy, and I think all of the experimenters would admit that we do not yet know whether it is worth it. Some of the kinds of questions we are trying to answer with very expensive experiments, like the Housing Supply Experiment, might have been answered by an appeal to natural experiments. For instance, when the baby boom increased the demand for housing naturally, one could have observed what happened to the supply. But of course no one is ever prepared and in there with a data collection system in advance to take advantage of that kind of natural experiment.

The other myth surrounding evaluation is that decisions get made quickly. Now some do, and Connie Newman was talking about a situation in which decisions do get made quickly where you have to evaluate safety of products. There are a lot of products; there are a few people making the decisions; and they have, of necessity, to do it quickly. Most of the social programs that we are talking about are not of that sort. Decisions are not made quickly; one could defend the proposition that they are not made at all. But what we are saddled with at the moment is the myth that decisions are made very quickly, that they are made periodically at budget time. Therefore, we must have quick evaluations, put out RFP's and get some stuff back very rapidly, and then do it again for the next cycle. If the myths are wrong, then evaluation ought to grow up and recognize that it is here to stay, that social programs are here to stay, and shift to a new mode which should contain some of the following elements:

- Maintain a continuing commitment to the collection of longitudinal information about a fairly large sample of people; presumably, a clustered sample, but a big, continuing round of panel studies, in which people and families stayed in the sample for some time. You would use this to monitor what is going on in the world. You would use it as a control group when you wanted to do some experiment, or when you had a natural phenomenon going on in a particular place which you could evaluate, but you had no way of knowing what was normal, which is often the problem. You would use this continuing panel to take sub-samples to do mini-experiments with–to give them different kinds of income maintenance, for example, or a different access to student aid or to housing, and to find out what happens. One would also switch on the production of services side, again to a continuing mode, not of evaluating programs.

- Switch from evaluating programs to finding out which inputs work in the human service area and which do not. I think this almost suggests moving away from Michael Scriven's model that evaluation should be cost-free in terms of a particular evaluation tied to a particular program. I guess I learned somewhere that there is no such thing as a free lunch, so that strikes me as an unlikely model anyway, at least maybe for a decade or so.

- Abandon our attempts at program evaluation as such and move to a more experimental mode not tied to the particular program. However, I think this raises all kinds of problems. It raises, among other things, the problem of the role of the non-governmental research organization–those who live on RFP's–where do they go from here? I think one could find a role for the non-governmental research organization in such a world.

The above also raises the problem of privacy and how you protect the people who are in the continuing panel, because a lot would be known about them. They would be in the panel for a long time and there would be some very difficult problems there.

CAPRON: It strikes me as a little odd to separate the two panels as they have been this afternoon. We are talking about the impact or payoff of evaluation; downstairs they are talking about the political impact, and it seems to me that it is all one ball of wax. It is hard for me, at least, to think about the subject that we are addressing here without recognizing the importance of the political impact. This was certainly illustrated in the discussion and even more so in that excellent paper which Lois-Ellin Datta presented, where she discussed the Westinghouse Head Start Study. It seems to me that those who have said, as she told us in writing, that this study did not have any impact, had a very odd measure of impact. For instance, the Westinghouse Study raised grave questions of whether Head Start was having any effect. Since there is still a Head Start program some said the Westinghouse Study had no impact, which seems to me to be an awfully limited conception of impact. That study has had a significant impact in a number of ways, directly involved in Head Start and otherwise. I would emphasize, however, that that study came along as a part of a growing pattern which influenced the academic, research, and political community; i.e., we had the Jensen results and we had Daniel Patrick Moynihan, saying some things that were widely heard, and certainly heard in the Oval Office. I think that the Westinghouse Study impact cannot be generalized; that is, another study like that will not have the same sort of fallout. I think it depends upon the context in which any one of these evaluations becomes more or less public.

In response to Ms. Newman, I would like to ask who is funding the evaluation? Is the agency conducting the program doing the sole monitoring of the evaluation? Also, the same question about the agency, typically the private contractor responding to an RFP who is doing the evaluation: What is the history of the evaluating organization? What is its track record? Has it always been the evaluator for the agency in question? Does it have other clients? What are the consumers' preconceptions about the program being evaluated? What were the criteria set up in the evaluation vis-a-vis the original objectives of the program, not only those that were stated in the legislation, but the de facto objectives in the actual design of the program. I would point out, for example, in the case of the Westinghouse Study that it seems to me a legitimate question about the focus of that evaluation to note that they completely ignored, as I understand it, what I would call the "community impact" effects of Head Start. Since I was around when that program was first being talked about, I know that some of us thought that quite apart from the direct effect on the children and their school performance in the next couple of years, there was a somewhat hidden agenda involved. And there is no question that Head Start programs, in some communities at least, had an important effect in organizing some portions of these communities in a way which has endured until today. It seems to me that a complete evaluation of Head Start would certainly pay attention to these effects. Of course, there were other things much narrower. It is true that they did, in the end, get some evidence on parent satisfaction, but the Westinghouse recommendation ignored the fact that at least the parents seemed to think Head Start was a dandy program.

As I read Mr. Scriven's paper, I thought that as he was using the term "cost-free evaluation" to mean subjectively that it would be very hard for anyone who had been involved in the evaluation to say that it was not cost-free. There are a lot of side benefits that he seems to accept as a typical result of an evaluation, and I am perfectly willing to agree. Indeed, I would say, as I understood the paper, as distinct from the oral remarks, that except where outright fraud is produced and, for example, an evaluation of Program A is cribbed to be the evaluation of Program B, which I suspect may have happened sometimes, that it is very hard in the way he is defining "cost" here, that they not be cost-free.

As a resident of a community nearby that is part of a METCO Program, all I can say to Dr. Zinberg is that I think it is virtually impossible to get an "objective" evaluation of a program as complex and dynamic as that one early in its lifetime. Maybe historically, we can do something in a generation or two. I do not envy anyone who attempts to take on the job of evaluating a program as complex and dynamic as that one has been. That does not mean we shouldn't try. Even though you cannot get what any of us would call an "objective" evaluation, the attempt to evaluate may produce important guides for improving the program and that, after all, is one of the main purposes of the game anyway. I think this notion that some of us in the academy get hung up on, that the evaluation must bend over backward to be "objective," is missing part of the payoff that I think has come from at least some evaluations which are defective. One might say that, for example, about the Westinghouse Study.

As Alice Rivlin said, there are a lot of natural experiments that can be done and we often spend a lot of money on designing overt planned experiments when we could learn many things by merely looking at what is going on in the world in the particular program area. I think that is true, within certain limitations. I do not think the major experiments we have seen so far have gone very far in the direction of the point I am about to make, but they have gone a little way. The one difficulty with many natural experiments is that they do not test directly what I would call the implementation problem, i.e., one thing that you get in a designed experiment is to see how well an agency, a contractor or federal agency, can administer a program and what the administrative problems will be, not the output or impact problems at the end of the line. What happens, for example, when you are actually making housing allowances or whatever the particular experiment may be? Now I would say that a major justification for experiments should be that they test not only the impact or effect but also the administrative feasibility and administrative design of a national program or a big program, following on after the experiment. Ms. Rivlin raised one problem, namely the privacy issue, but I think there is another one. I think we need to know more about this than we now do before we reach any kind of real judgment on it, and that is, what I guess would be referred to as the Hawthorne effect. It is obviously different to those people, those families, that are included in a panel, than to those who are not. The effect over time of a longitudinal study, where you have people in a panel for long periods of time, could be very important it seems to me. It could distort the results and make it much more difficult, therefore, to extrapolate from what you found in your panel to reaction of the general population should the experimental program be adopted as a regular program of government, affecting all eligible families in the population.

One other final caution about experiments generally, and that is that I do worry about the extrapolation problem. As far as I know, we have not yet gone "national" with any of the programs that started in the 1960's and early 70's that were first set up as these carefully controlled experiments—the income maintenance, the housing allowance and the health studies that are now underway. I think that we must be very careful in extrapolating to a national program from these experimental programs, because it is clear that there are some features of those experiments that will not be replicated when you go national.

ABT: Lois-ellin Datta's presentation was a valuable case study. It raised in my mind a certain hunger for an answer to the question of what constitutes causation in decision-making, and in particular, I think it would be useful to have more research on what part of the variance in decision-making is attributable to the absorbed evaluation research results. It was noteworthy that her case study showed how many impacts of evaluation research are unintended, specifically in this case program recommendations rather than policy recommendations—

essentially, the evaluation being somewhat out of control of the sponsors, which I think should give sponsors some pause and might stimulate some new ways of dealing with the control of the course of an evaluation.

I would like to tell you a little anecdote I heard last night, relevant to her point of the understandability of the information produced by evaluation research for the policymaker. A member of this conference, an old acquaintance of mine, used to work for General DeGaulle and he ran into a cognitive dissonance problem briefing the General on the need for some educational reforms in Latin America. He had the General's ear. He worked directly for him for several months and was highly respected by him. But he felt that the educational land reforms that the French Government should propose would have to be explained to the peasants in Spanish. And at that point the General shut off. If it was not going to be explained in French, the General really was not interested in the program any more. And he absolutely failed to make any further impact on the General, because he had really violated the rules of avoiding cognitive dissonance at that point.

We have to recognize that policymakers are people like other people, and they have certain very specific constraints on their perceptions. If we violate those and introduce cognitive dissonance, the pain of that will probably be resolved in disfavor of the evaluation researcher. Now I do not think that should be implied to mean that you can only communicate results that are already believed. It is a question of the relative distance and how quickly you move your audience to the point you want to make. And I think Ms. Newman's point that the researcher, particularly the evaluation researcher, has the responsibility to educate his or her client is terribly important. We frequently see evaluation researchers doing what I think is essentially copping out of their obligations to educate their clients by essentially following the moving target of client-policy needs around, instead of having their independent view, or if they are more stubborn types insisting upon their own point of view, and saying: "Well, I cannot keep up with this moving target of policy requirements; I'll go off my own way, let the chips fall where they may, and if the policymaker does not like it, I am doing honest research and it is just too bad." Neither of those are really viable solutions. The first fails to preserve the integrity and independence of the evaluation effort; the second fails to communicate that independence in a useful way.

What is needed is a continuous education effort to cover the cognitive distance and dissonance between the evaluator and the consumer of evaluation research. Connie also made an important point about timeliness, and here I think a practical suggestion is in order. Most evaluation researchers do not know what constitutes timely reporting of findings, and I do not think it is enough to assume that the end of the contract constitutes timely reporting. There are requirements of interim findings, and it would be most helpful if some kind of decision schedule plus the lead time required for absorbing evaluation results were provided as part of work statements to evaluation performers.

Finally, the problem of understandability is usually not addressed in the initial planning of the evaluation effort because the form of communication is not specified. Many evaluation clients would never fund the work if they had any idea of the kind of report they were going to get. This surprise could be avoided if right at the start there was required the submission of a policy paper saying these are the kind of findings we would expect and here is the way we would present them, and if that presentation of findings was negotiated at the start.

Michael Scriven raised some fascinating issues of the worth of evaluations, and I would like to suggest quickly six different ways of estimating the worth of evaluation, some of which overlap his.

- First, we might argue that evaluations are worth their market worth, i.e., what is paid for them—the accounting concept. Unfortunately, this does not reflect concepts of efficiency. Some things are worth less than paid for, because they are no good. Some things are worth more, because there is a consumer surplus generated, which brings us to the second method of establishing the work of an evaluation.

- Second, cost plus the consumer surplus, i.e., the difference between what it cost to produce and what the consumer would be willing to pay for it. What the consumer would be willing to pay for it is often a psychological concept, but conceivably for a rational consumer would be the opportunity cost of bad decisions avoided.

- Third is the direct benefit/cost return, the savings from better decision making which leaves us the problem of estimating the savings from better decision making.

- Fourth is to estimate the savings from better decision making and include the systems effects as well, with the indirect feedbacks that are involved.

- Fifth is shadow-pricing, essentially on the basis of the imputed price on the part of the decision-makers for the evaluation research in terms of the opportunity cost of that research to them. This opportunity cost is often much greater than the actual price of the research in terms of the time wasted, in terms of the administrative gyrations that are gone through, and the risks. We need to track some kind of expected value of the cost of a bad outcome, and the probability of that is a measure of risk here.

- Sixth is the use of some percentage efficiency of an ideal of evaluation efficacy, perhaps multiplied by some percentage of the ideal impact, as the market worth of that impact where the constituency is affected.

These are some ways of looking at the worth of evaluations and the budgeting problem. Another issue suggested by Professor Scriven was that of internalizing the currently externalized cost of evaluation, which I think is a general problem of internalizing externalized costs of various kinds of enterprises, and thereby confounding the correct evaluation of their payoffs. And finally, there was a suggestion of meta evaluation and the strategic mix.

Dr. Zinberg mentioned the psychological dimensions as being somewhat understated, with which I am very sympathetic, particularly the moving target nature of the psychological forces that affect both the subject of evaluation and the way it is carried out. I believe this requires some formative and process evaluation accompanying whatever summative evaluations we do, and the use of frequent crude measurements rather than infrequent precise measurements. It is a well-known finding of control theory that in goal-seeking behavior of a homing kind of system we get much more accurate seeking of a particular goal by frequent crude corrections of direction than by infrequent very precise ones. That implies some use of formative in-process evaluation, or at least summative evaluations chopped up into as many multiple stages as possible to feed into each other.

One method of solving the problem of getting value-free evaluations is to select two alternatively biased evaluations or evaluation teams. We might think here of adversary evaluators, somewhat in the role of adversary planners, and then perhaps attempt value-free evaluations of those two evaluations. In other words, get rid of the pretense of value-free evaluation and try and develop balanced biases.

Finally, the whole question of overall evaluation strategy that Alice Rivlin and Bill Capron referred to suggests the possibility of some other forms of overall evaluation allocation strategy to maximize payoff, meta-strategy if you will. First of all, the randomized selection of evaluation targets themselves may be something useful against our biases. The trouble here is that we may miss some high impact evaluation requirements. A second one would be to do uniform application of evaluation to all major programs, but here we run into the problem of limited resources or perhaps not having the necessary critical mass to address each of the relevant problems in sufficient depth. Probably in the long-term, the optimal strategy, if we had but the data necessary to apply it, would be to equalize the marginal utilities of a spectrum of evaluations with respect to the evaluation impacts. That requires some utility input or measurement of the relative worth of the different kinds of evaluations that we have discussed.

IV

RESEARCH VERSUS DECISION REQUIREMENTS AND BEST PRACTICES OF EVALUATION

TOWARD AVOIDING THE GOAL-TRAP IN EVALUATION RESEARCH[1]

Irwin Deutscher
Department of Sociology
The University of Akron

It is the purpose of this paper to discuss means which may be helpful in implementing two value assumptions. If one does not concur in either of these assumptions, much of the paper will not make sense. If one does concur in both assumptions, some of the paper may make some sense. I assume, first, that it is desirable to determine the consequences of deliberate efforts to alter ongoing social processes—educational, health, welfare or whatever—and to do so in as detached a manner as is possible. This determination is what I intend by the phrase "program evaluation." My second assumption is that a major criterion of the success of program evaluation is the extent to which it is taken into account in altering program policy, administration, or practice.

A CUE FROM ORGANIZATIONAL THEORY

I take as my point of departure, a cue provided by organizational theory and developed by Robert Bogdan (1972). From monographs published in the Chicago tradition during the early decades of this century to more recent organizational analyses such as those by Becker et al. (1968), Gouldner (1968), and Blau (1955), it seems that organizations are rarely what they pretend to be. The distinction between the formal and the informal or the stated and the real is made in various ways, but it is always made. Organizational theory suggests that the structure, the processes, and the goals of any organization must be assumed to vary in fact from their descriptions.

How organizations are built, what they do, and the consequences of this structure and process are frequently quite different from formal or public statements about such matters. In exploring how "original goals become bastardized," Bogdan observes that goal displacement is a key concept (Merton, 1957; Michels, 1959; Clark, 1956), while efforts to understand how organizations change their goals find the idea of goal succession most useful (Sills, 1957; Blau and Scott, 1961; Thompson and McEwen, 1958).

I have emphasized the likelihood of discrepancy between formal goals and actual goals, because it is at that point that these observations from organizational theory become central to program evaluation.[2] Partly because we live in an achievement-oriented society, partly because of the demands of funding agencies, and partly as a consequence of intimidation of program personnel by evaluators, a sometimes unwarranted and frequently unrealistic emphasis on program goals develops. Etzioni (1960) long ago noted the need for policy research to take account of the "illusory quality" of organizational goals. As a society, we tend to assume that there is no better way to judge the merits of an organization than by evaluating its output. If one hopes to obtain funds for a program, one must be able to specify what the program intends to achieve. If one is going to evaluate a program, then it is necessary to isolate precise and measureable goals in order to provide indexes of the "successes" of that program.

Peter Rossi reflects this position when he writes that ". . . any program which does not have clearly specified goals cannot be evaluated without specifying some measureable goals. This statement is obvious enough to be a truism." (Rossi and Williams, 1972, p. 18). I find the statement neither obvious nor true. Rather, it reflects what in my review of the theoretical and methodological literature in evaluation research I have come to think of as the goal-trap. Taking the opposite position from Rossi, Schulberg and Baker (1968) argue that there are two basic models of evaluation, goal attainment and systems. They suggest that the systems model provides a much better opportunity for implementation of the research findings. Although I applaud their search for alternatives to the goal-attainment model, I do not concur in the belief that systems analysis is the only one. In this paper I will suggest another.

In moving from organizational theory to a discussion of the goal trap, I would conclude with Bogdan (1972:37) that:

> It might be useful to think of a large number of organizational types as expressive rather than instrumental: they allow societies to act out their beliefs which may be unworkable in reality. Measures of success may serve the myth of the instrumental nature of organizations as well as myths societies hold in regard to the nature of certain problems.

THE GOAL TRAP

Unlike most traps, this one must ensnare the trapper as well as the victim. It is to be expected that funding agencies should be as much a captive of our societal achievement orientation as anyone else, and this is as true outside of government as within. In these post-MacNamara years of rational program accounting, it becomes necessary to know not only how money is being spent, but what the precise benefits of that expenditure are. It is not enough for competent and well-intended people to purport to be doing good, no matter how well they account for their expenditures. It is also necessary to know how much good they are doing. Efforts to deal with that question trap both the program people and the funding agencies.

In order for a proposed program to be funded, it must state clearly what it intends to do, how long it will take, how much of what kinds of personnel are needed, and how much it will cost. Let us leave aside, for the moment, proposals to continue ongoing programs and concentrate on proposals to create novel, innovative types of interventions. It is with the evaluation of such new programs that I am primarily concerned, and it is precisely such programs which are least likely to be specific about what they are attempting to do, how they intend to go about it, how much it will cost, etc. To the extent that their staff and management are creative and the program is indeed something new and different, there must inevitably be a great deal of flexibility—of winging it as the program and its problems develop. Competent program people understand this. Sometimes they also understand precisely what they are trying to do, but are rarely able to articulate it in the manner funding agencies require.

As a result of these conditions, program people feel that they must lie to funding people in order to meet the criteria required for a proposal to be funded. Sometimes they never intend to do what the proposal claims, but more often they begin by trying and end up by doing something that seems worthwhile to them even though it has nothing to do with the proposal which was funded. One of the officers in the job training program evaluated by Bogdan is openly cynical (1972, 35-36):

> You know what they do with a proposal after (a training program) gets started, they turn it face down on the desk and never look at it . . . Just as long as you write a nice neat package, just as long as it looks like its going to work all right. They just assume it works that way. Write how many hours the trainees are going to do this, how much they are going to do that. Just a lot of bullshit. But they can pay people to write these things up . . .

The result of such phony proposals is phantom programs. As Freeman and Sherwood put it (1965: 272): "To say that a program fails when it is not truly implemented is indeed misguided." Hyman and Wright (1967: 187-188) are equally straightforward: "Taking the word for the deed, an evaluator may try to observe the effects of a nonexistent treatment . . . Where a program has no input, no output . . . can ensue." And Rossi, discussing support for schools under Title I, notes (Rossi and Williams, 1972: 40) "the problem of 'nonprojects'." Reading a paper in 1966, Carol Weiss said that (1971: 138):

> Evaluators usually accept the description of the program given by practitioners as sufficient. They rarely attempt to . . . monitor its operation so that there is confidence that the program as officially described actually took place . . . It is possible that the evaluation is attributing the observed effects (or 'no effects') to a phantom program.

She finds no reason to alter her opinion seven years later (1973: 44): "Among the many reasons for the negative pall of evaluation results is that studies have accepted bloated promises and political rhetoric as authentic program goals."

It is a foolish evaluator indeed who attempts to study a program in terms of the goals which it proposed in order to get funded. Such an evaluation is most likely to show no effect as well as to alienate all parties involved. I doubt that this happens very often since I prefer to believe that most evaluators are not foolish. Evaluators probably do not generally fall into the goal-traps created by the demands of funding agencies; they are more likely to fall into those of their own making.

If it is necessary to provide an accounting for the effectiveness of a program, the evaluator usually feels that he must identify goals so that he can measure the extent to which the program appears to be achieving them. In fact, many distinguished evaluation researchers define program evaluation, as Rossi has, in terms of measurement of program goals (e.g., Brooks, 1965:51; Greenberg, 1968:155; Suchman, 1969:44). Most recently, Bernstein, Rieker, and Freeman (1973:51) insist that "the crux of evaluative research is the assessment of the degree to which the program . . . has achieved its specified goals . . ."

Frequently then the first task attempted by the evaluator is to specify measureable program goals. This may not be unreasonable except that just as frequently program people do not think in terms of specific measureable goals. They are trying to make the sick healthy, or the poor rich, or the ignorant wise. Furthermore, they may believe that their experience, their commitment, and their competence combine to provide them with an opportunity to achieve such desirable ends. And they may be correct, a matter to which I will return in the discussion of avoiding the goal-trap.

In pursuit of a clearcut evaluation design and the selection of appropriate measuring instruments, the evaluator is relentless in his quest for specific goals. He has to have something to measure and it must be something that is measurable. He scans the proposal; he interviews the administrator; he may even "have to observe some programs in order to identify what the objectives are" (Cain and Hollister, 1972:114). From such sources he evolves program goals. If they are not immediately apparent, he hounds program people: "Is this a goal?" "or this?" "or this?" As Freeman and Sherwood have put it (1965:268), those responsible for program design must be "forced" to specify clearly their objectives. Program people may resist at first, but eventually intimidated by the evaluators relentless pursuit of something he can measure, they will break down and weakly allow that such and such may be a goal: "I guess you could say that is one of our goals." The end result of this process is that, more often than not, the program is evaluated in terms of marginal goals which are unlikely to be achieved (if for no other reason, because no one is very serious about them) and are likely to be denied their legitimacy when the evaluator finally reports that the program does not seem to make any difference.

It may be that there are some kinds of programs where the goals are eminently clear and all interested parties are in accord regarding them. Pamela Krochalk, for example, has suggested to me that the goals of job training programs are perfectly clear. She is echoed by Peter Rossi (Rossi and Williams, 1972:18):

> Not all social welfare programs suffered to the same extent from ambiguity in the setting of goals. At the one extreme, manpower retraining programs were among the most clearly defined: A manpower retraining program is effective to the extent that it manages to impart marketable occupational skill.

But it was just such programs which Bogdan was studying when he drafted his provocative query on the theoretical viability of organizational goals (1972), and he provides a wide range of quantitative estimates of the success of the program. These estimates are all accurate enough even though some indicate tragic failure while others indicate massive success. The difference derives from subtle differences in the definition of program goals. Lerman (1968), although discussing delinquency control programs, makes the same point as Bogdan: "It all depends on how you count!" Goldstein, Hull, and Ostrander (1973) raise a series of related questions about job training. For example, if people are well trained for jobs which do not exist, is the program a success? Finally, Campbell considers some of the distorting factors which can occur in the definition of success of a training program (1969: 257).

Before turning to ways of avoiding the goal-trap, let me make an observation on the somewhat different consequences which can arise from the imposition of goals on ongoing programs (in contrast with innovative, experimental, or otherwise novel ones). Bogdan (1972:32), hitting close to home, says that measures of success are like the programs for professional meetings; they are something concrete in spite of the fact that they are largely irrelevant to what goes on. Although this may be true for novel programs, the reverse is possible for ongoing programs; the imposed measure of success can become the program's goal! Becker and his colleagues (1968) have documented the manner in which academic grades become transformed from a means of measuring academic success to ends in themselves. The prime aim of college students becomes not to get educated, but to make reasonably good grades. In a recent interview, (Salasin, 1973:12) Don Campbell has argued that the goals of people and of organizations can be changed when quantitative criteria of success are demanded. He suggests, for example, that the MacNamara PPBS system may have been self-sabotaging:

> By requiring quantitative statements of goals and quantitative reporting on how well they were met, PPBS probably increased rather than decreased the dishonesty of annual reports. These were inappropriate requirements for many, many agencies, probably for most agencies.

Campbell's prime example is the imposition of the criterion of a body count in Viet Nam in an effort to overcome the typically inflated estimates of enemy dead. The result of this neat quantitative index was to encourage the creation of bodies. Campbell suggests that this emerges as a new military goal. Lt. Calley was engaged in the legitimized military goal of getting bodies to count. Measures of success can and do become reified.

TOWARD AVOIDING THE GOAL TRAP

If the results of program evaluations are to be taken into account by practitioners, administrators, or policymakers, these results cannot be derived from phantom programs or spurious goals. Rossi (1969:99) mentions the "wonderfully varied ways in which practitioners and administrators welch on evaluation."

> Most often of all, it is 'discovered' (after finding negative results) that the 'real' goals of the social action program in question were not the goals that were being evaluated in the research after all.

Although tinged with a bit of sarcasm and implying that it is the program people who are at fault, Rossi's essential point is nevertheless true. In a more constructive vein, Carol Weiss (1973:40) states that "one of the reasons that evaluations are so readily disregarded is that they address only official goals." She goes on to suggest that it might be useful to assess other kinds of goals if the evaluation is to be taken seriously by decision-makers. Evaluations must be credible—they must make sense to those who could act upon them. If evaluations are not credible and thus not taken into account in decision-making processes, then there is no sense in doing them. Avoiding the goal-trap increases the probability of credible and useful evaluation research. In this section I will suggest three ways in which the trap may be avoided. They are presented in order from the most desirable to the least and, I suspect, in reverse order of their immediate feasibility.

1. *Input-Output vs. Social Process*. The ideal method of avoiding the goal-trap is to find alternative ways of thinking about evaluation—ways which do not hinge on measurable output and thus do not demand the identification of specific goals. Although it would require a terrible wrenching of our customary ways of thinking, it might be desirable to view success or failure in terms of process rather than of input and output. As Angrist puts it (1973:15): "The input-output model is not enough; what we need to keep track of is what happens in the black box." By "process," I do not intend the distinction sometimes made in evaluation research between studying a program's ouput and studying the functioning of the program organization. It is in this inaccurate sense that Cain and Hollister (1972: 110), for example, define process analysis as "mainly administrative monitoring." Nor do I intend by "process analysis" the procedure of systems analysis which is sometimes usefully employed in the study of organizations. What I do intend is that we alter the syntax of our evaluation questions, shifting from the past tense, "What happened?" to the present progressive, "What is happening?"

This syntactic shift carries with it a methodological shift. Exploring the relationships between input and output involves analysis of the relationship between independent and dependent variables. Exploring the process involves analysis of an ongoing social act—one which is seen as constantly in flux and constantly amenable to new definitions of the social situation. The act has no end except perhaps the mortality of the actor.[3] Herbert Blumer (1956) has provided the theoretical groundwork for such process analysis, and I have tried to elaborate his position as a basis for understanding attitudinal and behavioral change (1973, Ch. 11). It is precisely such change which I believe most intervention programs are all about. There are pressing methodological questions which accompany this theoretical position and the methodological solutions remain largely to be worked out. I believe the problems are soluble and I intend to address them over the next few years. I hope I am not alone in this task.[4]

Some clues close to home for the evaluation researchers can be found in the critique provided by Weiss and Rein which addresses

Broad-aim programs (1969), Guttentag's (1973) plea for attention to neglected intervening processes, or the more general cautionary advice provided by Mushkin (1973).[5] Scholars who customarily deal with developmental processes easily detect the inherent problems of output analyses in evaluation research. McDill, McDill and Sprehe (1972:159) relegate to a footnote this critical comment by H. Zimiles (1970):

> A more general criticism of measures of criterion variables for all preschool compensatory education programs has been leveled by Zimiles. His indictment has to do with a lack of knowledge base concerning the cognitive growth of young children which fosters an emphasis on "outcome" evaluation rather than "processual" evaluation; i.e., assessment of the cognitive processes and related personality variables which mediate and support the child's intellectual functioning at any given point in time.

Even the interrupted time series design, one of the quasi-experimental approaches advocated by Campbell (1969:247), takes into account the processual quality of social change. Another useful cue is provided by the concept of marginality which, as important as it is to comparative evaluations, seems to be taken seriously by no one but a few economists. Glennan provides a simple, persuasive, and graphic argument for the need to follow a program through time in an effort to determine at what point its incremental increases become marginal. His provision of a second hypothetical program which is discovered to be a slow starter with massive payoffs at later stages illustrates the dramatic errors which are possible when programs are viewed with an inadequate time perspective (Glennan, 1972:192-193).

Campbell, employing the term "process analysis" as I do, comments on the Weiss and Rein position. I think the comment is important because it raises an issue in my mind about what constitutes experimentation:

> Let me discuss process evaluation in general. What we need first are some clear-cut examples. At present, those such as Weiss and Rein who hold up process evaluation as an alternative may be making an argument in favor of common sense knowing, in which case I agree with them. Or, they may be arguing that we should not pretend we can do outcome evaluation when we can't, in which case I agree with them. But if they are arguing for an alternative that is as good as or superior to experimental design, then I have got to wait for an example to see whether or not I feel it would have been strengthened with more attention to experimental design. (Salasin, 1973:10)

I fail to understand what the logic of experimental design has to do with whether or not one chooses to undertake output (variable) analysis or process analysis. My emphasis on social process and the suggestion to seek alternative methodologies to conventional variable analysis in no way implies an abandonment of experimental methodology. I know of no better logic for establishing the fact that a program makes a difference from no program at all or from other programs.

There is, however, a difference between experimental methodology—a logic of procedure—and current experimental techniques. Although present techniques seem to imply the manipulation of static variables, employing doubtful measures of unlikely goals, this is not inherent in the logic of experimentation. One can think experimentally in any effort to establish causation by comparing any two or more phenomena through time. The data employed in those comparisons can be of any type. Max Weber employed experimental logic in his turn of the century comparative studies of religion, using ethnographic and historical data. Furthermore, as Weber illustrates, such designs need not be post-factum. One may entertain hypotheses concerning the expected nature of the world without a given historical event (such as the existence of the Protestant Ethic) and then seek out comparative societies which did not experience that event. Such societies may be located at some distant point in space or in time.

2. *Being Attentive to the Unintended.* If we do alter our syntax and ask what is happening rather than what happened, are we not dealing with a loaded question? After all, when we ask what happened and test a null hypothesis, our very methods force us to consider the likelihood that nothing happened. In fact, this is frequently the conclusion reached from rigorously designed evaluation research. Process analysis does pose a loaded question! It assumes that any effort to intervene in ongoing social processes will somehow and to some degree alter those processes. Programs, as we know them, comprise such deliberate efforts to intervene. This assumption renders nonsensical a question like "did anything happen?" and rules out as logically and empirically impossible a conclusion such as "nothing happened." By assuming that something is changing as a consequence of the program, our major research effort shifts from preordained goals to the discovery of processual consequences. One evaluation researcher states this assumption in a context of the constraints of organizational structure (Angrist, 1973:11):

At times . . . I despair and conclude that nothing helps, no remedy cures, no program changes people, no spending is justified. At such times, I mentally review what as social scientists we well know: that specific social contexts do have noticeable consequences. We take for granted . . . that social classes, ethnic and religious groups differentially shape their members; that prisons and mental hospitals mold their inmates; that boarding schools, colleges and sororities influence their recruits; that organizational structure constrains its functionaries.

The quest for program consequences can follow the conceptual guidelines provided by Merton (1957). When we ask, "what is happening," we are guided by several correlaries to the question: What is happening that was intended? What is happening that was not intended? Furthermore, what unintended consequences of the program were also unanticipated? It is these unanticipated consequences of the program which demand the greatest sensitivity of the evaluator. The unintended may be anticipated, but the unanticipated must be mysterious.

I cannot at this time provide any systematic guidelines for the discovery of *unanticipated* consequences, but the New Jersey Income Maintenance Experiment illustrates how *unintended* consequences can inform program evaluation. Rossi (1974) describes how the gravest concerns of dubious Congressmen are related to fears that income maintenance will result in a loss of interest in work on the part of those being maintained. Apparently there is little disagreement concerning the intended consequences of Income Maintenance; it is the unintended ones that are troublesome.[6] The investigators appropriately address themselves to such issues, for example by testing the hypothesis that there is no difference between the experimental and control groups in earned income after the introduction of minimum income levels into the experimental group. The failure to find sufficient evidence to reject this null hypothesis ought to help relieve the anxieties of opponents to the program. This evaluation of unintended consequences is more likely to have an impact on policy than would an evaluation of the intended consequences. A fringe benefit from the point of view of program proponents is that the testing of null hypotheses concerning undesirable consequences of a program reverses the burden of proof. For a change the conservative bias of tests of significance is working on the side of program advocates instead of against them. It is, as Rossi puts it, a case of "No Bananas Again," but this time it is the good guys who do not like bananas.

Although rarely giving them much emphasis, evaluation researchers sometimes reflect awareness of one or another kind of unintended program consequences. Cain and Hollister (1972:128-129) write of "third party effects"—those which affect other than the intended population. They mention negative as well as positive third party effects in youth training and job training programs. Greenberg (1968:163) discusses "side effects" of contraceptive devices and drugs—both desirable and undesirable. Heberlein (1973:3-4) considers "second order unplanned effects" of flood control efforts. While Suchman (1969:44) was concerned with unanticipated negative consequences, Mushkin (1973:33) writes of our neglect of the "side-benefits" inherent in some programs and Angrist (1973:5,7,14) elaborates on desirable but unintended program consequences of the introduction of evaluation research itself—the matter of reactivity which, important as it is, cannot be considered here.

Well over a decade ago, Hyman and Wright (1962) saw as one of the "major aspects" of evaluation research, "The conceptualization and measurement of . . . unanticipated relevant outcomes." A few years later they continue to argue the importance of such outcomes, employing Reiken's evaluation of a summer work camp as an example (Hyman and Wright, 1967:202-203). Nor do they believe it impossible to anticipate the unanticipated:

> Familiarity with previous studies of similar action programs and general scientific knowledge about the area involved—whether delinquency, attitudinal change, or voting behavior—can unlock the door to many of the relevant conceptualizations of unexpected results.

Houston (1972:61) observes that, "Evaluation studies are notorious for appending to negative results the assertion that effects were unquestionably produced, but that no provision was made for their measurement." He recommends pilot studies and fractional designs which permit examination of a large number of factors. But it is Don Campbell who seems to pursue the problem and its solution with the greatest deliberation. In a paper read at a professional meeting, (1971:54) he suggested that criticism focused "on past ameliorative efforts such as slum clearance, high-rise tenaments, aid to dependent children, automation, and the like, can generate an explicit list of noxious values, possible pernicious side-effects to be measured just in case they might be among the effects of a specific program." In a more recent interview (Salasin, 1973:12), Campbell says:

> I think if we regularly made it our business to interview the opponents of every new program ... we could get a list of feared undesirable side-effects ... By interviewing the people who oppose the program, brainstorming with them about possible indicators of their fears, we could do much better than we do now about setting in motion indicators that might pick up some of the anticipatable, understandable side-effects.

Although a shift in thinking from "goals" to "processes" might be the most desirable solution to the goal trap and a greater emphasis on unintended program consequences would be helpful, there is another possible solution which does not require such a great departure from our conventional modes of thinking about program evaluation. The procedure, although relatively simple and not novel, is costly in terms of time. I think it is worth it. Let us consider in the concluding section of this paper, the possibility of negotiating various alternative scenarios in a search for more meaningful program goals.

3. *Negotiating a Scenario.* Suppose that, rather than intimidating practitioners or administrators into confessing their goals (since they frequently cannot articulate them anyway), the evaluator joined with these people in a mutual effort to search out reasonable program goals and reasonable methods for assessing them? On the basis of his experience with the New Jersey Negative Income Tax Experiment, Kershaw (1972:226) recommends that, "Getting as many local people as possible to lose interest in the operation should be a primary goal." I am suggesting the reverse. I am not proposing the old fashioned social work game of conning people into feeling that they own part of the operation—that it is theirs, when in fact, they do not own it at all and it is not theirs. That kind of deception may be useful in temporarily gaining needed cooperation, but what is proposed here is a mutual endeavor, in which in fact, all parties have serious input. Such a negotiation can result in the identification of goals which all parties find acceptable and thus improve the probability that the results of the evaluation will also be acceptable to all parties. And, as Carol Weiss has pointed out (1971:141), there are fringe benefits:

> Not only does their participation (administrators and practitioners) help in the definition of evaluation goals and the maintenance of study procedures, but it may help change the image of evaluation from "critical spying" to collaborative effort to understand and improve.

To those who insist that there can be no negotiating of reality, that it is the *real* goals which must be assessed rather than the results of some political process, I would point out that "the decisions about program design . . . have usually been based upon (among other things) political bargaining" (Glennan, 1972:188). Mushkin (1973:32) writes that "objectives of social programs often are clouded by compromises along the path toward legislative enactment." Weiss has argued that the creation of programs and their evaluation is inherently the consequence of extensive give and take.

Perhaps more important is the fact that much of what we consider to be "reality" is the consequence of negotiations among interested parties. Recent introduction into the common parlance of the phrase "plea bargaining," has made it eminently clear that what crimes were committed by what persons is a matter which is negotiated between the defense and the prosecution with the assistance of the judge. Criminologists have always been aware of this element in the social creation of criminal statistics (Newman, 1966:76-330). The same order of social construction of data has been documented in clinic records (Garfinkel, 1967:186-207), suicide (Douglas, 1967), medical statistics (Rysman, 1973), welfare data (Beck, 1970), and generally in any kind of official statistics (Kitsuse and Cicourel, 1963).

It would be a mistake to consider these as instances of fudging data. These data are a negotiated reflection of a social order which they are at least in part responsible for creating. They are accurate. They do reflect reality. There are, of course, other sets of equally accurate data dealing with the same kinds of phenomena which also reflect reality, but then there are many realities. The negotiating of medical diagnoses has been documented in dealings between doctor and patient in a tuberculosis sanitarium (Roth, 1963) as well as in psychiatric interviews, both in America (Scheff, 1968) and in Britain (Herne, 1972) in which careful bargaining on the precise nature of the diagnosis appears to occur. In many areas, reality is little more than what interested parties can agree it is. Why not in the area of defining goals for the evaluation of programs?

The germ of the idea of negotiation is found from time to time in the literature. Rossi once suggested (1969:98-99) that action alternatives be developed for both contingencies—positive and negative findings. He believes that the development of such action alternatives enhances the commitment on the part of administrators and practitioners to alternative plans of action. Some years later, Glennan (1972:191) observed that planning decisions are the result of a complex bargaining process and that this is the way it should be. He too proposes a contingency analysis before the start of an evaluation: "If the evaluator and the planner were to sit down and ask what will happen if the results show one thing as opposed to another, the quality of evaluation would improve, its relevance would increase and its results would be more likely to be used" (p. 215).

The transition of these ideas from the application of evaluations to the discovery of goals is made by Cain and Hollister (1972) who talk about "search-evaluation." They argue that the first stages of an evaluation must involve a search for the objectives of the program: "The attempt to follow the usual dogma of evaluation, starting with the definition of a single objective—or a hierarchy of objectives—for the program, are bound to fail" (p. 114). Harper and Babigian propose an extensive negotiation aimed at the decision-making process. They begin by exploring with the administrator the whole range of possible recommendations as the first step in designing the evaluation. They then struggle together to find reasonable answers to such questions as:

> What kinds of data or information will lead to one or another of these decisions? and how does the evaluator obtain the best data that will enable the administrator to decide between making no change and making one of several possible changes (Harper and Babigian, 1971:152)?

If we extend their limited concept of an evaluator-administrator interaction so that it includes other relevant parties and if we extend the negotiable issues to include program goals and their measurement, then what follows is precisely what I mean by negotiating scenarios:

> The administrator and the evaluator should imagine themselves doing the evaluation and think through to its end—conjuring up possible sets of data or results and then making imaginary decisions based on the imaginary but alternative sets of data (Harper and Babigian, 1971:152).

These cues suggest to me that it is desirable for the evaluator to begin to learn what program people are trying to do by watching them do it and listening to them talk about it—in situ! There is a cumulating body of evidence from sociolinguistics that if one listens to people talk about what they are doing while they are doing it, chances of understanding the activity are maximized. An example of this principle applied to evaluation can be found in Wieder's study of a halfway house for drug addicts (1973).[7]

Experienced and competent practitioners (and I do not imply that all practitioners fall into that category) can be assumed to know what they are trying to do even though they may not be able to articulate those goals. Part of the evaluator's task then is to discover what in fact is being attempted. After watching and listening he will begin to speculate about what is happening and can then begin to engage practitioners or administrators in a dialogue in an effort to negotiate the reality of the situation. Alternative scenarios can be drawn, employing different conceptions of goals, different measuring devices, and alternative conclusions. Such scenarios can be negotiated one by one with the program people until reasonable agreement is reached as to goals, means of measuring them, and the credibility of alternative conclusions. This kind of involvement, as difficult and time consuming as it may be, will go a long way toward increasing the probability that practitioners, administrators, and policymakers will seriously take into account the findings of evaluation research. And that, after all, is what it is all about.

NOTES

1. This paper will appear in slightly revised form in Francis G. Caro (ed.), *Readings in Evaluation Research*. Russell Sage Foundation, 2nd ed. 1976 (forthcoming).

2. I do not intend to suggest that this is the only relevant facet of organizational theory in program evaluation. Systems theory, for example, with its concept of feedback loops, provides a built-in assurance that the evaluator will consider the reactive elements of the evaluation per se in the functioning of the program. However, as I have argued elsewhere (1974), it is toward social psychological theory that one must turn for guidelines in program development.

3. I say, "perhaps," since the influence of an actor and his actions generally transcends his death. As an extreme example, it may be that the most immortal action of the suicide is his suicide.

4. Blumer himself is working on the closely related problem of social indicators (Kesiel and Blumer, 1973).

5. I suspect that Robert A. Dentler's "The Phenomenology of the Evaluation Researcher" might inform this discussion, but I have not been able to obtain a copy and it remains unpublished since Rossi and Williams chose not to include it in their volume containing papers from the conference where it was presented (Rossi and Williams, 1972). Rossi discussed the Dentler paper on pp. 36-38.

6. In an earlier historical review, Rossi (1972:17) observes that the grounds for attacks on New Deal programs frequently had to do with "negative side effects."

7. Extensive references and some discussion of this issue can be found in Chapter 7 of Deutscher (1973). A comprehensive review of modern literature on sociolinguistics has been provided by Grimshaw (1973 and 1974).

REFERENCES

Angrist, Shirley S.
　　1973 "Limitations of Evaluation Research or Why 'No Effects'?" Pittsburgh: Carnegie-Mellon University, School of Public Affairs, Mimeographed.
Beck, Bernard
　　1970 "Cooking Welfare Stew." in Robert W. Habenstein (ed.), *Pathways to Data: Field Methods For Studying Ongoing Social Organization.* Chicago: Aldine Publishing Company.
Becker, Howard S., Blanche Geer, and Everett C. Hughes
　　1968 *Making the Grade: The Academic Side of College Life.* New York: John Wiley and Sons.
Bernstein, Ilene H., Patricia P. Rieker, and Howard E. Freeman
　　1973 "A Review of Evaluation Research: The State of the Art, Methodological Practices, and Dissemination of Research Findings." Presented at the American Sociological Association Meetings, New York.
Blau, Peter
　　1955 *The Dynamics of Bureaucracy.* Chicago: University of Chicago Press.
Blau, Peter and W. Richard Scott
　　1961 *Formal Organizations.* San Francisco: Chandler Publishing Co.
Blumer, Herbert
　　1956 "Sociological Analysis and the Variable." *American Sociological Review* 21: 683-690.
Bogdan, Robert
　　1972 "Organizational Goals and Success Measurement in a Job-Training Program." Syracuse: Syracuse University, Center on Human Policy, Mimeographed.
Brooks, Michael P.
　　1965 "The Community Action Program as a Setting for Applied Research." *Journal of Social Issues* 21: 29-40*

Cain, Glen G. and Robinson G. Hollister
   1972 "The Methodology of Evaluating Social Action Programs." in Peter H.
        Rossi and Walter Williams, pp. 109-137.
Campbell, Donald T.
   1969 "Reforms as Experiments." *American Psychologist* 24: 409-429.*
   1971 "Methods for the Experimenting Society." Presented at the Eastern
        Psychological Association, Washington, D.C., Mimeographed (Forth-
        coming in American Psychologist).
Caro, Francis G.
   1971 *Readings in Evaluation Research.* New York: Russell Sage Foundation.
Clark, Burton
   1956 "Organizational Adaptation and Precarious Values." *American Socio-
        logical Review,* 21: 327-336.
Deutscher, Irwin
   1973 *What We Say/What We Do: Sentiments and Acts.* Glenview, Ill.: Scott,
        Foresman and Company.
   1974 "Social Theory and Program Evaluation: A Metatheoretical Note."
        Cleveland: Case Western Reserve University, Department of Sociology,
        Mimeographed.
Douglas, Jack D.
   1967 *The Social Meaning of Suicide.* Princeton: Princeton University Press.
Etzioni, Amitai
   1960 "Two Approaches to Organizational Analysis." *Administrative Science
        Quarterly,* 5: 257-78.
Freeman, Howard E. and Clarence C. Sherwood
   1965 "Research in Large-Scale Intervention Programs." *The Journal of Social
        Issues* 21: 11-28.*
Garfinkel, Harold
   1967 *Studies in Ethnomethodology.* Englewood Cliffs, N.J.: Prentice-Hall
        (Chapter 6): 186-207.
Glennan, Thomas K., Jr.
   1972 "Evaluating Federal Manpower Programs: Notes and Observations." pp.
        187-220 in Peter H. Rossi and Walter Williams (1972).
Goldstein, Paul, Donald Hull, and Susan Ostrander
   1973 "The Evaluation of Urban Ameliorative Projects: Case Studies and
        Integrating Framework." Presented at the North Central Sociological
        Association Meetings, Cincinnati.
Gouldner, Alvin W.
   1968 "Organizational Analysis." pp. 400-28 in Robert Merton, et al. (eds.),
        Sociology Today. New York: Basic Books.
Greenberg, B.G.
   1968 "Evaluation of Social Programs." *Review of the International Statistical
        Institute,* 36: 260-77.*
Grimshaw, Allen D.
   1973 "On Language in Society: Part I." Contemporary Sociology, 2: 578-85.
   1974 "On Language in Society: Part II." Contemporary Sociology, 3: 3-11.

Guttentag, Marcia
1973 "Subjectivity and its Use in Evaluation Research." *Evaluation,* 1: 60-5.
Harper, Dean and Hartouton Babigian
1971 "Evaluation Research: The Consequences of Program Evaluation."
Mental Hygiene, 55: 151-6.
Heberlein, Thomas A.
1973 "The Three Fixes: Technological, Cognitive, and Structural." Presented
at the Water and Community Conference, Seattle, Mimeographed.
Houston, Tom R., Jr.
1972 "The Behavioral Sciences Impact-Effectiveness Model." pp. 51-65 in
Peter Rossi and Walter Williams (1972).
Hyman, Herbert H., Charles R. Wright, and Terence K. Hopkins
1967 *Applications of Methods of Evaluations: Four Studies of the Encamp-
ment for Citizenship.* Berkeley: University of California Press.
Kershaw, David N.
1972 "Issues in Income Maintenance Experimentation." pp. 221-45 in Peter
Rossi and Walter Williams (1972).
Kitsuse, John L. and Aaron V. Cicourel
1963 "A Note on the Use of Official Statistics." *Social Problems,* 11: 131-9.
Lerman, Paul
1968 "Evaluative Studies of Institutions for Delinquents: Implications for
Research and Social Policy." *Social Work,* 13: 55-64.*
McDill, Edward L., Mary S. McDill, and J. Timothy Sprehe
1972 "Evaluation in Practice: Compensatory Education." pp. 141-85 in Peter
Rossi and Walter Williams (1972).
Merton, Robert K.
1957 *Social Theory and Social Structure.* Glencoe, Ill.: The Free Press.
Michels, Robert
1959 *Political Parties.* New York: Dover Press.
Mushkin, Selma J.
1973 "Evaluations: Use with Caution." *Evaluation,* 1: 31-5.
Newman, Donald J.
1966 *Conviction: The Determination of Guilt or Innocence Without Trial.*
Boston: Little, Brown & Co. (Part III).
Rossi, Peter
1969 "Evaluating Educational Programs." *The Urban Review,* 3: 17-18.*
1972 "Testing for Success and Failure in Social Action." pp. 11-49 in Peter
Rossi and Walter Williams (1972).
1974 "No Bananas Again: The Non-Results of the New Jersey Income
Maintenance Experiment." Presented at Colloquia on Evaluation of
Policy Oriented Social Programs, University of California, Los Angeles.
Rossi, Peter and Walter Williams
1972 *Evaluating Social Programs: Theory, Practice, and Politics.* New York:
Seminar Press.
Roth, Julius A.
1963 *Timetables: Structuring the Passage of Time in Hospital Treatment and*

Other Careers. Indianapolis: Bobbs-Merrill.

Rysman, Alexander
  1973 "Ill?" in Jack D. Douglas (ed.), *Social Problems in a Revolutionary Age.* New York: Random House.

Salasin, Susan
  1973 "Experimentation Revisited: A Conversation with Donald T. Campbell." *Evaluation,* 1: 7-13.

Scheff, Thomas J.
  1968 "Negotiating Reality: Notes on Power in the Assessment of Responsibility." *Social Problems,* 16: 3-17.

Schulberg, Herbert C., and Frank Baker
  1968 "Program Evaluation Models and the Implementation of Research Findings." *American Journal of Public Health,* 58: 1248-55.*

Sills, David L.
  1957 *The Volunteers.* Glencoe, Ill.: The Free Press.

Suchman, Edward A.
  1969 "Evaluating Educational Programs." *The Urban Review,* 3: 15-17.*

Thompson, James and William McEwen
  1958 "Organizational Goals and Environment." *American Sociological Review,* 23: 23-31.

Weiss, Carol H.
  1971 "Utilization of Evaluation: Toward Comparative Study. pp. 136-42 in Francis Caro (1971).
  1973 "Where Politics and Evaluation Research Meet." *Evaluation,* 1: 37-45.

Weiss, Robert S. and Martin Rein
  1968 "The Evaluation of Broad-Aim Programs: A Cautionary Case and a Moral." *The Annals of the American Academy of Political and Social Science,* 385: 133-142.*

Wieder, D. Lawrence
  1973 *Language and Social Reality: The Case of Telling the Convict Code.* The Hague: Mouton.

Zimiles, H.
  1970 "Has Evaluation Failed Compensatory Education?" in J. Hellmuth (ed.), *Disadvantaged Child,* Vol. 3, New York: Brunner/Mazel.

---

*Note: These papers are reproduced in Caro (1971). Page references in text refer to Caro.

SOCIAL POLICY RESEARCH AND BAYESIAN INFERENCE

James Fennessey
Department of Social Relations
The Johns Hopkins University

BOUNDARY PROBLEMS BETWEEN
SOCIAL SCIENCE AND SOCIAL POLICY

Although this conference is focused specifically on the topic of social programs evaluation, many features of that activity are shared with a more general kind of applied social science research, one that may be described as social science research carried out to aid in the formation of public social policy. My paper will refer to this broader context as well as to the special case of evaluation research.

In many social policy areas where serious research has been done, perhaps most clearly in work on education policy and education program evaluation, there is a general sense of dissatisfaction with the results of the evaluation research. Often, serious inconsistencies between studies are apparent with respect to the specific results obtained or the accompanying interpretations made by the researchers. Also, there is confusion about, and variation in, the kinds of research techniques and inference paradigms used by different researchers. For these reasons, as well as others, those program administrators or policy-formers who wish to utilize the results of policy-oriented social research as an input to their practical decisions often become confused, suspicious, and eventually discouraged after exploring the available research material.

This problem is chronic and serious. From a practical viewpoint, important decisions are made with lesser amounts of reliable information than might have been used, and the cost of the research is largely wasted. In addition, the problem inhibits the progress of abstract social science knowledge, since the results of the research remain debatable among researchers also, and since the availability of public support for similar research is lessened.

Evidently then, there is a need for development of a better intellectual framework—one which can be used for designing, executing, and reporting the results of policy-oriented research projects. Any such new framework must (1) reveal rather than mask the sources of contradiction between different studies on the same topic, and (2) it must provide the results of research in a form more intuitively meaningful than those now in general use. Finally, (3) it would be desirable if the new framework also positively facilitated the *cumulation* of disciplinary knowledge as well as of public understanding about the phenomenon under investigation.

Admittedly, many reports from social science research which are aimed at the world of action (cf. Coleman, 1972) are treated unkindly by the intended audience for reasons that are consciously (if not publicly) political or ideological. There are substantial aspects of advocacy and propagandizing in most policy-oriented research undertakings, and these cannot be neglected in any comprehensive analysis (cf. Fennessey, 1972 or Coleman, 1972, for a discussion.) However, over and above those noncognitive components of the communication problem, too many research reports fail to have the anticipated impact or use because they mystify, mislead, or confuse the professional policy-former. They mystify because they are couched in an esoteric technical *jargon,* and because they are phrased in terms of a very indirect *logic* of inference. In short, their meaning is obscure. They mislead because the findings typically are presented in terms of statistical significance, or in terms of proportion of variation accounted for. However, the statistical significance style of reporting really indicates only whether the observed results should be regarded as only accidentally different from some specified pattern. Similarly, the proportion of variation accounted for style of reporting indicates only the closeness of the data to a predicted value. It does not provide any direct statement about the substantive applicability of the formal mechanism by which the prediction is generated. Obviously, a reader who is well versed in statistics is not likely to be confused or misled by these conventions. Also, many researchers do provide verbal interpretations in their reports to supplement their specific statistical results. However, the generalization remains: to the non-technical reader, the statistical jargon of social science tends to be a barrier and a source of confusion.

THE NATURE OF RESEARCH WORK AND RESEARCH REPORTS

Any piece of research can be described as an effort to use empirical data and specified rules of processing, coupled with a specified set of premises about the process under study (the substantive model) and other premises about the research operations (the model for the research) to derive inferences about the substantive model, and then to apply those inferences (without strictly rigorous logic) back to the real-world phenomenon. Thus, one central component in any research is the complete set of premises—including the substantive and the technical ones—which together make up the fixed portion of the model. These premises typically include some numerical constants known as the parameters of the model. The assumed values of parameters in these premises are an essential part of the model being used. Any changes in those parameter values would imply changes in the conclusions that would be drawn from the same data. At the same time, other parameters of the model are regarded as problematic. That is, in most cases, the major purpose of a research activity is to obtain good estimates of the value of certain selected parameters.

Accordingly, one of the most serious defects of the customary approach to statistical reporting of research results is that the report does not give clear emphasis to the particular parameters of the model which are being regarded as problematic in the research. Instead, although such parameters are recognized by the *researcher* as important, his report mingles them together in the discussion with F-ratios, critical levels, and other assorted statistical baggage, thus obscuring their importance.

The report from a typical policy-oriented research effort is likely also to have communicative difficulties which involve the fixed parameter values, the ones used as premises. In adopting any model for a research project, it would be ideally desirable to be explicit about the contents of all the premises. However, because the premises can be stated in such specificity as to become quite lengthy, full explicitness is not very feasible in practice. Therefore, the practical objective is to be explicit about as many as possible of the premises as are debatable or uncertain in a particular context. Note that this last phrase implies not only a particular topic of investigation, but also a well-defined community of discourse. In other words, only when the composition of the audience is known can there be an assessment of which premises are accepted and which are questionable.

In pure science research, that community of discourse is the other members of the discipline. In policy-oriented research, however, the community includes all to whom the results of the research are expected to be relevant—typically a much larger and more diverse group than in the pure science context. Thus, the relative susceptability to challenge of different premises depends upon the definition of the intended audience. Also, the need to maintain an awareness of the basic process parameters being assumed is more acute when the audience is wide and diverse.

Using these ideas about research in general, we can examine two additional sources of the confusion and apparent contradiction in much social policy research. First, in most such projects, the investigators in fact operate using a large number of beliefs about the substantive phenomenon being studied and about the research operations being employed. For example, in evaluating educational programs, the investigators typically assume that certain measurement instruments will be sensitive to the intended program effects. This includes an assumption (sometimes latent) that the possible sources of distortion on these instruments will not distort the central results of the research. Such an assumption, latent or not, is sometimes debatable. Note that we are not saying the investigator needs to have specific assumptions about what the results of the research will be, but only that he must and does adopt a variety of assumptions in order to draw any conclusions whatever (cf. Fennessey, 1974).

Research is a process of systematic empirical and logical argument (i.e., reasoning aimed to prove or disprove a proposition), but such argument can take place only after a set of relevant premises or assumptions have been established. These assumptions, unfortunately, may and often do differ from one investigator to another and also between investigator and audience. Such differences in turn influence the design, execution, and interpretation of the research project. Yet, these same beliefs or assumptions (the ones used as premises in the logic of the formal inference) too often remain only implicit. Consequently, the locus of disagreement about results or interpretation in turn remains invisible to most of the disputants.

A second source of confusion in policy-oriented research arises from properties of the actual data in relation to the models under consideration. In many cases, the data collected in a particular study are such that they might equally have been generated by any of several different phenomena. In other words, the data may have low value in providing for differential diagnosis between several different potential sets of parameters, i.e., several different models. Yet, the same data may be highly consistent with all of the competing models, thus yielding high proportions of variation accounted for.

Each of these difficulties is the kind that scientific training teaches one to recognize and avoid, not only in general (which is probably obvious) but, more importantly, professional research training teaches one to avoid them in the various specific ways they are likely to arise in a particular field of investigation. The point here, however, is that when the results of research must be communicated to an audience of nonresearchers, these interpretive difficulties do arise.

To summarize thus far, it has been argued that the disappointing utilization of evaluation research (and of policy-oriented social research more generally) arises in part from simple unfamiliarity with the nonintuitive technical logic of traditional statistical inference and its associated jargon, in part from the unrecognized use of diverse premises with respect to substantive and technical matters, and in part from weak data, where "weak" is used to mean data which do not distinguish well between alternate models.

An obvious implication of this claim is that any proposed remedy, i.e., any new approach to policy-oriented research practice, should be more intuitive so that communication between researchers and the consumers of policy research is improved. The remedy should draw attention and emphasis to the content and the confidence of the premises being used by the researcher in his argument (i.e., to the "model" being used), and it should also highlight the diagnostic power of the data at hand with respect to the research questions being addressed. Such an approach would provide benefits to the researchers and to their disciplines as well as to the policy-formers. When awareness of the limitations of many current research styles becomes more widespread, not only among researchers but also among the potential sponsors of such research, there is likely to be greater support, both financial and administrative, for research efforts of higher quality and greater power. This in turn will lead not only to better inputs to the policy-formation process, but also to more rapid advances in disciplinary knowledge about the phenomena under study.

The question thus arises: can an improved approach to policy-oriented social research inference—one which meets the desiderata just mentioned—be found?

THE BAYESIAN INFERENCE VIEWPOINT

Within the last decade or so, as the communications gap between applied social science researchers and practitioners in social programs has grown and become manifest (cf. Coleman, 1972), there have been important developments occurring in other intellectual areas of work, developments which appear to offer a promising solution to the problems just described. These developments center around Bayesian statistics, which is a general style of inference, a paradigm (cf. Kuhn, 1970), as well as a body of specific analytical procedures and theorems. This approach possesses, it is argued, the desirable characteristics needed to deal with the problems described earlier, plus other advantages as well.

The general ideas and the technical machinery of the Bayesian perspective have been developed and applied almost entirely apart from policy-oriented social research and social policy studies. The basic work was initiated some years ago by mathematical statisticians; important contributions have been made by deFinetti, Jeffreys, Savage, and Lindley. The approach has been fleshed out and applied mainly by specialists in the quantitative analysis of business and military decisions (leading figures include Howard Raiffa and Robert Schlaifer of the Harvard Business School). Bayesian ideas have become closely linked with the field of decision analysis, where the notion of utilities of outcomes is essential. Their applicability was enhanced by the work of vonNeumann and Morganstern (1947) on estimation of utilities. However, my own judgment is that there is much to be gained now by considering separately the Bayesian inference logic, thus separating the notion of decision from the notion of conclusion. In this, I draw upon a distinction made some years ago by John Tukey (1960), though with somewhat different purposes and results.

The Bayesian approach to inference has been used hardly at all thus far in the study of public social programs. For example, at present, there is only one group in education research making visible use of these ideas. Melvin Novick and his colleagues at the American College Testing Program in Iowa have been developing and using such techniques in educational measurement, but there have been (to my knowledge) no other applications to date in applied educational research.

One effort to remedy that situation will take shape in a project I am just now beginning. The aim in that project will be to use the Bayesian perspective to reformulate and reinterpret the results of a set of recent educational research and evaluation studies. The project will seek to clarify the meaning of the results from various educational outcomes studies in more intuitively acceptable terms, to show the degree and specific ways these results depend upon the premises and also upon the diagnostic power of the data, and finally to produce a formal cumulation of the results from the separate studies in terms of the Bayesian perspective. Of course, it may be that such a cumulation, though possible in principle, will be unfeasible in practice. This may happen because of the degree of vagueness or the degree of diversity of the premises, or even because the different sets of data may be fundamentally inconsistent. However, regardless of the outcome, the concrete attempt to develop such a cumulation will shed light on the importance of two factors as they affect efforts at cumulation of knowledge: (1) the limitations of informal procedures of synthesis and cognitive cumulation for handling the complexity of the evidence; and (2) the real inconsistency between different results and/or premises. It will also help to pinpoint specific sources of inconsistency.

ADVANTAGES OF THE BAYESIAN INFERENCE APPROACH

The Bayesian approach is quite straightforward and attractive, and more and more persons charged with policy-oriented social research can be expected to make use of it (cf. Finsterbush and Weitzell-O'Neill, 1974). Toward this end, there may be value in enumerating a few specific advantages of this still-new approach, of which some may not be immediately apparent.

First, the Bayesian approach is, for the contexts in which policy-oriented social research is conducted, *more intuitive* than the traditional, sampling-theory approach to research inference with statistical models. The result of a Bayesian data analysis typically is a posterior distribution for a parameter of interest. That is, the Bayesian result speaks directly about the parameter being investigated, rather than about significance levels, proportion of variation accounted for, etc. Also, by presenting results as a distribution, the Bayesian approach makes clear that the parameter is not known exactly and thus avoids the trap of appearing more precise than it is, or can be. On the other hand, the Bayesian approach is more precise than the "confidence interval" formulation, since the Bayesian analysis provides and highlights not just the boundaries of an indirectly relevant interval, but instead the relative probabilities for different parameter values within the boundaries of possibility. In short, the result of a Bayesian analysis, typically expressible in a graph that can be understood at a glance, more truly reflects the kind of commonsense judgments ordinarily made by policy-formers. To that degree and for that reason, it is more intuitive, more direct, and simpler.

The traditional statistics approach is less direct because its results are stated with respect to a hypothetical sampling distribution. The concept of such a distribution is (judging by the experience of most introductory statistics students) emphatically not intuitive for most people. In any case, the traditional concept is more complex, even when it is understood. Of course, there are situations where a sampling distribution approach to inference can be highly intuitive. Everything depends on the context of the study. For example, in quality control of a manufacturing process, a repeated samples approach can be readily concretized. However, when the process under study is a real-world educational program, or a health services program, then the entire notion of hypothetical repeated samples from a universe of hypothetical worlds becomes painfully artificial and (to many minds) absurd. For such applications, the commonsense approach is much closer to that used by the Bayesian.

Like the traditional statistical inference approaches, the Bayesian approach does have its own jargon. However, the main ideas of the Bayesian approach and, in particular, the form its results take are quite straightforward, so that learning the jargon is easy and does not become an obstacle to understanding the import of the Bayesian analysis. Thus, although the technical details of the analysis are typically complex and nonintuitive in both the classical and the Bayesian approaches, this does not provide any grounds for preferring one over the other.

In short, it appears that the Bayesian approach offers greater communicability of results to a nontechnical but interested and informed audience than does the classical approach, primarily because its results are expressed in the intuitively meaningful form of a posterior distribution for the parameter of interest.

A second major advantage of the Bayesian approach is that it brings to the surface the problem of diversity and disagreement about the content of the research premises. In the traditional approaches to inference, such disagreements most often remain latent. Perhaps they are not explicated because explication would lead only to overt conflict. That is, the inference paradigm of traditional statistics provides no convenient way of embracing and handling such disagreements as part of its formal structure. Thus, it is entirely natural that they are allowed to remain implicit, subsumed as part of the "judgment" or "wisdom" of the investigator. Therefore, with the traditional approach, disagreements about the content of the premises tend to take the shape of disagreements (sometimes bitter and personal in tone) between different scientists. This has a number of obvious dysfunctions.

The Bayesian viewpoint, however, allows for some of the research and/or substantive premises to be expressed as distributions rather than as point values. In this sense, there is a parallelism with the corresponding difference in the way conclusions are expressed. Consequently, if two investigators hold differing premises, each can, using the Bayesian approach, express his opinion in such a way as to admit the possibility that the other may be correct. The Bayesian technique, if judiciously applied, then can (at least in principle) yield results which are conditional upon either set of premises or upon some mixture of the premises. It can also indicate the evidence provided by the data as to the plausibility of either investigator's premise.

So, just as the first advantage of the Bayesian approach derives from the fact that it expresses *results* in terms of a posterior probability distribution for the parameter of interest, this second advantage derives from the fact that it expresses the research *questions,* and (if necessary) selected *premises,* as prior distributions of probability for parameters.

A possible drawback of the Bayesian paradigm sometimes alleged is the need to specify the prior distributions. However, this is an empty objection. Even if such prior distributions are not dealt with explicitly, they continue to exist. More important, they continue to exercise a major influence on the receptivity felt by the audience toward the stated conclusions. Thus, by making these priors more explicit and by allowing their impact on the conclusions to be derived formally, the

Bayesian approach provides for more productive informal discussion about them and removes from the informal discussion the question as to whether the premises were properly used in the inference. In short, discussion of their content becomes explicit, and discussion of their utilization becomes unnecessary.

Related to this is another point about the Bayesian approach. It can be shown as a formal theorem that the Bayesian approach will eventually lead to nearly identical posterior distributions regardless of the diversity of initial prior distribution, provided the data that are collected do have diagnostic value. In other words, the Bayesian approach, at least in principle, can lead men of good will who believe in the relevance of empirical evidence eventually to come to agreement about a phenomenon. This may seem to be so obviously necessary a property as not to deserve mention, but it cannot be shown to be true for the traditional statistical inference methods.

The third major advantage of the Bayesian approach for applications in policy-oriented social research is that it mercilessly exposes weak data. That is, the Bayesian approach structures the question not in terms of testing whether a particular hypothesis is compatible with the data, but instead focuses on *comparing* the relative likelihood of the observed data under two or more alternate explanations. Again, this is exactly what most non-technical persons would intuitively want from a research analysis. To be fair, one should say that this same comparison of likelihoods is possible in the traditional inference frameworks and is in fact sometimes used. Unfortunately, in the traditional framework, the real meaning of this operation often is obscure to the lay reader. This is not the case in the Bayesian approach. Thus, the difference between the approaches here is not one of essentials, but one of prominence.

Notice that the "likelihoods" (i.e., the probability of the observed data given a specific set of parameter values) may be calculated individually for each possible set of parameters (i.e., each explanatory model). Thus, the likelihoods as a function of the parameters may be presented for inspection and judged to be high or low, as well as being compared with each other. The clear distinction between these two kinds of analysis (which might be described as indicating either the absolute or the comparative goodness of fit) is much more apparent in the Bayesian approach than it is in the traditional style of inference.

To the extent that both absolute and comparative analysis have their place, it is important that they be understood clearly. For instance, regardless of the absolute likelihoods, if a number of alternative models generate nearly equal likelihoods, then the data have low diagnosticity, and the research usually is of little value to the policy administrator. Conversely, even if there is a clear difference in magnitude of the likelihoods, with one being substantially higher than the others, but all likelihoods are quite low, then the research, though perhaps useful to the policymaker, usually indicates that the substantive process is poorly modeled and that the discipline needs to devote further attention to understanding it. By drawing attention to the strengths and weaknesses of particular studies in this way, the Bayesian approach will tend to stimulate research that is more focused and more powerful and policies that are more adapted to needs.

THE BROADER BAYESIAN PERSPECTIVE

The features discussed above are inherent in the Bayesian perspective and reflect themselves no matter how it is applied. However, there are some further advantages to be gained by considering the Bayesian approach somewhat more generally, and in particular by considering its applicability to contemporary work in policy-oriented social research.

In some discussions, it is more or less taken for granted that the Bayesian approach is applicable only when the model for the data-generating process is formalized and analytically solvable. Our position is that, for applications in social science and evaluation research, this is excessively narrow. It does simplify derivations and calculations, but the availability of large computing resources makes that a less weighty consideration than it formerly was. Rather than a simple, analytically solvable model (such as the Bernoulli process for dichotomous outcomes), it is possible to use at least three other approaches as a means of assessing likelihoods. The first of these is simple subjective likelihood assessments. Such assessments can be obtained from individuals (cf. Edwards, 1968), or from groups (as in the Delphi technique and others like it). These assessments leave the nature of the process fully implicit; we deal with a strictly "black box" model. A second approach is to simulate the process in such a way that part of it is explicit and part is left to black box decisions. This approach can be operationalized via activities such as man-machine simulations or by simulation games. A third approach is possible when the model is fully explicit, but too complex or intractable to lend itself to analytic solutions. This is the 'Monte Carlo' approach, based upon computer simulations of the process which are run repeatedly and thus allow distributions of the outcomes to be empirically obtained.

The point here is that these different procedures for likelihood estimation provide not only a way to implement the Bayesian approach for drawing inferences from data, but provide also a natural, intuitive sequence of theory-building, in which more and more of the phenomenon becomes the subject of an explicit and dynamic model, while less and less of it remains tractable only to those with detailed familiarity and personal expertise. These two extremes (i.e., black box models versus purely mathematical models) too often become conflicting ideological positions in the efforts of a discipline to deal with complex phenomena. The Bayesian approach to statistical and scientific inference, coupled with a model-building strategy which allows for judgments where systematic knowledge is incomplete, provides for a gradual mediation and synthesis of these distinct styles of research.

A second point about the general Bayesian approach concerns the matter of subjective probabilities. This is one of the major points of contention between the traditional and the Bayesian schools. In my judgment, the issue is irrelevant to the program administrator or the policy-oriented social researcher. Regardless of which academic philosophy they may espouse about probability, persons involved with social programs find themselves working with concepts which are operationally identical to the probability as degree-of-belief used by the Bayesians. This subjective-probability approach can be shown to be internally consistent. Moreover, from the point of view of the mathematics, probability is simply a number with some specified formal properties (cf. Chacko, 1971). How those numbers are interpreted and how they are assigned to events are outside the formal logic of the mathematical analysis system. Thus, it becomes possible to take an eclectic position, to admit that probabilities, as used in policy-oriented social research, need only to be agreed upon by all concerned. How that agreement is reached or rationalized is a pragmatic, not a formal, question. Agreement may rest on arguments of relative frequency or symmetry, or it may rest on implicit, consensual judgments. In either case, the numerical probabilities are used the same way by the Bayesian paradigm. Thus, attention should be devoted not to subtleties of probability definitions but to gaining greater agreements about actual probability assignments.

Note that this point suggests, for example, that randomization in experimental design is only one (albeit a highly persuasive) rationale for assigning equal probability distributions of potentially confounding variables to each cell of a research design. However, a Bayesian might wish to argue that such distributions are equal, while using a different rationale for that claim. The quality of his argument would then depend on its specific content. This kind of distinction (between a premise and its rationale), though easily abused, would seem to open up a variety of new possibilities for policy-oriented research design and use.

A third direction in which the Bayesian approach can be used broadly begins with the notion that data constitute only one of several alternative kinds of justification for believing in a premise. Thus, other kinds of justification can be expressed in terms of the data pattern to which they are equivalent. The basic formal idea of this sort is the notion of conjugate distributions for a parameter. That is, it is sometimes possible to express one's prior beliefs about a parameter value using a shape which is identical to the shape of the likelihood function associated with one particular pattern of data. For instance, if one is dealing with a Bernoulli process, it may be that the prior beliefs about the parameter, call it P, take the same shape as a likelihood function of P, given the observation of, say, 8 successes in 13 trials, and no other information. In fact, when this is possible, the distribution of the parameter for that case is a Beta distribution. Thus, the Beta distribution is said to be "conjugate" to the binomial for a Bernoulli process model (cf. Winkler, 1972, pp. 143-162).

But, if a person's total beliefs can be expressed as equivalent to a given set of data, then it is also possible to consider whether the separate influences leading him to hold those beliefs can also be equated to specific data. An example of this for the use of expert judges (instead of data) has been developed imaginatively by Peter A. Morris (1974). In my own project, I plan to apply a similar approach to the evaluation of particular pieces of research evidence. In other words, a policy-former can be influenced by the report of an expert judge; he also can be influenced by the contents of an empirical study or by his own experiences. In each case, it should usually be possible to express that influence as equivalent to the observation of a specific pattern of data, provided the beliefs can be put into a conjugate distribution. Thus, not only cumulation, but also analysis of evidence is possible.

The real advantage of all this is that such influences are then not only made comparable in a nominal sense, but also operationally, since it is a property of the Bayesian approach that evidence can be cumulated or decomposed in a formal way. Moreover, this can be done quite easily if there is a conjugate distribution.

The last point to be mentioned here about the Bayesian inference framework relates to the earlier idea that it is closely linked with the new discipline of decision analysis (Raiffa, 1968). Although the linkage is close and natural, it is not a necessary or intrinsic one. For the application of the Bayesian approach to research and social policy, the important point is that the conclusions of the researcher can be made distinct from, but compatible with, the decisions of the administrator. The additional elements that must be introduced for decision analysis are, of course, a loss function or utility function over the possible policy outcomes and a set of action options. However, constructing this utility function or the set of options is not the province of the social science researcher, and the Bayesian approach neatly allows him to report his conclusions—including the conclusion that no specific substantive model can be chosen (cf. Tukey, 1960) without adopting any specific social "values" or advocating a particular action. By allowing this distinction to be maintained clearly, cleanly, and operationally, the Bayesian approach circumvents a number of problems frequently faced by the policy researcher (cf. Fennessey, 1972).

This paper has attempted to indicate some attractions of the Bayesian approach to statistical inference, particularly for work in policy-oriented social research. There has been a deliberate emphasis on its positive features; this should not be taken to imply that there are no technical and practical difficulties in attempting to use this approach. Such difficulties—some foreseeable, others not—plainly do exist. Nevertheless, the many advantages of the Bayesian approach (not all of which have been mentioned or detailed here) quite clearly make it a prime candidate for serious use in future policy-oriented social research.

RESEARCH DESIGN AND POLICY INFERENCES

Richard J. Light
Harvard University

Both federal and local agencies seem to want more evaluation research done than ever before. This has created a new bull market in methodological debate, a debate that cuts across many specific fields of social science. I would like to present and briefly comment upon three issues that I believe will occupy much of the attention in this debate. The first issue is about experimental designs for evaluations, the second is about how to disentangle seemingly conflicting research findings, and the third is about caveats on inferences that come even from well designed studies.

RANDOMIZED CONTROLLED EXPERIMENTAL DESIGNS
VERSUS OBSERVATIONAL STUDIES

In some areas of social research, strikingly little progress has been made in learning which programs work and why they work. For example, a report issued earlier this year by the National Academy of Sciences found that between 1963 and 1973 6.8 billion dollars had been spent on 6.1 million trainees in a wide variety of federally sponsored manpower training programs. These programs included, for example, The Neighborhood Youth Corps, Job Corps, and Concentrated Employment Program. Further, the N.A.S. reported, more than 180 million dollars had been spent on commissioned program evaluation. The net result, after hundreds of studies and hundreds of millions of taxpayers' dollars, is that we still don't know, reliably, the effects of these programs. Indeed, the *one* evaluation study that the N.A.S. found to be well designed was carried out in 1969 on young women job trainees in Cincinatti, and a statistically significant effect was found for the training. The women receiving training did significantly *worse* in the job market than a comparison group getting *no* training. The N.A.S. report found this state of affairs discouraging. I agree. The key ingredient that seems to be missing in most of these studies, and that could have been built into at least some, is the straightforward concept of random assignment. Without this crucial lynchpin of research design, statisticians can adjust and touch up and standardize data indefinitely, but each adjustment will ultimately boil down to an effort to approximate what would have happened in a randomized trial.

Contrast the state of manpower evaluations with work recently completed by Educational Testing Service of Princeton, New Jersey, who studied Sesame Street and The Electric Company, two educational television programs for children. The studies were designed as randomized, controlled field trials. While the work was not easy to carry out and monitor, the evaluators made a major effort every step of the way to guard against threats to the actual implementation of the randomization. The result is that while there may be plenty of political argument about the import of the findings, the basic substantive results, showing that kids who watch Sesame Street have better number and letter recognition than those who don't, appear firmly grounded. These findings cost a tiny fraction of what all the manpower studies cost, and I see no reason, ethical, political, or statistical, that manpower programs cannot do just as well. Indeed, my colleagues John Gilbert and Frederick Mosteller have argued that observational studies are frequently not even "neutral" in a value sense—they may be actually harmful. The argument here is that poorly designed studies can hold up, often for many years, the carrying out of a well designed evaluation effort. I find this argument compelling; perhaps the area of manpower programs provides a good example of this conjecture.

One final point here. The argument is occasionally made that carrying out randomized, controlled, field studies is too difficult, or ethically indefensible, or too costly, or impractical for some other reason. These arguments are no doubt sometimes correct. But recent work of Alice Rivlin; Henry Riecken and Robert Boruch; Gilbert, Light, and Mosteller; Stuart Adams in the area of criminal justice reform; and others, illustrates the large number of areas and circumstances where controlled trials *have been carried out successfully.* These early well-done studies should serve as beacons for future work.

ISSUES IN BUILDING RANDOMIZATION INTO AN EVALUATION

I don't want to give the impression that just because a study has randomization somehow built into it all other problems pale in importance. This is not so. Indeed, I would like to indicate two areas where more work needs to be done to guide evaluators in their analyses.

First, randomization is a single word. But in many research studies it is not obvious *what* should be randomized. Some people call this the "unit of analysis" problem. Let me take an example. Suppose we wish to do a simple test between two drugs meant to lower blood pressure. Let's call them A and B. We have a medium-sized city. It has ten hospitals currently functioning. Now, if we wish to compare these drugs, what should get randomly assigned to whom, and where? There are surprisingly many alternatives.

a. We could, within *each* of the ten hospitals, randomly assign drugs A and B between all hypertensive patients currently in each hospital.

b. We could assign drug A to all hypertensive patients currently in five hospitals selected at random, and drug B to all hypertensive patients currently in the other five.

c. Instead of only assigning drugs to hospitals but keeping the patient populations undisturbed and uncontrolled by the study, we could, at least starting next week, randomly assign hypertensive patients in this city among the ten hospitals. Since some hospitals are currently using drug A and others are using drug B, we would not have to change any hospital procedures or drug routines this way.

d. We could, at least in principle, assign *both* drugs and patients randomly among the ten hospitals.

Now, the question is which design is best? Is there a clear ordering of preferences? Does the ordering of preferences change if we are especially interested in discovering subject-by-treatment interactions? Anyone who believes that randomization is just a trivial idea should work through the implications of these alternatives to inferences that might be ultimately drawn about drugs A and B.

A *second area* where more work is needed involves combining results from small randomized and observational studies to generate the strongest possible inferences overall about a large population. Let us stay with drugs A and B for a moment. Assume we search through the medical literature and find two studies that compare the two drugs. One study is a randomized, controlled trial, done on volunteers for the trial who have given their informed consent. The other study is an observational, retrospective, sample survey with no experimental manipulation.

What might we find? We could find that the results of the two studies agree; for example, that both find drug A preferable to B. In this event, we might assert with reasonable confidence that A is genuinely more effective. But what if the experimental study on volunteers finds A preferable to B, while the sample survey finds B preferable to A? Then we have a conflict. It is at this point—not an uncommon point—that three distinct lines of argument emerge. One line is that this conflict merely illustrates once again how hopeless the whole enterprise is because it is so difficult to disentangle contradictions among research findings. Let us reject this line. A second approach is to observe that if forced to choose between a randomized, controlled study and a nonrandomized, uncontrolled one, the former is preferable. This line has some merit, but it may not get us all the way home. A third approach is to notice that the randomized trial might have what Donald Campbell calls a "threat to external validity." That is, since the randomized trial was done only with volunteers who had to give informed consent, perhaps the results are not generalizable to the full population. This may well be correct. But how can we find out? A group of young statisticians led by David Oakes, meeting at the Harvard School of Public Health, have developed an attractive model for checking whether "volunteer effects" have clouded the generalizability of the randomized trial. Their basic suggestion is that, in the early stages of a randomized trial using volunteers, the volunteers should be randomly segregated into two subgroups. One subgroup should participate in the randomized experiment, just as they expected. The other subgroup of volunteers should be told "thank you for volunteering, but your services are not needed after all. Let your doctor treat you (i.e., assign you to drug A or B) according to his best judgment."

This second subgroup, then, has two known features. First, each patient was treated by his own doctor and given drug A or B. In other words, as a group, these rejected volunteers were treated just like the patients in the non-experimental study. But the second fact we know is simply that each of these patients was a volunteer for the randomized study, even though he didn't "get in." Why is that valuable knowledge? Because by comparing this second subgroup with the original *non*-volunteers, and seeing how the drug A versus drug B comparison looks in each group, we can estimate the *volunteer effect* and see if there is a problem of external validity. For example, if A outperforms B for the non-volunteers, while B outperforms A for the volunteers who were not selected for the randomized study, this would be a strong indication of a substantial "volunteer effect." On the other hand, finding similar results for the two groups would indicate no volunteer effect.

SHIFTING RESPONSE SURFACES

My final point has more to do with common sense than with advanced mathematics. While much debate in evaluation research focuses on what designs are most powerful in the statistical sense (i.e., minimizing risk of Type II error for fixed risk of Type I error), I have seen surprisingly little discussion of *pitfalls of inference* that occur when evaluators *generalize* from small studies to large populations. My colleague Paul Smith has called this the problem of "shifting response surfaces." Perhaps an example will illustrate the point.

Suppose a program is developed in a city to train paramedics and doctors' assistants who work closely under the supervision of MD's. We wish to evaluate it, and we wish to do so using the best research design possible. So, from a pool of 40 people we randomly assign 20 people to the training program and 20 to a control group. One year after the program we compare the two groups. The results are clear; the 20 trainees are all employed, at good salaries, and their doctors and patients all report high satisfaction. The control group is nowhere near as well off. Conclusion? The training program is a success, as determined by a well-done randomized field trial. Policy implication? Generalize this to a larger population. Give more people the same excellent training.

Next year the program is implemented. All 20,000 unemployed but trainable people in this city are given the paramedic training. What happens? The program is a mass failure. A year later almost all of the trainees are unemployed. Why? Because while there was demand for the 20 trained paramedics, there was not demand for 20,000 trained paramedics. So the highly successful micro-program, even though nicely evaluated in an experimental paradigm, *broke down when expanded into a large scale program.* Many people might consider this an obvious and trivial example. Yet the concept that it illustrates is, I think, an important one. This example is illustrative of a large class of social programs where the benefit that the program confers to any one recipient is a function of how many other people got the program! In this case, the more widely the training program gets disseminated, the lower the expected gain of any one trainee. While this point appears obvious, I have rarely, if ever, seen it made in write-ups of manpower programs. It is representative of a type of faulty inferential leap that a researcher may not remember to include as a *caveat* in an evaluation report, yet this is precisely the sort of caution that evaluators making policy recommendations cannot afford to forget.

RESEARCH VERSUS
DECISION REQUIREMENTS AND
BEST PRACTICE OF EVALUATION

Keith Marvin
Associate Director
Division of Financial and General Management Studies
United States General Accounting Office
(currently in the Program Analysis Division)

The U.S. General Accounting Office was thrust into the methods of evaluation by the 1967 amendments to the Economic Opportunity Act which required GAO to review the extent to which programs authorized by the Act were achieving the intended objectives. This sort of review has grown rapidly to over one-third of our total effort. A statement on June 19, 1974, by the Comptroller General before the Joint Committee on Congressional Operations has an appendix that lists about 38 representative reviews of program results, which one might call evaluation, that have been reported by GAO in about an 18-month period. Of that 38, about one-third deal with social programs.

Observation of GAO reports on these reviews reveals a general problem which has been referred to several times in this conference and by this panel—the lack of data. We have frequently concluded that we were not able to find adequate data or data of enough validity that we could make an evaluation and that no one else could.

There have been cases where GAO has created measures and collected its own data. If we do not believe the data are valid or if there are not any, we have no other choice if we want to evaluate the program. For example, a report issued in June 1973 on social services—do they help eliminate or reduce dependence on welfare; that is, make people more self-sufficient—is a case where we collected our own data. A recent report on a review of Upward Bound is a case where GAO developed its own measures, proxy measures, for motivation and success in college. These reviews are done, by and large, by our eight major divisions that have resident audit sites in the agencies.

The division that I represent, the Division of Financial and General Management Studies, has a variety of functions, from approval of accounting systems that the GAO is required by law to do to provision of technical assistance in the review work done by other divisions. There is a multi-disciplinary staff of about 50 people in our division, including mathematicians, statisticians, some sociologists and psychologists, engineers, and computer scientists, that are available to go out and work directly with the audit teams on reviews. That is one of the key ways that we have used to get this kind of methodology into more of our reviews.

We have had also an internal training program, in which we have given a number of our higher level people an orientation in these subjects and their applications. We have had also a hiring program at the college level, in which about half of the people hired are non-accountants, whereas prior to 1966 all hired were accountants. The result of these actions is that scattered in GAO divisions and the regional offices are approximately 400 people who have a fairly high level of quantitative skills. This is beginning to have more impact, and I think you will see this reflected in our reports in the next two-to-five years.

We also do some developmental reviews. We try to pick areas where we have the resources to try to make a state-of-the-art advance and to show how advanced techniques could be used in reviews. For example, in the case of an Indian reservation, we conducted a household survey on the reservation; and we found, perhaps contrary to some popular belief, that there was a desire by most of the population to be employed and, furthermore, to accept non-Indian ownership if that was required to obtain this employment. This is a reservation that does have potential for economic development, and some of it, such as timber and cattle, had been developed. We were interested in finding out more about what affected employment and income, and the Indian's perceived indicators of quality of life; and we looked at education, health, alcoholism and other things.

With regard to education and the problem of alcoholism, we looked at three different measures of employment: whether or not they were employed when they were interviewed, the days worked in the last year, and job tenure or length of time in the last job. There appeared to be differences in the relative effect of education and the problem of alcoholism, depending upon the choice of measure.

With regard to education, obviously important, we found that the condition of the family housing, the parents' level of education and a measure we developed to indicate cultural adaptability all seemed to have important effects on the achievement level. We also found that whether there was a car present that the family could use, whether there was a TV set, whether both parents were present in the home, and whether the parents had received training in the past year were important.

To indicate the cultural adaptation, we used data from the household survey, whether or not the English language was used in the home, the extent to which the family had contact with non-Indians, and whether or not the family believed that Indians and non-Indians can live together peacefully. We had an interesting experience in this study in being able to merge our study data with another study that was going on when we arrived—a study of cases of infant morbidity and mortality. We were able to work with that project, merge our data on condition of housing with their data and to show in this case, fairly conclusively, that housing condition was definitely related to infant health. In some of the other work done by GAO, it was concluded that housing condition might be related to health on the Indian reservations generally.

We have not finalized our conclusions in this experimental study as yet, but I believe it is quite obvious, that if there are this many interactions going on in this many different areas, that policymakers are going to need to be concerned about improving many things, perhaps simultaneously, if they expect to improve some of the quality-of-life issues.

I want to speak briefly about the Congressional Budget Act of 1974, which has been mentioned before at this meeting. It establishes a new budget process for the Congress, a new Congressional Budget Office, and a Budget committee in each House.

As for GAO, the Act amends provisions that affect GAO in the Legislative Reorganization Act of 1970. New provisions require GAO, at the request of any committee, to help in developing goals and objectives and methods of evaluating programs. Specifically, the Act now requires that we shall develop and recommend to the Congress methods for review and evaluation of government programs and activities carried on under existing law.

GAO is required also to conduct a continuing program to identify and specify the needs of the committees and the members of the Congress for fiscal, budgetary and program-related information. We are required to maintain an inventory of information sources and data. We interpret that inventory to include program evaluation studies, and we intend to work on developing a service for the Congress that would make more readily available the evaluations that are relevant to the needs of the Congress and GAO. We do not have the intention of duplicating anybody else's clearinghouse. We like to see those developments going on and being improved too.

As I see it, it is really a question of resources. The Congress and the GAO must make use of the evaluations that the agencies are doing. We found in a survey in May that about $150 million was currently being expended per year by the non-defense federal agencies. This much could be identified directly at the federal level and does not include money that might be used from program funds at the state level or money provided by the states from their own budgets for evaluations. I heard here yesterday of single social experiments costing as much as the GAO annual budget. Consider that we can spend only a portion of our budget for this kind of activity—the program results or evaluation work—and it is obvious that we are going to have to make use of information that other people have developed. GAO can help see that this information improves through better methods.

With regard to evaluation methods, we see our job involving several things. One thing we want to do is write a pamphlet, in layman's language, to help the committee staffs and the Congressmen understand what evaluation is. We do not believe that we can send them a package of formal, complex evaluation principles and standards and expect them to know what we are doing to respond to this requirement to recommend methods.

We want to have a dialogue with the technical evaluation community on what the principles and standards ought to be. That would be something, as we see it, similar to the dialogue we had in developing standards issued by GAO in 1972, for audit of Governmental Organizations, Programs, Activities, and Functions. Those standards are intended for application to programs at any level of government; and, in developing them, an intergovernmental group of federal agency representatives and state and local representatives was involved. A number of states have adopted these standards officially as their state audit standards.

There is similarity between program audit and program evaluation, as I am sure you can see, so there will be similarities among standards. Our audit standards really say to the auditor that he should include a review of the results of the program in his audit. What we want to develop as the principles and standards for evaluation are more specific criteria for auditors, GAO included, so that when they get into the results area there are criteria to judge when an evaluation is good enough to be used or so bad it should be disregarded. In addition, there should be criteria for auditors to use in their management audits, as to whether evaluation is being done properly as a management function. When it comes to statements of policy on the subject, the Comptroller General has said that we believe evaluation is a function of good program administration.

I want to close with mention of the states. I think there should be more of an effort to get state people involved. The evaluation activity is growing in the states. Several state legislatures have established new offices—New York has had one for a long time; Texas, New Jersey and Illinois have taken on this job; there are fiscal and expenditure commissions established as part of the legislative structure in North Carolina, Florida, and Virginia. There is a new Legislative Program Evaluation Section established by these leaders as part of the Governmental Research Association (currently as a section of the National Conference of State Legislatures). The National Association of State Budget Officers is providing training and education in the area.

STEADY SOCIAL PROGRESS REQUIRES QUANTITATIVE EVALUATION TO BE SEARCHING

John P. Gilbert
Computer Center and Department of Statistics, Harvard University

Frederick Mosteller
Harvard University and University of California, Berkeley

John W. Tukey
Princeton University and Bell Laboratories

Presented by: John W. Tukey

Without insightful qualitative evaluation and sturdy quantitative evaluation, social progress is likely to resemble wandering in the dark—occasionally running into something so large that no one can miss it. This paper is about the second of these key activities—quantitative evaluation.

We hold these truths about quantitative evaluation to be either self-evident or established by experience:

A) Sound evaluation is essential to relatively rapid social progress.

B) Managers are understandably reluctant to accept incisive evaluations of overall programs.

C) Social modifications which make large changes (a) are very rare and (b) may well not need formal evaluation. (Unless all concerned are really hit between the eyes with the effect, it is not large, in this sense.)

D) A large share of important, large-scale social progress will come from an accumulation of small improvements—evaluation, to be effective, must detect small improvement with considerable reliability.

E) Many modifications that do not live up to large planned-for changes may show smaller but important gains—the hope that a large change will occur cannot be a good reason for failing to plan for its evaluation in a way adequate to detect such valuable but modest effects.

F) The Hawthorne effect—that people who know they are being treated differently may do better for that reason—cannot be neglected.

G) In view of (B), (C), (D) and (F), the most important evaluations will compare "seemingly minor" differences between two versions of a program.

H) Reliable evaluation can hardly ever be attained without a randomization process determining which treatments—in view of (G), often which modification—are applied where.

I) The costs, in time or money, of incorporating a randomized comparison of modifications in an ongoing program can often be much smaller than is usually feared. The costs, especially the social costs, of not doing this are usually very much greater.

J) Ethical justification for failing to make a randomized trial is never easy and often impossible. Inadequately evaluated programs can usually be regarded as "just fooling around" with the people involved.

K) The statistical evaluation of "natural experiments" will always be fraught with difficultues—but statisticians must do what they can to see that such analyses are well conducted and reported with suitable caveats.

L) Any attempt to infer what will be caused by an active intervention from data involving either no intervention ("natural experiments") or unrandomized intervention has to be subject to possibilities of error that are hard to evaluate. Any attempt to assert that the statistical significance or confidence associated with such an analysis allows us to conclude reliably what active intervention will do is dangerous and unsound.

M) The best we know how to do in such a situation is to seek out alternative methods of fallible inference, use up to several of them, and then, recognizing their fallibility, trust moderately in their combined message.

N) Results of trials involving people seem to be clearer and more precise when the people are not conscious of either the purpose of the trial or the distinctive character of treatment with which they are associated. Thus trustworthy medical experiments, for example, often must be conducted at least "double blind" so that both patient and attending physician are unaware which treatment the patient is receiving. (If the evaluator of the quality of success is not the attending physician, it may also be as vital that this evaluator is also unaware.)

P) Difficulties, such as one variable camouflaging itself as another, will be at least as great in social experimentation as in medical experimentation, so we must take to heart the lamentable experience in medical investigations, where, all too frequently, as many as 20 parallel unrandomized studies of a new treatment have led to what was later found to be entirely unwarranted optimism about it.

THE IMPORTANCE OF PRE-CONFIRMATION WORK

Before expanding on these truths, describing them in more detail, and giving some supporting evidence for them, we emphasize the importance of the efforts that must precede the kinds of studies we recommend. Before these confirmatory studies are carried out, extensive preparation must already have gone on, preparation that may be much more difficult and time consuming than carrying out the confirmatory studies. Preliminary information about the process under study, information that leads someone to have insights about the sorts of programs that are needed, is absolutely essential. These insights often come from theory and from good anecdotal evidence—that is, careful case studies—and they may also come from other sorts of qualitative and quantitative investigations. Without such insights leading to programs, there will be no programs to test.

But good ideas are not enough either. After such ideas must come the often tiresome work of developing them into a going program, something very concrete that can be taken to the field and tried out, not in competition with anything, but just to get the bugs out. These steps may be called pilot studies or they may be demonstration studies. And some fields may have other names for them. Sometimes years of work are required to bring ideas to this level of practicality. Thus the aspect of the work we treat in this paper comes after a great deal of solid initial work has gone on. That such initial work is essential must not go without saying, even though the present paper emphasizes a different aspect of program evaluation.

Thus, we need a true partnership between innovation, development, execution, and evaluation or progress will always falter. To sum up, not only must insight and exploration come before evaluation, but after exploration must come development and feasibility studies.

Equally, confirmation—either positive or negative—has to be the foundation from which the next generation of insight, perception, and anecdote development climbs to new improvements. A good example is given in Gilbert, Light, Mosteller (1974), where a particular new surgical treatment was found *not* to be successful, but the investigation that showed this to be so has been the rock upon which the next 10 years of successful research in that area was built.

To some, our emphasis on progress by very occasional large steps forward, whose importance is obvious and a relatively steady (if we all do our best) accumulation of small gains denies the needs of our society. Not at all. We are very conscious of the needs and deeply concerned that there be real progress toward meeting them—real progress.

When we look at any major human activity—for example, health care, production of objects, management of businesses—what we see is just a combination of very occasional large steps forward (which sometimes like Pasteur in medicine, or water power and the steam engine for factories, or computers for management, are not absorbed either rapidly or without pain) and a more-or-less steady accumulation of small gains. Why should social progress be any different?

There seems to be every reason to believe that this pattern has to be typical of any human activity where a substantial number of able people have been involved for decades. It is unlikely that any gold will be found at the grass roots, except where new ground has been broken. The occasional very large step forward is almost always when we do something new. It is only the new whose larger opportunities have not been skimmed off by progress guided by the insights and perceptions of able investigators and administrators.

What careful quantitative evaluation can do is to work with the small effects, cumulating them to larger and larger gains. This is all that people of wisdom and perception have left for us to do in any long practiced—and consequently long thought about—area.

To say this is not to deny the importance of qualitative evaluation. Two roles for qualitative evaluation are unchallenged:

> Agreement on those large and easily replicated effects that are "interocular" that do "hit us between the eyes"—effects so large that surely we must put them into use without waiting for quantitative evaluation, and

> Presentation for quantitative evaluation of those modifications which human perception and insight, often those of unusually sensitive or usually well-guided people, have identified as either plausible improvements or possible improvements.

Without the second role, quantitative evaluation would have no grist to grind and could do little to aid social progress.

The three authors of this paper are quantitative people—we know quite a lot about the strengths and the weaknesses of our quantitative colleagues. We would not take seriously the thought of giving these colleagues the sole responsibility for progress in any major substantive field, social or not. Without the crucial input from sensitive qualitative people, our quantitative colleagues could make only unsatisfactory progress.

In the same way, we cannot leave the responsibility for social progress entirely to qualitative people either. In medicine and surgery, qualitative evaluations (and even some partly controlled quantitative investigations) have often been misleading. Medicine and surgery do offer a model for the social area to emulate, however, because for some reason they have managed to introduce a considerable amount of quantitative work during the last 20 years. The use of randomized controlled clinical trials has increased, not as much as we would like to see, but nevertheless much more than in the social area.

With the help of large-scale, carefully controlled trials with broad bases, surgeons and physicians are making substantial progress; the social area has a parallel opportunity and a parallel obligation.

SOME FURTHER ISSUES

It has been common, at this conference as (we presume) elsewhere, to attack or defend program managers for actions that may plausibly have been taken for understandable reasons. We would think that not enough attention has been given to the reasons why managers tend to blur the lines—lines which we consider it vital to maintain—between three quite distinct kinds of input:

wise advice,

anecdotes, and

quantitative evaluation.

Without wise advice, from outside or in, hardly any program can function well. Where there is general concurrence among those reputed to be wise (including the Congress), the program is almost sure to follow this common lead—we may hope for the better.

When the wise disagree, the first step is to bring in anecdotes, anecdotes which may be very relevant or very misleading. One topic at the conference involved differences in the efficacy of a treatment between volunteers and non-volunteers. Who would be so rash as to say that if we make everyone volunteer, the treatment will work as well as it did for true volunteers? All anecdotes are subject to doubts, of which this example illustrates one. Much progress has been made with the aid of some anecdotes—and much only after overriding the apparent, but misleading, implications of others.

We can understand the desire of a manager for a combination of wise advice and anecdotes—something that lets him describe his actions as based upon "evidence." But we feel that he ought to understand how rapidly his certainty fades away as:

the size of the anecdotal effect diminishes,

the typicality of the situation to which the anecdote applies diminishes, and

the extent to which the anecdote depends on "natural experiments"—a dangerous misnomer—rather than on situations where it has been possible to impose the treatment on some and not others in a suitably controlled way.

Only as he recognizes this will the manager be able to perform effectively his highest and most difficult function: balancing the political realities against the available knowledge.

To be done well, quantitative evaluation should, in particular, be careful as to the apparent degree of generalizability of its reported results. Random selection of sites to compare volunteers and non-volunteers, combined with appropriate forms of analysis, can give not only a central value but a valid confidence interval for the average national difference of behavior between volunteers and non-volunteers. But this result, if intended to guide action that might make more people volunteer, is still subject to a very real uncertainty—not usually approachable by any merely statistical assessment—about what would happen if we intervene. Without due emphasis on such questions, quantitative evaluation can become only a few quantitative anecdotes. Failure to recognize this works to everyone's disadvantage.

The discussions of the conference have pointed up a phenomenon common in quite different fields. The results from fertilizer depend not only upon kind and amount but on time of application and post-application tillage—and, often, rainfall. The results obtained in a face-to-face questionnaire depend not only on the questions and the inter-viewee, but significantly on the training and other characteristics of the interviewer. What is a treatment often requires very careful consideration.

It would seem to be clear that in social programs a treatment needs to be described in many more aspects than just what is supposed to happen. The nature of the administrative and operating structures, the doctrines written down, the doctrines conveyed less visibly, the extent to which the operators understand what they are to do, and the extent to which they do it—all these are part of the treatment. While this makes the problem of either qualitative or quantitative evaluators more difficult and threatens the generalizability of the results, sweeping such problems under the rug does no good.

Social scientists concerned with either social anecdote or social experiments have an opportunity and, we suggest, a responsibility to concern themselves with the influences of the administrative/opera-tional mechanisms of what happens. Confining oneself to what was supposed to happen and the consequences of what did happen is taking a narrow road that may miss the target.

Until we learn to be effective in describing the administrative and operational aspects of our treatments, what should we do? Obviously, the best that we can.

In calling for confirmation as one major activity, we do not diminish the difficulties as to the degree to which "a treatment" is in any way the same at two sites. Learning better how to arrange for treatments to be closer to what they are supposed to be—learning better how to measure what a treatment has been—these are matters of the highest importance.

Decision-makers must make decisions about the names of treat-ments, using the best evaluation available. Evaluators cannot avoid twin responsibilities to name the treatments studies in sufficient detail and to point out any reasonable doubts about differences between the treatments evaluated and what would be likely to occur in a larger-scale program.

SOUND EVALUATION AND SOCIAL PROGRESS

Sound evaluation is essential to relatively rapid social progress. The variability of performance of social innovations from site to site and from one group of people to another is easy to document. When, for example, investigators in the field of education have tried to decide whether one treatment was superior to another, they repeatedly have found—as agricultural experimenters found long ago (see Pearson and Wishart 1942)—that some treatments seem to work better in one place and some in another. Clearly, if we do not know when we have found a good thing, we will likely lose it; and, if we think we have a good thing when we do not, we will be the losers. The field of manpower training is an example where we have spent very large amounts of funds with little or no evidence of solid benefit from the training itself.

MANAGERS AND INCISIVE EVALUATION OF OVERALL PROGRAMS

The effectiveness of a program depends not only on the effectiveness of the treatment delivered but also upon the efficiency and skill of the delivery. For this reason any searching evaluation will tend to appraise both the abstract scientific question of whether the treatment works and also the technical practical question of whether the manner of delivery was such that the treatment had a chance to work. Because this second question carries a very real possibility of criticism of the personnel managing the study, managers often perceive a really effective form of evaluation as a threat. This perception can be particularly troublesome when, to reduce "bias," outside evaluators are used. In some programs, the personnel running them are the only ones who are in a position to collect accurately the data needed for evaluation. For such programs, there is little chance of getting an accurate picture of program effectiveness without the close and full cooperation of the management. In order to minimize the natural antagonism between program management and its evaluators, some goals and consequences need to be clearly stated and understood by the policymakers responsible for the program, the administrators, and its evaluators. These are, first, the evaluation can provide a means of documenting the effectiveness of management's delivery of the treatment independently of how effective the treatment is once delivered; second, the evaluation can be used to pinpoint those variations in treatment (or its delivery) that are most effective, thus allowing management to tune the program for high effectiveness; and third, if it does turn out that the treatment is not effective, the evaluation should point out clearly that this is due to the treatment and not its delivery whenever that is true.

It will and must remain true that good evaluation will pose a serious threat to the poorly administered program and its administrators. However, the administrator who can implement a program so that it has the strong chance of working, who can document that he has done so, and who, finally, can present a strong evaluation of the effectiveness of the program, will have a successful career independent of the success of the individual programs that he administers. Such a manager will have enough healthy skepticism to be able to evaluate the program critically rather than being blindly and totally committed to his program on a priori grounds.

SOCIAL MODIFICATIONS THAT MAKE LARGE CHANGES

Social modifications which make huge improvements are very rare and may well not need formal evaluations. In an attempt to get at the frequency of large improvements owing to social innovations, Gilbert, Light, and Mosteller (1974) evaluated the frequency of very strong improvements. They found, among those that were carefully appraised, fewer than a third were outstanding in their effects. Figuring that only the best would have been so well evaluated to begin with and that large additional numbers died silent deaths because they were obviously poor or deleterious, one can see empirically that large improvements are rare.

That they may not need formal evaluation when they occur arises because the effects are so large and so directly traceable to the new procedure that there is no gain-saying them. For example, when the hospitals empty of tuberculosis patients, that is convincing evidence that a cure has been found. When good soup kitchens get no takers, clearly something else is handling the hunger of the poor. But it is important that such "large" effects be so large as to be "interocular," as that term has been used by Edwards, Lindman, and Savage (1963).

We have much experience, in both the social and medical areas, of selection effects producing appearances of worthwhile treatments that later proved illusory. In education, for example, sometimes the control group is at a different level of attainment from the experimental group and, when this is not recognized, one can easily be misled. When it is recognized, one is still faced with the problem of direction and appraisal, and this is not a well-solved problem, nor will it ever be. Instead, we know that we have troubles with it, and that we are more able to enumerate the troubles than to get rid of the difficulty.

In the absence of control and experimental groups, the givers of a treatment will ordinarily report on their pleasure and that of the participants in the study with the treatment. For some reason, this pleasure usually, but not always, seems to be positive, and so one gets the initial impression that the treatment is doing some good. This sort of impression is not what we mean when we speak of interocular effects. We mean unusual improvement or change that registers on large fractions of the people and has not formerly been obtainable.

THE ACCUMULATION OF SMALL IMPROVEMENTS

Although we always hope for big breakthroughs and new programs with slam-bang effects, most progress comes as the result of cumulating many individual small gains. This appears to hold true in many fields of endeavor but is certainly as true of social progress as, say, that in engineering or medicine. In order not to lose a small but perhaps important effect that a program does have, even though it may not fulfill all its proponents' initial expectations, it is necessary that its effects be carefully evaluated using methods powerful enough to detect such small effects. It is particularly important to document small effects well since otherwise the programs that brought them about will go out of style and their effects will be lost rather than built-upon.

SMALLER BUT IMPORTANT GAINS

Most social modifications are intended to produce large improvements. But we can expect few modifications to live up to such great expectations. Neither the unrealistic expectation of huge success nor the realistic expectation of failure to achieve large gains is good reason for failing to plan for evaluation that will adequately detect valuable but modest effects if these occur. In the Gilbert, Light, Mosteller study mentioned above, there were substantial numbers of studies that offered small positive effects. In order to note such gains, it was necessary to be able to assess them carefully. Small gains are hard to assess and require substantial studies. Since small gains are the rule and since much of the advance we see in society accrues from collections of small gains rather than from one mighty jump, it is vital to recognize, hold onto, and build upon those small gains we have.

THE HAWTHORNE EFFECT

The Hawthorne effect, originally thought of as "improvement in the experimental group, no matter which way you shift the variable" has been almost a platitude of social research for decades. More recently, some have begun to stress how much the Hawthorne effect has been overstated. No matter how much or how little stress we may eventually learn it deserves, today we have to take it as a real possibility and design our studies to make it threaten our evaluations little or not at all.

Some experience with human experimentation suggests that studies that seem to be testing noticeable things of little interest can often give better assessments of little things of real interest. This sort of camouflage is frequently ethical and practical.

COMPARISON OF MINOR PROGRAM DIFFERENCES

We have already seen that (B) overall programs may not be evaluatable, (C) really large improvements are likely not to need formal evaluation, (D) most important progress will come in small steps, and (F) we may be able to measure the less noticeable changes with less confusion. All these points push us to a clear conviction that many, if not nearly all, of the most important evaluations will compare "seemingly minor" differences between two versions of a program.

Unless these small differences are appraised and appraised carefully, we have entrusted our entire hope of progress to "playing for the drop," to a hope, all too often vain, that we will be the rare group to which a large difference will happen—and will happen to be favorable.

RANDOMIZATION PROCESS

Some of the reasons for point H will be discussed under K, L, and M. The most important thing to do here is to reiterate the point: *reliable evaluation can hardly ever be attained without a randomization process determining which treatment or modification is applied where.* Restricted randomization, using blocks and other controls, will often be desirable—almost anything we can do to strengthen a comparison can be made compatible with an appropriate kind of randomization. We must, of course, be wary whenever the candidates for randomization are only those who are willing to submit to either of two treatments, so that our evaluation is of a subpopulation of volunteers. Until the non-volunteers become willing to participate in either treatment also, we cannot compare the alternatives for them.

Random selection from natural strata allows a clean comparison of one natural stratum with another and is thus desirable, but does nothing more to deal with the question of "What will happen when we intervene?" than would a complete census. It is not the kind of randomization that concerns us here.

COSTS OF RANDOMIZATION

The incremental costs, in time or money, of implementing a randomized comparison of different modifications of an existing program are much smaller than is usually feared. Since nonrandomized studies are almost always susceptible to the selection biases that randomization is designed to prevent, they are always subject to the additional criticism that such a bias and not the treatment was the cause of the observed effect or lack of effect. Thus, a randomized study will provide the decision-maker with a more reliable estimate of the effects studied than a comparably well-done nonrandomized study. The uncertainties of nonrandomized trials have been repeatedly documented in medical investigation where all too frequently 10 to 20 nonrandomized clinical trials have enthusiastically supported the use of a new treatment that was later found to have little or no therapeutic value (see Gilbert, Light and Mosteller).

INADEQUATELY EVALUATED PROGRAMS

Often there is considerable complaint that it is unethical not to give the new treatment or good to all those who "need" it. One of the weaknesses of this argument is that that is exactly what a careful investigation is designed to find out—whether the new treatment is a positive contribution. Sometimes it is just the reverse.

What is unethical is trying this treatment and then haphazardly and unsystematically changing to other treatments, as is common, for example, in the field of education, without having a basic evaluation that tells whether the contribution is positive, let alone whether it is cost beneficial. Usually these changes are made in such an unsystematic way that every evaluation is ambiguous. This manner of making improvements can usually only be regarded as "fooling around with people" rather than experimenting with them.

The real need is for more randomized controlled field trials to measure carefully the effects that social innovations actually deliver. An ethical problem that must be more squarely faced is this: When is it ethical to fail to make a randomized controlled field trial? The answer is not easy—one example, of course, is when it would be unethical to try the new treatment at all, another is when the program is so small that its careful evaluation might have costs out of proportion to the program itself. Such small programs may well be thought of as pilot studies, if they are capable of expansion later. If they are not, then we may have to be satisfied with other forms of evaluation.

STATISTICAL EVALUATION OF NATURAL EXPERIMENTS

In his recent Presidential Address to the Royal Statistical Society, David Finney (1974) stressed the statistician's responsibility to pitch in and work with dirty data on important problems—no matter how unstatistical the key problems may prove to be. In spite of the many concerns we express in the present paper, we heartily support this point of view. (Many applied statisticians have come close to feeling that "salvage" is the statistician's main way of life).

In helping with such problems, statisticians must not forget their professional obligations, which compel them both:

To urge the inclusion of adequate caveats, including dishearteningly large estimates of uncertainty, where these are appropriate; and

For crucial issues, to help in finding a variety or ways, subject to different sources of error, to approach the directions and sizes of effects.

It is not easy to be a statistician. One friend and colleague says "to be a statistician you must be schizoid on certainty and uncertainty." This is not only true as regards mathematical deduction and statistical intro-duction; it is also true as regards desirable and actual quality of data.

ACTIVE INTERVENTION

George Box has (almost) said (1966): "The only way to find out what will happen when a complex system is disturbed is to disturb the system, not merely to passively observe it." These words of caution about "natural experiments" are uncomfortably strong. Some would read them as being in conflict with our acceptance of the statistician's obligation to help deal with bad data.

In today's world, there seems to us no alternative to accepting the words of caution as, if anything, too weak and the obligation of involvement as overriding. Under these cross-pressures, however, the obligations of adequate caveats and diversified approaches gain new importance. We neglect them at our peril.

Regression is probably the most powerful technique we have for analyzing data. Correspondingly, it often seems to tell us more of what we want to know than our data possibly could provide. Some examples of what can happen may help us all to understand point L, which covers these as well as many others.

First, suppose that what we would like to do is measure people (or items) in a population and use the regression coefficients to assess how much a unit change in a background variable (say x_1) will change a response variable (say y). Since the regression coefficient of x_1 depends upon what other variables are used in the forecast, we cannot hope to buy the information about the quantitative effect of x_1 so cheaply. These remarks do not deny the potential use of forecasting the value of y from several variables x_1, x_2, and so on in the population *as it stands*. What they do cast grave doubt on is the use to forecast a change in y when x_1 is changed for an individual (class, city, state, country), when no controlled trial making such a change has been tried.

The idea that such regression-as-measurement methods are successful in the physical sciences is seriously misleading for a variety of reasons. First, because most physical-science applications of regression-as-measurement are to experimental data. And second, because the relatively few useful applications that remain involve systems in which "the variables" are few in number, well clarified, and measured with small error. When one fits $A+BT+CT^2$ to data on heat capacity as a function of temperature, for example, he takes advantage (1) of knowledge that only temperature is involved, (2) of knowledge that temperature and only temperature is changing and that many decades of work have gone into the definition of the temperature scale, and (3) of measurement precision that is very high, compared to the changes in T. Analogs of any one of these three supports, to say nothing of all three, are not common in social, economic, or medico-surgical analyses.

Some, who realize certain of these difficulties keenly, try to use regression in a more qualitative way. They admit they cannot really use it to measure the size of the effects involved, but they hope that they can use it to show that some effect or other actually exists. They, too, are likely to fail—often without knowing that they have failed.

Why might they fail? Because, if we fear that what we measure with error as x_2 may also contribute to the "causation of y" alongside what we measure with error as x_1, it is not enough to do multiple regression of y on x_1 and x_2. The coefficient of x_1 may be reliably—and in the population—different from zero when what we measure with error as x_1 has no effect on y whatsoever (see Tukey 1973 and 1974).

What does this condensed paragraph mean? Suppose we are studying some aspect, y, of children's development as a response to some out-of-home variable, x_1, and we are quite properly concerned with separating any response to x_1 from the varied responses to home atmosphere, either material or mental. The first thing to do—clearly—is to choose as appropriate a measure of home atmosphere as we can, call it x_2, and start doing multiple regression of y on x_1 and x_2. If now we still find that x_1 clearly contributes to regression-as-prediction, can we be certain that "even with home conditions held constant" x_1 contributes to y?

Regrettably, we need not be able to be certain at all. There are two reasons whose combination leaves us in trouble. First, while we may have used much wisdom and insight in choosing our x_2, only a limited number of measures of home atmosphere could be considered for measurement, so that, at best the x_2 we choose is an imperfect measure of the aspect of home atmosphere that matters. And, second, the two x's we are using—x_1, whose effect we are probing, and x_2, which falters under the burden of carrying all relevant home atmosphere—these two x's turn out to be correlated in the population our data come from. The condensed paragraph says that, under such circumstances, the trustworthy appearance of x_1 in regression-as-prediction does not ensure that x_1 has an effect "with home atmosphere held constant." A sad and grievous statement—but a true one. We all have a responsibility to communicate it more widely, especially to unsuspecting analysts who are doing their best to use quantitative methods to untangle confusing variables.

ALTERNATIVE METHODS OF FALLIBLE INFERENCE

Even if we are able to follow the best guidance we now have—when we must evaluate either a natural experiment or an unrandomized trial—namely, to seek out alternative methods of error-prone inference, to use a few or even several that appear likely to be prone to separate sources of error, and then to discuss their results together, recognizing their fallibility—even if we do all this we cannot be sure of our results, only somewhat less uncertain. But we have an obligation to do as well as we may with the data we have—only rarely can we indulge ourselves in the luxury of saying "the data are lousy, forget the whole thing." Often the error bounds will still say something close to this, even after good hard work and some originality have gone into the analysis, but when this happens, our obligation as analysts of data has been met, once the error bounds are both calculated and adequately reported.

The grave danger always present in either subjective or parallel approach analyses is that we fool ourselves about the magnitudes of errors and we forget to include important sources. And when parallel approaches seem to agree we may become overconfident because we have paid no attention at all to some common, maybe false, assumption that makes them all agree. The assumption of independence of measurements is often such a source of overconfidence.

THE EFFECT OF AWARENESS ON TRIAL RESULTS

Because people often respond to stimuli that they believe are present, the results of trials involving people seem to be clearer and more precise when the people are not conscious of the distinctive character of the treatment given or the purpose of the trial. Thus, trustworthy medical experiments, for example, often must be conducted at least "double blind" so that both patient and attending physician are unaware of the treatment the patient is receiving. (If the evaluator of the quality of success is not the attending physician, it may also be vital that this evaluator is also unaware of the treatment—thus "triple blind.")

As Michael Polanyi (1958) says, "believing is seeing." An "unblind" evaluator cannot help showing his prejudices, at least to a degree, overcompensation included. It would be good if more social innovations could be studied in equally veiled circumstances, not for the purpose of keeping the existence of the investigation from the public, but to keep the appraisal of improvement less contaminated with prior prejudices. Often in social investigations, as in medical ones, it may be impossible to keep the recipient in ignorance of the treatment. But as medical investigations have improved, their investigators have become more and more imaginative about ways of carrying out investigations maintaining both scientific and ethical standards. We may hope that social investigators will be similarly successful.

IDENTIFYING VARIABLES ACTUALLY BEING MEASURED

In researching social experimentation, it is often difficult to identify what variables are in fact being measured. Thus, for example, if one finds that children's performance in school relates to their parent's level of educational attainment, is it the parent's education—or the social and economic factors that determined the parent's opportunity to obtain a higher education—or other parallel consequences of grandparents who motivated the parents strongly enough to get that education that affects the children's level of achievement? This difficulty of not knowing for sure what we are really observing is one of the reasons that it is so hard to infer from a purely observational study what will happen if, instead of passively observing, we actively change a social situation by altering, directly or indirectly, some of the variables.

We are well aware that the evaluation of social programs, whether by randomized experiments or otherwise, often raises complex ethical questions and equally complex emotions—more or less as unevaluated trials of the same programs would have. Nothing for the sake of a trial that teaches us little or for one that teaches us much. We do believe, however, that if we are going to change peoples' lives we must make sure that the unfavorable consequences of such changes, if any, shall not have been in vain. Two of us are currently working out the implications of this position for social evaluation, but we are not ready to develop more of these implications here.

REFERENCES

G. E. P. Box (1966). "Use and Abuse of Regression." *Technometrics 8:* 625-629.

W. Edwards, H. Lindman and L. Savage (1963). "Bayesian Statistical Inference in Psychological Research." *Psychological Review 70:* 193-242. ". . . a procedure that statisticians of all schools find important but elusive. It has been called the interocular traumatic test;[1] you know what the data mean when the conclusion hits you between the eyes. The interocular traumatic test is simple, commands general agreement, and is often applicable; well-conducted experiments often come out that way. But the enthusiast's interocular trauma may be the skeptic's random error. A little arithmetic to verify the extent of the trauma can yield great peace of mind for little cost." (page 217)

D. J. Finney (1974). "Problems, Data and Inference." *Journal of the Royal Statistical Society, Series A, Vol. 137.* 1: 1-23.

J. P. Gilbert, R. J. Light and F. Mosteller (1975). "Assessing social innovations: An empirical base for policy." *Evaluation and Experiment: Some Critical Issues in Assessing Social Programs.* ed. C. A. Bennet and A. A. Lumsdaine. New York: Academic Press Inc., pp. 139-173.

E. S. Pearson and J. Wishart (1942). *"Student's" Collected Papers.* Biometrika Office, University College, London, England.

M. Polanyi (1958). *Personal Knowledge: Towards a Post-Critical Philosophy.* University of Chicago Press, Chicago, Illinois. Polanyi used this expression in a lecture at the Center for Advanced Study in the Behavioral Sciences in the fall of 1962 (FM). The quotation from his book *Personal Knowledge* is "According to the logic of commitment, truth is something that can be thought of only by believing it." (p. 305) on p. 266 Polanyi has a footnote: St. Augustine, *De libero arbitrio* Book I, par. 4: "The steps are laid down by the prophet who says unless ye believe, ye shall not understand." Finally, Cleo Youtz who kindly searched out the above quotations, also informs us that Isaiah VII, 9 (King James) gives "If ye will not believe, surely ye shall not be established."

J. W. Tukey (1973). "The zig-zagging climb from initial observation to successful improvement." *Frontiers of Educational Measurement and Information Systems.* ed. W. E. Coffman, Houghton-Mifflin, 113-120.

J. W. Tukey (1975). "Instead of Gauss-Markov Least Squares, What?" Published in *Applied Statistics. (Proceedings of the Conference on Applied Statistics* at Dalhousie University, Halifax, Nova Scotia: May 2-4, 1974.) Ed. R. P. Gupta. North Holland Publishing Co. pp. 351-372.

NOTE

1. Berkson, personal communication, July 14, 1958.

DISCUSSION: Research versus Decision Requirements and Best Practices of Evaluation

Discussants: Mancur Olson, University of Maryland
Michael Scriven, University of California, Berkeley
Paul Wortman, Northwestern University

OLSON: I would like to discuss only the two papers which I received in full in advance of the meeting. These were the papers presented by Professor Deutscher and by Professor Tukey. Let me deal first with what seems to me to be unsatisfactory about Professor Deutscher's paper—that is, the resistance in the paper to studies that, in a clearcut way, try to relate goals to means and ends to means. At several points in his written paper, Professor Deutscher states that it is very hard to know what the goals are; that program administrators may state goals in an ambiguous fashion; and that, when results are different than the ostensible goals, possibly the proper interpretation is that the goals were different than what they were initially said to be and that the program is, in fact, an effective means for attaining the true, if not the ostensible end. Although it is often the case that the goals of a particular program are complex and ambiguous, and that sometimes we find that the goals were different than we thought after seeing what the real outcomes were, it is very important not to press this too far, as Deutscher does. Napoleon didn't lose at Waterloo because he liked to lose or was looking for a vacation on a remote island. One very important part of evaluation is that it deals with the consistency of means and ends. Professor Deutscher's emphasis on the process approach may take us too far away from that.

At the same time, Professor Deutscher makes an important contribution in criticizing the widely-held view that nothing works. He points out that that is a meaningless statement, that substantial interventions into any ongoing social process are almost certain to have some substantial effects, even if they are not what was intended or even if they are not consistent with the goals. We ought to stop saying that nothing works; we ought to be saying that things are working in very different ways than we expected. We ought, for example, to be alert to the substantial distributional consequences of public programs that are not effective in attaining the goals they are supposed to attain. These distributional consequences may not always be favorable to the poor as a class. They may favor the civil servants as a class, or the construction companies and the cement companies, or even indeed, the evaluators of social programs. But in any event, they all have consequences and we need to study them, and Professor Deutscher's emphasis on process helps us there.

Turning now to the papers presented by Professor John Tukey and his collaborators I would like to say that I think all of us here are indebted to one or more or all of them, for we are all, in one way or another, students of one or more or all of them. They are, it seems to me, particularly distinguished statisticians, and it is wonderful that their talents turn to these problems. Theirs is not a bad paper, but it is not, in every respect, original, nor even at every point, fresh—there is a little too much of the elder-statesman, with warnings about Hawthorne effects and so on. It is even, in a couple of cases, true I think that the argument is not as technically precise as it might have been. In point B, for example, they state that program managers, presumably in general, will resist the evaluation of public programs or social programs because these evaluations may show that the administrators of these programs are in fact poor administrators. Surely, it follows by definition that half of the administrators are above the median level of quality—so how then can we get the conclusion that, in general, administrators are poor? While it may be the case that program administrators are opposed to evaluations of their programs, that opposition needs to be analyzed in a more detailed and precise way than I think has been done in the paper. What we need to do is look at the fact that the output of any social program is a result not only of the treatment or program itself, but also of the quality with which it is administered, and many other things as well. Therefore, it is logically impossible to get information about the quality of the administration or about the effectiveness of the treatment unless one has independent information about both the quality of the administration and the nature of the treatment. These things must be distinguished. You could, of course, have one administrator who had administered a great number of social programs, each of them evaluated carefully, in which case one could then arrive at a judgment about the quality of this administrator's administration of a social program. There may be other ways too of solving this problem, but in any event, it is a problem that has got to be confronted in more detail.

SCRIVEN: I wanted to start by making some comments on Irwin Deutscher's paper and discussing the somewhat more radical approach to getting into the goals trap that he was talking about, the so-called goal-free evaluation approach. Professor Deutscher does us an extremely valuable service by assembling a magnificent collection of quotes that the people who wrote them would surely by now love to be able to suppress. In all of them it is said that of course it is stupid to mention the fact that there can't be any evaluation without knowing exactly what the goals are. It is clear you do not need to use goals at all. It is also clear that it is very important not to use them in some cases. Now goal-free evaluation is perhaps best understood in terms of the procedure, which I use in my training stations, where I simply show a movie or a slice of television tape on a screen to show what is happening in a classroom where the experimental treatment is being provided and to show what is happening in the control classroom where the experimental, not defined, is not being provided. Then we discuss what it is that distinguishes the two classrooms. Later we see clips of film where what happens a month later or a year later is also shown, and we distribute a hand-out which indicates test results. At the end of all this, you are in a position to be able to say what the difference is between these two groups and you are also able to say what the treatment was as it actually reached the classroom. This avoids much of the evaluation of phantom treatments as well as evaluation of phantom goals. In fact, the typical procedure of evaluation is much too elusive.

If the evaluator is allowed to talk to program people and is allowed to look at the background material which tells about how eminent foundations and distinguished boards of reviewers have put their stamp of approval on a particular project and that it is committed to the welfare of the Indian child, the black child, the white child, and all other right-thinking children and so on, he can hardly be described as entirely unbiased. If, in addition, he gets some information about where to look for results, then it is amazing how easy it is to find them. It should hardly surprise people who are sophisticated about social psychology that the set achieved by the briefing sessions that almost all evaluators go through on the morning after they have been met at the plane, had their boots licked, and been taken to a nice dinner, during which it is revealed that almost everybody on project staff has assidu-ously read every item in their bibliography and can quote quite lavishly from it, then we have this meeting where we are briefed as to what we will be looking for, and then we are told to get out there and really lay it on. Well, there is not much hope of doing any such thing. You have been provided with the instant co-option which it normally takes months to achieve. So, on the whole, I think something could be said for goal-free evaluation on the grounds that it avoids that sort of biasing.

What it does, perhaps most importantly, is to give the evaluator a chance to pick up side effects which he otherwise would not pick up. The real problem of that set is not only the favorable bias but the directional bias. It is favorable, which is one problem and can be handled by avoiding social contacts with the program people being evaluated. It is also directional, which really deters the evaluator from picking up side effects. What he needs is an opportunity to find out what is happening, without any hints—which makes the work a whole lot harder. My approach is different from Deutscher's approach in that it does not focus on process and can be totally outcome-based. You can be looking at the process because you want to get an independent reading on what the treatment really is, but it can also be based purely on outcome inspection, with outcome results, so it can be a very payoff-oriented type of evaluation.

Now, I want to tend to Richard Light and the mysterious phantom box in his little contingency table. You may have wondered after his systematic development why we finally finished up with nothing in the mysterious box in his contingency table. It might have occurred to you that that was perhaps because we did not want to be randomly assigning things to the non-volunteer group. I think probably in practice what we need is clearly, simply, a random assignment to those who did not volunteer for a random assignment. I think we can probably best cope with this by having staff members specifically committed to the unethical activities of the research program—the unethical associate, who can appear perhaps in phantom writing on the top of the paper. Such people would, of course, resolve the conflict here. Our investigation would be dismissed. We could then have an Office of Unethical Affairs. Results could perhaps be published in the Journal of Unethical Results. One way or another we clearly need to fill in this column in the contingency table and make the whole interest much simpler than it is at the moment. I suggest that a little systematic thought about this could probably lead to a constructive solution.

I would now like to comment upon Keith Marvin's approach. The emphasis he was placing on the necessity to start looking at the situation on the state level is really important, particularly in California, and our own Post Office is perhaps the nation's largest of these independent GAO-like organizations. It has an enormous budget and has a magnificent record with the Congress. To mention the educational counterpart of that, in California Alex Law has that office—he has 43 Ph.D.'s in the educational evaluation office now. That is a fairly substantial staff, at the state level, and it is a pretty prominent-looking group. I heartily endorse the suggestion about the setting up of a resource center for program evaluations for Congress. A number of years ago I was talking around a suggestion which, not surprisingly, met with no support at all, that we should introduce something to compete with ERIC, and the something was going to be called Elmer. Elmer's advantages over ERIC were a number, but they were very strong in the cost-effectiveness area. Elmer was restricted by definition to being a four-door filing cabinet, with no computerization allowed. Elmer stands for Evaluation of Learning Materials Resource and what it contains is simply the latest, most reliable, alternatives where there are competitive ones, and evaluations of each of the program materials or curriculum materials that are available to school people. The task of Elmer was to be able to answer 90% of the questions that come in requesting advice from Congress or from schools looking for implementation advice. The read-out time was extremely fast, the turnaround time was extremely fast, and duplication costs were extremely low. Such a thing would be of great use to Congress, which might even understand how to use it.

I just want to reinforce something that Dr. Tukey said about the history of medicine. There is a good deal too much tendency to think that agricultural agents and medical research are somehow paradigms for us. The truth is far from this.

WORTMAN: In many of the papers presented during the past two days we have learned that a non-experimental approach to program evaluation that omits randomized assignment of the treatment program is equivalent to Original Sin. And, at this session, the papers by Professors Light and Tukey have reiterated the need for randomized experiments. While I whole-heartedly support this position, we should be aware that randomization is not just a slogan for success, but often a complex and difficult process. In particular, there are methodological and managerial problems that can subvert this process. It is important that an evaluator be familiar with these threats to experimental validity in order to avoid them. In the brief remarks that follow I would like to deal with a few of the more important problems in successfully implementing randomization.

REACTIVE EFFECTS

(a) *Blind Procedures.* We have all heard of experimenter bias and how it can undermine and contaminate the observations we make. As Professor Scriven has just noted, it is useful and important to keep the hypothesis or goals of the program concealed from the evaluators (his so-called "goal-free" evaluation). This is a small extension of the more traditional, double-blind procedures where both experimenter and subject are kept from knowing who is assigned to the treatment condition. However, in program evaluation there are some risks involved in such secrecy. For example, in one health-care experiment involving rehabilitation therapies, nurses and patients were assigned to either a control or experimental treatment condition without being informed that this was part of a research project. As a result, one nurse in the control condition noting the apparently superior alternative treatment decided to sneak her patients in for treatment when her superiors were not present. As is obvious, such behavior eliminated the randomization procedure's intended effects.

There are equivalent situations where alternative treatments are made available to experimental populations. Project Follow Through, a national program to continue the Head Start program through grade school, had its comparison schools undermined in this fashion. In this case, these control schools were eligible for and received Title I funds to establish programs similar to those of the Follow Through schools.

(b) *Ethical Conflicts.* One way of dealing with the problem of concealment, just discussed, is to obtain prior consent of participants before randomly assigning them to conditions. This also eliminates a serious problem in attrition caused by those persons who are first assigned, and then invited but refuse the invitation to participate in the program. Of course, in this case, one is dealing entirely with volunteers who may be atypical of the population at-large. Incidentally, this problem in external validity is not dealt with in Light's paper. Since only volunteers are available, we could only learn by his procedures whether or not random assignment has a systematic effect on the observed outcomes (as opposed to non-random assignment). It is apparent then that the point at which random assignment is accomplished can vary and does have different ramifications.

Prior consent, however, does not remove all reactive threats. It may, in some instances, produce the serious ethical conflicts it seeks to avoid. In one national study examining the effects of special treatment for cardiac-prone persons prior consent was obtained. But, when the first subject at one of the sites was assigned to the control group, he broke down and started to cry. The experimenter was thus confronted with an extremely difficult and delicate ethical problem. In order to overcome human fraility and avoid pressures to undermine the assignment of treatments, the randomization was entrusted to a computer that was safely located many miles from the site. The conflict between scientific rigor and human compassion, of course, is not unique to this particular evaluation. It is an important problem that must be confronted and resolved prior to implementing the randomization procedure.

MANAGEMENT PROBLEMS

Most of the programs that have been discussed at this conference such as Title I and Follow Through have been extremely large, if not immense, with thousands of participants and millions of collected data. We have also learned that these large-scale projects have been, unfortunately, remiss in their omission of randomization. The implicit assumption in this methodological critique is that the results of these massive undertakings would have been interpretable had proper design procedures been invoked beforehand. It is this thesis that needs re-examination, so that millions of dollars not be spent on well-designed programs that also fail to yield useful information. It seems to me there are two crucial management problems that increase with increasingly large programs. They are organizational scale and treatment complexity.

(a) *Program Scale.* As programs attain large-scale status, they may reach a point where managerial problems swamp methodological concerns so that even the best designed programs will fail. This can happen through lack of staff coordination in both implementing and evaluating a program as occurred in Follow Through. Moreover, there are serious problems in staff continuity and attrition that parallel those for participant attrition noted in Professor Robins' paper. While Professor Deutscher refers to the "goal-trap" as a sort of guiding fiction, there are real goals that emerge in large-scale programs that are antithetical to proper evaluation. The first is that such organizations take on identity of their own and, as a result, become primarily concerned with perpetuating their existence. This creates pressures for favorable findings so that the program can continue and expand. Secondly, with large, complex programs involving many persons—program staff, funding agencies, communities, and the like—there will, of necessity, be a diversity of goals often in conflict with one another. More often than not, these goals will be hidden agendas not communicated to the research staff or others involved in the program. These goals have to be revealed and reconciled prior to the imposition of a large and costly study.

(b) *Treatment Complexity.* Treatments as well as organization vary in complexity in a manner that interacts with the scale of the program. In particular, there appear to be at least two categories of treatments—one dealing with services, and the other with products such as vaccines, machines, and money. Most of the programs we have considered and practically all educational programs are service treatments. These are complex programs involving many steps or processes (often unspecified) and many people. Such service programs are barely manageable on a small scale, and, as noted above, have been unmanageable on a large scale. Moreover, the problem of ensuring uniformity of treatment implementation and delivery is probably neither possible nor desirable on the national level. In addition to the staff problems already mentioned, it is unrealistic to expect a single program or small set of programs to be appropriate to the widely diverse populations receiving them. In most cases, such an approach has been undermined through degradations in treatment uniformity caused by local adaptation or tailoring of the programs.

For these reasons, it would seem appropriate to keep innovative programs as small, and hence as manageable, as possible. In the case of service programs, this should be made the rule; otherwise program evaluation is likely to founder in a sea of organizational red tape. The policy maker's need for generalizability or external validity can be dealt with through local replications realistically tailored to the needs of the communities involved. There may be exceptions such as medical research on diseases with low incidence, but then the treatments are often uniform products such as the Salk polio vaccine that make management practicable. In addition to small-scale, local experiments, I would also urge organizational parsimony as well. Too many groups involved in the program can only hinder its operation and assessment. If it is desired to separate program administrative effects from program outcomes as Tukey has urged, then additional staff should be added. However, great care and training should be added too.

SUMMARY

In conclusion, I would like to reiterate a commitment to randomized experiments wherever possible as the most appropriate means for program evaluation. While there are difficult problems in achieving this goal, they are manageable once they are recognized. To underline that point, at Northwestern we have been cataloguing successful instances of randomized experiments in the health, education, and human welfare fields. Our archive now has almost two hundred entries in it. Thus it is possible to conduct such evaluations once there is an awareness of the problems involved in implementing true, randomized experiments to assess social programs.

V

EVALUATION OF HEALTH PROGRAMS

PART V □ CONTENTS

EVALUATION OF HEALTH PROGRAMS

Chairperson: RALPH BERRY, Harvard School of Public Health

HEALTH PROGRAMS EVALUATION:
A Budget Examiner's Perspective

Martha O. Blaxall
Institute of Medicine

In the days when Abt Associates had less than 20 employees—I was the twelfth employee back in 1965—we used to have a motto that we never forgot as we went around Washington trying to sell evaluation research with a company and a staff that was still relatively unknown. That motto, which is of some relevance to the deliberations here, was "ignorance is no bar to action."

Several years later, when I became a budget examiner for health programs in the then Bureau of the Budget (now the Office of Management and Budget, OMB), I was struck by the relevance of that motto to the way in which decisions were made at OMB; few and far between were the times that health policy research or evaluation were brought into the decision-making process in any kind of meaningful way. I would like to pursue the reasons for this—namely, why health program evaluation has not been used to any significant extent in OMB for making budget or legislative decisions, and the directions which evaluation research might take to become more useful to policy makers at that level.

There are four basic reasons why evaluation research has been of limited utility to OMB. All of these are worth some emphasis, since only when we all fully understand and accept these reasons will we begin taking the kinds of action that will make evaluation research more useful. The first of these relates to the methodological limitations of evaluation research in health. Three examples come to mind.

1) Lack of accepted criteria for measuring health status.

Except for a few programs, such as those in the maternal and child health area, we do not really know what we should be using to measure the impact of a health services' program. Mortality is the only hard index and is relevant in only a few areas, such as cancer research or financing of kidney dialysis. Morbidity is much more difficult to deal with. Moreover, even if the impact on health could be determined, how would the social and economic utility of a particular program be measured? How can we get at the marginal changes, when there are no base lines from which to begin measuring? And how do we value the change? Using the traditional economic methods of measuring human capital in terms of the amount of the wages and salaries (or GNP) which would have been lost without particular health programs seems grossly inadequate to get at the full value of health.

2) Difficulties in measuring the impact of non-health care factors on health status.

Secondly, many of us at OMB and elsewhere believed that it probably did not matter what the precise budget level was in many of our program areas, since housing and environmental factors were also important in affecting health status. Unless a coordinated comprehensive attack was mounted, the outlays for health services would cause only short-term improvements in health status. However, the Health Branch did not participate in developing budget recommendations or the legislative programs for housing, or alcoholism and driving (in those days it was a DOT program); and decisions on air pollution and occupational safety were made elsewhere in separate councils at separate times. And, even though we were aware of the need for a more coordinated approach, the program evaluations were also done along categorical lines, and the impetus for comprehensive planning did not materialize. Thus, we went about our recommendations for marginal increases or decreases with our usual sense of hunches.

3) Impact of health programs on other social programs.

By the same token, although we never had any hard data, we were conscious of the fact that decisions about other federal programs should be taking into consideration the effect that the health dollars were going to have on their constituents. Family planning support expanded rapidly during the years I was the budget examiner for that program; but even though we had extensive data on the number of people served, until the Report of the National Commission on Population, I was not aware of any evaluation work done on the impact of the family planning program on demographic trends or reductions in welfare payments. If we had been able to obtain that kind of evaluation information, we might have been able to provide more substance to much of the discussion in Director's review sessions. I remember one incident during Director's review where our Division was recommending an increase in the Budget. The general tone of the Director's response was, "well, we just went up $X million in cancer research, we'd better go down $X million in family planning."

Secondly, much evaluation research in health is self-serving and concerned only with measuring inputs, not the quality of a program or its impact. The evaluation research of Regional Medical Programs (RMP) falls into this category. Further, as was mentioned above, since we have not developed any standard measurement indices, the evaluation tends to be anecdotal and not useful for making budget tradeoffs.

Thirdly, much of the evaluation research which we saw was too late, because the objectives of the program had changed before the evaluation of the old objectives could be completed. Although this is not really a fair criticism of the evaluation itself since the policymakers, not the evaluators, were responsible for the change, it is a fair criticism of the way in which evaluation was carried out in many cases. Too often, ex post evaluations were undertaken on contract when much more useful results might have been obtained if evaluation techniques had been built into the program to begin with and modified as the program goals were modified. RMP again fits the bill here, although I would also include the support of health manpower training through capitation grants. Financial stability of the nation's health professional schools, which was the ringing cry of the 1971 Comprehensive Health Manpower Training Act, no longer carries the same level of importance in 1974. The overriding goal, now, is to link health manpower support to a more equitable geographic and specialty distribution of physicians. Thus, the Institute of Medicine Study in which I participated on the costs of health professional education and the relationship of these cost data to capitation support was limited even before it came out, because the goal that the Congress had asked us to address in 1971 was only a small part of the issues which the Congress was debating in 1974.

Oftentimes, results of evaluation research are not in line with policy objectives or political ideology, and the research results are therefore ignored. The best example that I can think of concerns the Maternity and Infant Care Centers and the Children and Youth Centers of the Maternal and Child Health programs. Despite their relatively sophisticated evaluation systems and the impressive longitudinal data that had been collected which "proved" the positive impact of these programs on child health indicators, revenue sharing was upon us, and the party line was to fold project grants into formula grants and "let the states decide how to spend this money."

Given these obstacles, it is no surprise that many OMB analysts have had few kind words for evaluation research. Left with little in the way of hard research, even when we tried hard to find it, we were forced to rely on ad hoc or longer term impressions, political judgments (drug abuse and cancer are two obvious recent examples of large increases based largely on political considerations), and the occasional GAO reports if they provide further fuel for an a priori decision. (I am reminded particularly of the recent study of the GAO on the health professions' student loans' program which illustrated the basic failure of that program. Yet both the Administration and the Congress are calling for expansion of student loan programs tied to even more specific conditions.) While we were making our recommendations on the basis of our Abt Associates' motto, we were lamenting the lack of good evaluation research and saying, what we really need are social experiments and a better data base to help us understand what the impact of decisions will be. Four areas where evaluation research is particularly needed in the health sector are cited below.

First of all, we need more and better basic and applied research on defining health status and how to measure it. We need to know more about how different combinations of health care services and environmental conditions affect the health status of different population groups. To do this we need to reexamine our current data collection systems and to develop a uniform set of data that everyone agrees can be most useful for answering our policy and research needs. If every time we want to evaluate something we have to go out and gather fresh data on even some of the most basic issues—the current situation in many cases—it slows down progress considerably. Certainly my experience with the big survey studies that Ruth Hanft directs at the Institute of Medicine bears this out. Since we do not have nationwide data on utilization of services for the general population, data that are needed for our analytical work in determining an appropriate distribution of physicians by specialty and geographic area, we shall probably have to use Canadian data, unless individual states can provide the information we need.

Similarly, in attempting to define health status we need to identify the thresholds where additional amounts of health care services do not make any difference in health status. There have been some studies on this already, but without an adequate data base to warrant translating the decisions into policy action. Unless we can determine where additional health care services do not make any difference, so that we can impose some kind of aggregate limit on demand, we cannot begin to get a handle on containing costs or developing the kinds of incentives in new financing mechanisms that will guide people's behavior in the directions that we want. Joe Newhouse's work will be essential here, but it is only one piece of the needed research.

Thirdly, we need to understand better the effects of income levels on health status. I have recently heard some decision-makers say that if we had a workable income maintenance program in this country, the attention of those developing National Health Insurance could shift towards the issues of how much society is prepared collectively to pay for health care, and for what type of services, rather than being directed towards designing differential programs for the poor. Once again the national health insurance experiments will provide some insights into this problem, although much more remains to be researched.

Finally, in the area of biomedical research, we need to reexamine our analytical skills and bring them to bear on the thorny question of how do we allocate our biomedical research dollars so as to increase the probability of scientific breakthroughs which will have positive impact on health status, without at the same time minimizing the scientific value of a breakthrough. Some kind of Delphi-like technique may be useful to help scientists and policymakers establish a common ground for communicating on these issues. We need to figure out how to achieve more breakthroughs in what Lewis Thomas calls the high-level technology—the polio vaccines which cure—and not become captives of the high-cost supportive care modalities which Dr. Thomas calls the midway technology—the expensive iron lungs of yesteryear or the kidney machines of today.

In conclusion, many of these suggestions are long term in nature.

However, I refuse to accept the position that it is inevitable that research is always too late for policy relevance. I take the position that the research and evaluation industry has a responsibility to educate policymakers to the fact that sometimes they need to wait for more information.

At OMB I saw numerous examples of the use of insufficient hard information as a rationale for not moving ahead at a given moment, when political considerations or ideology were the real reasons. I think it is equally important that lack of good information be seen as a perfectly *legitimate* reason to wait. I support the position of my former colleague, Paul O'Neill, that some way must be found to insulate important long-term research and data collection activities from the political process and the vagaries of annual appropriations. I am impressed by the way in which the Institute of Medicine has come to serve the role of evaluator/researcher for the Congress in certain policy areas where the "decision to wait" was made. Enough attention was raised by the teaching hospitals with respect to Section 227 of the Social Security Amendments of 1972 (that would have affected the payment of teaching physicians under Medicare and Medicaid in a detrimental way, according to the teaching hospitals), that implementation of that section was deferred pending the results of an Institute of Medicine study. Results of the study, which will be available in 1976, should improve the quality of the final decision by the Senate Finance Committee and the Ways and Means Committee on how to reimburse physicians for care delivered in teaching hospitals.

In short, the policymakers need to sort out what it is they want to find out from long-term prospective evaluation research. Then, they must work with the evaluators in the design of the experiments and be prepared to use the information when it becomes available. Although this takes time and money, can we really continue to afford the alternatives? Maybe, if we can move in this direction, we can discard my old Abt Associates' motto or at least modify it into a testable hypothesis: ignorance may be no bar to action, but does knowledge do very much to improve the results?

HOSPITAL PRODUCTIVITY TRENDS IN SHORT-TERM GENERAL NON-TEACHING HOSPITALS

Jerry Cromwell
Abt Associates Inc.

Over the last decade the health sector of the U.S. economy has experienced a rate of inflation considerably higher than that of the rest of the economy. Moreover, since 1967 the hospital daily service charge has risen at nearly 13.5 percent per year, or over twice the rate of inflation in the medical care sector as a whole.[1]

Recently, two causes of hospital inflation have been singled out for empirical analysis—growing third-party payment schemes and limited productivity change. Martin Feldstein[2] and Salkever[3] both have shown the importance of increasing demand on medical care and hospital process, emphasizing the role of net patient cost after adjusting for third-party coverage. Lower net prices to consumers reflect the immediate cost of care, thereby encouraging greater utilization of services. Hospitals and physicians also are more inclined to raise average fees as price discrimination becomes less common.

Less empirical work has been done on hospital productivity, although Feldstein has done some pioneering theoretical and quantitative work in the field both for British and American hospitals.[4] While the existing literature measuring hospital productivity trends over time is not extensive, there are two studies, one by Feldstein and one by Elnicki, that are instructive. Feldstein constructed real capital and labor input indexes per patient day between 1955 and 1968 and found that real inputs rose at 3.8 percent per year, implying a 3.8 percent annual decline in productivity unless, as Feldstein notes, there has been a change in the nature of the product.[5] The problem with putting inputs on a patient day basis is an obvious one. A day of patient care today requires a considerably greater intensity of resources and is viewed by patients more favorably than a day of care 10 or 20 years ago.

Using Feldstein's estimated rate of real resource growth per patient day, we can deduce the rates of productivity growth that would be consistent with hypothesized changes in the quality of care. Total factor productivity in the initial year would simply be the ration of patient days (PD_0) to factor inputs (F_0) aggregated by relative shares. If we assume that patient days have been growing at q percent and real factor inputs at r percent per year, then productivity in any year t would be:

$$(1) \quad P_t = e^{(q-r)t} \cdot PD_0/F_0$$

According to Feldstein's figures, the rate of productivity growth (q-r) stands at a -3.8 percent per year, or an increase in real factor inputs per patient day of 3.8 percent yearly. We can incorporate quality into Equation (1) by making an upward adjustment in the growth of PD_0 beyond the simple growth in the number of days, say, s percent annually. The growth of the productivity index will be (q+s-r) percent yearly. While a universally accepted definition of "quality care" does not currently exist, formulating productivity change as the composite of changes in real resources per patient day (q-r) and quality change (s) clearly differentiates the increasing intensity of resources used from quality improvement. They are not necessarily the same, although often viewed as synonymous.

Knowing (q-r) already permits us to establish trade-offs between the change in productivity and s, the rate of quality growth. For example, the rate of quality improvement would have to be 3.8 percent yearly if total factor productivity growth were to be as high as zero, and 5 percent if productivity were to rise at 1.2 percent. A 3.8 percent quality change, however, would imply a "doubling" of hospital quality every 19 years.[6] While it is difficult to imagine any general hospital or health indicator recording such an increase, there may be extenuating circumstances that might still allow for positive productivity growth. One possibility might be the changing case-mix of hospitals requiring greater intensity of services per patient day. If such were the case, it would reflect a basic change in the nature of the product. In a different vein, we might use a broader measure of health care which would include such psychological concepts as reduced anxiety and pain relief. Although we do not know their quantitative importance, it is conceivable that significant contributions have been made in this area in the last 20 years that are not taken into account in published health statistics.

Elnicki's study addressed the problem of a growing intensity of services per patient day (which was ignored in Feldstein's work) by defining hospital output as the aggregated outputs of each department of the hospital. Departmental outputs for 1960 and 1969 were aggregated by unit costs in the two periods and then divided by the respective man-hours of labor to arrive at Laspeyres and Paasche indexes of labor productivity ranging from .62 percent to 1.54 percent per year.[7]

Besides problems in output definitions, discussed later, these results are not generally applicable nationally because they cover only a very limited sample, i.e., three Connecticut hospitals, and require disaggregated data in a degree of detail unavailable at the national level.

The plan of this paper is to adapt the general methodology used by Elnicki in his study to readily available, published data provided by the Hospital Administrative Services (HAS) program of the American Hospital Association. In the next section, we discuss some theoretical aspects of the method, concentrating in particular on the definition of department output, the measurement of input flows, the alternatives for valuing output, and finally the ubiquitous problem of quality. Then, we discuss the data base used for the analysis and provide a summary of the results of our analysis. Finally, we outline some important areas of future research.

ESTIMATING HOSPITAL PRODUCTIVITY BY DEPARTMENT

The major theoretical (and practical) difficulty in measuring hospital productivity has been the determination of a quality-constant definition of output. The growing body of literature on the question has concentrated either on patients served or illnesses treated. The former, and most often used, involves measures of patient time spent in the hospital itself. The patient day or more preferably, the episode of illness, both fall into this category. The strength of these measures lies in their simplicity and availability.

A second set of output definitions involves various forms of end-product indicators.[8] These indicators have an advantage over duration-of-stay variables in that they reflect the impact health services have on health status, e.g., changes in infant mortality rates as a result of hospitalization. The problem with such indicators is that while they do measure changes in health (and thus the quality of services provided), it is quite difficult to appropriate any general change in health status only to hospitalization. Improved nutrition, reduced poverty, increased education, all can contribute to better health as well. End-product measures are unsatisfactory for productivity estimation because of the lack of a clearly defined relationship between hospital services and changed community health status. Of course, patient days is also an unsatisfactory measure unless some generally accepted technique can be devised to make them comparable over time. Moreover, contributions to psychological need such as reduced anxiety and pain are not included in any end-product or patient day indicator, but these are important services provided in all health care institutions.

Selected Hospital Services. A third alternative, and one which we employ in the present study, is to concentrate on a selected number of hospital services (usually categorized by department) where it is believed that the quality change in service provision has been minor. We have in mind the more routine services of the hospital such as administration, dietary, laundry, housekeeping, plant, medical records, and pharmacy. It is in the departments where hospital personnel have either direct (nursing, operating, and delivery rooms), or indirect (radiology, laboratory) responsibility for improving patient health that we expect most quality change to be taking place. Thus, it would seem feasible to estimate an overall productivity trend for the routine services of the hospital without incurring too serious a downward bias due to resource-using quality improvements. Also, by concentrating on the routine services of the hospital, the problem of measuring department output as something other than labor input is significantly reduced.[9] Dietary, laundry, medical records, and pharmacy all have an easily definable unit of output, while housekeeping and operation of plant require the servicing of a specified number of square feet of hospital space.

Defining administrative output, in comparison to the other six routine areas, is much more difficult. For many years, the HAS program simply used the number of beds in the hospital as a measure of administrative "output," no doubt influenced by the administrator's end goal of serving bedridden patients. But if we regard the administrator as a coordinator of people, equipment, and supplies and as the hospital's link with the community it serves, then the changing number of beds in a hospital may not adequately reflect his growing administrative responsibilities. Several alternative measures of output have been suggested to us, including total hospital costs (suggested by Paul Ginsburg), and a weighted average of the outputs of the other departments of the hospital (suggested by John Kendrick). While both measures have their advantages, we have chosen to adjust the published administrative productivity indexes by the change in "personnel per bed," arguing that the administrator's responsibilities and functions increase roughly proportionately with the staff under him. (Research by Neuhauser and Andersen[10] actually shows a declining ratio of managers to employees as the number of hospital personnel increases, implying non-proportional growth; but this does not include clerical personnel, which are

.Table 1

ANNUAL RATES OF GROWTH OF PERSONNEL PER BED
AND BEDS PER ADMINSTRATIVE MAN-HOUR BY BED SIZE,
1964-1971

Bed size	Growth rate of personnel	Growth rate of beds per adminis-trative man-hour	Growth rate of personnel per admin-istrative man-hour*
<50	3.11	-0.04	3.07
50-74	2.23	-1.80	0.43
75-99	2.23	-2.06	0.17
100-149	2.15	-4.17	-2.02
150-199	2.15	-5.31	-3.16
200-299	2.74	-4.91	-2.17
300-399	2.86	-4.58	-1.72
400+	4.16	-2.60	1.56

*Column 3 equals column 1 plus column 2. Source: Journal of the American Hospital Association, Guide Issues, 1964 and 1971.

reflect both unit costs and intensity of service per discharge; that is to say,

(2) $EXP_i = TC_i/Q_i \cdot Q_i/D \cdot D/TC = TC_i/TC$,

where

EXP_i = Percent of total hospital costs originating in the "i"th department

TC_i = Total yearly costs of "i"th department

Q_i = Units of output of "i"th department

D   = Number of hospital discharges per year

believed to have increased as a percent of hospital personnel since the advent of Medicare). Also by using a physical dimension of output, we are avoiding the problem of inflation of costs, a problem that would occur if total hospital costs were used.

We adjusted the growth in administrative productivity, defined by HAS as the change in the number of beds serviced per administrative man-hour, by adding to it the growth in personnel per bed (see Table 1). This has the effect of putting administrative productivity on a "personal managed" basis. The decline in productivity as reported by HAS (Table 1, column 2) is completely offset in the three smallest and the largest bed size category by the growth in personnel per bed, while in the middle bed sizes the decline is reduced by approximately 50 percent.

Once the departments were selected and the adjustment in administration carried out, each department's published productivity index was weighted by the department's expense percent of total costs to arrive at a weighted average index for all routine services combined. Department expense percents were used as weights because they reflect both unit costs and intensity of service per discharge; that is to say,

(2) $EXP_i = TC_i/Q_i \cdot Q_i/D \cdot D/TC = TC_i/TC,$

where

EXP_i = Percent of total hospital costs originating in the "i"th department

TC_i = Total yearly costs of "i"th department

Q_i = Units of output of "i"th department

D = Number of hospital discharges per year

TC = Total hospital costs = $\Sigma_i TC_i$

Now unit costs (TC_i/Q_i) may not accurately reflect the true contribution to patient care made by one unit (e.g., a pound of laundry) produced by any particular department, and given the wide variations in accounting procedures, they may not perfectly measure even the costs incurred; but as averages they probably are not too far off, at least in relative terms.

Intensity of output per discharge (Q_i/D) is another question. If certain departments have considerably increased their output per discharge without actually affecting patient health (surgery, for example), then the true expense percent for the department (as a product of average cost and average product) would be an *overestimate* of the value of output. We have reduced the impact of such misleading changes in our study by using base period expense percents throughout (final period expense percents did not significantly alter the results), but this does not take care of imperfections in the original expense percents themselves.

Before turning to a description of the data and our results, it would be instructive to summarize our methodology in the light of the existing literature on hospital goals and objectives. Because most hospitals are not profit-maximizers, some might argue that the usual analysis of productivity change cannot be applied. But such arguments seem spurious, in that no matter what objective function hospitals attempt to maximize, e.g., specialized personnel, prestige, etc., cost minimization for every level of goal attainment would still be the only rational decision-making criterion. Admitting this, the concept of weighting departmental productivity indices by corresponding expense percents seems justified. Only if the cost minimization criterion were applied very unevenly over the different cost centers would expense percents be inappropriate weights in a *relative* sense. In the absence of knowledge to the contrary, it is reasonable to assume that the reported expense percents accurately represent actual input costs, if not absolutely at least relatively.

THE DATA

The HAS program of the American Hospital Association collects, processes, and disseminates information on costs, revenues, and productivity trends for over 3,000 member hospitals. Data are categorized by hospital types, bed size, and region. All short-term, general, non-teaching hospitals were included in the present study, or over 2,000 hospitals. HAS coverage has grown considerably over the study period and we do not know the impact such changes have on our results. The following analysis is done by bed size, however, which at least reduces the effects of changing participation rates by this important variable. Still, other factors might possibly have varied with changing participation rates of which we are unaware, but a more detailed study of sample size is beyond the scope of the study.

The actual data used were taken from published national comparative reports for the month of June (a three-month running average) for the years 1964 through 1971. The man-hours per activity included all paid time—regular salaried, vacation, and overtime. Man-hours were allocated to each department on a basis of time spent in each department. Expenses reflect only direct costs; indirect costs, including capital, are not allocated to departments.[11] The fact that our study focuses exclusively on *labor* productivity reduces the allocation problem somewhat in that non-labor costs are more difficult to appropriate to particular departments. Finally, there is the more general question of the accuracy and uniformity of hospital reporting. The lack of any HAS data control detracts from our confidence in the following analysis, but the data are certainly adequate to illustrate the potential in the estimating technique.

National Trends in Hospital Productivity. Table 2 presents the adjusted growth rates for all 12 departments for the eight bed sizes over the 1964-1971 period. The last column provides a weighted average across the eight bed sizes and thus represents a national productivity growth rate for 12 cost centers of the short-term, general, non-teaching hospital. The weights used to arrive at this column were the percent of patient days in each bed size category to total patients days for 1971.[12] A routine-service and all-department productivity growth rate for each of the bed sizes appears in rows 8 and 14, using 1964 departmental expense percents as weights.

Redefinitions of department output occurred in three departments in 1969. Housekeeping and operation of plant were changed from "beds" to "square feet," while pharmacy was changed to "line items." To arrive at an estimate of productivity change for the entire 1964-1971 period, we assumed that the growth rates realized in housekeeping, plant and pharmacy in the 1969-1971 period were also attained in the earlier period. Obviously, we have no way of knowing how accurate this assumption is, but it is the only way we can combine data for the two periods in a way that reflects the results using the preferred productivity indicators of the post-1969 period.

Nationally, productivity change was positive in housekeeping, laundry, plant, pharmacy, radiology, and laboratory and negative in administration, dietary, nursing, medical records, operating, and delivery. For all departments taken together, labor productivity growth amounted to .17 percent per year. While not a very impressive figure, it must be remembered that quality change in certain included departments such as nursing is obscuring much of the productivity growth. In fact, any

Table 2--Growth rates of hospital productivity by department by bed size for short-term general hospitals, 1964-1971

Department (Units per man-hour)	<50	50-74	75-99	100-149	150-199	200-299	300-399	400+	All Bed Sizes
Administration (personnel)	3.07	0.43	0.17	-2.02	-3.16	-2.17	-1.72	1.56	-0.30
Dietary (meals)	-1.67	-2.44	-0.82	-1.33	-0.09	-0.86	-0.76	-0.69	-0.89
Housekeeping (square feet)	3.90	3.60	5.10	4.50	5.30	2.30	4.10	3.20	3.70
Laundry (pounds)	-0.76	0.71	-0.33	-0.26	2.43	1.53	1.58	3.03	1.71
Plant (square feet)	4.70	4.80	3.20	3.50	4.30	-0.30	7.30	0.00	2.40
Pharmacy (line-items)	7.70	6.70	3.70	-1.50	-0.60	1.40	0.80	8.00	4.00
Medical records (beds)	NA	NA	NA	-3.53	-3.27	-4.19	-1.87	-2.86	-2.53
Routine Services	2.42	1.42	1.10	-0.27	0.16	-0.54	0.81	1.65	0.88
Nursing (beds)	0.69	-0.77	-1.08	-2.14	-2.15	-2.16	-1.89	-2.28	-1.38
Operating (visits)	NA	NA	NA	0.88	-0.63	-0.11	-0.96	-0.30	-0.24
Delivery (deliveries)	NA	NA	NA	1.43	0.34	2.02	-3.72	-0.85	-0.99
Radiology (procedures)	3.94	1.11	1.41	0.86	2.62	2.36	-2.50	2.64	1.60
Laboratory (tests	-0.20	0.00	2.93	2.93	2.64	3.01	2.46	3.35	2.66
All departments	1.79	0.51	0.45	-0.42	-0.15	-0.46	-0.29	0.53	0.17

Source: HAS Comparative Reports, June 1964-1971.

positive estimate at all is very indicative of significant productivity growth and should be regarded as a minimum figure. Productivity growth in the routine services, which are less sensitive to quality changes, is significantly higher, approximating .9 percent per year. Growth was highest in the small and very large bed sizes, but the figures for the smaller bed sizes have an unknown upward bias due to the lack of productivity data for three departments—medical records, operating rooms, and delivery rooms. Still, productivity growth for administration, plant, nursing, pharmacy, and radiology was relatively high for the less-than-50 bed size. Possibly the greater number of profit-oriented hospitals in this category would explain some of the increase.

The significant productivity growth in the over-400 bed size may have been due to a combination of growing economies-of-scale and the substitution of capital for labor. The high rates of labor productivity growth in radiology and laboratory, for instance, can be explained by the increased utilization of auto-analyzers and other equipment which have significantly raised the capital-output ratio in these departments.

DISCUSSION

The rapid rise in hospital costs beginning in 1966 has accentuated the need for empirical and theoretical research on hospital efficiency. We have tried in this paper to estimate trends in hospital labor productivity using a method that reduces the problem of quality change by concentrating only on a limited number of departments. To the extent that routine services in their contribution to patient care have not significantly improved care over the last eight years, our estimate of productivity growth using just these services is unbiased. Focusing on these services alone, we found the rate of productivity growth to be nearly 1 percent per year. How applicable this percentage is to the entire hospital is unknown, as the included routine services account for only 50 percent of total costs.

This study has only touched the surface of the measurement of hospital productivity change, restricted to readily available HAS publications. Considerable theoretical and empirical work still must be done, not only to verify the accuracy of available data, but to devise ways of measuring productivity in departments where service quality is improving at a significant rate. More thought needs to be given to the definition of department output as well as the measurement of non-labor inputs by department so that a total factor productivity index can be devised.

Most of the empirical research in the field so far has been of a cross-sectional nature. Work now is in progress by Ralph Berry to estimate production functions for all U.S. general hospitals by service mix. Still, practically no econometric analysis of productivity trends within hospital cost centers has been carried out. Such research could explain the impact size, incentive systems, service mix, and technical advance have on changes in efficiency over time.

NOTES

1. Department of Health, Education and Welfare, Social Security Administration. *Medical Care Costs and Prices: Background Book,* 1972, p. 10.

2. Feldstein, M. "Hospital Cost Inflation: A Study of Nonprofit Price Dynamics," *American Economic Review* (December 1971).

3. Salkever, D. "A Microeconomic Study of Hospital Cost Inflation," *Journal of Political Economy* (November/December 1972).

4. Feldstein, M. *Economic Analysis for Health Service Efficiency: Econometric Studies of the British National Health Service* (Amsterdam: North Holland Publishing Co., 1967).

5. Feldstein, M. *The Rising Cost of Hospital Care* (Washington, D.C.: National Center for Health Statistics Research and Development, December 1971) p. 25. Ralph Berry has updated Feldstein's figures for the last four years. His results show that between 1969-1972, real inputs per patient day have been increasing at a rate of 6.4 percent per year. See: Berry, R. "Perspectives on Rate Regulation," paper presented at the Conference on Regulation in the Health Industry, Institute of Medicine, Washington, D.C., January 1974, Table 6.

6. We adjusted Feldstein's factor input figures downward to account for the substitution of lesser skilled personnel in the hospital. This reduced the apparent productivity decline to 3.2 percent. Still this would imply a doubling of quality every 22 years.

7. Elnicki, R. "Effect of Phase II Controls on Hospital Services," *Health Services Research* 7:114 (Summer 1972).

8. Donabedian, A. "Evaluating the Quality of Medical Care," *Milbank Memorial Fund Quarterly* (July 1966); Shapiro, S. "End-Result Measurement of Quality of Medical Care," *Milbank Memorial Fund Quarterly* (April 1967).

9. Many of the departments in Elnicki's study had some dimensions of labor time as an output measure. Thus, as time spent in these departments increased so did output, but we are not sure how much of this increase was due to increased activity and how much to inefficiency. The use of an input dimension as an output measure can lead to serious problems of interpretation.

10. Neuhauser, D. and Andersen, R. "Structural-Comparative Studies of Hospitals." In: Georgopoulos, B. *Organizational Research on Health Institutions* (Ann Arbor: Institute of Social Research, 1972) pp. 83-114.

11. Hospital Administrative Services. *The Guide to Uniform Reporting.*

12. These percentages were 4.7, 6.25, 6.25, 8.7, 8.7, 15.7, 14.1, and 35.4 for the smallest to largest bed sizes, respectively.

SHORT TERM DEMONSTRATION PROJECTS

George Nash
Montclair State College

Demonstration grants and experiments are rightly designed attempts to answer questions about process and impact. If the answers were known with absolute assurance, then programs could begin on a larger scale. The problem with most social experiments and demonstration programs is that they are extremely costly and the answers are a long time a-coming.

This paper will discuss two short-term demonstration projects operated by the Vera Institute of Justice in New York City and evaluated by the author. One was in the field of criminal justice and the other involved the delivery of health services. One lasted one day and the other four days. The results of one of the demonstrations were completely positive and the idea was eventually adopted. The other resulted in mixed reviews and it was not adopted.

This paper will discuss the specifics of each of the projects and describe the advantages of short-term projects with built-in evaluations.

THE ANTECEDENTS

Both projects were run by the Vera Institute of Justice in New York City, an organization with a successful record of innovation. It pioneered a system of release on recognizance which reformed bail procedures for low-income persons, and its evaluation of its demonstration project proved that the system worked and saved money. Vera, operating under Mayor John Lindsay's Criminal Justice Coordinating Council, was able to tap the resources of the New York City Police Department, obtain cooperation from other New York City agencies, utilize volunteers, and get a good press.

The two programs tackled the public distress of inebriated Skid Row alcoholics and street crime in Central Harlem. Each was a highly visible problem which had stirred widespread concern.

Columbia University's Bureau of Applied Social Research became involved with Vera because of its long-term study of the residents and institutions of Manhattan's Bowery Skid Row District. This research had shown that there were fewer hard-core alcoholics than had previously been assumed and that police procedures which had attempted to control the problem produced impressive statistics, but wasted large amounts of manpower and did not help to solve the problem of intoxicated men lying in the streets.

We started with a Mayor who wanted to do something, an action agency that was well accepted, and a knowledge of the basic problem because of our research. We had found that the total number of men who lived in the Bowery was smaller than people had thought and was declining. Second of all, the number of "public nuisance" alcoholics who laid down on the sidewalks was much smaller than people thought. Despite this, there were a tremendous number of arrests—something like 50,000 per year—because of police practices. The police had worked out a very efficient system. Several times a day they took a paddy wagon out and filled it up with people. One of the best times to do this was in the middle of the afternoon because a lot of men were coming home from work and the streets were crowded. To the Bowery men the arrival of the paddy wagon was the entertainment of the day. Men scurried out of the way so they would not get picked up. The one way to be sure not to be picked up was to be lying asleep on the street because then a person was too much of a bother. The policeman would come up with a nightstick, tap the man on the sole of the shoe, and if he did not move, he was left because the policeman wanted to avoid people who were difficult. The people who were arrested, many of whom were not even intoxicated at the time they were arrested, were usually released that same day, and it did nothing to help clean up the Bowery.

THE BOWERY DETOXIFICATION CENTER

In a joint planning effort, the Vera planners and the Bureau of Applied Social Research researchers determined that one solution to the problems of the Bowery would be a short-term inpatient hospital type detoxification center which would have an outreach arm—a team which would voluntarily help distressed Bowery denizens off the sidewalk and bring them in to the Detox Center.

It was decided to hold a one-day demonstration project both to see if the concept was viable and to answer the following key questions:

1. Could the men be persuaded to come to such a center voluntarily, and as a corollary, would the police therefore be able to stop arresting them?

2. Would it be possible to run the detoxification center inside the city's Men's Shelter, which had many useful backup services, but which was widely distrusted and disliked by the Skid Row men?

3. Would the men actually be helped by a detoxification center? It wasn't anticipated that it would bring about long-term rehabilitation, but would the men at least stay until they had recovered if it was operated on a purely voluntary basis?

4. Finally, there were many process-oriented questions. How should the center and the pickup team be staffed? What kind of medicines, medical care, and facilities would be needed? Would violence be a problem?

With about six weeks of planning in the fall of 1966, it was possible to set up and operate the detoxification center on a one-day basis. An underutilized floor of the Men's Shelter was cleaned up and made into a makeshift infirmary. Staff was laid on and trained. Supplies were gotten in.

A large number of operation people and observers were on hand on a chilly fall morning when the street team went out to attempt to round up volunteer patients.

The team, which was composed of two former alcoholics and a policeman, approached the first downed, inebriated man and asked him if he wanted to be cleaned up and detoxified. "Go away and leave me alone," was his indignant response when he finally stirred. Somewhat discouraged, the team reconsidered its approach.

The approach finally settled on had one of the paraprofessionals shaking the man gently and offering him a cigarette. Once he had sat up and lit up, the potential client was asked how he felt. Inevitably, his response was some variation of the word terrible. Once that admission had been secured, and the man was awake and involved in a trusting relationship with the team member, he was usually quite willing to accept the offer of bed, bath, meals, and medicine.

During the first day, approximately 12 of the 15 men approached on the street accepted the offer to come to the center and all but one stayed when he got there. Bowery men usually have a host of complaints about how they are treated by official agencies, including the Men's Shelter in which the detoxification center was located. Extra care was taken to make sure that the men were treated with dignity. They were called "Mr." The intake procedure prior to being showered and put in bed was cut to a bare minimum, taking no more than two or three minutes from entry into the reception area. The clients were treated with dignity in all phases of the operation.

By the end of the day, it was clear that men would come to such a center voluntarily and that the center had the potential to help the men. At that point, with the day's experience complete, the facility was shut down. The men were shifted to hospital facilities elsewhere to complete their detoxification, they were interviewed at length, and they were subject to followup. Two weeks after the completion of the one-day experiment, the evaluation report was turned in.

Everyone connected with the venture concluded that it was a feasible alternative to the arrest of disabled public intoxicants. The next problem was to secure funding. It actually took almost one year after the one-day demonstration project for long-term funding to be arranged. The fact that the project had proven feasible in actual operation gave the Vera people heart in pursuing the funds and made the project more graphic to potential funders. Once long-range funding was assured, the project began and operated in much the same manner as it had during the one-day demonstration project.

As of this date, the project has endured for seven years, has expanded to other parts of New York City, and is hailed as a model. The short-term demonstration project probably played a major role in its birth and growth.

THE COMMUNITY PATROL CORPS

The idea was to try to use a team of inner city young men to work in conjunction with the police in an effort to cut street crime and improve police community relations.

Again the project was undertaken under the auspices of a special committee of the Mayor's Criminal Justice Coordinating Council. The positive experience of the one-day demonstration project alluded to above led to the idea of another short-term demonstration. A brief one-day recognizance effort involving two young people in January led to the decision to hold a large four-day demonstration project in March.

The questions that the demonstration project sought to answer included:

1. Would a community patrol corps reduce crime, especially street crime?

2. Would it help to alleviate other problems such as false alarms and littering?

3. How would city agencies including the police, the fire department, and the sanitation department respond to such a community organization?

4. What kind of response would there be from the citizens of the inner city community?

5. What would the operational problems of the program be and how much would it cost on an ongoing basis?

The Community Patrol Corps was a much bigger operation than the experiment involving the Bowery Detoxification Center because of the number of people involved and the need for the residents of the community to understand what was happening. A luncheon was held at a Central Harlem restaurant to explain the proposed program to Harlem leaders. The program was publicized ahead of time and press coverage was allowed at the two-day training session that preceded the four days of patrol. Mayor Lindsay himself addressed those involved with the project before the Corps Members started off on their first foot patrol.

Approximately 30 young men were recruited and paid to undergo two days of training and to participate in four days of patrol. A number of leaders of organizations in the area were picked to serve in cadres. Those who began training with the experiment completed a questionnaire which revealed that most of the young men involved were employed, but would have preferred employment in an organization like the Community Patrol Corps or the police to the work they were doing.

The training was fairly extensive covering aspects of the law, communication, self defense, first aid, and descriptions of the relevant city agencies. The Corps Members were issued special khaki jackets which they got to keep. Two cars were rented as command vehicles, and the Motorola Corporation donated walkie-talkies. A vacant store front was donated by the City Housing Authority and spruced up. Two police sergeants were assigned to the unit to handle communications out of the store front.

The attitudes of the experimental Corps Members were interesting. By and large, they shared the general community apprehension of the police. Before beginning their tours, the young men (who were generally between the ages of 18 and 25 and all either black or Puerto Rican) were convinced that the police did not really try hard enough to prevent crime and did not really patrol the streets with sufficient vigilance. The attitude of the young experimental Corps Members before beginning the program was "We're going to get out there and stop crime because we're honest and we're not afraid."

There were problems in the definition of the Corps Members' status. They were unarmed. They did not have the right to arrest. They did not necessarily have the obligation to report crime. In case of trouble, they were expected to call the police. A number of the men said that they had reservations about the criminal justice system and that if they saw someone breaking the law they would tell them to stop it, but they would not do anything to lead to a person's being arrested.

The four days of patrol covered the high-crime times from early afternoon to early morning and included a weekend and two weekday evenings. The area covered included seven high-crime patrol posts in one precinct. At the end, the evaluators attempted to assess the impact of the program.

Basically, the results as far as impact on crime were disappointing. Comparing the number of arrests made in the area to the same four days in several preceding weeks, there was no difference in reported crimes or arrests. Furthermore, there was no other way of proving that the patrol had had any impact on crime. Most of their efforts were devoted to routine problems or minor incidents, things that often do involve the police. Stalled cars were helped out of intersections they were blocking. The authorities were called to remove several dogs hit by cars and several abandoned vehicles. Several drunks were returned home. Some sick people were helped to the hospital. A number of women called or came by the store front to request escort service home from night work or evening meetings. Corps Members spotted problems relating to refuse and building safety and filled out the appropriate forms to get the various city agencies to deal with these problems.

The program ran into serious operating difficulties. Several of the Corps Members drank on duty. Girl friends appeared and were given rides in the command cars. There were reports of reckless and dangerous driving. The Corps Members had numerous complaints about the various agencies with which they interacted. The Corps Member who called the police when he witnessed a fight which he mistakenly reported as a knife attack refused to give the police his name or any information about the incident.

In summary, the Community Patrol Corps performed a number of useful community services, but did not become involved with crime nor apparently did it diminish the amount of criminal activity. It had a host of operating problems.

To have operated the program on an ongoing basis would have proven to be extremely expensive. To be effective, the program would have had to have enlisted the cooperation of the relevant city agencies who would have done the work, such as the police and the sanitation department. However, these departments already complained that they were underbudgeted for their work in the Central Harlem area; and they did not relish the formation of a new organization. Furthermore, members of the Auxiliary Police Department who for years had been paying for their own uniforms and doing volunteer police work on an almost no budget basis were extremely upset at the attention given the budding program.

A team of researchers headed by the author covered all aspects of the program and interviewed area residents and businessmen before and during the program. The research report was turned in two weeks after the end of the project and widely circulated among all who had helped to plan it.

Excellent community response to the program was the only absolutely positive result of the four-day operational experiment. When the program was over and the research report digested, there was very little enthusiasm on the part of those who originally promoted the idea to pursue it. It was felt that it was a good idea, but one which would not necessarily cut street crime and would be very expensive to run as a long-term official city program.

The short-term demonstration project concluded that the program was not as promising as was originally hoped. Plans to develop the program were abandoned. Interestingly enough, this program in 1968 generally preceded the whole movement of citizen involvement in the areas of public safety and the criminal justice system. Since that time, a number of programs involving citizens in the protection of their communities have sprung up around the country, but most have not been official city endeavors involving public funds for full-time employees.

CONCLUSIONS

What was learned from these two short-term demonstration projects aside from the fact that one led to the adoption of an innovation and the other did not? These two programs conclusively demonstrated to this author, the Vera Institute of Justice, and the Mayor of New York City's Criminal Justice Coordinating Council that short-term demonstration projects are a viable means of testing ideas and getting quick answers about the potential impact of new programs.

In retrospect the advantages are as follows:

1. Low cost. Very little out-of-pocket money was required. Most of the people who participated in the two projects either borrowed time from their regular assignments or were volunteers. Only a small number of people were actually hired and their employment was brief. Even the research funds were modest.

2. Planning for real events. The people who worked to set up the two projects were not just writing proposals which might or might not be acted upon at some uncertain time in the future. They were planning a real program that was actually going to take place in the imminent future. The focus was on activities rather than phrases.

3. The demonstrations were graphic. Because those who were involved in policymaking and funding decisions were able to see something concrete happening, they were able to learn much more about the possibility of the ideas becoming realities than would have been the case from reading proposals. The actual projects and their planning were intense, exciting affairs which allowed for deep involvement.

4. Basic questions were answered quickly. The demonstration projects focused on specific questions. Because the researchers were involved in the planning they were able to make their questions and observations relevant. The small-scale nature of the work allowed the reports to be rendered quickly. In each case, the draft reports were turned in in a matter of two-to-three weeks after the completion of the

demonstration. Suggestions for revisions were quickly forthcoming because of the clients' interest in the studies.

For all those involved in the research, the short-term demonstration projects were meaningful experiences that were extremely rewarding. A tremendous amount of activity and planning was concentrated in a brief period of time. In less time than it usually takes to get a response to a proposal from a federal agency, the projects were conceived, executed, evaluated, and the outcomes of the evaluations were acted upon.

REFERENCES

The Draft Report, "The Planning and Operation of the Experimental Detoxification Center" is available from the author, 33 pp, 1966.

"The Community Patrol Corps: A Descriptive Evaluation of the One-Week Experiment" by the author is available from the Columbia University Bureau of Applied Social Research, 64 pp + 20 photographs, 1968.

IN-HOUSE EVALUATION CAPABILITY

John C. Sessler, Ph.D.
Senior Program Analyst
Drug Abuse Council, Inc.

More than 10 years ago there was much discussion and movement focused on bringing the experience the Department of Defense had with its unique operations research and study group organizations into other departments of the federal government. The idea being that as organizations such as RAND, the Institute for Defense Analyses, and the Johns Hopkins Operations Research Office had been very important in the development of programs within the Air Force, Navy, etc. so similar organizations should be useful in HEW, Justice, etc. One result of this was the establishment of the Urban Institute, now with more than five years of experience providing this kind of support to federal and local governments.

These efforts to extend operations research applications overlooked one quite successful kind of organization that is in some ways similar to the RAND Corporation but in other ways very different. This difference is operating forces of the Navy. The organization is called the Operations Evaluation Group (OEG) of the Center for Naval Analyses (CNA). Today I would like to take some of my experiences with the Operations Evaluation Group and the experiences of others who were in OEG before me, put this together with the experience of some of the other organizations like the RAND Corporation, the Institute for Defense Analyses, and the Weapon Systems Evaluation Group to indicate a broad model for the type of organization which may be useful in evaluating our social programs.

First, I want to point out that I am not really optimistic that such an organization will ever be established within other federal departments, as for example in the National Institute for Drug Abuse. Furthermore, federal spending on evaluation and research, at least in the area I am most familiar with, drug abuse, seems to be on a decline. So it seems unlikely that even the modest amount of new money that would be required will be made available for the long-term funding needed. On the other hand, this seems like a good time to be thinking of improving the quality, timeliness, and impact of evaluation on our social programs.

A small amount of background information on the Operations Evaluation Group will be useful since many of you may be unfamiliar with that organization. OEG was established about 1942, the early days of World War II, from a small group of physical scientists at the Massachusetts Institute of Technology who were working on anti-submarine warfare problems for the Navy. The Navy at that time was undergoing a rather traumatic experience from the German submarine threat in the Atlantic and was ready to try just about anything—organizational or otherwise—to solve this problem. The group grew in size to about 40 or 50 professionals, shrank following World War II, and increased again during the Korean War. Over the first 20 years of its existence it had a maximum of approximately 60 professionals. In 1962, it was organized into a much larger entity called the Center for Naval Analyses which took on a wider variety of problems for the Navy and Marine Corps, including cost-effectiveness studies and long-term policy analysis. Within the Center, the OEG continued to do its work pretty much unchanged from what it had been previously, although its role became somewhat more specialized. Thus, for over 30 years OEG provided the Navy with an independent in-house evaluation capability.

What are the important characteristics for this organization? I think there are two, and they work in opposition to each other. One is a large degree of independence and the second is a close working relationship. Pairing these attributes is perhaps difficult, but it provides a utility to the organization which I do not believe has been achieved in other ways. Support groups seem to move either too close, becoming a captive group absorbed in the clients' work (thereby losing the freedom to question), or they emphasize independence and thereby lose the access needed for substantial work. These attributes of independence and a close relationship have been characterized in another way by Dr. Steinhardt who led the OEG during most of its first 20 years. Dr. Steinhardt describes the relationship as similar to that between the client and counselor or patient and doctor.[1] The implications of this relationship are privileged communication, freedom for the evaluation group to conduct its own affairs in the interest of the client, and access to all relevant information. One would imagine then that it requires a lot of tact and diplomacy for such an organization to exist in association with a federal agency.

I would like to discuss the independence side of this relationship first. The three main ways in which independence is achieved are through the funding, through the process of selecting projects, and in the agreement on distribution of reports. Forward funding is a necessity to the independence of the organization. This was recognized, for example, in the establishment of the Urban Institute where three years of funding was provided initially, although at present the evaluation division is funded on a project basis. Forward funding is important in two ways: (1) it permits longer-term planning so that projects can be undertaken that look to the future needs of the client, and (2) it provides the stability that enables recruitment of individuals of high caliber to work in the group. Along the lines of recruitment of individuals and the maintenance of professional standards, I would like to add one point. Many of those selected will be educated in scientific discipline outside of evaluation. There is a need to provide some form of rotation through the academic community so these individuals can maintain their professional skills.

The process used for selecting projects shows very clearly the degree of independence allowed to an organization. In the Institute for Defense Analyses, RAND Corporation, and CNA, for example, projects are mutually agreed upon with provision in the charter for some self-initiated projects. Thus, all projects are not the result of a direct request from the client. These self-initiated investigations are along the lines of the clients' area of activity, and many arise as a result of attempts to anticipate future needs. Within the OEG, prior to the formation of the Center for Naval Analyses, up to one-third of the projects could have been self-initiated. At present, the Center for Naval Analyses contract provides for about 15% of the projects to be self-initiated. In practice, self-initiated projects have represented less than 5% of the CNA budget, since most suggestions become supported by the Navy. However, it has been an important lever in the selection process.

Third, and of equal importance in maintaining independence, is the policy on publication of evaluation results. The analogy to a client-counselor relationship immediately suggests that the client would control distribution of all reports, although this should not restrict publication of professional papers free of client data. Such was the case in the OEG. This was coupled, however, with the requirement that reports may not be changed in any way by the client. Thus, published work by the group represents their findings and must be judged on this merit. On the other hand, the client is fully assured that information that he did not wish to have disclosed will not be disclosed.

Some alternative publication policies exist; such as, all major reports are published but with objections by the sponsoring organization presented in a cover letter preceding the report itself. This policy satisfies the requirement for results where studies are mandated from outside the sponsoring organization.

In opposition to the need for independence there is the need to develop and maintain a close working relationship. However, the relationship must not develop into a partnership with the two sides working too closely toward the same goals, forgetting the importance of questioning the assumptions. The relationship should be sufficiently close to provide not only access to data and information for specific evaluations, but the evaluation group should be privy to the pertinent ideas of the client which may become important in the future.

While in the evaluation of an ongoing project the primary need is for data, if an evaluation organization is to have a continuing relationship, it must participate in the planning of projects so that evaluation is a part of the project itself and so there is sufficient time to critique the underlying assumptions of the project. In addition to this, the evaluation organization needs to be close enough to the client so as to understand his ideas and purposes and to anticipate his needs so that longer termed and preparatory analyses can be undertaken.

I would like at this point to discuss one way in which a close working relationship has been maintained. In the OEG a tradition developed of providing analysts to different portions of the operating Navy, both at the headquarters in Washington and with the Fleets. In Washington, analysts are assigned as contact points for various divisions. These analysts provide a ready-response (without a formal request) for division needs as they occur. They participate in staff meetings and receive routed material, but they are not a part of the staff for day-to-day problems. Through this relationship, the analyst is able to keep abreast of projects and concerns while maintaining objectivity. For the operating forces, analysts are assigned to major staffs for periods of one-to-two years. While assigned they work on individual evaluations initiated by the command, on larger projects required of the command, and serve as consultants. At the same time, they report their work to the Washington office, receiving professional review and support from the parent organization. OEG to my knowledge is unique in this practice of providing field analysts to operating forces on this continuing and large scale. The Institute for Defense Analyses maintains a close relationship with their client, the Office of the Secretary of Defense, through the assignment of analysts to the various panels working within the office.

In summary then, what I am suggesting is an organization which will work closely with one branch of a federal department, serving as consultants to that organization but with an independence achieved through long-term forward funding and a strong charter. Long-term funding would free the group from depending upon the outcome of each immediate request for continued existence. The charter, perhaps with the backing of a large educational institution, such as the University of Rochester, provides for the Center for Naval Analyses, adds substance to this funding.

The group would be composed of professionals, perhaps with the same kind of skills as the advisors who now make up the invisible colleges of consultants.

It would give immediate assistance on evaluation aspects of projects, addressing not only the technical needs of each evaluation project but also looking at the underlying assumptions and forming precise statements for the questions that are being asked of evaluations. It would also undertake a small, long-term research program in support of the sponsor's evaluation needs.

I am under no illusion that something like this can be started readily, and I am not sure there is a way to start one at all. It is certainly true that we are not now experiencing in the social programs the trauma that the Navy experienced in 1942, that led them to try any type of organization they thought would help. Perhaps, if Congress were in a position to understand better the need and utility for this kind of organization, it would be in a position to support the formation of such organizations within our social program administrations. In any case, I am at a loss as to how something like this can get started.

NOTE

1. Steinhardt, "A Plan for the Future"; Proceedings of the Vicennial Conference on Operations Research, May 1962.

Discussants: Helen Nowlis, U.S. Office of Education
Henry Riecken, University of Pennsylvania
Mildred Shapiro, Bureau of Economic Analysis,
State Department of Health, N.Y.
Jerry Cromwell, Abt Associates Inc.

NOWLIS: I would like to point out something that is very important to me—both as a former researcher and as an administrator in the government trying to persuade OMB that we do have some data that mean something—and that is the pervasive theme that ran through all of the discussions: being able to agree on a definition of health, of success, of productivity, etc. You cannot measure something without knowing what it is you are measuring. I think we have a lot of technology in terms of measurement capability, but we cannot agree. By "we" I mean people in substantive areas, people in service areas, people in administrative areas, all of whom have a great deal of difficulty agreeing on success criteria. This reminds me of Paul Frawley's discussion of the need for—at least in a given evaluated study—agreement between the administrator (that is, program administrator), project staff, and evaluators on a measurable criterion of success, a measurable definition of health, a measurable definition of the outcomes of an educational program, whatever it is. I see this as a problem of, but not by, evaluators; and I think that the professional evaluator cannot make progress in the field until we go through a tortuous process of refining definitions, refining measurements, and making sure that projects do indeed have objectives and goals which relate in some way to the definition of the measurement that somebody else wants measured. Drug education has been evaluated to death by measures which have nothing to do with drug use behavior.

The other thing I would like to mention, just briefly, is an insight that I have gained in my brief government experience as to why we do not have better evaluations from a program point of view. If, for instance, we talk about health, health in the federal government is so fragmented that all you are doing is taking one little piece, one little action program, and trying to apply it to a broad, general concept. It makes such a little difference in the broad, general concept. Another problem is that, given the legislative situation, given the budget situation, given the administrative situation, it is impossible—in any program that I know about—to plan really adequate long-range evaluation. I let two contracts last year. They had to be one-year contracts because (a) I did not know whether I was going to be in existence or not, and (b) I did not know how much budget I would have. But I took the bull by the horns and wrote that one-year RFP as if it were the first year of a three- to five-year RFP, hoping that I would be able to continue it, or if I did not, that I would be able to persuade some other program in some other department interested in this area to do it. I do not see a way to get the kind of data the policymakers need if the data collection has to be on an ad hoc basis or if it has to be done on demand in the middle of a process that has not been completed.

RIECKEN: I would like to say, in regard to George Nash's major conclusion in his paper on the alcoholic detoxification experiment, that it certainly is a strong argument to say that one of the principal values of a true experiment is that it gives practical experience with program design, implementation, operation; that one learns, on a small scale, what he is going to have to write in the way of regulations, definitions and so forth, on a larger scale when the thing gets going. On the basis of Dr. Nash's comments, I would call the event a demonstration and not an experiment, simply because it was not controlled, it was infrequent, and because of the kind of measurement that came afterward.

I was interested in Mr. Sessler's paper, particularly his remarks on the relationship between evaluation and program direction or action. There are some interesting problems connected with the structural relationships between program action and evaluation or collecting data about the effectiveness, the impact of the program, and the various kinds of arrangements of closeness and distance, subordination, equality, superordination that may obtain usefully between "evaluators" and people who actually run programs. There are several different roles that appear in social experimentation. First is the initiator or sponsor who specifies the general dimensions of the experiment, its purpose, and the output expected; this is often an agency role which may require, in addition to administrative responsibility, a certain amount of expertise in supervising and monitoring the work of the second major role, which we call the designer/researcher. The designer/researcher is usually the social scientist who actually designs the experiment and collects the data.

Two roles that are often ignored and sometimes combined are those of program developer and treatment administrator. Now in an experiment, the role of program developer sometimes gets combined with that of either the initiator/sponsor, the designer/researcher, or the treatment administrator. In fact, it often seems in social programs that nobody pays a great deal of attention to program development. This is unfortunate because you must work very hard to get a program developed if it is to meet the sponsor's requirements.

Martha Blaxall's paper has an air of verisimilitude about it; it reminded me of some of my discussions with her colleagues when I was trying to sell the NSF budget to the Bureau of the Budget. I have sympathy for her position and I am comforted that it happens to all of us. I think her remarks on the absence of accepted criteria for measuring health status and the need for research were right on target. I do not think it is so difficult to get a measure of the socio-economic benefits of an experiment even though you do not know everything you need to know about health status. I am thinking here about David Kestner's study for the Institute of Medicine which undertook to examine the effectiveness of the treatment of otitis media, a very common, prevalent childhood disease, which is easily treated by accepted methods that are well known and well defined. Kestner used otitis media as a "tracer disease" to examine the effectiveness of various forms of health care delivery; that is, the school nurse, the private practitioner, the public clinic, the HMO, to examine their relative effectiveness in dealing with a single disease entity that is widely prevalent and conventionally well treated by the available technology.

I think it is probably the case that impact studies are missing in a great many areas of health services research, but they do not need to be. For example, in the area of family planning, many of the studies concentrate on the number of people processed through the clinic and are basically head-counting kinds of studies, which should not be dignified by the term evaluation. However, there are experiments on family planning counseling that demonstrate the possibility of doing good impact studies; for instance, the Taiwan experiment—a randomized study of several thousand families which showed conclusively that one method of birth control advocacy and information delivery was quite superior to others and was reflected in the demographic data.

SHAPIRO: I wanted to discuss a few points in Jerry Cromwell's paper. One of his conclusions was that, in 1964 to 1968, there was actually a decline in productivity in many of the hospital service departments, while there was an increase in the 1969-to-1971 period. The author, being unable to explain that, attributed it to possibly a downward bias in the figures. Well, I have more confidence in the figures than the author does and would like to offer two explanations. Let us look at the staffing ratios, the longitudinal data, in the year 1966 (the years 1964-1968 span the period when Medicaid and Medicare were introduced). In 1966, the staffing ratio (personnel to patients) increased in New York State by 16%. Since then, while the overall rate keeps increasing, it does so at a decreasing rate. The last figure was sixth-tenths of 1%. Now why? There are probably a couple of reasons. In 1966, the hospitals were preparing for increased demand for Medicaid and Medicare. Possibly they were eyeing some of those juicy goodies, those cost-plus retrospective reimbursement formulas and were looking forward to this infusion of new federal dollars. The other reason is that labor was relatively cheap in 1966 and employment criteria not so strict. Since that time, in New York at least, the wages have doubled and fringe benefits have probably quadrupled, and hospitals are much more discriminating in their hiring policies. The fact that reimbursement formulas have been tightened, with its impact on staffing ratios, would account for increased productivity per man-hour in the 1968-1971 period.

There were two words which Jerry Cromwell used which I would like to applaud. The words are "redundant output" and "wasted output." The Hospital Association does not use those words at all. They call it "intensity of care coupled with technology," and they want an increase or a plus factor to their formula; Cromwell suggests some sort of subtraction. The problem is deciding at what point medical care is no longer medically appropriate and becomes, therefore, redundant productivity. The number of laboratory tests are now doubling every five years; I think we would be hard pressed to prove that medical care is doubling in quality every five years.

The final point I would like to make concerns one of the recommendations of Cromwell's paper: since man-hours are increasing, roughly about 1% per year, there should be a deduction from prices up to 1% per year, based on output per man-hour. I realize that the Cost of Living Council accepted that, but I do not think an industrial engineer would. There is a cost to productivity, there is capital investment; and the money you invest in capital equipment is the substitutor of machinery for men. There is a cost of operation and maintenance of capital equipment. Even though you may displace a large number of skilled and unskilled people, you often have to replace them with small numbers of highly skilled people, either engineers or programmers.

CROMWELL: Mildred Shapiro is exactly right that a real measure of productivity ought to include all the inputs in production. The productivity indicators used by the Cost of Living Council have dealt only with labor inputs and, to the extent that firms can substitute capital for labor, they can appear to raise the productivity faster than it really is increasing, and of course there is a capital cost associated with that substitution. So to the extent that we have, in this country, overtime and increase in capital/labor ratio or more machinery working with us on our jobs, labor productivity will rise faster than it would have had we had to work with the same machinery that our parents used in their operations. The Cost of Living Council is being extremely pragmatic, however, in using these labor productivity indicators to get on with the job of regulating industry and has shied away from using the more complex indicators that would include other factors of production.

VI

EVALUATION OF EDUCATION PROGRAMS

THE "WHAT" WITHOUT THE "WHY" OR EVALUATION WITHOUT POLICY RELEVANCE

Marvin Gerry Cline
Abt Associates Inc.

The analytic designs used in the evaluation of education programs often look like those used in experimental research. That is, two similar groups of subjects are chosen in a way that allows them to be judged equivalent on some dimensions. One group is given Treatment (experience, stimulus) A and the other is given something else. The researcher then tries to determine whether the groups are still equivalent on the original dimensions. It is at the point where these findings are available that evaluation and experimental research begin to function differently. For example, the evaluator often stops the analysis at this point because he now knows what happened as a result of the administration of Treatment A. He can then report to the policymaker that an event of a certain magnitude, associated with a certain cost, occurred following the administration of Treatment A. His only concern about the control group of subjects is that they did less "well" on the posttest than the subjects who received Treatment A. On this basis, the evaluator is ready to bring the evaluative task to fruition, i.e., to recommend to the policymaker that it is or is not worth supporting Treatment A in those places over which the policymaker has administrative control.

On the other hand, the experimental researcher has a good deal more to do once the findings are in. The purpose in doing the experiment is, after all, to test the adequacy of a Causal model. Treatment A and

Treatment B were selected by the experimenter precisely because the Causal model requires that subjects behave differently under these two conditions. The findings allow the experimenter to reject or to refuse to reject the efficacy of the model. The focus is on the model which may be a developmental process, or the interaction of several processes (e.g., memorial and affective), or the receptors (central or peripheral) of certain stimuli, or several other psychological structures. The treatments provide an occasion for testing the model. The researcher is, in other words, testing a hypothesis, not the treatment.

The evaluator rarely gets involved with models. The evaluation is focused on the treatment, which may be an educational program or a means of delivering educational experiences to children. Rarely does an evaluator ask why a program works or does not work, and he is never concerned with the efficacy of Treatment A for any group of subjects other than those over whom the policymaker has administrative control. Further, I have never seen an evaluator become interested in why Treatment B does not work as well as Treatment A, or, in the more intriguing situation, why B works better than A. The researcher, of course, must account for all events associated with both A and B in order to test his theory. If a model can predict behavior under one set of conditions but not under another set, it is at best rather weak and at worst fatally flawed.

It is the thesis of this paper that many kinds of social experiment, particularly outside the educational system, can efficiently and meaningfully be *evaluated* in the sense that I am using the term here. The reason for this is that the causal constructs underlying many social programs are reasonably well known and the problem for the social experiment is one of implementation of solutions. On the other hand, well-established developmental theories which can be translated into pedagogical techniques do not yet exist. I suggest that the kind of evaluation strategy described earlier will not provide the educational policymaker with the kind of information he needs to make decisions at the moments when he is required to do so. Let me look quickly at a major educational issue about which evaluation techniques have been creating problems for the policymaker. This is the issue of compensatory education for the disadvantaged child.

There is a wide variety of explanations offered for the generally poor performance of low-income children in school. These explanations include the psychic damage suffered by low-income, particularly black children, in the course of their isolation from wider society; the lack of a "relevant" curriculum; the lack of sensitive teachers with positive expectations; the damage done by an understimulating and/or inadequately verbal environment; the lack of appropriately involved and motivated parents who also fail to socialize adequately the problem-solving skills of their children; and the lack of curricula which reflect the developmental needs of children in general, and disadvantaged children in particular. In all of these explanations, the underlying assumption is that membership in the low-income, minority stratum produces both intellectual and emotional consequences which inhibit the learning of children and this is reflected in lower scores on standard tests of achievement. Note the causal chain here: minority membership brings with it certain experiences which damage learning abilities or skills; the quality or quantity of information processed in school by the children is reduced; this results in the students' inability to solve certain test problems in school.

In the case of most hypotheses about the sources of low achievement, some work has been done attempting to associate the hypothetical explanation/cause (e.g., segregation, negative teacher expectations, black English, parental teaching style, etc.) with low academic performance. In almost no instance has any attempt been made to test any of the links in the causal chain which connects the hypothetical cause to the final consequence of low achievement. Segregation is a good example. If we assume that the relationship between racial isolation and poor achievement has been established and note that there is still nothing in the literature which identifies the specific steps by which such isolation produces poor test performance, then we ought not to be surprised to find that a deliberately manipulated segregation variable has not generally had much of an effect on the academic achievement of children. Note that natural occurring variation in segregation *is* associated with differences in black children's performance, but deliberate manipulation of segregation does not appear to *change* their performance. This is not to say that segregation does not inhibit several important functions in black children and spuriously inflates the sense of self worth in white children; rather the manner by which the social insult of segregation is translated into a cognitive event which can interfere with test-taking behavior is not yet sufficiently well understood to enable us to use the knowledge to change test-taking behavior. It is entirely possible that the segregation-desegregation-integration variables provide an opportunity for certain social comparison processes to operate so that manipulating the isolation variable alone, without manipulating the social comparison processes by which black children set standards for themselves, may not lead to changed school performance.

Again, in the case of hypotheses involving lack of intellectual stimulation as the cause of low achievement, very little work has been done to test the causal links. Since these causal hypotheses have not been investigated or tested, it is not surprising that the "cures" suggested are vaguely stated, inconsistently implemented, and generally ineffective. Head Start and Title I programs are prime examples of such solutions; there is no evidence that any appreciable changes have been produced by them. Once again, this is not to say that the hypotheses upon which these solutions are based are not reasonable; it is that the steps in the sequence leading to pupil change have not been followed.

The evaluation of programs does not involve testing causal hypotheses. Rather, the hypotheses remain as *assumptions,* so that when the evaluator finds that he cannot accept Treatment A (Head Start, Title I) as a better set of procedures than Treatment B, it is not surprising that he turns to his evaluation design as the source of the problem. His task is to find out if something happened as the result of Treatment A; and, since he assumes that A contains the active ingredient necessary to effect the cure, then it must be that something in the evaluation design is obscuring the phenomenon he assumes is there. The typical solution to this problem is for the evaluator to try to reduce the noise in the design to allow the signal to come through, to increase the power of the test of effects, to decrease the error variance. All of this means that the evaluator continues to use the "what happened" strategy—build a better microscope in the hope that the increase in resolution power will bring the effect into focus.

In the course of trying to make a design more powerful, for one large evaluation project, an Abt Associates team now has a somewhat different view of the situation. Rather than a uniform set of null effects, what seems to be emerging is a kaleidoscopic pattern of effects which are time bound, place bound, child bound, and bound to the politics of local school administrations. This is the most general conclusion from the recently completed Abt Associates study of the Follow Through Programs, a planned variation experiment in early childhood education.

The design, which was developed by the Office of Education, is probably the most sophisticated yet produced for a major education study. It involves 10 major early childhood educational models administered by their advocates at a variety of sites around the country. The models range from behavior modification, computer assisted instruction, parent involvement, cognitive stimulation, to open classroom approaches. Clearly there is variation of the treatment but not *along any dimensions* relevant to hypotheses about the treatments. Thus, the treatments do not represent levels of a variable or a set of variables assumed to be related to classroom learning. The treatments are a set of nominal variables. In order to know how these treatments work therefore, it is necessary to know levels of the critical dimensions within each treatment category. This can be accomplished by design, or one can allow the treatments to vary naturally, influenced by local conditions which need then to be taken into account. Unfortunately, neither of these conditions was established for the design, so that each model was administered in a variety of sites, but we have no idea how the implementation of treatments varied over sites. There was no measure of the independent variable and no attempt to control its administration.

Further, although there is variation in location of the models around the country, there is no crossing of models with sites. Thus each model is administered in its own unique set of sites, which makes model-to-model comparisons almost impossible. If sites were measured, then some kind of categorization of models by site could have been accomplished; but such data are not available either.

Despite these problems, the attempt to apply a planned variation experiment in a variety of sites is a major step forward in educational evaluation. Clearly, the policymaker is constrained from making a decision about a single best or worst model. The conditions of implementation are so varied that what is accomplished by one model in one set of sites cannot be compared to what is accomplished by another model in another set of sites.

This kind of event was anticipated by the planners of the Follow Through Experiment. They did not want information about a single winner or loser; rather, they were interested in a directory for consumers which would specify the effects produced by each model under a variety of conditions. The consumer could then make the most informed choice possible by selecting the model which he felt would work best in his community. Unfortunately, this plan has some severe problems as well.

The findings of a two-year (k and 1st) longitudinal study indicate a very large amount of site-specific effects for almost every model. For example, the behavior modification models, which showed rather impressive gains in reading and math skills in kindergarten are considerably less impressive in first grade. However, their overall patterns are simply means of quite variable patterns found in each of their sites. These show gains in some sites, losses in others, and a maintenance of kindergarten gains in others. At the same time, one of the behavior modification models shows gains with high-achieving children and losses with low-achieving children, and the other behavior modification model shows just the opposite. Further, one shows gains in math while the other shows its biggest losses in math.

The open classroom models, which showed very little gain in kindergarten, reveal almost as much variability across their sites in first grade as the behavior modification models. One model, based on the British Infant School, showed gains in math in two sites, but gains in reading in only one. One of the cognitive stimulation models, which showed rather strong gains in kindergarten, showed gains in reading in two of these sites and losses in three. Another responsive environment model showed a different kindergarten to first grade pattern in each site on each outcome test.

There were a few consistencies in the findings, but it is hard to deal with them at this point. The computer-assisted model adds nothing to the performance of children in a moderately high-achieving site; that is, the experimental children perform at the same levels as their comparisons. At the same time, this model adds nothing to the performance of low-achieving children who are falling further behind average children each year. The bilingual model which did little for children in the kindergarten year shows gains in two sites in first grade.

These findings place the policymaker in something of a bind. There is *no model which can be offered to consumers.* A directory of effects which would tell the consumer how a local site might interact with any given model to produce given effects on particular children is far from complete. To be sure, a great many more interactions can and should be studied each year. But the prospect appears to be that a very large matrix of cells will have to be filled before the policymaker can offer choices to consumers with confidence in the consequences.

Further, filling such a matrix is both costly and time consuming. And because of the multitude of site specific effects, one might believe that every effect is dependent upon specific conditions and that there is, therefore, no lawfulness to such data. As a working analyst, I cannot accept that notion.

I would suggest that the reason the data seem chaotic (note, this does not mean null findings; there is much evidence for change, but it is not cast in the form that allows for a lot of decision-making) is that we have focused only on *what* has happened without asking *why*. We have not asked why the data are site specific and child specific.

There are at least three possible reasons why models have different effects in different sites. The first has to do with the selection of the model by each site. This was done through a complicated process of self-selection which reflected a wide variety of community and school relationships across the sites. The result was a very political decision (in the sense of an accommodation of groups to each other) at each site. How this process influenced the implementation of the model at each site needs to be examined carefully in order to compare effects of a model across sites.

The second issue is the degree of LEA cooperation or resistance to the models. Some models produce strong resistance and others invite cooperation. Neither of these responses is necessarily a virtue or a vice, but both severely contribute to the character of the model in operation.

The final subject which needs to be examined at the site level is teacher training, which varies substantially between sites. The problem of the dependency of model effects upon the kind of children to whom the model is applied has to do with the developmental processes which are being influenced by the models. Obviously, each model attempts to intervene in the developmental process in a different way. But no one has yet identified the processes which are being attacked or the expected effects of each model at each level of child development. For example, some models clearly manipulate associative skills and others attempt to influence concept learning. But the developmental pattern of associative skills differs from that of concept learning and can be expected to show different growth rates depending upon when and how they are stimulated. I am sure that the variability of our findings will disappear when we look at the developmental stages of the children and then try to understand the kind of impact of each model at each grade level.

This is not the place to identify all the questions which should be examined in order to make sure of these data. I am suggesting, however, that the most effective way to generate a useful directory of effects which the policymaker can offer to the educational consumer is to engage in a search for the reasons for effects, a search which can only be accomplished by testing hypotheses. This is not impossible to blend with a national evaluation although it requires that we pay attention more to the test of the hypothesis than to the generalization of the results. Generalization will come with the accumulation of systematic knowledge. Without such knowledge however we may be no further along at the end of the evaluations than we were at the beginning. Clearly we are well past the time when this kind of costly error needs to be excused. It is time to bring research strategies into the arena of public-policy decisions.

SIMULTANEOUS EQUATIONS MODELS OF THE EDUCATIONAL PROCESS:
A Reanalysis of the Coleman Data

Anthony E. Boardman
Peggy R. Sanday
University of Pennsylvania
Otto A. Davis
Norman Johnson
Carnegie-Mellon University
Presented by: Anthony E. Boardman

INTRODUCTION

This paper considers the educational process as a simultaneous equations model. Modeling via this format permits variables to be jointly and interdependently determined. This approach diverges sharply from the more traditional approach which models the education process as a single equation production function in which pupil achievement depends linearly on a number of pupil, teacher, and school variables. Achievement is certainly an important output, but it is not the only one. Estimated simultaneous equations models seem to provide a better understanding of the educational process as well as to strengthen the ability to devise more appropriate policy guidelines.

The estimated model includes six endogenous variables: achievement, motivation, expectations, efficacy (self esteem and control of environment), student's perceived parents' expectations and student's perceived teachers' expectations. This model also includes 42 exogenous variables. Among the exogenous variables are measures of pupil demographics such as, sex, ethnic group, and age; family background characteristics such as, socioeconomic status, information in the home, family structure, order of birth, and reading before school; stability characteristics such as number of times and the last time the pupil changed school; school peer group characteristics such as the racial composition of the school and classroom and the average socioeconomic background level of the students; teacher characteristics such as the average achievement level of the teachers, teachers' experience, and the number of teachers per pupil; and school characteristics such as school facilities, problems in the school, and school age.

The basic model was estimated separately for seven ethnic and racial groups: White Americans, Black Americans, Puerto Rican Americans, Mexican Americans, Native Americans, Asian Americans, and students not ethnically identifying themselves. The total sample consists of over 16,000 twelfth grade students from the *Equality of Educational Opportunity Survey* [9] (EEOS), the Coleman data.

The estimated simultaneous equations models suggest an extremely complex educational process. First, variables which promote achievement may decrease rather than increase other endogenous variables, such as, motivation and expectations. Consequently, focusing on achievement solely may incline persons to lose a sensitivity for other possible tradeoffs. Second, the endogenous structure does indeed differ in activity and complexity for the several "ethnic" groups identified in this study. The difference tells us to avoid the simplistic "do this, do that" answer. Further, differences among these ethnic structures suggest that multi-cultural models of the education structure appear to be more productive than a homogenous model of that structure. The endogenous structure, while it gives insight into the structure of the educational process, by itself sheds little light on possible policy directions. The following policy suggestions result from considerations of both the reduced and structural form equations.

On the issue of integration for the purpose of improving achievement, black and white students do better in either mainly white or mainly black schools and perform worst when the schools are integrated (30%-69% white). This finding suggests that for some ethnic groups desegregation is a mixed blessing at best. The achievement of all ethnic groups improves significantly, except perhaps for whites, if one improves the quantity and quality of teacher-related variables (class size, teacher ability, teacher experience, etc.). For all ethnics except whites, the school appears to compensate for what whites normally receive at home; that is, smaller family size, two parents living at home, incomes allowing for an abundance of informational materials, parents reading to children before school, and other structural home supports.

Given these major findings, we turn now to several limitations. The endogenous structure excludes variables of considerable importance, such as perceived peer and reference group expectations and the affective growth of pupils. These are omitted measures of classroom level variables such as student-teacher interaction, methods of teaching, or style and structure of classroom material. Students were not identified with particular teachers. Our failure to deal with these matters resulted from inadequate data on the Coleman tapes. Some researchers might quarrel with the present form of our indices for efficacy and motivation. In fact, we plan to split efficacy into two variables (self esteem and belief in the ability to control one's environment). Motivation will be broken into two components also. Finally, we are acutely aware of the hazards of drawing implications in 1975 from 1965 data. Over a 10-year period, America has changed. Consequently, the usefulness and validity of the findings and their implications must be considered in the light of the 10-year time lapse. An elaboration of our thinking on the modeling and other matters follows.

APPROACHES TO SIMULTANEOUS EQUATION MODELING IN EDUCATION

Previous Work. In the past, many educators and educational researchers may have perceived multiple, jointly-determined outputs in the educational process. Unfortunately, these persons lacked the statistical power to handle jointly-determined variables, and thus they promoted the use of single-equation production function models. In education, these statistical inadequacies resulted in a focus on achievement and all those variables most likely to contribute to a higher R^2.

Mosteller and Moynihan [17] articulated descriptively the possibility for jointly-determined variables. They suggested that feelings of control might be essentially a feedback from reality. Bright students who achieved good marks might feel good about themselves. Thus, achievement and efficacy are jointly determined.

Levin [16] moved beyond description and modeled empirically the educational process with simultaneous equations. His jointly-determined endogenous variables were: students' verbal achievement, efficacy, motivation, and (perceived) parents' attitudes. While Levin models parents' attitudes as an endogenous variable, it should be treated as exogenous in the estimation of the structure because Levin finds no empirical evidence of any feedback to this variable. Finally, the sample of only 618 whites from the urban Northeast limits the reliability of any generalizations. These shortcomings aside, Levin's empirical analysis, which includes feedback effects (interdependent as opposed to a recursive model), forms a good basis for a model. It is better than the more recent recursive simultaneous equations models by Gordon [11], Anderson and Evans [1] or Parti and Adelman [21]. These latter authors disregard Levin's work and exclude feedback effects. Thus, they fail to contribute significantly to the literature.

Boardman, Davis, Johnson and Sanday Model of the Educational Process: The endogenous structure. While building on Levin's research, this analysis does not simply assert a recursive or interdependent relationship as has been the practice in the past. The analysis goes beyond assertion to the behavioral sciences and educational theory for insights into the relationships among the variables comprising the structure of the educational process. We postulate eight endogenous variables: achievement, an index[1] of five tests—verbal, nonverbal, reading, mathematical, and general information—is designed to tap those skills leading to a good job and moving up to a better one, not intelligence; efficacy, an index combining variables related to self esteem and belief in the ability to control one's environment; motivation, an index combining variables related to desires and wants and variables indicating the behavioral manifestations of those wants and desires; pupil expectations, a measure of what the student expects to achieve as a result of high school—his future hopes; perceived teachers' expectations, hopes and behavior which the pupil believes his teachers have and expect for him; perceived parents' expectations, hopes and behavior a student believes his parents have and expect for him; perceived peer and reference group expectation, hopes and behavior a student believes his significant others (other than parents and teachers) have and expect for him; and affective growth, a capacity here meaning the ability to recognize, as well as the freedom from inhibition, feelings in self and others so that these feelings manifest themselves in the fullness of one's personality and the parties engaged understand the dynamics behind these feelings. Given these endogenous variables, the following discussion considers the relationships among them.

Achievement, expectations, and efficacy seem "naturally" jointly determined. As Mosteller and Moynihan [18] suggest, high achievement results in high efficacy and high efficacy leads to higher achievement. Similarly, a student who expects to succeed probably achieves better than one who does not expect to succeed [5]. One's expectations about future success are in large part structured by one's present achievement. These three would seem, then, to be in a jointly-determined simultaneous relationship.

In a society like America, where the Protestant work ethic and "up by the bootstraps" are normative imperatives, motivation would also appear to come into the above "natural" jointure. The work ethic suggests that, the harder a person works, the better he will do. Also, in an academic setting, good achievement should lead to greater motivation. Thus, achievement and motivation are jointly-determined. Focusing for the moment on these four variables of the endogenous structure, the following statements can be made about the expected relationships among the variables.

Efficacy (self esteem and control) should affect achievement strongly and vice versa.

Expectations should affect achievement strongly and vice versa.

Motivation should affect achievement strongly and vice versa.

Motivation should affect expectations strongly.

Efficacy should affect motivation weakly.

Denoting achievement by ACH, motivation by MOT, efficacy by EFF, expectations by EXP, strong a priori causality by solid lines, and weak a priori causality by dotted lines with arrows indicating direction, the discussion might be represented thus.

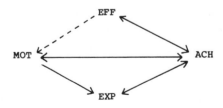

Figure 1

Now, adding perceived parent and teacher expectations to this structure, we postulate that a child's attitudes depend upon his parent's attitudes. [22] Perceived parental attitudes, then, are relevant for pupil expectations. Pupils' expectations may also depend on teachers' expectations. However, a priori, we suspect children probably believe their parents more than their teachers. Consequently, the relationship from teachers' expectations to pupils' expectations should be weak unless, of course, teachers are seen as a part of the larger adult community who are generally respected. Children probably respond to high-perceived parental and teacher expectations with greater effort and generally higher motivation. Similarly, low-perceived parental and teacher expectations may not provide the student with a challenge and probably lead to lower motivation. A pupil may also base the feelings about himself on what he perceives his parents and teachers expect of him. However, no a priori reason exists why pupil achievement should depend directly on perceived teachers' and parents' expectations. These effects upon achievement should operate through intervening variables: efficacy, expectations, and motivation. The addition of perceived parent and teacher expectations allows us now to make these statements about the relationships among six of the variables in the endogenous structure.

Perceived teacher expectations should affect motivation strongly.

Perceived teacher expectations should affect efficacy strongly.

Perceived teacher expectations should affect pupil expectations weakly.

Perceived teacher expectations should affect perceived parent expectations strongly and vice versa.

Perceived parent expectations should affect efficacy strongly.

Perceived parent expectations should affect motivation strongly.

Perceived parent expectations should affect pupil expectations strongly.

Denoting perceived teachers' expectations by PTEXP and perceived parents' expectations by PPAEXP, the figures below summarizes the discussion thus far.

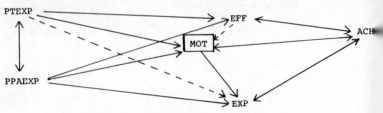

Figure 2 (2)

The literature clearly suggests that perceived peer and reference groups have profound impacts on adolescents. Whyte [24] believes that the younger generation builds up its own society relatively independent of the influence of its elders. Thus, parents' expectations may have little effect on peer expectations. Indeed, Whyte argues that the home plays a very small role in the group activities of the corner boy. A person's associations frequently persist into the late twenties despite movement out of the district. Physical movement does not seem to take the corner boy away from his corner. While the street corner may be an extreme manifestation of the impact of peers and reference groups, the direction is unmistakable. Peers and reference groups clearly affect the individual and his expectations. Similarly, the norms of these groups determine how much a student will "put out." In short, peer expectations should affect motivation. Perceived teacher expectations should also be affected by perceived peer expectations. The argument goes something like this . . . If I perceive my teachers as believing that my friends are not very "cool," then in all probability I perceive my teachers as viewing me in the same light.

The affective growth literature lacks clarity. In educational circles it is not entirely clear what the concept means. It is clear though that many educators today see affective growth as an important output of the educational process. In a recent speech, Dean James Kelley of the School of Education, University of Pittsburgh, stated: "Being a high achiever is fine but it's not good enough. It is the context of that achieving that is important. If our achieving is done in a negative context, that is, we destroy others to get ahead, or we pop pills essentially destroying ourselves, so as to be number one in the classroom, education has failed in the human feeling sense." In thinking it through, perceived teachers', peers', and parents' expectations should affect this variable directly as well as through student expectations; and there should be feedback to these variables. Efficacy should also affect affective growth with feedback. Thus:

Perceived peer and reference group expectations should affect expectations strongly and vice versa.

Perceived peer and reference group expectations should affect perceived teacher expectations strongly.

Perceived peer and reference group expectations should affect perceived parent expectations weakly.

Perceived peer and reference group expectations should affect motivation strongly.

Perceived peer and reference group expectations should affect efficacy strongly.

Perceived peer and reference group expectations affect affective growth strongly.

Affective growth affects efficacy strongly and vice versa.

Affective growth affects expectations strongly and vice versa.

Affective growth affects achievement weakly and vice versa.

Perceived teachers' expectations affect affective growth strongly.

Perceived parents' expectations affect affective growth strongly.

Designating perceived peer and reference group expectations by PPEERXP and affective growth as AFF, the relationships among all eight variables might be represented and summarized as follows:

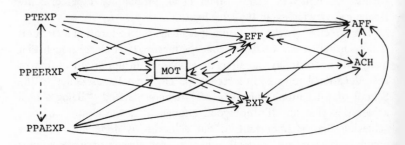

Figure 3 (3)

Figure 3 portrays the total system for the hypothesized structural relationships among the endogenous variables. Unfortunately, the EEOS data (the best available data source on the educational process) do not contain measures of affective growth and perceived peer and reference group expectations. In all subsequent discussions, these two variables will not appear. Hereafter, the variables of focus are: ACHIEVEMENT, PUPIL EXPECTATIONS, EFFICACY, MOTIVATION, AND PERCEIVED PARENT and TEACHER EXPECTATIONS—a total of six variables whose relationships were summarized previously by Figure 2.

The exogenous structure. The above discussion focuses on the endogenous structure. However, the formulation is incomplete without consideration of the exogenous variables. For a quick review, these variables are summarized in Table 1 along with a priori estimates of their relationship in each of the six equations.[4] The following key explains the notation found in the table:[5]

Abbreviations	*Description*
++	Variable must have a positive or zero coefficient. Otherwise it is excluded from the equation. The expected sign of the coefficient is positive.
++?	Same as "++" except that a zero coefficient is expected.
+	Probably positive—no constraint.
——	Same as "++" except negative instead of positive.
——?	Same as "++?" except that negative instead of positive.
—	Probably negative—no constraint.
0	Probably zero—no constraint.
00	Must have zero coefficient—i.e., this variable is excluded on a priori grounds.
?	Don't know—probably not zero, though.

Table 1 shows that identification is not guaranteed by a priori exclusion restrictions. Of course, one could restrict all "++?" and "?" to "00" in which case the structure satisfies the rank and order conditions. However, instead of imposing the constraints that some variable must have zero coefficients, constraints apply to the signs of the endogenous variables. All endogenous variables must have positive and significant coefficients. Exogenous variables appear in an equation if the associated t-statistic exceeds unity in absolute value.

The reasons for this procedure come from educational theory. The theory does not allow one to exclude an endogenous variable from an equation. At the same time, the theory does suggest that an endogenous variable should not enter any one of the equations with a negative sign.

This procedure for obtaining an identified structure is novel. To show the relationship of this procedure to the more usual method of

TABLE 1   THE A PRIORI MODEL: A SUMMARY OF THE
A PRIORI HYPOTHESES

Dependent Variables

Explanatory Variables	ACH	MOT	EXP	EFF	PPAEXP	PTEXP
ACH	1	++	++	++	++	++
MOT	++	1	++	++?	++	++
EXP	++	++?	1	++?	++	++
EFF	++	++	++?	1	++	++
PPAEXP	++?	++	++	++	1	++
PTEXP	++?	++	++?	++	++	1
SEX	-	+	-	+	?	?
AGE	-	?	-	-	?	?
SES	?	-	+	+	+	+
INFO	+	+	+	+	?	?
TWOP	+	?	+?	+	+	?
NOBAS	+	?	?	?	?	?
FL	?	?	?	+	0	0
RBS	++	+	+	+	+	?
PTAAT	++	+	+	?	+	?
PTAS	--	-	?	?	-	?
TC	?	+	-	?	?	?
NTCHSCL	-	?	?	-	?	?
LSTCHSCL	+	?	?	+	?	?
AVSES	+	-	+	+	+	?
PWPICLY	+	?	+	?	+	?
MYLBLCK	-	+?	-	-	-	?
MIX	-	?	?	?	?	?

TABLE 1 (CONTINUED)
Dependent Variables

Explanatory Variables	ACH	MOT	EXP	EFF	PPAEXP	PTEXP
TAVR	+	+	+	+	?	?
NTPRPUP	+	+	+	+	+	+
TANYTCH	?	?	?	?	?	?
TANYTCH2	?	?	?	?	?	?
PWTCHLY	+	?	?	+	?	?
TASEX	+	?	?	?	?	?
TPTC	?	?	−	?	?	+
TPADTN	−	?	?	?	?	−
FACILITS	+	?	+	+	?	?
PROBLEMS	−	?	−	−	?	?
AGES	−	?	−	−	−	−
TEST	++	00	00	00	00	00
NTCHLV	?	?	−	?	?	?
PRNMADEG	?	++	+	?	?	?
SMSA	?	−	−	+	?	?
NEWENG	?	?	?	?	?	?
MIDATL	?	?	?	?	?	?
LAKES	?	?	?	?	?	?
PLAINS	?	?	?	?	?	?
SEAST	−	+	−	?	?	?
SWEST	−	+	−	?	?	?
NTLKGC	+	+	+	+	?	+
NHWTV	+	+	+	+	?	?
NHWTV2	−	−	−	−	?	?
CONST	?	?	?	?	?	?

postulating exclusion restrictions, let us consider the estimation of economic demand and supply equations. One way of identifying a demand equation is to postulate that the supply equation varies with the weather (or a land tax) while the demand equation remains unaffected. One way to identify a supply equation is to postulate that the demand equation varies with the disposable real income of the buyer while the supply equation is unaffected. Thus, both the demand and supply equations are identified. However, in most circumstances, the real test of whether the estimated equations are identified is if the demand equation has a negative coefficient for quantity and the supply equation has a positive coefficient for quantity (in both cases, price is the dependent variable). Thus, identification occurs a posteriori.

Finally, taking a clue from Johnson and Sanday, [20] we postulate important structural differences among ethnic groups. For this reason, the total sample of over 16,000 twelfth grade students was subdivided ethnically according to the ethnic group that pupils selected. Seven such groups were identified: White Americans, Americans electing no ethnic classification, Black Americans, Native Americans, Asian Americans, Puerto Rican Americans and Mexican Americans. Using two-stage least squares regression, the model was estimated for the combined sample and for each ethnic sub-sample. Our results appear next. A more detailed discussion of the results for the combined sample appears in Boardman et al. [6].

THE RESULTS

It is difficult to discuss the results clearly and succinctly. All of the estimated structural equations are discussed next followed by diagrammatic presentations of the endogenous structure for the combined sample and for the ethnic sub-samples. The final section concentrates on two important issues: integration and compensation to reduce the differences among the output levels of different ethnic groups.

Summary of the Structural Form Estimates of the Exogenous Structure. Table 2 summarizes most of the information provided by all of the estimated structural form coefficients. Appendix B summarizes the findings for all of the estimated reduced form equations. Specifically, Table 2 shows the number of times a variable significantly enters each one of the structural form equations. The following key enables one to read the table.

Key for Table 2 and Appendix B

Abbreviation	Description
++	The explanatory variable enters this equation six or more times (out of a possible 8) with a positive and significant coefficient and in no case enters with a negative and significant coefficient.[6]
+	The variable enters significantly this equation at least 4 times but does not qualify for a "++."
(+)	The variable enters significantly the equation at least three times, but does not qualify for a "++" or a "+."
——	The same as "++" except the variable is negative.
—	The same as "+" except the variable is negative.
(—)	The same as "(+)" except the variable is negative.
?	The variable enters with a positive and significant coefficient on at least two occasions, and it enters with a negative and significant coefficient on at least two occasions.
1	The variable is the dependent variable.
0	This category covers all other possibilities. The explanatory variable rarely or never enters with a significant coefficient.

These categories are not mutually exclusive. In general, a "?" dominates a "+," "(+)," "—," or "(—)."

TABLE 2: A SUMMARY OF THE ESTIMATED STRUCTURAL FORM EQUATIONS
FOR ALL OF THE ETHNIC GROUPS AND FOR THE COMBINED SAMPLE (7)

Dependent Variables

Explanatory Variables	ACH	MOT	EXP	EFF	PPAEXP	PTEXP
ACH	1	0	+	++	0	0
MOT	0	1	+	+	++	0
EXP	0	0	1	0	++	+
EFF	++	(+)	(+)	1	0	+
PPAEXP	0	++	++	0	1	+
PTEXP	0	+	0	+	++	1
SEX	--	++	(-)	++	--	0
AGE	--	-	-	-	?	0
SES	++	--	++	(+)	++	-
INFO	+	++	++	0	0	0
TWOP	+	0	0	0	++	(-)
NOBAS	--	0	0	(-)	(-)	+
FL	0	0	--	+	0	0
RBS	0	(+)	0	++	0	0
PTAAT	0	0	++	0	?	0
PTAS	0	0	0	0	--	0
TC	+	+	-	0	0	0
NTCHSCL	(+)	0	?	0	(+)	0
LSTCHSCL	+	++	?	++	-	0
AVSES	++	-	+	0	0	-
PWPICLY	?	?	(-)	0	0	-
MYLBLCK	-	++	(-)	-	0	+
MIX	--	+	0	0	0	(+)

7. The reduced form equations tables as well as ethnic tables are available on request.

TABLE 2 (CONTINUED)
Dependent Variables

Explanatory Variables	ACH	MOT	EXP	EFF	PPAEXP	PTEXP
TAVR	++	0	0	0	0	0
NTPRPUP	+	0	0	(-)	(-)	+
TANYTCH	--	?	0	-	0	+
TANYTCH2	++	?	0	+	0	(-)
PWTCHLY	0	++	(-)	+	0	(-)
TASEX	0	0	0	(-)	(+)	0
TPTC	0	0	0	0	(-)	+
TPADTN	+	(+)	+	0	0	-
FACILITS	0	0	0	0	0	-
PROBLEMS	--	(-)	-	+	0	0
AGES	0	+	0	0	--	0
TEST	+	0	0	0	0	0
NTCHLV	+	(-)	0	(+)	0	0
PRNMADEG	0	0	0	?	0	0
SMSA	0	0	0	+	-	0
NEWENG	(+)	0	0	0	-	?
MITATL	?	0	-	+	0	0
LAKES	0	?	-	(+)	0	0
PLAINS	+	0	(-)	++	0	0
SEAST	?	?	(-)	0	0	+
SWEST	-	++	0	0	0	0
NTLKGC	0	0	++	++	-	(+)
NHWTV	(-)	++	(+)	+	-	-
NHWTV2	0	--	-	-	(+)	-
CONST	+	0	+	0	+	--

This table provides an interesting overview of the educational process. Looking down the columns shows that few exogenous variables enter the perceived parents' expectations equations while even fewer variables enter the perceived teachers' expectations equations. Looking across the rows shows that the marginal contributions of the exogenous variables do not always act in the same direction. For example, speaking frequently a foreign language appears to result in a marginal increase in expectations and a marginal decrease in efficacy. Spending most of one's life in one place seems to improve a pupil's motivation, but it lowers his expectations. It is interesting to note that sex (female) affects the endogenous variable achievement significantly and negatively while it affects motivation, another endogenous variable, in another direction significantly and positively. The upshot of all of this is that, as was suggested in the introduction, the educational process is extremely complex and tampering with it, without an appreciation for its complexity, may produce undesirable outcomes. Caution and care are probably better watchwords than full steam ahead.

The Endogenous Structure. If we switch from the tabular form to a diagrammatic form and focus exclusively on the endogenous structure, we can quickly glean the differences found between what we postulated for this structure (Figure 2) and what the empirical estimates yielded for the combined sample (Figure 4).

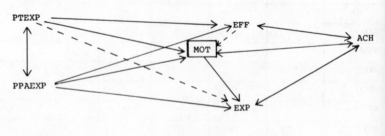

Figure 2 (2)

The estimations based on the entire sample yield the following empirical structure.

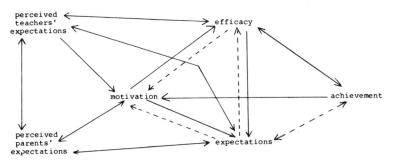

Figure 4

The empirical results make it clear that only two variables, efficacy and expectation, affect achievement directly, while achievement feeds back to efficacy, expectations, and motivation. Perceived parent and teacher expectations affect achievement through intervening variables: efficacy, motivation, and expectations, but do not affect it directly nor does achievement feedback to these two. Table 3 allows us to quickly confirm or deny empirically our original hypotheses. Four of our affect statements did not hold up, while four of our hypotheses were not empirically supported. Additional findings appear in Table 4.

Focusing on the endogenous structure alone reinforces our earlier statements about the complexity of the educational process.

The Endogenous Structure Viewed Ethnically. Disassembling the sample into seven ethnic samples allows us to portray the varying complexity as well as point out endogenous structural differences among ethnics. The relationships among the endogenous variables are portrayed ethnically in Figures 4-A to 4-G. The figures are listed in decreasing order of complexity and activity. (The notation in Figure 4 is the same as that in Figure 1.)

TABLE 3: A Priori Predictions Compared to Empirical Results

Assertion	Affect	Impact
1) Efficacy should affect achievement strongly and vice versa.	yes yes	strong strong
2) Expectation should affect achievement strongly and vice versa.	yes yes	weak weak
3) Motivation should affect achievement strongly and vice versa.	no yes	weak strong

4) Motivation should affect expectations strongly.	yes	strong
5) Efficacy should affect motivation weakly.	yes	weak
6) Perceived teacher expectations should affect motivation strongly	yes	strong
7) Perceived teacher expectations should affect efficacy strongly.	yes	strong
8) Perceived teacher expectations should affect pupil expectations weakly.	no	strong
9) Perceived parents expectations should affect motivation strongly.	yes	strong
10) Perceived parent expectations should affect efficacy strongly.	no	weak
11) Perceived parent expectations should affect pupil expectations strongly.	yes	strong
12) Perceived teacher expectations should affect perceived parent expectations strongly	yes	strong
13) Perceived parent expectations should affect perceived teacher expectations strongly	yes	strong

TABLE 4: Results Not Hypothesized

Assertion	Affect	Impact
1) Efficacy affects perceived teacher expectations strongly.	yes	strong
2) Pupil expectations affect perceived teacher expectations strongly.	yes	strong
3) Efficacy affects expectations strongly.	yes	strong
4) Expectations affect efficacy weakly.	yes	weak
5) Motivation affects efficacy strongly.	yes	strong
6) Expectations affect motivation weakly.	yes	weak
7) Motivation affects efficacy strongly.	yes	strong
8) Motivation affects perceived parents' expectations strongly	yes	strong
9) Expectations affect perceived parents' expectations strongly.	yes	strong

WHITE AMERICANS

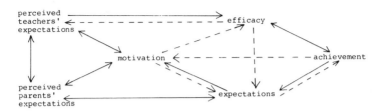

Fig. 4-A

AMERICANS ELECTING NO ETHNIC DESIGNATION

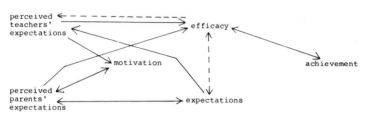

Fig. 4-B

BLACK AMERICANS

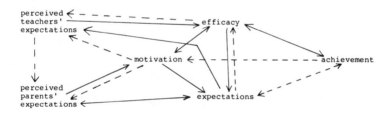

Fig. 4-C

NATIVE AMERICANS

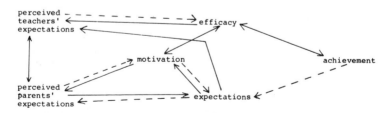

Fig. 4-D

ASIAN AMERICANS

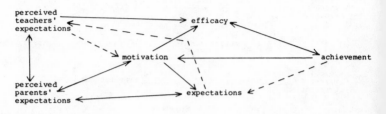

Fig. 4-E

PUERTO RICAN AMERICANS

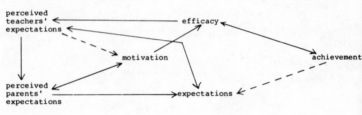

Fig. 4-F

MEXICAN AMERICANS

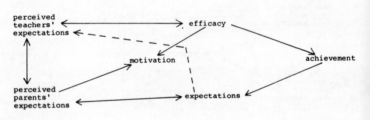

Fig. 4-G

Summary of Results. Although a summary is difficult at this point, the following major results emerge:

1) The educational process should be modeled by interdependent simultaneous equations. This model allows for joint determination of variables as well as feedback.

2) The complexity of the endogenous structure varies according to ethnic group. White Americans are the most complex while Mexican Americans are the least complex.

3) In school, the child who does best in terms of achievement, expectations, motivation and efficacy has the following characteristics: a) younger, b) high socioeconomic status, c) is the oldest child in the family, d) has changed schools a long time ago, e) has a home with an abundant supply of information, and f) in the expectations and achievement equation is male. The findings for the reduced form equations are summarized in Appendix B.

In short, the school structure is built, as has frequently been charged, on a model that favors males, stability, and upwardly mobile persons—mainstreamers. In this form the school is exclusionary. This does not readily square with our democratic ideals in which we, as a society, view education as a basic right for our citizens as well as an avenue for upward mobility. Further, if the disaggregation of the data suggests anything, it clearly says America is pluralistic, although each ethnic group has its mainstreamers who are making it. Pluralism suggests it may be necessary to have alternative models of the educational structure, if indeed, more than a few (mainstreamers) shall benefit from education as we view it in a democratic context. On this note, we conclude the discussion of the variables and turn now to two policy issues—integration and compensation.

PUBLIC POLICY ISSUES

The discussion to this point has indicated the extreme complexity of the educational process. It has also called attention to the possibilities of reconciling our belief about education in a democratic society with our behavior, perhaps, by proceeding pluralistically. Frankly, as we pointed out, the schools as presently (1965) constituted, work for "mainstreamers" independent of ethnic identification. If we proceed pluralistically, two questions emerge. Is there a racial pupil mix that will produce better results, and are there compensation strategies which might be better? These two questions are not easily answered, for variables which promote achievement may decrease rather than increase motivation and expectation. Further, perhaps achievement is so completely dominant in our society that people are unwilling (parents particularly) to sacrifice for other outputs. Bailey [3] speculates that this is not entirely the case with all ethnic groups. In short, tradeoffs exist; it seldom is either this or that. These tradeoffs require extreme sensitivity.

Integration. Unfortunately, these results do not give a clear policy prescription. They do indicate that the situation is much more complicated than had previously been imagined. Bluntly, for some minority groups, integration is, at best, a mixed blessing, all trade-offs considered. Let us focus first on the results for blacks and whites.

In terms of achievement, black students do better in either white or mainly black middle class schools and perform at their worst when the schools are integrated, all other variables held constant. A second look confuses the story. The coefficient for the variable which indicates the percentage of white pupils in last year's class is positive and significant. Hence, in terms of achievement, all other things being held constant, these results tend to indicate that a black student will do best, in terms of achievement by either attending a predominantly (more than 70%) white school or being in a *class* which is mostly white but which is in a mostly black *school,* a scenario rather impossible to achieve. On the other hand, in terms of motivation and expectations, black students tend to be better off in schools that are racially integrated. In the structural form equation for efficacy, the coefficients for integrated schools, mainly black schools, and the percentage of whites in class year are all negative and significant. From this, one might conclude that, in terms of a black student's self-esteem and sense of control, he would be best off, other things held constant, by being in a class which is mostly black but which is contained within a mostly white *school.* It is clear that there is not a straightforward tradeoff that one can make in terms of integrating blacks and whites.

Now consider the situation for whites. In terms of the structural form achievement equation, the coefficient for mainly black schools does not even enter significantly. It does enter negatively for integrated schools although not very significantly. Hence, in terms of achievement, white students appear to be best off, other things held constant, in mostly white schools, followed by mostly black schools, and relatively worse off in integrated schools. It is clear that the negative effect of integration upon achievement is not nearly so significant for whites as it is for blacks. In addition, other things being controlled, attendance at either an integrated or a non-white, middle class school tends to improve the motivation of white students. On the whole, these white students are unlikely to suffer very much in terms of achievement from having integration.

These results suggest the deep complexity of the integration issue.

White students appear to have little to lose or to gain from integration. Black students present an expremely complicated set of tradeoffs between the various educational outputs. Johnson, et al. [19] suggest that conflict accounts for the relatively poor achievement for students in integrated schools. The severity and intensity of the conflict, they argue, is determined by the size of the minority group and the social class mix of the school. Our results clearly support the importance of socioeconomic status and home and school stability in the achievement equation for all groups. Conflict in the school, to our way of thinking, destroys school stability. Let us explore this further.

In 1965, despite the school desegregation ruling of 1954, most schools North and South were still segregated and so were most residential neighborhoods. Mixing immediately presents turf and status problems. In instances where a significant minority is present, these turf problems probably exacerbate the conflict, which disturbs stability. On the other hand—if integration were natural, in 1965, with blacks and whites living in the same neighborhood, sharing neighborhood schools— the context most generally was one where whites (poor) were trapped in neighborhoods going rapidly black. Essentially whites were in a place they had no desire to be. Dissonance, racism, and black pride coalesce to produce conflicts which disrupt stability. The conflict situation is heightened when, as Zeigler and Boss [25] point out, there is a condition in which policy responses to racial problems are characterized by ambiguity and lack of clear corrective action. In short, the school is ill-prepared to cope with conflict. Unplanned racial and class mixing generates conflict.

What is being suggested is that conflict potential is a major exogenous determinant when considering black-white racial integration. This potential for conflict is enhanced where minority size and overall socioeconomic class considerations are not considered, particularly as that relates to the achievement equation. If students spend their time preparing for conflict, then little time is available for concentrating on reading, writing, and arithmetic. Further, it is even conceivable that the dissonance resultant from the discrepancy between pupil and perceived peer, parents, and teachers expectations might become so severe that problems at the individual level may begin to emerge. As we said when we started, the issue is not an easy one and ought to be approached delicately. Clear knowledge of preferred tradeoffs coupled with a clear strategy for controlling conflict by paying attention to minority group size and socioeconomic mix appears to be a small step in the right direction.

The results for other ethnic groups on the issue of racial integration are not nearly so striking as those for blacks and whites. Nevertheless, there are important and complicated tradeoffs across the various educational outputs.

In terms of achievement, both Native American and Mexican American students appear to gain by attending mostly white schools. The coefficients in the structural equations for both integrated and mainly non-white schools are negative and significant in each instance. This result suggests that these two groups achieve higher in a predominantly white school. Efficacy decreases if these students attend mostly non-white schools, while there is some gain in motivation if they attend mostly non-white schools. On the whole, the evidence suggests that these two ethnic groups have the simplest and most straightforward argument for complete integration with the white majority within the schools. While probably few, if any, situations existed in 1965 where either of these groups comprised a significant minority in a public school system, thus reducing potential for conflict, care still needs to be given to socioeconomic considerations in the mixing.

In terms of achievement, Puerto Rican students also appear to gain from complete integration with the white majority. The coefficient for mainly non-white schools was negative and significant in the structural form equation. It should be remembered that Puerto Ricans, mainly New York based, under the neighborhood school concept would share schools with blacks in 1964. The situation is ripe for conflict as a function of minority group size and social class mix. The coefficients for integrated schools are negative in terms of both motivation and efficacy. The significantly negative constant terms in both of these instances indicate that there may be tradeoff sacrifices from complete integration. Asian Americans appear to achieve less well, other things being held constant, if they are students in mostly non-white schools. On the other hand, they seem to gain in terms of motivation and lose in terms of expectations through attendance at such schools. We call attention to a recurring theme—for all ethnics, going to school with other ethnics (except whites) appears to lead to lower achievement results. Racism may in part account for this finding, but we suggest that conflict produced by minority group size and socioeconomic mix are probably the most instructive with regards to understanding what is going on. Further, it is interesting to note that the ethnic group which may be the most emotionally up-tight about integration, the white majority, appears to have the least to worry about, no matter what the integration policy. Blacks present the most complicated situation on this issue.

In closing on this issue, the approaches have been far too simplistic. Existing policies have plunged headlong toward fully integrated schools in a society where those with decision-making authority (the courts) can control few of the all-important social variables which appear to determine the final outcomes for the educational process. Since the legal and symbolic supports for segregation have been abolished, now may be the time to begin thinking anew about the policy on this issue. Lofty ideals on this critical issue must not allow policymakers to miss the forest for the trees.

Compensation. The question is simple. Given that White Americans and Asian Americans achieve higher in 1965 than the other ethnic groups in our society, is it possible to compensate in some way so that achievement difference might be minimized between ethnics? Our data allow us to make a few suggestions on the compensation question.

If one begins again by comparing the results for the black and white ethnic samples, one is immediately struck by the fact that the average score of the teachers within a school on the verbal achievement test has a much more significant and a larger coefficient in the achievement equation for blacks as opposed to whites. This suggests that the intellectual competence of the teacher appears to be much more important for the achievement of black students than it is for whites. The average verbal achievement score for the teachers of black students was 22.836. The comparable average for the teachers of white students was 25.25. If, for example, the average competence of the teachers of black students could be raised to that of the teachers of white students as it is measured by this score, then the performance of black students would be increased by approximately 20% of the difference between the mean achievement levels between blacks and whites after one controls for all other variables. Hence, there appears to be an important potential payoff in terms of student achievement by increasing the average competence of the teachers, especially the teachers of black students. However, tradeoffs may be involved here too. Note, for example, that the coefficient for teachers average verbal right is negatively significant in the motivation equation for white students and positive and significant in the expectation equation. On the other hand, it is negative and significant in the expectations for black students. Yet, these tradeoffs do not appear to detract significantly from the potential improvement which could be obtained by improving the competence of the teachers of black students.

Similar results emerge when one examines the effects of the number of teachers per pupil. While this ratio appears to have a positive and significant effect upon the achievement of white students, its coefficient is even larger and more significant in the structural form of the achievement equation for black students. Since average class size is larger for black students (by approximately two students per teacher) than it is for whites, the mere reduction of the average class size for black students to the level for white students, other things being equal, would reduce the difference in mean achievement levels between whites and blacks by approximately 2%. In short, the evidence suggests that, other things being held constant, black students tend to gain more in terms of achievement from smaller classes than do whites.

One might note in passing that, while the coefficient for teachers average verbal right is positive and significant in the reduced form and structural achievement equations for all ethnic groups, the same is not true for the teacher-pupil ratio. Class size does not appear to be significantly associated with achievement in the cases of American Indians and Asian Americans.

The reduced form achievement equations suggest that teaching experience, as measured by the average number of years that the teachers have spent teaching, generally has a quadratic effect upon achievement. Young teachers and those with much experience are generally more effective than teachers with some but not a lot of experience. However, except for Black Americans, American Indians and Mexican Americans, this conclusion does not stand up in the structural form equations. Again the evidence suggests that experience may be more important for Black Americans than for any other ethnic group. Briefly, it might be said that in many respects the school is a home surrogate for ethnics except whites, excluding perhaps poor whites. Perhaps, manipulating teacher-related variables to obtain the best quality teachers is the way to improve the endogenous variables of the educational process for ethnics. Programs such as Upward Bound and other compulsory education programs, unless teacher variables are controlled, are probably inappropriate compensation approaches.

Simultaneous equations models seem applicable to the educational process, representing the best approach to that process to date. The results suggest a complex system of tradeoffs that must be viewed and considered for each ethnic group individually. Future decision-makers, unable to control many of the exogenous variables, particularly those that enhance potential conflict, ought to be mindful of the maxim: "Fools rush in where angels fear to tread."

NOTES

1. The indices are constructed by principal components analyses from the answers to questions in the EEOS.

2. The notation for Figure 2 is the same as that for Figure 1.

3. The notation for Figure 3 is the same as that for Figure 1.

4. For more information on the model, reasons for the inclusion of variables in the model, and reasons for hypothesizing that a variable enters an equation with a particular sign, see Boardman [4].

5. See Appendix A for variables' descriptions.

6. Significance means the t-statistic of the structural form coefficient exceeds 1.645 in absolute value.

7. The reduced form equations tables as well as ethnic tables are available on request, and appear in Boardman [4] pp. 146-160.

REFERENCES

1)   Anderson, J. G., and Evans, F. B. "Causal Models in Educational Research: Recursive Models." *American Educational Research Journal*, 11, 1974, 29-39.

2)   Armor, David J., "The Evidence on Busing." *The Public Interest*, 28 Summer 1972, 90-126.

3)   Bailey, Peter, "An 'Integrated' Youngster." *Ebony Magazine*, August 1974.

4)   Boardman, Anthony E., "Simultaneous Equations Models of the Educational Process." Unpublished Ph.D. dissertation, Carnegie-Mellon University, 1975.

5)   Boardman, Anthony E., Otto A. Davis and Peggy R. Sanday, "A Simultaneous Equations Model of the Educational Process: The Coleman Data Revisited With an Emphasis upon Achievement." *American Statistical Association Proceedings of the Social Statistics Section*, 1973.

6)   Boardman, Anthony E., Otto A. Davis and Peggy R. Sanday, "A Simultaneous Equations Model of the Educational Process." Forthcoming in the *Journal of Public Economics*.

7)   Bowles, Samuel and Henry M. Levin, "The Determinants of Scholastic Achievement: An Appraisal of Some Recent Evidence." *Journal of Human Resources*, 3, November 1968, 3-24.

8)   Cain, Glen C. and Harold W. Watts, "Problems in Making Policy Inferences from the Coleman Report." *American Sociological Review*, 35, April 1970, 228-241.

9)   Coleman, James S., Ernest Q. Campbell, Carol J. Hobson, James McPartland, Alexander M. Mood, Frederick D. Weinfield and Robert L. York, *Equality of Educational Opportunity*, Washington, D.C., U.S. Gov't. Printing Office, 1969.

10)   Dhrymes, Phoebus J., *Econometrics*, Harper and Row, 1970.

11)   Gordon, C., "Looking Ahead: Self-Conceptions, Race and Family as Determinants of Adolescent Orientation to Achievement." Arnold M. and Caroline Rose Monograph Series, American Sociological Association, 1973.

12)   Hanushek, Eric A., "Teacher Characteristics and Gains in Student Achievement: Estimation Using Micro Data." *American Economic Review*, 61, May 1971, 280-288.

13)   Hanushek, Eric A., *Education and Race*, Lexington: D.C. Heath, 1972.

14)   Jencks, Christopher, et al., *Inequality*, Basic Books, 1972.

15)   Johnson, Norman J., Neil Bilbert and Robert Wyer, "Quality Education and Integration: An Exploratory Study." Fall 1967.

16)   Johnson, Norman J., and Peggy R. Sanday, "Subcultural Variations in an Urban Poor Population." *American Anthropologist*, Vol. 73, No. 1, 1971.

17)   Leacock, Eleanor, *Teaching and Learning in City Schools: A Comparative Study*, New York, Basic Books, 1969.

18)   Levin, Henry M., "A New Model of School Effectiveness," in *Do Teachers Make a Difference?*, U.S. Gov't. Printing Office, 1970, 25-78.

19)   Mayeske, George W., et al., "A Study of Our Nations Schools," working paper, U.S. Dept. of Health, Educational and Welfare, Office of Education.

20)   Mosteller, Frederick and Daniel P. Moynihan, (Eds.) *On Equality of Educational Opportunity, (OEOEO)*, Random House, 1972.

21)   Parti, M., and I. Adelman, "An Empirical Analysis of Urban Primary Education in the United States." *Social Science Research*, 3, 1974, 61-78.

22)   Pouissant, A. F., "The Black Child's Image of the Future." In Toffler, A. (Ed.) *Learning for Tomorrow*, New York: Vintage Books, 1974, 56-71.

23)   U.S. Commission on Civil Rights, *Racial Isolation in the Public Schools*, 2 Vols., Washington, D.C., 1967.

24)   Whyte, William Foote, *Street Corner Society*, Univ. of Chicago Press, Chicago, Ill., 1943.

25)   Zeigler, Harman and Michael Boss, "Racial Problems and Policy in the American Public Schools." *Sociology of Education*, Vol. 47, No. 3, Summer 1974, 319-336.

APPENDIX A
DESCRIPTION OF THE VARIABLES

Abbreviation	*Description*
ACH	Achievement
MOT	Motivation
EXP	Expectations
EFF	Efficacy
PPAEXP	Perceived Parents' Expectations
PTEXP	Perceived Teachers' Expectations
SEX	Sex
AGE	Age
SES	Socioeconomic status
INFO	Information Available
TWOP	Two parents
NOBAS	Number of older brothers and sisters
PTAS	Parents talking about school
FL	Foreign Language
RBS	Reading before school
PTAAT	Parents attend PTA
TC	This city
NTCHSCL	Number of times changed school
LSTCHSCL	Last time changed school
AVSES	Average socioeconomic status
PWPICLY	Proportion of white pupils in class last year
MYBLCK	Mainly black school
MIX	Integrated school
TAVR	Teachers' average verbal right
NTPRPUP	Number of teachers per pupil
TANYTCH	Teachers' average number of years teaching
TANYTCH2	(Teachers' average number of years teaching)^2
PWTCHLY	Proportion of white teachers in class last year

TASEX	Teachers' sex
TPTC	Proportion of teachers from this city
TPADTN	Teachers' problems with administration
FACILITS	School facilities
PROBLEMS	Problems in the school
AGES	Age of school
TEST	Testing experience
NTCHLV	Number of teachers who leave
PRNMADEG	Principal has Master's degree
NTLKGC	Number of times talk to guidance counsellor last year
NEWENG	New England
MIDATL	Mid-Atlantic
PLAINS	Plains
SEAST	Southeast
SWEST	Southwest
NGWTV	Watching television
NHWTV2	(Watching TV)^2
CONST	Constant

APPENDIX B

A SUMMARY OF THE ESTIMATED REDUCED FORM EQUATIONS FOR ALL OF THE ETHNIC GROUPS AND FOR THE COMBINED SAMPLE

Dependent Variables

Explanatory Variables	ACH	MOT	EXP	EFF	PPAEXP	PTEXP
ACH	1	0	0	0	0	0
MOT	0	1	0	0	0	0
EXP	0	0	1	0	0	0
EFF	0	0.	0	1	0	0
PPAEXP	0	0	0	0	1	0
PTEXP	0	0	0	0	0	1
SEX	--	++	-	++	--	0
AGE	--	--	--	-	--	--
SES	++	++	++	++	++	+
INFO	+	++	++	++	++	++
TWOP	(+)	0	0	0	+	0
NOBAS	--	-	--	-	-	0
FL	(-)	(-)	-	0	-	0
RBS	+	++	++	++	++	+
PTAAT	--	+	+	0	+	+
PTAS	++	--	--	0	--	-
TC	+	(-)	(-)	0	0	0
NTCHSCL	(+)	0	(-)	0	0	0
LSTCHSCL	++	+	+	++	+	0
AVSES	++	(-)	+	0	(-)	(-)
PWPICLY	?	0	0	0	0	0
MYLBLCK	-	+	?	0	+	(+)
MIX	(-)	(+)	0	0	0	(+)

Dependent Variables (Continued)

Explanatory Variables	ACH	MOT	EXP	EFF	PPAEXP	PTEXP
TAVR	++	0	0	0	0	0
NTPRUPUP	+	0	0	(-)	(-)	+
TANYTCH	--	?	0	-	0	+
TANYTCH2	++	?	0	+	0	(-)
PWTCHLY	0	++	(-)	+	0	(-)
TASEX	0	0	0	(-)	(+)	0
TPTC	0	0	0	0	(-)	+
TPADTN	+	(+)	+	0	0	-
FACILITS	0	0	0	0	0	-
PROBLEMS	--	(-)	-	+	0	0
AGES	0	+	0	0	--	0
TEST	+	0	0	0	0	0
NTCHLV	+	(-)	0	(+)	0	0
PRNMADEG	0	0	0	?	0	0
SMSA	0	0	0	+	-	0
NEWENG	(+)	0	0	0	-	?
MITATL	?	0	-	+	0	0
LAKES	0	?	-	(+)	0	0
PLAINS	+	0	(-)	++	0	0
SEAST	?	?	(-)	0	0	+
SWEST	-	++	0	0	0	0
NTLKGC	0	0	++	++	-	(+)
NHWTV	(-)	++	(+)	+	-	-
NHWTV2	0	--	-	-	(+)	-
CONST	+	0	+	0	+	--

EVALUATION OF EDUCATION PROJECTS FINANCED BY THE WORLD BANK GROUP[1]

Mats Hultin, Senior Advisor
Education Department
International Bank for Reconstruction
and Development

The World Bank Group (WBG) granted its first education loan in 1962. Thereafter, about 100 education loans and credits have been approved, covering 60% of a total project amount of $1,900 million.[2] Of a typical loan or credit, some 60% of the funds would be used for construction of buildings, 30% for equipment, and 10% for technical assistance. As an illustration, a project might in this way support a vocational education reform in a developing country through provision of new vocational schools and vocational teacher training institutes, through curriculum reform and through the writing, printing, distribution and introduction of the appropriate textbooks. Other levels or areas of education might also be supported.

The implementation of WBG-financed education projects requires generally 3-to-5 years. Another 4-to-6 years may pass until the first cohort of students has gone through the project institutions and entered the labor market. As much as a decade has therefore to pass until the full impact of an education project can be measured. Consequently, a comprehensive evaluation of the WBG-financed education activities has only recently started and a handful only of projects has so far been assessed. The emphasis has been on so-called summative evaluation.

It is now generally agreed that education project evaluation should be a comprehensive and continuous process. It might be formative as well as summative. The formative evaluation provides information during the project execution and provides the management with a tool for necessary project revisions. The summative evaluation is carried out after the project's completion and describes the project's success or failure and should provide a lesson for future projects.

In WBG-financed activities the project outcome is of interest to the borrower as well as to the Bank. Bank involvement in the evaluation is therefore justified. Ideally, evaluation should be the borrowing country's full and own responsibility and should be carried out by local bodies which are independent of those authorities which are directly responsible for the project. However, such local bodies are often nonexistent. The evaluation of WBG-financing education projects would, therefore, have two major functions: (a) the specific project assessment and (b) assistance to establish local bodies capable of continuous evaluation.

The WBG-financed education projects might be evaluated at five related levels:

(i) whether the intended construction, equipment, staffing, and technical assistance, etc. were achieved (a process assessment);

(ii) whether the intended student enrollments and school outputs were achieved—considering the distribution of the students by sex, race, ethnic groups, catchment areas, socioeconomic backgrounds, reduction in drop-out and repetition rates, etc. (a production target);

(iii) whether the attainments of the project institution students—they may be adults in farmer training centers, pupils in primary schools, university students, vocational school trainees, etc.—reached expectations (a second subgoal);

(iv) whether and how soon the project school leavers found gainful employment or were accepted by the next level education institutions (a first subgoal);

(v) whether the education projects have contributed to economic, social, cultural and environmental development (a main goal).

The performance at the first level mentioned in (i) above is as a routine assessed by the Bank through so-called supervision missions. Student enrollments and school outputs (ii) are also assessed by supervision missions, although insufficient attention has been given to the distribution of students by sex, race, catchment areas, ethnic groups, socioeconomic backgrounds, etc. Less attention has also been paid so far by the WBG to the assessments of (iii), (iv), and (v). Those tasks have not been undertaken by the supervision missions, which possess neither the time nor appropriate manpower for them. An Evaluation Department was established in the Bank some years ago, but it was soon realized that more had to be done in advance during project preparation if the Evaluation Department would be able to assess in a fully satisfactory way student attainments, school-leaver employments, and the education projects' overall impact on development.

For the assessment of student attainments and some other education objectives, it was decided in 1973 to finance a research study of WBG-financed education projects. The objective would be to arrive at methodologies which could be built into the Bank-financed education projects as a routine and provide formative as well as summative evaluation.[3] The Bank asked the research team to study the WBG's education appraisal reports, the loan/credit agreements, and other documents with a view to see the extent to which the education objectives of the projects had been defined in such a way that they could be properly evaluated. Furthermore, the research team was requested to suggest evaluation machineries which could answer the following questions: (a) Have the education objectives as agreed upon with the borrower been met? (b) Did the attainments of the students of the project institutions reach expectations? This study will thus primarily help the Bank to deal with the evaluation issue listed under paragraph (iii) above. It will deal less with the employment of the school leavers and not at all with the general impact of the education projects on development. The latter issues will be dealt with in other ways.

The attainment study has so far indicated that WBG-financed education projects often lack precise statements of education objectives. This renders appropriate evaluation difficult. The report of the first phase of the research criticizes the definition of education objectives in WBG's education projects and states "by conventional standards of curriculum workers, the projects fall extremely short of what is desirable and feasible as far as specificity is concerned." In this context, it is emphasized that measurements of the attainments of the learning objectives (the student performance) should be criterion referenced rather than norm referenced. Criterion-referenced measurements are difficult to conduct, but they are objective and permit longitudinal studies. Bank projects should, furthermore, according to the research team, be exposed to formative rather than to summative evaluations which implies that full evaluation machineries must be defined at the conceptual stage of the projects.

During the discussions of the research team's recommendation in the Bank, the feasibility of introducing sophisticated evaluation methods in developing countries was questioned. It was furthermore stated that some of the evaluation methods developed by the IEA and recommended by the research team for Bank-financed projects would require research skills which might not be available in many developing countries.[4] This is true, but it is feasible to develop those skills as a part of the establishment of evaluation machineries in the education projects. The scarcity of human and financial resources in the developing countries makes it, in fact, particularly necessary to measure as accurately as possible the efficiency and productivity of the education systems of those countries to avoid costly mistakes and waste. More than many developed countries, the developing countries may thus need evaluation machineries of a fairly sophisticated nature as well as well-trained evaluators. But the machineries and the staff must be geared to the specific local needs and circumstances; ready-made methods and expatriates cannot easily be used.

The research study also devotes a chapter to education statistics and the composition of the student body. The latter is a part of education project evaluation which has often been neglected in the past. In Bank-financed education projects, the national aggregates have been considered rather than the individual target groups (broken down by sex, race, ethnic groups, socioeconomic background, etc.). The current WBG's emphasis on "the 40% poor," on equity and income distribution has changed the Bank's approach, and considerable interest is now focused on the target groups. The question of who are the students receiving the education in the project schools has become important. The first study of the student background was made in a recent project evaluation in Ethiopia. It was found that two-thirds of the Ethiopian students in the last grade of secondary education had illiterate parents and 50% of the parents were working in agriculture. Such information provides, of course, a useful feedback for a discussion about instruction methods, provision of learning materials in the schools, etc. It is thus important to study both the intake and output of the education systems as a part of a project evaluation.

A new evaluation development is the cohort analysis in which the whole age group of a region or a country is followed year by year, whether in or out of school. This technique requires access to census data, but there are a number of developing countries in which the quality of the demographic and educational statistics would permit cohort analysis.

Tracer studies are related to cohort analysis, and they form an important part of education evaluation. In developing countries, tracer studies are a new concept but some 10 Bank-financed projects include tracer studies. So far only one of the Bank tracer studies has been completed—in Thailand in connection with a vocational school project. It provided significant information and showed that the graduates from the Bank-financed vocational schools had no difficulty in obtaining employment but that an increasing percentage of the graduates proceeded to higher education, which is not an objective of vocational education and implies a waste of an expensive instruction. It might be said that the tracer study in Thailand showed that the vocational schools were too good. They attracted considerably more applicants per place than did other schools and the academic ability of the student body was perhaps unnecessarily high. The tracer study thus provided an important feedback to forthcoming vocational education projects in Thailand.

Education projects are supposed to contribute to economic, social, cultural, and environmental development. An increased productivity in agriculture, industry, and business by the school leavers is an expected outcome of education projects. The quantitative assessments of this contribution of education projects to development is difficult and more research is needed. In the Bank, the Development Policy Staff is working on this aspect of Bank projects, but so far no education projects have been measured as regards their impact on development in general. It is unsatisfactory to admit that we assume that the education projects will contribute to development by the provision of educated and trained manpower to meet specific labor market needs but that we have no solid quantitative proof of such contribution. The major justification for education projects is still the basic sense about education's necessity for development. We can perhaps agree that we know less about the true quantitative correlation between education and economic growth today than we thought we knew at the time of the famous OECD conference in Washington in the early 1960s.

Few developed and developing countries have established evaluation machineries in education and conducted education assessments on a nationwide scale. Countries with planned economies have used manpower studies for a long time and developed education systems to meet those manpower demands, and they have also assessed the outcomes. But otherwise systematic education evaluations on a national scale are rare. In some countries examination systems at the exit levels are referred to as evaluation machineries. But examination systems do not meet the requirements of an appropriate evaluation of an education system. It is, therefore, important to build in evaluation machineries as a routine in education projects. The evaluation systems so established should ideally develop and eventually serve on a nationwide scale at all levels of the education and training system.

I would like to summarize my paper by saying:

(i) education projects which have been financed by the WBG have often not been defined in such operational terms that they can easily permit a fully quantified evaluation;

(ii) evaluation is, however, a necessary part of any activity in education and the objectives of education projects should, therefore, be defined in such a way that they lend themselves to an appropriate evaluation;

(iii) evaluation machineries should ideally be built into projects as a routine and they should primarily be formative;

(iv) the evaluation machineries should ideally, among other issues, include an analysis of the student body by sex, social background, etc., a measurement of the students' achievements and a follow-up of the students in the labor market through appropriate tracer studies;

(v) when data permit, a full cohort analysis would often be an important evaluation tool;

(vi) the quantitative measurement of the impact of an education project on development and productivity in general is not yet possible to carry out in a fully satisfactory way and it is, therefore, an important task for education researchers to continue their work in this area and find the quantitative correlations between education and development and provide the tools for the measurements of those correlations.

NOTES

1. The views are those of the author and not necessarily those of the Bank.
2. The term "loan" is used in the World Bank Group for the Bank loans while

the term "credit" is used for the soft financing by the World Bank affiliate, the International Development Association (IDA).

3. The Research is conducted by a team at the International Institute for Education Planning (IIEP), Paris, under the leadership of Dr. N. Postlethwaite, formerly director of the well-known 20-country comparative education study by the International Association for the Evaluation of Education Achievement (IEA).

4. See footnote number 3.

EVALUATING TITLE I AGAIN?

Michael Timpane
The Rand Corporation

Every few years, someone asks me to sum up the effects of federal education evaluation activities, particularly those concerning the federal compensatory education programs funded under ESEA Title I. I have found this report the most difficult to compose. In part, this is because I have not been closely involved with federal decision-making in this area for the past two years; in part, the difficulty stems from a great awakening that I have experienced serving as a local school board member. Surely, too, the incomplete and often contradictory nature of recent evidence is simply hard to interpret. For example, I believe that, in examining the effects of Title I, we now know more about the dimensions and significance of such questions as:

- How long does policy or theory suggest that we can or must wait to observe effects?
- What size effects are significant for policy?
- What difference do organizational or personal attributes make in the implementation and therefore effectiveness of nominally equivalent programs?

The problem is—all of these questions seem to apply also to evaluating the effectiveness of evaluations themselves.

[415]

THE TANGLED SKEIN REVISITED

There are already several versions of the history and impact of Title I evaluations.[1] The story begins with the objectives of the legislation Congress declared in 1965:[2]

> In recognition of the special educational needs of children of low income families and the impact that concentrations of low income families have on the ability of local educational agencies to support adequate educational programs the Congress hereby declares it to be the policy of the United States to provide financial assistance to local educational areas serving areas with concentrations of children of low income families to expend and improve their educational programs by various means which contribute particularly by meeting special educational needs of educationally deprived children.

To carry out this policy, a formula grant awarded monies through the states to localities on the basis of the number of low-income students. Local educational agencies would use the money to meet the special educational needs of educationally deprived children in school attendance areas serving high concentrations of children from low-income families, in projects which gave reasonable promise of success. The Congressional action carried forward some very major and diverse political and societal objectives:

- To establish the principle of large-scale federal aid to education.
- To provide especially significant fiscal assistance to hard pressed city schools.
- To create a large within-school component of the anti-poverty program to improve the education of poor children (and at the same time to substitute for more general forms of federal education aid).
- To stimulate educational institutions generally toward reform of educational practice resulting in increased attention to the needs of the disadvantaged.

Each of these objectives implies, of course, different criteria for program success.

What was *not* an objective of the legislation was the establishment of particular forms of compensatory education to enhance the achievement of poor children. This was an understandable omission. There was, at the time, almost no evidence either theoretical or empirical pointing to specific compensatory and remedial educational services that were sure bets to accelerate the academic achievement of poor youngsters. Furthermore, following the political tradition of American education, Congress provided local educational authorities with great discretion in selecting the types of program they thought would best suit local educational needs. Annual appropriations for the program started off near $1 billion per year and have increased gradually to $1.8 billion each fiscal year. The program provides services to 7-8 million children in 16,000 school districts.

Title I was also the first federal education law to mandate annual effectiveness evaluations. Thus, from the outset, evaluative efforts and related research endeavors sought to ascertain the program's effects. None has been entirely successful, but each has succeeded what had gone previously, improving our understanding of the program's political and intellectual prospective inch-by-inch.

Three statements seem to sum up the course of events:

- A sizable "first wave" of evaluative studies of Title I were all flawed in conception (as much from political innocence as from methodological choice) and were, in their primary objectives of defining program effectiveness, failures.

- These studies produced substantial side effects, not just in painful learning from their failure, but also in suggestions for program management improvements and educational research initiatives.

- A new generation of studies and programs, better than the last but not perfect, has begun.

THE WAVE OF FAILURES

The *GE Tempo* evaluation (1967) was a pilot cost-effectiveness study that tried to ascertain Title I impact in 11 school districts, in terms of increased reading and mathematics skills.[3] It found few such effects and was widely (and wrongly) cited at the outset of the Nixon administration as proof that Title I did not yet work and should be held down in size.

The *Belmont* evaluative information system (1968 through the present), was a huge attempt to secure cost, process, pupil background and achievement data through a federal-state-local reporting system.[4] Conducted largely as an intergovernmental bureaucratic intrigue, with a hidden agenda for educational reform, Belmont foundered, as a federal evaluation on the states' unwillingness to report achievement data honestly and fully, as well as on its own overambition. It continues as a developmental information system, largely controlled by and useful to the states.

National project surveys (1968-69), covered several hundred representative compensatory programs. They also encountered state and local reluctance to provide achievement data and federal reluctance to report their discouraging results.[5]

Searches for exemplary Title I projects (1968 and 1970) turned up a few handfuls of projects that were increasing achievement scores significantly, but these projects were only a small percentage of reported successes and not many of them showed consistently high gains over several years.[6]

A synthesis of programs and evaluative data for the first five years (1972) concluded that (1) federal, state, and local management performance was lackluster; (2) the program's resources got to eligible children, but not in proper relation to their educational needs or to the financial needs of the school districts and states which served them; and (3) evidence of program effectiveness was scattered and slim.[7]

√ *State and local evaluations* required by the federal statute were of little use for federal program decisions. Most of the local evaluations had no scientific character, nor, in the questions they asked, were they even potentially useful for local purposes; and the few state-wide evaluations were of uneven quality. HEW's compensatory education review of 1972, the only serious attempt to use state and local results— together with the exemplary study findings, was hurried and mixed up in anti-busing politics; it built up the available positive evidence to much the same extent that earlier political requirements had exaggerated GE Tempo's negative purport.[8]

There is plenty of reason for dismay in reviewing these results. At the end of all these studies, the effectiveness of Title I as an educational program was still unknown. Politics had frustrated federal evaluation efforts at both ends; states and localities had brushed off federal requests for essential achievement data, and federal policymakers had picked and chosen among evaluation findings, depending upon which policy they wished to promote. Fortunately, there are several mitigating circumstances that make the tale less hopeless and forlorn. The first is that Congress never took the whole business too seriously, and Title I was never in danger of either abrupt decline or expansion on account of either real or exalted claims. For one thing, the evaluations were mostly concerned with just one among several legislative objectives—educational effectiveness. This objective was by no means preeminent in Congressional minds in what seemed to them the early years of a program which was doing pretty well, they thought, in several other important respects—getting money to poor districts and districts serving poor children, sustaining national initiatives toward equal educational opportunity, and holding together a grand legislative compromise that stopped short of general aid to education. So long as no one was stealing the money, and in the absence of an alternative, Congress was not yet ready to condemn the program at all.[9] Title I's annual appropriations have grown at a relatively constant rate, year in and year out, and its appropriation levels were rarely an issue in the frequent veto battles of the Nixon years.

Moreover, the federal offices worrying about Title I, in analyzing and reflecting on these evaluations, found many important lessons for federal program development.

CONSEQUENCES, CONSEQUENCES . . .

In Title I itself, the evaluation reports have made key contributions to major program improvements. For example, GE Tempo investigators reported persistent difficulty in finding school districts where they could identify the Title I program for purposes of measurement. This finding was soon reinforced by the Washington Research Group's report (1970) that many school districts had failed to apply Title I funds to "special educational needs" but had used Title I as general aid—as a substitute for state and local resources and had thereby simply brought the resources of poor schools, which had previously been shortchanged, up near the expenditure range of the more well-off schools in the district.[10] These findings helped convince reluctant educators and Congressmen that Title I needed a provision for *comparability,* so all localities would use Title I funds as truly extra—on top of an equalized allocation of state and local resources among schools. The Lawyer's Committee for Civil Rights Under Law reported recently that comparability is actually being enforced with discernible fiscal effect.[11]

Many of the early evaluations also found a wide dispersion of compensatory education funds among pupils and activities so that in some cases the dollars per pupils served were trivial and so were the purposes of the expenditure. Several also found, not surprisingly, some indication that higher dollar levels per pupil were associated with greater program effectiveness. These findings contributed to two distinct program decisions that both fall under the rubric *concentration:* namely, program guidelines that concentrate available funds in adequate per pupil amounts until the dollars run out (even if some eligible children are thereby left unserved) and guidelines that concentrate educational activities on the so-called basic skills of reading and math. These decisions may be arguable, but they were defensible and improved the program in my judgment.[12]

Another important area which the evaluations spotlighted but where less progress was made was the *actual distributive characteristics* of the Title I formula. Title I had a built-in bafflement here: district entitlements were based on numbers of low-income and welfare children, but services were to be delivered to a non-identical group of educationally disadvantaged students. The evaluations helped reveal the problems with both counts: educationally disadvantaged meant remarkably different things to different people; and counts of low-income and welfare students were not accurate or not available at all in many districts, since the data collected—on census tract and county bases, respectively, and, in the case of the census collected only every 10 years and that collected on low-income students—were counted differently again (on such bases as free and reduced price lunch eligibility), in determining which school buildings received funds. There were reports from several evaluations that the dollars available per pupil varied significantly by district, for no legitimate reason. In general, the Title I funds seemed to be headed in the intended direction, but there was plenty of room for improvement. These problems were not resolved much, until this year's legislative renewal, when they were the principal topic of Congressional scrutiny.

Beyond the program itself, because the findings were at once disappointing and methodologically suspect, the several Title I evaluations also helped focus federal educational research more than ever upon education for the disadvantaged and upon more elaborate and sometimes more rigorous tests of various educational techniques. To say the least, the studies indicated that effective compensatory education would be hard to accomplish until it was better understood. Thus, for good or ill, came the reorientation of Follow Through to Planned

Variations, the NIE and its charter for experimentation, the OEO experiments with educational vouchers and performance contracting. Sad to say, there was failure mingled with success in these efforts too—but out of them, we may finally have learned how to evaluate an educational intervention like compensatory education, in a real school setting. Without going into detail, let me mention four such instances of progress:

- Understanding of the political and bureaucratic requirements of field testing and evaluation,

- Appreciation of the importance of program implementation as an independent variable in evaluation,

- Realization that there was no agreed upon basis for comparing prominent education reforms which were based on disparate conceptions of human nature, and

- Finding the effectiveness of these reforms in specific dimensions of students' development, more than across-the-board progress.

Any future evaluation of Title I will be—politically, administratively, and methodologically—a far cry from the models and techniques we started with seven years ago. And think about that—only seven years! We are not even sure that the main effect of the program should occur in that period of time; how can we judge the ultimate promise of evaluation methodology.

WHAT HAS HAPPENED LATELY

For our purposes, two recent happenings should be noted. First, OE and HEW have not tried to evaluate the program impact of Title I lately. Instead, they have undertaken further review of program management[13] and an extensive but very careful study of compensatory reading programs in some 500 schools.[14] Initially, the latter study is having better than expected success in securing cooperation and information from school districts, and its documentation and analysis are far more fine-grained than any previous evaluation.

Second, Congress has recently renewed Title I's legislative authority.[15] The main change in the legislation was a new formula that was thought to be fairer and more administrable. With respect to educational results, Congress remained patient. The House Committee said:

"... Here we are dealing with measuring the effects on human beings of the program, instead of simply stating the dollars and cents impact on school districts of this aid. And the deficiencies of education and the social sciences in measuring human results have been amply documented elsewhere.

Many early proponents of Title I compounded the problem by hailing it as a quick solution to the problem of providing equal educational opportunity for all children. We have learned, though, within the past several years that this goal, so simple to state, is extraordinarily difficult to achieve. However, that growing realization has not stopped some people from measuring the program in terms of that rhetoric...

We have, undoubtedly, expected too much too soon from the Title I program. For most of us our expectations were rooted in a strong desire to give young people a chance to break the cycle of poverty and poor education that so many of them and their parents have known.

A more realistic appraisal of our ability to bring about change, however, should not lead to disillusionment and the rhetoric of defeat. Schooling does make a difference in the lives of the poor; and Title I can—and in many instances has—broken the cycle of poor education and low income. To be able to help a child overcome social and economic disadvantages requires many years of patient work and many varieties of teaching expertise. Therefore, we must all learn to be patient for results ..."[16]

Finally with respect to evaluation, Congress noted past failures[17] but went on to authorize many new studies and evaluations—22 for the legislation altogether and five for Title I alone, including three studies of effectiveness and a new charter for experiementation.

On your marks, get set, go!

NOTES

1. By far the most extensive is Milbrey W. McLaughlin, *Evaluation and Reform: The Elementary and Secondary Education Act of 1965, Title I* (Santa Monica: The Rand Corporation, 1974). See also Joseph S. Wholey and Bayla F. White, *The Impact of Evaluation on Title I Elementary and Secondary Education Program Management* (Washington, D.C. The Urban Institute, 1973) and Bayla F. White, "The Role of Evaluation in Title I Program Management," remarks delivered at the National Academy of Public Administration Conference on Evaluation of Educational Programs (Washington, D.C., The Urban Institute, 1972). My own earlier version of this history is contained in "Hard Lessons in the Assessment of Social Action Programs: The Case of ESEA Title I." Remarks delivered at the Annual Meeting of the American Sociological Association (Processed, 1972).

2. U.S. Congress, House Committee on Education and Labor, *A Compilation of Federal Education Laws,* 91st Congress, 1st Session. (Washington, D.C., G.P.O., 1969), p. 13.

3. E. J. Mosback et al. "Analysis of Compensatory Education in Five School Districts: Summary." (TEMPO The General Electric Company, n.d.) McLaughlin, op. cit is a thorough analysis of the development and utilization of this and the succeeding evaluations through 1972.

4. U.S. Office of Education, *Joint Federal/State Task Force on Evaluation: An Overview* (Belmont System), February 1971.

5. See U.S. Office of Education, *Education of the Disadvantaged: An Evaluative Report on Title I Elementary and Secondary Education Act of 1965, Fiscal Year 1968;* and Gene V. Glass et al. *Data Analysis of the 1968-1969 Survey of Compensatory Education* (U.S. Office of Education, 1970).

6. D. G. Hawkridge et al. *A Study of Selected Exemplary Programs for the Education of Disadvantaged Children* (Palo Alto: American Institute for Research, 1968) and Michael J. Wargo et al., *Further Examination of Exemplary Programs for Educating Disadvantaged Children* (Palo Alto: American Institute for Research, 1971).

7. Michael J. Wargo et al. *ESEA Title I; A Reanalysis and Synthesis of Evaluation Data from Fiscal Year 1965 through 1970* (Palo Alto: American Institute for Research, 1972).

8. U.S. Department of Health, Education, and Welfare, *The Effectiveness of Compensatory Education* (Washington, D.C., 1972).

9. Looking at this situation from the perspective of a school board member, I do not take umbrage. First of all, in a scientific sense, local schools know the effectiveness of very few elements of their education program. This is so, not just for traditional and bureaucratic reasons, but (we should now realize) for reasons of technical difficulty. The problem of gauging effectiveness for a universe of several thousand children, participating in a mixture of programs is far beyond the capacity of most school districts; with less training and more distractions, it is not surprising they cannot do what evaluators also cannot do.

10. Washington Research Project, *Title I of ESEA: Is It Helping Poor Children?* (Washington, 1970).

11. Daniel Badger and R. Stephen Browning, "Title I Comparability: One Year Later," Washington, D.C. Lawyer's Committee for Civil Rights Under Law, 1973.

12. From a local perspective, comparability and concentration requirements have an unfortunate side effect on local decision-making. To ensure that these provisions are enforceable, strict accounting requirements hold the monies, and thus the programs, apart from the main education enterprise, and the uncertainty of annual federal appropriations reinforces this trend. Believe me, it's easy for local officials to ignore Title I and absorb themselves in the myriad of matters that parents and taxpayers are always concerned about.

13. Peter J. Briggs, *A Perspective on Change: The Administration of Title I of the Elementary and Secondary Education Act* (Washington, D.C., The Planar Corporation, 1973.)

14. U.S. Office of Education (PBE) "A Descriptive and Analytic Study of Compensatory Reading Programs: Phase I Summary" (Washington, D.C., 1973) processed.

15. P. L., 93-380 "The Elementary and Secondary Education Amendment of 1974," Aug. 21, 1974.

16. U.S. Congress, House Committee on Education and Labor, "Report on the Elementary and Secondary Education Amendment of 1974" (House Report 93-805, February 21, 1974), pp. 5-6.

17. Ibid, p. 6.

EVANS: I would just add a few demurs from Mr. Hultin's proposals as to how to go about evaluation. He advocated the development of a built-in evaluation process. I would like to urge some caution there. It is an illusion that the best way to handle evaluation is to begin at the beginning of the program and to build in, via a program information system, a mechanism for collecting the data needed for evaluation. Program information systems are inherently untrustworthy, likely to be invalid and often irrelevant to simple evaluation needs because not only do they require the collection of high-quality data that are controversial, self-evaluative, and therefore possibly incriminating, from the standpoint of program administrator; but most importantly, they do not contain a design. Program information systems obviously do not allow for the possibility of aggregation which we certainly should try to achieve whenever we can; and they do not contain, and cannot contain by their very nature, a built-in estimate of the effects of non-treatment; that is, some control group estimate.

I would like also to respond to another of Mr. Hultin's points—that the best way to evaluate these programs is to allow the local country which is the grant recipient to do the evaluation procedure. If you want to produce at the end of some reasonable period of time an evaluation of these loans and grants, do the evaluation yourself. In other words, develop your own, centralized, independent, objective and professional evaluation mechanism, which would accomplish that task while simultaneously, but for different reasons and purposes, building up the evaluation capability of the local recipient.

I think the analysis in the Boardman/Davis paper is important because it seems to be based upon some solid empirical data and some sophisticated analysis, while providing possibly an encouraging antidote to some of the dismal findings of the Coleman analysis. They are right in the conclusions that they support.

Mike Timpane's paper raises some of the larger issues with which this conference has dealt. His not-so-pessimistic conclusions about the very erratic history of evaluation with respect to Title I are very encouraging, and they indicate that program evaluations are important. I would have to disagree with Alice Rivlin's conclusions that we put that mode of analysis aside and go instead, more profitably, to a general analytical survey. Those are useful, but they cannot substitute for direct program assessment. I think that the history of Title I bears that out.

Mr. Timpane raised the issue of Go/No-Go type of decision-promoting evaluation. It is very clear what some of the disadvantages and limitations of those kind of evaluations are. They do not, if they merely focus on identifying whether the program is effective or not, tell us how to improve the program. Ideally, what we want is evaluation which indicates an overall assessment and also contains data on the relative effectiveness of alternative models or different variables. The need for internal program improvement is often illuminated through some fairly shocking data or finding about the overall program.

Finally, there can and should be no debate about the inherent superiority of randomized design. We should put that issue aside as an issue of principle or an issue of methodology. One of the things that Gerry Cline pointed out in his discussion of the Follow Through evaluation is that the program is essentially a black box. Any program is made up of an infinite number of independent variables. There is the color of the pages in the book. There is the personality of the teacher. There is anything else you can think of or conceptually create out of all the enormous number of activities that are going on. When we find a positive or negative effect, we do not know what the relative contributions of the variance is, to those infinite number of independent variables, and the task of finding out is an enormous methodological one.

With respect to the lessons that relate to Follow Through, it seems to be quite clear that we would do a number of things quite differently than we were doing them the first time around. We would try to lay out a situation where we could make all those comparisons that cannot be made, makeable. We would have an adequate number of replications, we would have clearly distinguishable treatments, make all those things clearer, and I think that an indication of social experimentation is potentially an enormously valuable tool for policy analysis and program decision.

PORTER: I want to share one main thought which is related to all four papers, but with perhaps a slight weighting toward Gerry Cline's and Mike Timpane's. It comes, in part, from my experiences at NIE and, in part, from a theme that has run through the past couple days at this conference.

Let me start by saying I am in general agreement with Mike Timpane's point that we have learned a great deal from evaluations over the past few years and that an important part of what we have learned is how to do better evaluations. In that regard, however, I would like to challenge one trend that I perceive has developed, that is, the trend toward large-scale social evaluations. The Follow Through evaluation Gerry talked about and the Title I evaluation Mike described are both cases in point. I believe there are some important advantages to small-scale evaluations and I am convinced that these advantages have received too little attention in the past couple days.

Let me list just a few of the advantages that I believe small-scale evaluations can have. The most obvious is cost, but of course cost alone is insufficient justification for reversing the trend I perceive toward doing large-scale evaluations. My second point concerns experimentation. Earlier in the conference, Tukey argued the utility of randomized studies for investigations of program outcomes. My guess is that the usual obstacles to doing randomized field experiments are more easily overcome in small-scale efforts. Small-scale evaluations require smaller pools of willing subjects and are less likely to arouse wide spread criticism. Third, if we really do have programs that have potential for large effects, either positive or negative, small-scale evaluations place fewer subjects at risk. Fourth, one of the things we have learned is that large-scale data collection efforts are very difficult to conduct. A smaller effort allows much greater attention to the quality of data collected from each subject. Fifth, a small-scale evaluation makes it much easier to look carefully at the data, to study process and side effects as Gerry Cline wants to do. In practice, the administrative and data processing problems inherent in large-scale evaluations make it nearly impossible to have a good feel for the data. Sixth, I suspect that, as a whole, small-scale studies require less lag time. For example, in the Follow Through study typically a year or more goes by between completed data collection and the availability of an analysis report. This is an important consideration if evaluations are to inform policy decisions.

It is also important to note that many of the things we've learned from large-scale evaluations might well have been learned through smaller efforts. For example, Mike Timpane says that we learned Title I funds are hard to trace. I think we would have found out the same thing pretty quickly if we had simply gone out to a few sites and tried to see where those funds were going. As another example, all of those different Follow Through sites, all of those different programs and all of those thousands of children probably get in the way of what Gerry really wants to do. If he is interested in making sense out of the "black boxes" to which he referred, he would probably do better if he had only one or two boxes at which to look.

Yet another example is provided by an evaluation which I recently conducted of the Hilda Taba teaching strategies. The request was for a comprehensive study of student outcomes and the results were quite conclusive in documenting no effect. The results from a fifteen minute teacher interview at the end of the school year, however, strongly suggested that the relatively expensive evaluation of student outcomes was premature. The teachers reported that they had not been using the Taba strategies nor did they feel they had good understanding of those strategies. A smaller-scale evaluation focusing on the implementation of the Taba strategies would have been more appropriate as a first year effort.

Another point I want to make is only partially on target, but I think still worth sharing. There are several cases where large-scale evaluations have been launched only to find at the end that there were serious flaws in the design, measurement and analysis which prevented reaching conclusions about some of the questions of interest. This seems particularly true in demonstration projects, such as Vouchers. It would be nice if detailed plans and prototypic conclusions complete with necessary caveats were published prior to the final decision to go ahead with an evaluation. This procedure might diminish some of the emphasis on large-scale evaluation. Where large-scale evaluations are appropriate their quality might be improved and at a minimum they could be launched with more realistic expectations.

I do not mean, however, to be calling for a moratorium on large-scale evaluations since some questions can be answered only by large-scale efforts. For example, I disagree with Paul Wortman's position, shared earlier in this conference, that large-scale evaluations should not be conducted on programs that are difficult to implement. If a program is a candidate for wide use, then an important evaluation question is "can it be implemented on a large-scale?" By definition this requires a large-scale evaluation, and one that focuses on the implementation question rather than outcomes. This seems somewhat consistent with Mats Hultin's call for emphasis on formative evaluation. As an aside though, I wonder if we should ever do large-scale summative evaluations. Instead we might first conduct small-scale evaluations to see if the program has the desired effect under conditions favorable to program implementation. If the program appears effective then the remaining question is "can it be implemented on a large-scale?"

Another type of question which requires relatively large-scale evaluations is whether there are interactions between types of programs and other dimensions, such as characteristics of the units being exposed to the programs or settings in which the programs are implemented.

I suppose it might also be true that large-scale evaluations are sometimes necessary because of their apparent validity. By this I mean that if decision makers are convinced only by large-scale evaluations, at least in the short run that is what must be done even if in fact smaller evaluations would yield just as good or better data. Of course, if that is the case it might also be desirable to attempt to change the climate of opinion.

As a related point, when large-scale evaluations are done I suggest that the expensive data bases should be made available to others for secondary analysis. I think a good example of where this has taken place is on the Equality of Educational Opportunity survey data, i.e., *Inequality* and *On Equality of Educational Opportunity*. On that particular example, however, I am skeptical that further secondary analyses are likely to yield important new insights.

To sum up I hope that large-scale evaluations will not be done simply because they are in vogue. I would much rather that it be fashionable to do small-scale evaluations. Then large-scale evaluations would only be undertaken to answer important questions that, for one reason or another, cannot be answered otherwise.

SMITH: I generally agree with Andy Porter that we should encourage more small-scale studies, that we should be more careful and that we've got to consider the cumulative nature of results more than we have before.

And, I share his sense that we have learned some things from the past. I'd like to talk a little about some of those things. While my remarks are not entirely responsive to the papers in this session they were triggered off by them.

Mike Timpane talked about what we've learned from the large evaluations of Title I. He lumped together those large evaluations with the recent ETS work on reading. I think you could also include the Right to Read work with exemplary programs, the other AIR studies of exemplary programs, and the Follow-Through and Head Start Planned Variations Evaluations. From the data collected in these studies, I think we're beginning to muddle into some ideas about what works in schools, what makes some schools better than others. For those of us who've been watching the studies, a number of variables are becoming familiar.

Let me suggest three variables which we can't measure very well right now, but which make some sense. The first is something we might call "Shared Purposefulness." It seems to turn out that in many of the schools which do particularly well in reading that just about everybody shares and understands their particular approach to teaching reading. Principals, teachers, parents, and kids all seem to have a common framework. A lot of people have toyed with the idea that there may be three or four different conceptions of reading within a single school. Perhaps in many schools students have one conception of reading, teachers have another and principals have still another. In schools characterized by "Shared Purposefulness," you may have a match between the various notions that the kids, teachers, principals and parents have in the school. All groups agree on the goal and move toward it, in a purposeful way.

The second variable is called "Closeness." It's a generic term and seems to apply, for example, to the choice of time of intervention. That is, if you're going to try to get a person into college, a more efficient time to intervene may be shortly before he's going to go into college, rather than in early childhood. The concept of "Closeness" also applies to things like reading instruction. If we want to teach a child to read, it appears as if we should teach him reading in a directed fashion rather than try to change his self-concept and through that his reading skills though we may develop a reading program that is better because it changes his self-concept. I think we are finding out that teaching reading affects reading more than teaching self-concept affects reading. This is again obvious, but the history of school instruction is filled with attempts to affect reading achievement by attempts to manipulate self-concept. Still another way to think about "Closeness" is by considering the distance from the intervention to the goal in terms of number of people. If we really want to change the way instruction goes on in school, particularly in the short run, it seems that we should work with the teachers rather than with the parents, who would then apply some political pressure on the principal, who would then in turn attempt to influence the teachers. We get a filtering process that goes on in the latter case and I think we lose effectiveness. In successful schools the intervention seems appropriately "close" to its purpose.

Thus one general concept is of "Shared Purposefulness," and a second one is "Closeness." The third is "Time." Time on task. Again an obvious idea. It's something we've overlooked greviously, however, in many of our studies. In many evaluations we just haven't looked to see how much time children spend reading or spend in small group reading instruction. It's insane when you think of it that way, but it seems to have happened. However, over the past eight or nine years, we have gathered together a bunch of small studies which suggest that if you spend a little bit of time instructing a child he will learn a little bit, if you spend a bit more, he will learn a bit more.

In summary I think we are discovering that if we want to raise some achievement scores in a particular content area, we should make sure that our purpose is clear, we should try to intervene by focusing directly on the content area, and we should spend more time on it than we might have done otherwise.

Bill Cooley is doing some nice work on this, using Jack Carroll's model of School Learning. Cooley has looked at a number of IPI classrooms from the Pittsburgh model of Follow-Through. This has allowed him to control for the kind of curriculum and the kind of instructional strategy. He has measured the natural variations among the teachers in the amount of time they spend teaching reading, and teaching math and so on. He's found some strong positive relationships between time spent in instruction and student achievement.

All right, some generic concepts are beginning to seep out and I think they can be communicated to the school people. These ideas transcend the traditional idea that a particular curriculum might be a panacea. Though this idea has dominated evaluative research it has not been very fruitful. Most comparisons among curricula aimed at similiar objectives show few important differences. Perhaps this form of evaluation should be replaced by assessment of more global variables of the sort I have suggested.

In a different vein I want to make two specific points about the Boardman/Davis paper. It is in a long line of highly respectable analyses of the Coleman data. I guess as I get older and grayer about this, I tend to believe them less and less. First, I'm bothered by Boardman and Davis's use of 12th grade data. One reason that most people carrying out re-analyses of the EEOS data never looked much at the 12th grade data was that there was no real concern—I think it was just an oversight—by the people who collected the data, to be able to separate the technical high schools from the academic high schools and from the multipurpose high schools. When you get a situation like that, you've got schools really trying to do different things. When you throw together schools with different purposes in an analysis and assess them on the same outcomes you are guaranteed to get confused results. Even if we really knew what was going to produce academic achievement in one kind of school, we would imagine that different kinds of relationships would occur in the four year college oriented school than in a technical high school—we should expect different production functions for the different kinds of schools. But, beyond that I don't believe that we ever had any clear idea about how to determine the production function in any type of school. That leads to the second specific point while I will make as part of a story.

Stephan Michelson, a very talented economist, worked with us at the Center for Educational Policy Research. Stephan brought us all into the econometrics literature with a passion. He challenged our use of single stage least squares and argued that we should move into simultaneous equations and two stage least squares models. Stephan analyzed the 6th grade Philadelphia data from the Coleman survey. It was one of the larger SMSA's in the data. It had a lot of schools in it. He carried out some elegant analyses using two stage least squares, and lo and behold he found that a couple of teacher variables had strong effects on achievement. He was very pleased. He found in particular that teacher experience seemed powerful, and concluded that more experienced teachers would raise achievement scores. The variable seemed to work both for blacks and whites, and it seemed to make sense to him.

He was careful, though, and he applied his equations to a sample of EEOS data from Detroit using the same measures as he did for Philadelphia. He found that nothing worked. The coefficients went in different directions. What was positive in Philadelphia was negative in Detroit, etc. He toyed for awhile with a notion he called the Specificity Hypothesis. He even wrote a short paper about it. The specificity hypothesis held that the production function was different in Philadelphia than in Detroit, and by analogy different in every other site.

But nobody really bought that. So he began to get hold of new information from Philadelphia to try to figure out whether or not there was an institutional reason to explain his results. He found out that in the middle sixties in Philadelphia, that experienced teachers were often transferred to schools with high achieving kids. His findings of the relationship between teacher experience with achievement was explained. This may be an obvious point, but it demonstrates the problems, I think, with the Coleman data. They are one-shot survey data, appropriate for general descriptive purposes but at present a disaster for drawing causal inferences, no matter how sophisticated the methodology. It also shows that it's nice to replicate results.

Finally, let me make a few comments about Gerry Cline's paper. This takes us back to Follow-Through. The second year (First Grade) results are somewhat disappointing, I think. In the kindergarten data it really looked as though we had some strong effects. Now we find that those effects are tapering off.

But even though the findings are somewhat discouraging the evaluation may still be productive. Gerry has not stopped with just the comparison question—he is asking "why" the effects are appearing or not appearing. One of the things that many evaluations suffer from is a lack of attention paid to existing knowledge about how kids learn and about the principles of instructional practice. Much of the discussion at this conference has been dominated by people who lack systematic training in either cognitive or instructional psychology. This seems naive to me. At the very least it seems silly that the sociologists, economists and methodologists among us don't collaborate more with some of the psychologists who are thinking hard about educational intervention.

Let me just suggest a couple of ideas that might indicate some ways to collaborate. Gerry Cline mentioned the potential importance of stage theory. Over the past four or five years scientists have pulled together a large number of studies which indicate that children pass through a number of growth periods which might be called stages. Sheldon White talks about cognitive shifts in the 5-7 age period. In the 9-10 age range area, particularly for boys, I understand there are some dramatic changes going on. Then in the 12 to 14 age range adolescence happens and children change cognitively in a variety of different ways.

Thus we have some indication that there are cognitive shifts in a number of age ranges. At the same time, we also find that for some reason the instructional systems in schools are changing at exactly those periods. Between 5 and 7 children move into first grade. They are expected to learn something systematic about reading and math. In reading, the instruction is focused on the task of learning the code—of making word-sound correspondences. By the age of 9 or 10 they are asked to move from this task to the task of comprehending written language. They move from decoding into reading for meaning—a task which has clearly different cognitive demands.

Then, for 12 to 14 year olds in junior high school, a lot of new pressures (social and cognitive) are apparent. The system is changing at precisely the same time as the student is changing.

This raises questions in my mind about a variety of things. The clearest question, I think, is the way we go about measuring effects of interventions, particularly if we are looking at interventions which happen at the same time as the developmental changes. I don't know what it means to measure, for instance, the effect on a child's concept of something like bigness or tallness when we've got data that suggest that a four year old cannot distinguish between bigness and tallness, but a two or three year old can.

The second thing it seems to me that we should really think about, is when we should intervene. Should you intervene before the shifts, during them, or after them? I think this is the sort of question that we have to begin seriously asking before we carry out any serious program evaluation.

VII

RESEARCH ALLOCATION STRATEGIES

SOCIAL PROGRAMS EVALUATION
Research Allocation Strategies for
Maximizing Policy Payoffs

Clark C. Abt
Abt Associates Inc.

My objective is to talk about the evaluation of evaluations for purposes of maximizing their benefits, or policy payoffs, to the users. It is assumed that the main source of waste in policy evaluations today is the result of a sub-optimal mix of program evaluations; that is, the wrong ones were selected and the issues that they addressed and the way they addressed them are also sub-optimally organized. I am going to propose a set of measures of effectiveness for evaluating the relative efficiency of program evaluations with respect to some specific policy goals, and then some strategies for improving the selection mechanism. I am not going to bore you with repeating the various criteria that have already been stated in this conference for program evaluation, and I will try to concentrate on those that I have not heard much mention of.

Research in general, and certainly policy research, can only be justified by the value of the information that it produces for decision-making of some kind. I think that one can argue with that point of view for basic research, but there is little argument possible for policy research. Assume then, that the value of policy research is a function of the value of the information produced by some criteria I am going to mention and of the relevance of that information or the utility of that information for policy application. One of the criteria for information

value that I have not heard mentioned is *uniqueness,* or improbability—
a measure of newsworthiness. Validity, relevance, stability have already
been mentioned. Precision, or the ability to discriminate, and reliability
have already been mentioned, as have impact and applicability. I would
like to suggest some measures, quantitative or at least numerical, of
these kinds of criteria, so we can evaluate evaluations for the degree to
which they meet them.

But before that, I want to draw a larger framework, in which these
measures of information and utility have to be considered. That is the
matrix here (see chart below). It is a matrix of information utility
criteria. First are evaluation objectives. Evaluation objectives have been
described ad nauseum. They are both overt and covert. The point is
they are usually different for different people. There are usually a
multitude of them, and they have different priority weights for different policy audiences. That little matrix is essentially a set of intersects
of information utility criteria and evaluation objectives.

Those little profiles that are there at the margins are the relative
weightings on the horizontal evaluation objectives—weightings of different information utility objectives. The top and left profiles are what
you might get out of a specific matrix. The bottom and right profiles
somewhat in parallel with it define an effectively designed evaluation,
where both the evaluation objectives and the information utility criteria
match well those of the policy users. In some places, they are obviously
in contrast. One can even make that into a numerical measure of
program evaluation efficiency, in terms of the degree to which evaluation objectives and information utility criteria defined by the user are
met or unmet.

Now, the problem is, how do we fill in the cells? What is our metric
for the different information utility criteria and evaluation objectives? I
think that you can see that if we fill in that matrix we could begin to
produce *a production function for evaluations.* And, if you can produce
a production function for alternative evaluations, you can select the
optimum mix of evaluations for a particular policy program; or if one
has a set of policies that need to be evaluated by equalizing marginal
returns from evaluation, one can optimize the mix of overall evaluations. That is, one can maximize the results for a fixed level of
investment, or minimize the costs for a fixed level of information
utility required. It is my assertion that this is where the major waste is
in policy evaluation research today, that there is nothing like this in

EVALUATION CRITERIA PROFILE

INFORMATION UTILITY/EVALUATION OBJECTIVES MATRIX

EVALUATION OBJECTIVES PROFILE

Evaluation Objectives / Utility of Information Criteria

	A Inventory?	B Effectiveness?	C Benefits?	D Costs?	E Efficiency?	F Comparative Efficiency?	G Most Effective Aspects?	H Least Affective Aspects?	I Side Effects?	J Continue?	K Expand/Contract?	L Terminate?	M Change?	N How Change?	O Causal Relations?
1. Uniqueness															
2. Relevance															
3. Validity															
4. Precision/Detail															
5. Stability															
6. Generaliz-ability															
7. Reliability															
8. Impact															
9. Applicability															
10. Feasibility															
PROBABLE TOTAL BENEFIT															
COST															
BENEFIT/COST															

1.0 .75 .5 .25 .00

practice, except very informally and perhaps in many cases not even informally.

Returning to the question, how do we fill in that matrix with actual numbers, let me just describe some of the more unusual ones. For example, if we are talking about uniqueness, it is that part of the policy space that is unknown. And how does one quantify that? Well, one can decompose the policy space into sub-policy issues that are of roughly subjectively equal import, and then determine what percentage of them are actually addressed. One can think of uniqueness as a measure of counter-intuitiveness or of the inverse of the probability that the evaluation finding would have been identified or was available without evaluation research.

For example, the discussion of Indian education was very lacking in uniqueness because most of those findings were available from previous research.

One of the scarce resources of policy research is the attention space of the user, or of the audience, and that attention space is polluted by information that is unasked or uninteresting or irrelevant. So more information than what is usable means actually less information getting transmitted. I take some issue here with Coleman's distinction between policy and disciplinary research in which he thinks it is the proper role of policy research to be redundant. The lack of elegance, the lack of parsimony in policy research actually reduces the communicability of the results, because it reduces the attention to the signal that we want to transmit compared to the noise that is associated with it. And policy findings that may be perfectly valid, but that do not speak to the policy issues, are noise from the point of view of the policy audience.

The validity of the research is also a function of the percentage of the theoretical maximum channel capacity achieved, and this is a function of both data and theory validity and any interaction effects that there are between the two, of which there frequently are some. And this is multiplicative, because you can just imagine if you are dealing with an issue in which half the data is garbage and half the theory is garbage, and assuming that theory is randomly applied across all the data, what you get out is at best only a quarter right, not half right.

In summary, if we can elicit from the users of policy research some kind of profile of evaluation objectives and information criteria that best serve their needs, we can select the, if not optimal, at least

EXAMPLES OF EFFICIENT AND INEFFICIENT MATCHING
OF EVALUATION OBJECTIVES AND INFORMATION
UTILITY CRITERIA PROFILES
WITH THOSE OF EVALUATION USERS

EFFICIENT   (Good design/user match)

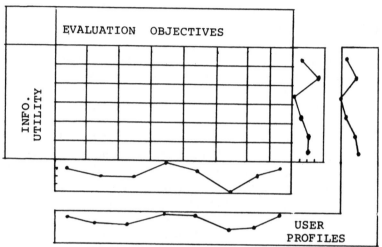

INEFFICIENT   (Poor design/user match)

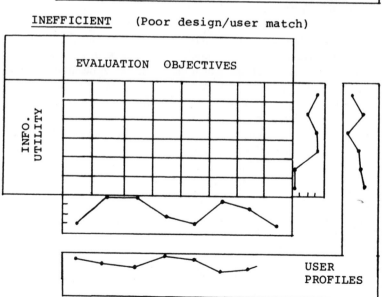

satisfactory design for evaluation research for that particular user profile. Or, if one has the problem of allocating resources among many policy evaluation studies, one can maximize the overall result by getting the best mix of policy evaluations to maximize the overall impact.

There are a number of specific steps the government can take in its funding of policy research that would address the scarce resources on the producer side. That is dear to some of our hearts, particularly because of the great waste in the policy evaluation of human resources that is incurred as a result of proposal writing in the annual "crunch." I have been talking mainly about conserving the consumption attention space, but there are also human production resources to be conserved.

Some of these steps readily accessible to the government are: reduce the number of selective bidders; select bidders in a two-stage process; keep records of the quality of bidders for feedback from the quality of performance to the selection process; spread out the bidding process over the year so better resource planning can be done; increase the funding period beyond a year to three years so there is more stable research possible; restrict the length of proposals to 50 pages; insist on face-to-face briefings of finalists, thereby doing double duty of reducing the proposal efforts of scarce evaluator resources and the evaluation of proposal efforts by the scarce government resources; and increase the lead time to allow a small number of people to spend more time developing high quality proposals with less communication friction. All of those measures would probably reduce the roughly 30% of current human evaluation resources applied to the marketing of that work to 10 or 15% and make that much more resource available for technical problem solving.

I have covered some of the measures that can conserve the attention space of the decision-makers using evaluations and the human resources that provide the evaluations, in the interests of a more efficient overall allocation of evaluation resources.

SOME COMMENTS ON STRATEGIES OF R&D FUNDING[1]

Harvey Averch
Deputy Assistant Director for Analysis and Planning
Research Applications
The National Science Foundation

I would like to provide some comment from a purchaser's or funder's perspective on R&D allocation. I will be rather crude and not discuss any kind of elegant resource allocation scheme, because I believe we can make significant improvements in R&D funding without very elegant schemes.

First, let me give you some idea of the resources we are allocating. The federal R&D budget has been running about $17 billion a year; $9 billion is roughly defense related; $8 billion is civilian sector research. Four to seven hundred million dollars of the civilian sector research money is estimated to be spent on social research, including basic, applied, and evaluation research. And the very crude question that funders have received in Congress and elsewhere for the last few years is how much return for this investment. Research funders search constantly for reasonable answers, not elegant answers.

There are three strategies used in allocating this sum. There is first the "pure" science strategy. With this strategy, the ideas originating in the research community are sent into a central funding agency; the ideas are evaluated by knowledgeable researchers; and the research is executed. The final product most often appears in a refereed professional journal. A crucial assumption is that the knowledge aggregation process and the knowledge utilization process are inherent in this procedure.

The second strategy is mission-oriented research. Research funding is correlated and articulated with respect to the "mission" of an agency. For example, HUD has $60 to $70 million a year that is related to housing and urban development. In this strategy, the criteria for funding are supposed to be derived from actual decision-making in a given agency and information requirements in decision-making. Several allegations are made about mission-oriented research, especially by the research community. It is alleged that such research can be biased and that it can be myopic, since very important issues span the responsibility of a number of different agencies.

The third strategy is exemplified by various proposals to set up departments of science and technology, or on a much smaller scale, by NSF/RANN—funding through a "freestanding" research agency. In FY 1974, RANN represents a $150 million experiment which funds evaluation research, policy research, hard technology research, and so on. Its mission is to "cross-cut" the mission agency research as well as disciplinary research.

Within RANN, and in most other parts of the government, there are various procedures for obtaining research. The procedural mix varies with the funding strategy. There is the assistance procedure.

In assistance, the federal government helps a researcher execute his idea on the ground that some public benefit is or will be created. Assistance is most commonly exemplified in a grant, and the product is usually a paper or technical report.

In the procurement procedure, a federal agency knows what it wants, writes an RFP, and obtains specific responses to the RFP.

RANN has invented a hybrid procedure called a "program solicitation." In solicitations, categories of research are called out, but the idea is still to help the proposer execute his research idea. What RANN says is, that if a researcher has a good idea within a category of interest, he should be willing to enter it in competition with other ideas in the specified category.

Eventually, RANN and other federal agencies may experiment with a "two-stage solicitation" whereby we obtain very short prospectuses on research ideas, then evaluate the prospectuses and select five, ten, fifteen proposers as appropriate to present very refined and rigorous proposals. Some research funders and researchers believe that such a procedure would improve cost-effectiveness of all parties to research transactions.

Whatever the procedure of funding, I do want to give you some sense of what people look for on the funding side of the desk. First of all, a clear statement of the problem is required. Most proposals that are received for the first time do not tell the funder what the problem is. Second, a clear statement of the research procedure is searched for. Most proposals that I see, and that most federal agencies see, have the following kind of language. People will "identify" X or "develop" X or apply multivariate statistical analyses to X, but they are not really very articulate about what research procedures or "algorithms" they are going to use. And if researchers do not have some kind of "map" to take one from here to there, funders become suspicious.

An issue that has become very important throughout the federal government, no matter the kind of research being considered, is utilization. Most researchers do not have a comparative advantage in getting their research utilized, and most proposals do not address utilization very well. I think somebody yesterday mentioned that most research is written in a very technical kind of language; and, in many research reports, there is no preface or executive summary. I expect that researchers will be pressed more and more by the funding agencies on what will be done about utilization. Now it is recognized that good researchers do not necessarily make good utilization agents, but many agencies are making funds available to hire specialists for that. It is a tricky job, but there is a deep suspicion in Congress, and in the OMB, that one of the reasons we are not getting as much return as we would like is the lack of explicit attention to utilization and the lack of utilization considerations in research designs.

Another thing funders look for is "track record." There is no government-wide way of keeping track of people's performance on grants and contracts, and there is quite a bit of resistance to doing that. In RANN, we are now beginning to evaluate what researchers have done. There are large conceptual and operational issues in carrying out research evaluations and complex issues of equity. I would suggest to all the evaluation people in the audience that the evaluation of research products is itself a worthy topic of attention, especially the evaluation of payoff or utility. Not too much has been written on this subject.

Let me close with some action recommendations for improving

policy research funding and evaluation research funding. The basic unit of funding is the proposal, and we need a good deal of improvement in research proposals. We need improvement just in the logic of what is laid out, and we need a good deal of improvement in syntax and grammar. Many proposals are written in a language that is not easily understood. When that happens, the funding staff has to spend a lot of time translating proposals into English.

We need improvement in monitoring proposals, on finding procedures that are fair and equitable and do not get in the way of research but still keep funders informed. It has happened in the funding community that investigators never give their sponsors a final report. The first thing a sponsor may find out about results from an award is that a report has been published in a journal or that there is a Congressional inquiry.

A third area where we can improve performance is in utilization. Utilization raises complicated questions in research design that are not addressed in proposals. This may be a caricature, but proposals come with the following structure. The first year is to be spent designing a data collection effort; in the second year, data are to be collected; and in the third year, the investigator analyzes data; and the fourth year he reports. I do not believe that kind of design, at least for applied social research, will get entirely favorable action any more. How one designs proposals and research to get sequential information that is useful is something that I would hope is thought about.

NOTE

1. The views expressed are the author's own and do not represent those of the NSF.

REQUIREMENTS FOR VALID RESEARCH VERSUS REQUIREMENTS FOR SHORT-TERM DECISION MAKING
A Research Allocation Strategy of Phased Evaluations in Criminal Justice

Dr. Richard T. Barnes
National Institute of Law Enforcement
and Criminal Justice
Law Enforcement Assistance Administration

The National Institute of Law Enforcement and Criminal Justice (the National Institute) in the Law Enforcement Assistance Administration (LEAA) shares the problem posed by the dilemma on which the panel focuses its attention with other research and development arms of large government agencies. It is appropriate and encouraging that the Congress recognizes the need for research as it creates or continues agencies whose primary mandates are in specific problem areas of national significance (e.g., education, health, crime). On the other hand, the proximity of these research arms to their host agencies leads, quite naturally, to their utilization in the short-term decision-making process. Thus, there is a constant demand for "right now" information placed on these "think tanks" which, if not firmly kept in check, can result in disruption of basic research efforts.

An example of an area of activity where these two requirements come in conflict is evaluation. In fact, the impossibility of giving a definition to this term to which everyone can agree is attributable to this conflict. "Evaluation" is interpreted as anything from what might better be called fiscal monitoring to an indepth research study. This in turn is reflected in the intended use of evaluation as a management tool or a research methodology.

The National Institute has designed a concept of "phased evaluations" in the criminal justice field which we hope will meet the needs of both of these requirements. This concept underlies our National Evaluation Program (NEP) which is presently being implemented through the Institute's Office of Research Programs.

BACKGROUND

The Law Enforcement Assistance Administration (LEAA), in its first five years of existence, has distributed more than three billion dollars to state and local criminal justice agencies in support of their efforts to reduce crime in America. The complexities involved in establishing an appropriate planning and funding mechanism for carrying out this program have been enormous, and it is not surprising that careful evaluation planning took a back seat to program implementation during the early years.

Nevertheless, for the past two years the need for determining the Agency's achievements and failures has received the increased attention it deserves. The 1973 Guidelines to the State Planning Agencies (SPAs) included a section pointing out the responsibilities each state has in evaluating the projects and programs supported with LEAA funds. States were encouraged to begin the development of an evaluation strategy that would meet their needs. The 10 Regional Offices of LEAA, recognizing their role of providing leadership, have supported numerous training and technical assistance efforts in the area of evaluation. The central offices of the Agency, and particularly the National Institute, have become more active in sponsoring evaluations of programs having national significance. In addition, the latest legislation gives the National Institute a broadened responsibility in the evaluation of programs and projects funded with federal monies.

By late 1973 then, LEAA and the State Planning Agencies were implementing numerous evaluation activities. Still, the efforts were fragmented, and it became clear that a comprehensive program design was needed. As a result, an Evaluation Policy Task Force, representing both LEAA and the states, was established in the fall of 1973 and charged with the responsibility of developing an overall Evaluation Program to be carried out by LEAA in partnership with the states.

One of the basic problems addressed by the Task Force was that of specifying appropriate functions for federal and state agencies in a New Federalism block grant program. It seems inconsistent with the program's philosophy to centralize all evaluation efforts in Washington. On the other hand, it is inefficient for each state to be testing the effectiveness of the same types of programs. The Task Force's resolution was to assign the federal government (the National Institute) the function of determining general norms for typical types of criminal justice activities—both internal efficiencies and external effectiveness. The states' role would be to apply the standards to their own programs, to provide new information to update the standards, and to undertake more sophisticated evaluation of programs not studied at the federal level.

The Task Force completed its report in March 1, 1974, and the component programs recommended have been endorsed by both the Agency and the National Conference of State Criminal Justice Planning Administrators. The program to carry out the federal level knowledge-gathering function has become known as the National Evaluation Program. It is this program which will attempt to satisfy both short-term management needs, at all levels, and long-term answers to more basic research questions.

THE NATIONAL EVALUATION PROGRAM[1]

National policymakers and state and local decision-makers need sound information concerning major criminal justice hypotheses, project results, and nationally applicable standards. The National Evaluation Program will involve both short-term assessments and major research studies to evaluate various areas of criminal justice activity, including those LEAA supports through its block grant program.

Specifically, the National Evaluation Program will help:

—To provide a timely, objective, and reliable assessment to Congress and the public of the effectiveness of typical programs funded with federal monies.

—To extend our present knowledge and technical capability in all aspects of criminal justice.

—To test criminal justice standards and goals and, through critical research, refine and evaluate them.

—To provide criminal justice administrators with relevant information which they can use to administer their programs more effectively.

An underlying assumption of the Program is that the types of information which can best be produced through nationally coordinated evaluations are those which indicate whether a particular idea for reducing crime or a particular approach for improving criminal justice is likely to be successful under a variety of conditions, organizations, and management.

Although particular types of projects are now often operated with some frequency throughout the country, it is difficult for a SPA or criminal justice system administrator to obtain comparison data on similar projects to determine in advance whether a type of project under consideration has been generally successful or unsuccessful in other communities, or to find out what effect emphasizing particular components of a project may have on its success or failure. The major reason for this problem has been a lack of comprehensive evaluations that covered similar types of projects and collected similar information about each project. In effect, to date we have failed to mine this resource of natural variation available to us.

The thrust of the National Evaluation Program is, therefore, to concentrate on particular *topic areas* commonly encountered by SPAs and local administrators. Each *topic area* will contain a group of projects that appear to have similar goals and methods and which are common enough to be of interest to many SPAs and local administrators.

In each topic area, an attempt will be made to assemble what is known about the methods, outcomes, and effectiveness of projects of that general type and to determine if the present knowledge—when assembled—is sufficient to be useful in planning and funding decisions by the SPAs and local agencies. If the present knowledge does not appear sufficient, designs will be developed specifying how such information could be obtained and at what cost. Thus, in attempting to provide inputs to short-term decision-making, the research needs in each area will also be uncovered. This initial work in each topic area is referred to as a "Phase I Assessment." The implementation of the research designs developed would represent a major research study of the Topic Area and will be conducted as a Phase II Evaluation. In each topic area examined then, the Phase I investigation will cover the collection, synthesis, and assessment of what is already known and one or more designs for evaluations that would fill any gaps in that knowledge, if such gaps appear to exist.

It is expected that some of the Phase I investigations will either be adequate in themselves, will demonstrate the infeasibility of further evaluation in that topic area, or will indicate that the cost of obtaining more accurate knowledge is higher than its possible value to LEAA, the SPAs, and the local administrators. In the other cases, however, a Phase II (an actual field evaluation) will be implemented based upon the design developed during Phase I, or selected portions of that design.

The products anticipated from the Phase I investigation of a particular topic area may be summarized as follows (numbers in parentheses refer to Exhibit 1):

(1) Paper outlining the issues and substance of expert views and opinions in the topic area drawn from available general knowledge and past findings.

(2) For projects in the topic area, a process flow diagram of the intervention actually made by the project and an accompanying description of the project keyed to the flow diagram.

(3) A framework (s) that represents a synthesis of the assumptions that underlie the projects (or families of projects) in the topic area and can be used to describe the chains of assumptions linking the expenditure of funds to project activity or intervention, the project activity or intervention to immediate outcome, and the immediate outcome to the impact on the problem addressed by the topic area. Included will be potential measurement points, suggested data elements to be measured, and methods of measurement for testing the assumptions. Also included will be a listing of those factors affecting a project that are believed to be under control of the project and those likely intervening factors not under the control of the project.

(4) A judgmental assessment in terms of the framework, its operating assumptions, and the specified data elements of the success or failure in the topic area and a statement of the quality, reliability, and accuracy of this assessment made on the basis of present knowledge. This assessment will also point up gaps in present knowledge and the importance (or unimportance) of these gaps in making an authoritative assessment of success or failure.

There will be a publishable summary of the known quantitative results in the topic area. It should include the best data available on both the costs and effectiveness of projects in the topic area.

(5) An evaluation design based on the framework developed above for filling gaps found in present knowledge in order to produce an authoritative and

Exhibit 1: Relationship of the Various Phase I Tasks for One Topic Area

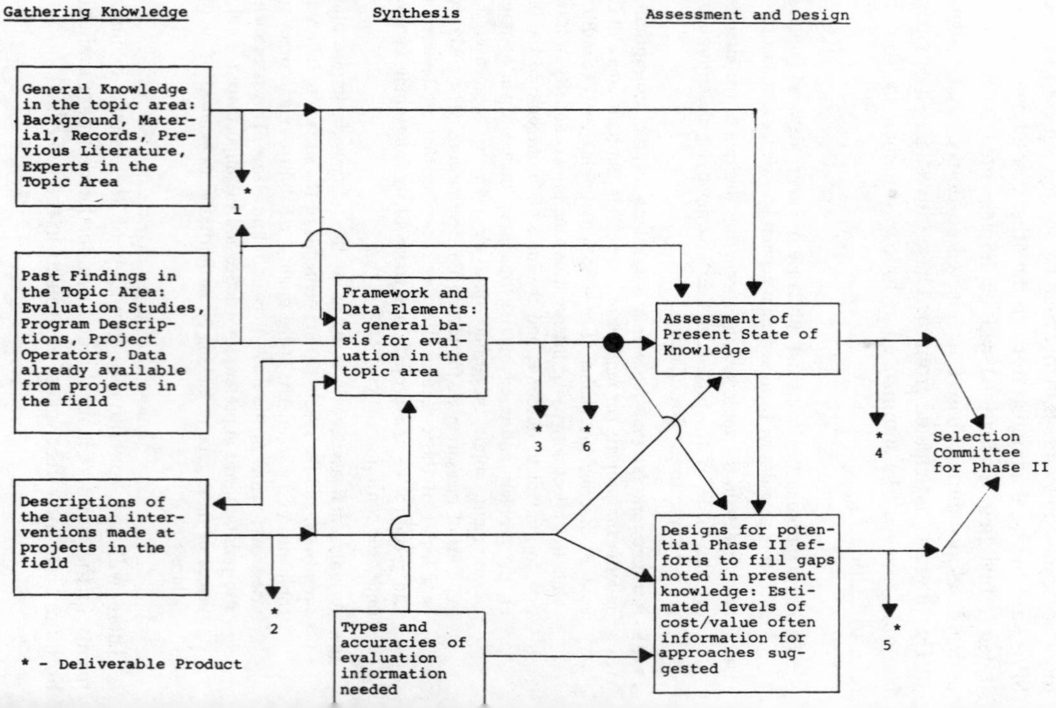

Gathering Knowledge   Synthesis   Assessment and Design

Gathering Knowledge

General Knowledge in the topic area: Background, Material, Records, Previous Literature, Experts in the Topic Area

Past Findings in the Topic Area: Evaluation Studies, Program Descriptions, Project Operators, Data already available from projects in the field

Descriptions of the actual interventions made at projects in the field

Synthesis

Framework and Data Elements: a general basis for evaluation in the topic area

Types and accuracies of evaluation information needed

Assessment and Design

Assessment of Present State of Knowledge

Designs for potential Phase II efforts to fill gaps noted in present knowledge: Estimated levels of cost/value of information for approaches suggested

Selection Committee for Phase II

* - Deliverable Product

useful assessment of success or failure. This design should estimate the importance, feasibility, methods, and costs of obtaining measurements to test further the assumptions laid out in the framework (where that appears to be necessary).

(6) A model data collection and evaluation design for use with single projects of the type included in the topic area at the state and local level. This represents an adaptation of the same framework developed in (3) to a single, local project.

SUMMARY

Like all agencies, then, LEAA is faced with the need for quick (a few days to a few weeks) answers to specific questions, short-term, (a few months) requirements for the best information available on particular topic areas, and the need for longer term, definitive answers about the efficacy of the underlying assumptions of particular approaches to reducing crime.

At present, the quick answers must in every case be provided by special staff efforts that are often disruptive of longer-term research. The Phase I studies of the National Evaluation Program represent an intentional, designed effort to perform in a few months an assessment of what is being done in a chosen topic area and to ascertain what is presently known about success and failure. Since they are available in a few months, these results can be tailored to upcoming knowledge requirements. If successful, they can, of course, also serve as a sound basis for answering future quick requests for information in a topic area. In addition, each Phase I study assesses the needs for (and costs of) further evaluation and research in the topic area.

By buying its information sequentially, LEAA hopes to have a working knowledge available in the short-term and to be in a position to commit larger blocks of its research and evaluation money to questions where both the requirement for further information has been established and where the value of that further information can be weighed against the estimated costs of acquiring it (Phase II).

The first phase of each NEP topic area investigation might be thought of as a spotlight that can be turned upon particular key areas of the criminal justice system to illuminate what is being done, what is presently known about it, and what time and money will be required to learn more. Our experiment will assess whether this can be accomplished in enough depth and in a short enough time period to also meet the short-term decision-making requirements of the agency.

NOTE

1. Descriptive material about the program in this section has been extracted from various papers developed by the National Institute's NEP Coordinator, Dr. Richard T. Barnes, and Mr. Joe Nay of the Urban Institute, an advisor to the program.

REFERENCES FOR NATIONAL EVALUATION PROGRAM

"The Report of the LEAA Evaluation Policy Task Force"; Draft; March 1, 1974; Law Enforcement Assistance Administration.

"The National Evaluation Program"; July 1974; Gerald M. Caplan, Director, National Institute of Law Enforcement and Criminal Justice; LEAA.

"The National Evaluation Program of the Law Enforcement Assistance Administration"; July 1974; Office of Research Programs; National Institute of Law Enforcement and Criminal Justice; LEAA.

"Work Description for a Phase I Study" under the National Evaluation Program; LEAA/National Institute of Law Enforcement and Criminal Justice; Revised August 1974.

POLICY RESEARCH PLANNING[1]

Bette Silver Mahoney
Director, Office of Research, Evaluation and Data Systems
Office of the Assistant Secretary for Planning and
Evaluation Department of Health, Education and Welfare

Economists believe that rational allocation decisions should be based on the analysis of costs and benefits from alternative decisions in such a fashion as to maximize the returns from the decisions. The difficulties arise not from the maximization principal but usually in the measurement of the returns. Research allocations could also be based on the assessment of returns from alternative possibilities. However, I know of no example where there has been an explicit analysis of the payoffs from different types of research except in the quite limited trade-offs between responses to an RFP or other solicitation for proposals. Here the trade-off usually compares cost and methodological soundness but does not really assess the return from the research. Explicit comparisons with research in other subject areas or even in the same subject area which asks a different question or uses a substantially different methodology are usually not made. This is not to suggest that such comparisons are not implicitly made but rather that no description of the assumptions and assessments are explicitly stated for further comment or examination. I intend to argue that the attempt to analyze better the alternative returns from different types of research, despite its extreme difficulty, might increase the "payoff" from research. Policy analysis should be as much a part of the research process as we argue it should be in other program areas.

Research "quality" is a factor which most reviewers believe can be assessed. By quality here I am referring to "technical quality" or methodological adequacy, the methodological or scientific rigor or merit. Thus, the complaints one hears about having to assess 30 proposals responding to a single RFP are usually complaints about the paper work and not concerns about the difficulties in differentiating the research quality among proposals. Even so, raters vary in their assessment of research quality.[2] In a study supported in part by SRS, one project was rated by 239 reviewers. On a scale where 1 was "Far above average," 2 "Somewhat better than average," 3 "About average," 4 "Somewhat below average," and 5 "Far below average," the mean equaled 2.886 with a standard deviation of 1.209. This suggests that, with a probability of 95%, the project was somewhere between "far above average" and "far below average." No completely satisfactory explanation of this variance has yet emerged. However, rater characteristics, like courses in research methodology and quantitative techniques, explain a significant if small amount of variance. Another important variable in explaining the variance was the order-of-rating the project. Raters who rated the benchmark either second or third tended to be much less strict than those who rated it first. It also appears that there is more agreement among raters on the methodological quality of substandard projects than among the high quality projects.

Although limited to a single agency, a recent study by Minnesota Systems Research found, in a probability sample of 179 of 532 projects considered by staff of the responsible funding agency to have at least some research component, that only 6.7% were completely able to achieve their stated objectives; another 34.1% were judged to hold reasonable promise of doing so in fact of time, resource, or study constraints beyond the investigator's control.[3] Still one proceeds under the assumption that technical quality may be judged and uses sufficient numbers of reviewers to reduce the variance. Research funded in response to broad program solicitations or RFPs is usually chosen by peer review teams which assess "research quality" but only infrequently can make explicit trade-offs based on the policy returns from different research.

Technical quality is a necessary but not a sufficient condition for the good allocation of research funds. The relevance of research project findings is easily as important as methodological quality. To be useful, research should be both of a high technical quality and relevant.

Although assuring high technical quality is not an easy process, it appears to be easier than assuring relevance. Perhaps this is because relevance requires forecasting both the issues that will be important in the future and the outcomes of the research. Although there have been many high quality, relevant research projects, it is my contention that there could be more if we were more systematic in our attempts to make our research relevant as well as of a high quality. I believe that a better analysis of alternatives considered in a broader context would increase our relevance potential.

In considering the spectrum of areas for analysis of research funding, one can view the spectrum as ranging from "Guns and Butter" questions like comparing health, education and welfare funding to the "brand of toothpaste" question which can be compared to the responses to a single RFP. It would be nice to be able to answer the full spectrum of questions. However, we are unlikely to be able to resolve the "Guns and Butter" questions by any satisfactory analytic means currently available to us and the "toothpaste" question which is more likely to be answered may not be broad enough to expand our analytic insight into the choices available. Also, if we fail to analyze the larger issue, we may not correctly establish the criteria even for judging the best toothpaste. The art of analysis may well be the choice of the question to be addressed.

In order to move from generalities, a specific example may be useful. I will draw on research funded under the Poverty Program. This is a subject which has been heavily funded in recent years, where major alternative programs have been proposed, and which I happen to know something about. It is also a subject to which high quality analytic skills have been applied. That it is still an area where we must depend so heavily on the serendipitous nature of research speaks to the problems we have in allocating research funds.

"How do we solve the poverty problem?" is a question which has been seriously addressed by many. Analysis of all of the alternatives suggests potential research topics too numerous to be funded in any short period of time even by a research program as generous as the Poverty Research Program. A listing of programs proposed in the first National Anti-Poverty Plan prepared in October 1965 suggested a large number of areas of anti-poverty potential: Jobs including Public Employment, Work Experience, Programs for Youth (Job Corps and Neighborhood Youth Corps) and Mobility Programs; Education;

Health; Rural and Urban Programs including Economic Development; Housing; Social Action Programs like CAP and VISTA; Legal Assistance; and Transfer Programs. The research topics suggested by these programs are numerous even though the list of possible programs was limited to those which it was felt we knew enough about to put in place. If we were to extend that list to all potential programs and to include also those researchable ideas relating to basic causes and measurement issues, the list would clearly be staggering. Explicitly attempting to assess the trade-offs among topics is just an impossible task.

However, it is possible to think more about trade-offs as one moves down the scale of generality. Thus, for example, the early OEO policy-makers determined that a negative income tax was the best form for an income maintenance program to take. Even assuming that the analytic base for the negative income tax decision was sufficient (i.e., it was not necessary to explore childrens' allowances, other demogrants, wage subsidies, guaranteed employment, etc. more thoroughly), there are a number of questions of implementation, costs, and impact which should be addressed in a new program proposal. However, one expects to refine such estimates as one proceeds and such has been the case. It is as we get to the narrower questions that it becomes feasible to make the trade-offs between research approaches.

For example, cost estimates for any new program depend upon a set of base statistics and a model which incorporates behavioral assumptions and makes projections of behavior as it affects costs in the future. Reducing the variance in the errors of such estimates may be highly desirable (although there is some not insignificant range of error that we clearly can live with.) For the negative income tax, the more sophisticated estimates of costs were determined as early as 1968 by using a microfile containing income and demographic characteristics, aging the population and income estimates, and then simulating the continuation of the existing program and comparing it with a simulation of the new program. Clearly a number of assumptions about behavior like the changes in labor force participation of participants, alterations in family composition, program participation by the eligible population, and affecting behavior like the economic conditions prevailing in the future were made. Frequently, these assumptions were made with little real knowledge about what alters behavior. Concern about the necessity of making some of these assumptions led to additional research. It is at this point that some analysis of the impact of additional research on the cost estimates would have seemed appropriate. Drawing upon the information we had about some of the behaviorial relations, it would have been possible to assess what the refinement of our estimates of these relations would do to reduce the variance of our cost estimates. An assessment of the cost of producing information (i.e., the research costs) to reduce the variance could then be compared to the returns from this reduction; and, after consideration of all of the unmeasurable benefits (including those not related to answering the cost question), a research agenda could have been selected.

In fact, a research agenda was selected and implicitly some of these concerns were incorporated. The agenda included a heavy expenditure which addressed the behavioral question on the labor force participation of participants, particularly males (the income maintenance experiments as well as a number of econometric studies using existing data), improvements to the projection model (including a number of alterations to those sectors upon which behavior is dependent like economic conditions), and some small improvements in the data base. Parenthetically, I should note that documentation of this agenda is almost impossible to find. I suspect that if an explicit assessment had been developed to model the costs and returns of research projects as they affected our ability to reduce the variance of our cost estimates for a negative income tax our agenda would have been different. For example, the statistical base for most of the estimates is the *March Current Population Survey*. Estimates of the difference between the total amount of welfare income collected from the CPS and the benchmark total are as high as 30%. Improving the income estimates is neither an easy or inexpensive task. However, even without an explicit model for allocating research, it seems likely that some of the $70 million which will eventually be spent on the income maintenance experiments might have been more fruitfully spent on improving the income statistics base. Another example, of an assumption which was more likely to alter the variance of our cost estimates but which we still do not understand, is the extent of program participation by the eligible population. During much of the recent income maintenance history, the participation rates of potential AFDC recipients has altered quite dramatically. It is a change which we are not now able to explain. What is also clear is that our initial estimates of the SSI program are off either because we over-estimated the participation rates of the potential SSI population or because we understated that potential population or both. Actual participation in the program is significantly lower than our initial projections. Should not our allocation of research funds have been more directed towards this question?

Even when we look at narrower questions, we frequently do not examine the alternatives available. For example, a question which we have expended large amounts of research funds to answer is "What would be the labor force impact of various tax rates and guarantee levels in income maintenance schemes?" Three alternative research approaches come to mind: (1) an experiment with controlled variation; (2) econometric modeling of existing large data sources; and (3) evaluation of existing programs. The costs of each of the alternative approaches is different as are the potential returns. None of the alternatives is likely to give an answer which cannot be challenged on the grounds that the real program might produce different results. However, of the three research approaches, only the first two have been thoroughly explored, and I know of no analysis which suggests that the costs of the third are so high as to make such exploration infeasible. For example, at the time the income maintenance experiments were being designed there were programs in place for male-headed families in a few sites which might have been evaluated. If what you need to know is only whether or not large-scale withdrawal will occur, such evaluation is feasible.

Why don't we explore alternatives more carefully before we fund research activities? Why don't documents presenting research strategies based on an exploration of alternatives exist? There are several reasons that I can think of. One is that such documents are difficult to write, and frequently the press of getting the funds out or managing existing projects or doing the program analyses just does not permit time to be spent on the less pressing needs—like long-range strategies. A second reason is that much of our research is oriented towards professional and academic research and interests. Thus, the labor force participation question is more interesting to economists than improving our statistics, and economists were organizing much of the research. Peer review in some ways provides the extreme of this. What is likely to be funded is what the peers find relevant and useful—not necessarily what appears to be useful to the government analyst. Another is that much of our research funding is reactive based on unsolicited proposals. Perhaps most important, there are not requirements or incentives to do such analyses. Neither the requirements of the competitive procurement process nor any penalties for an inefficient use of research funds exist, and it may be that without such incentives and a few good examples there will not be any in the future.

NOTES

1. Paper prepared for conference on Social Programs Evaluation, sponsored by Abt Associates, September 24, 1974.

2. Willy DeGeyndt, *Methodological Adequacy of Federal R&D Projects,* Minnesota Systems Research, Inc. March, 1974. "Analysis of Rater Variance" by Jan Parkinson.

3. Minnesota Systems Research, Inc. December 1973 executive summary, p. 1. and Appendix Table 10.

Discussants: *Daniel Bell, Harvard University*
Joseph Newhouse, Rand Corporation
William Pollin, National Institute on Drug Abuse
Albert Biderman, Bureau of Social Science Research Inc.
Clark C. Abt, Abt Associates Inc.
Daniel Bell, Harvard University
Harvey Averch, National Science Foundation

BELL: My comments are going to be addressed almost entirely to Clark Abt's paper. It is a measure of our friendship that I will be as "harsh" as I am on that paper. What I find wrong is the fact that Clark—who is a much wiser man—takes an engineering approach to the whole question of evaluation and research, even to the extent of trying to get production functions of research based on matrices, utilities, etc. Is life like that? It reminds me of the time that George Bernard Shaw was being taken through the plant of THE NEW YORK TIMES. He saw typewriters typing, the teletype moving, the linotype jumping back and forth. Taken downstairs, he saw the paper coming out all neat and clean, and said, "My God, you mean to tell me all this is premeditated?"

I am going to make three points, which stress what might be called the non-rational considerations in evaluation research. The entire discussion here concentrates on so-called rational, or what might be called engineering, or even economic, approaches. Yet it strikes me that to anybody who has ever been engaged, either in watching Washington or looking at policy research, or trying to do it, non-rational considerations become almost overriding.

My first point deals with the meaning of semantics and symbols. Let me take an anecdote and then give you an apropos situation. The anecdote is that of a caliph who calls in a soothsayer and says, "Read me my fortune. If you read it well, I will reward you well." And the soothsayer looks into the crystal ball, and he says, "Sire, great news: all your relatives will die before you." And the caliph says, "Kill that man." And he calls another soothsayer and says, "Tell me my fortune. Tell it well; I'll reward you well. But I warn you: someone has already told me my fortune and if yours is the reverse of what his said, I will know you are a liar." The man looks into the crystal ball and says, "Sire, great news: you will outlive all your relatives." He says, "Reward that man."

Semantics and symbols often count more than the literal fact. A large portion of the welfare rolls in the country have been substantially reduced because of legislation—the blind and the disabled have been moved over to Social Security. The payments now come from Social Security rather than Welfare. Does that mean a change? It is semantic and symbolic; we no longer have people on welfare; we have people on Social Security. What is the meaning of that kind of policy and social change? That is to me an important illustration of the role of semantics and symbols.

The second point is the relation between economic rationality of the kind that Ms. Mahoney was talking about—maximization, allocation, etc., and what might be called the political rationality. Some years ago there was a sanitation commissioner in New York City who wanted to establish a good record so he could run for mayor of the city. Previously, when there were heavy snowfalls, the commissioners would hire trucks in which to load the snow and dump it into the river. The new commissioner had the snow pushed into the middle of the streets where the taxis ran over it and turned it to slush. It turned out that the drycleaning bills of the people in the city went up substantially because they were splashed by the slush, but the tax bills were reduced because fewer trucks were used to carry the slush. What is the more rational method—the economic rationality or the political rationality? In the first instance, we have greater "efficiency" and lower costs. In the second a "randomized" tax on individuals and lower municipal costs. Do we always want "economic" rationality?

The third point is on the semantics of the word evaluation. I keep hearing the word evaluation, but I find myself dulled by the repetition of the term. There seems to be an inability to distinguish between evaluation relating to facts and to values. The distinction is important if we make clear what it is we are evaluating. Take a particular illustration, the question of workers' discontent. How does one evaluate it in research. There is a question of choice in the problem. Now you can discuss the problem in terms of productivity or speed-up. In one case it means productivity; that is, the viewpoint of the manager. Or it is speed-up; this is the point of view of the worker. What is the appropriate choice of term? The problem is *not* one of fact but formulation. You can call it either a restriction of output or a fair day's work. In this example, you have problems of valuation and evaluations which are given not by any single objective standard, but by contrasting viewpoints.

NEWHOUSE: I think that from the point of view of people like Harvey Averch there are some real issues to be faced in how to allocate research and development (R&D) monies. I think the issues that are probably most productive to look at, at least for now, are issues of process. There is a tendency, I think, among people at this kind of conference to treat the evaluation of the evaluation, if you will, as a kind of gut issue—if you cannot evaluate the evaluation, how can you hold yourself out to the world as being able to evaluate whatever it is that the world is doing. That reduction is clearly a little simplistic, because there are some things that are easier to evaluate than others.

There are problems in trying to look at what evaluation is, what the output is, and in trying to understand the relationship of the process that allocates R&D funds to the results. What is the type of support that is most productive or, more precisely, what is the nexus of support? Project grants, program grants, institutional support, contracts? Associated with that, what is the right kind of distribution of term size in the research and development industry? What is the optimal length of support? This would impact on how much overhead there is in the system in terms of writing proposals, as well as what kind of incentives there are to the researchers to produce. There is a question of what the process is for reviewing what you get. Do you review with an in-house review?

I would like to conclude by talking about a study that one of my colleagues, Grace Carter, has done that addresses some of the issues we are discussing and, in particular, addresses the problem of research resource allocation at the National Institute of Health. The major bugaboo, of course, in doing this kind of work is what one assumes about what the output measure is. In this case the measure used is a citation index; that is to say, the number of citations to articles produced under the grant, on the assumption that if articles are cited they are of use to the scientific community. I think that may be about as well as one can do at the present time in getting an output measure. This work has led to two conclusions that I think are noteworthy. It does give support to the notion that technical quality can be assessed, and I think with considerably more reliability than other speakers implied.

Second, the original study section priority score on the research application correlated significantly with the citation index, indicating that study sections ratings were not a random process. Even more interesting is the subset (which is almost all) of the grants that come back for renewal. The correlation was even stronger between the renewal priority score and the citation index, indicating that study sections were objectively rating contributions to the scientific litera-ture. This study suggests that the allocation of research funds is subject to quantitative evaluation.

POLLIN: After listening to the papers today I would like to describe three problem areas which I find the evaluation community has failed to conceptualize adequately and to come to grips with.

The first one is derived from a paper which many of you are familiar with—John Platt's eloquent paper in *Science* some years ago in which he made the persuasive suggestion that one of the major dynamics in pushing any scientific theory ahead is actually the accumulation of negative findings in that part of the research. It is this accumulation of negative findings that shuts off fallacious hypotheses and wasteful avenues of research and enable one to decide where to go with ones' efforts. I do not hear in any of the evaluations any suggestion as to a method for putting proper value to a negative rather than a positive finding.

A second point is that I think that there are rather persuasive studies which suggest that a huge preponderance of truly breakthrough findings have, in most cases, come either directly from, or one or two steps removed from, sets of findings. Those kinds of findings which have resulted in the development of antibiotics, tranquilizers, Salk vaccine, etc., really make huge differences in our ability to deal with major medical issues. Most cases either come directly from or one or two steps removed from sets of findings wherein an investigator is trying to go here and answer question A, and almost accidently observes relationship B. How do we set up evaluation C, taking into account this empiric fact as to how progress has indeed been made in this country?

A third point which concerns me is the question of practicality and trade off concepts. Clark Abt's paper discussed the situation where half of one's data are reliable and valid, and suggests that you can multiply one-half by one-half and come up with a quarter. There is an implication there that evaluation research is subject to the same kinds of constraints that other high quality research is subject to. If any significant part of your data are not reliable and not valid, you end up with a partial result or you end up with the other situation which Clark Abt alluded to in his paper—garbage in, garbage out. The questions as to whether poor research is better than no research or actually a lot worse than no research deserves considerable attention.

One last point I would like to make refers to Joe Newhouse's question concerning the use of citation indexes as one way of evaluating research. We were very interested in this possibility, and we still think it has much to offer. However, when we looked at some fields that we were very familiar with we found that there were two categories of papers which tended very frequently to end up in the top 5% of most frequently cited papers. Papers which so infuriate and exercise a research community that a great many people set out to disprove the claim tend to be cited frequently. The second type of paper which receives a very high number of citations is a paper which has made some relatively minor but useful methodological suggestion. The contribution to the field may be quite far removed from the frequency of the citation.

The last point which I would like to make is a request to the evaluation community to consider very seriously not only the advisability but the necessity of trying to break down the sociology of the process as it now exists so that one has teams of evaluators looking at products of a research community. It seems to me that there are tremendous and inevitable problems that flow from that kind of a situation and that it is almost essential that there be communications between the researchers and the evaluating team if the work is to be both productive and realistic.

BIDERMAN: If we take at all seriously and literally the word "Social" in the title of this Conference, a large part of the discussion that has taken place is close to irrelevant in that it has been concerned with individual matters, not social ones. It is paradoxical that social research should be dominated by fundamentally non-social value orientations because our enterprise—research—is itself directed toward producing a type of good that has in ideal form every one of the features of a "public good"—that is, products that diverge from classic economic goods or those conceived in other individualistic models of rational choice. Harvey Averch, however, has just happily suggested several kinds of evaluation research that could be directed to social problems, as distinguished from problems of individuals—for example, the regulation of energy.

Interestingly, evaluations of programs dealing with individuals seem more often to go in the direction of finding social system costs and benefits as contrasted with evaluations of truly social (or societal) programs which more exclusively look at costs and benefits to concrete individuals rather than social system consequences.

The important point is that whenever we are dealing with *social* research or with *social* problems, we are inherently involved in realms that fit poorly the calculus of rationality which is applicable to individually divisible goods and services. A social calculus should apply better both to what we do and to what we are studying. But since we lack adequate rationalities for dealing with social or public values, we tend to convert problems into the form to which the rationality of private values and purposes can be applied. Evaluation research itself tends to be institutionally structured as if it were a commodity in which personified consumers buy it from a market created by producers—a structure which doesn't fit the situation very well. The product of research—knowledge—tends to be valuable as a public good in inverse ratio to the degree that it is (or can be made) valuable as a private good. There are a host of reasons for this being the case, but note that from the science standpoint a particularly relevant property is that knowledge is important and useful to the extent that it is generalized—that is, to the degree that it is nobody's peculiar business because it is of value to so many people (if not everybody) and to so many situations (ideally every situation). For someone in an agency to allocate funds to getting knowledge, however, there must be the rationale of special and peculiar interest.

Knowledge is also valuable to the extent that it forms part of some integrated system. There is a problem involved in tracing the value of some increment to knowledge because the value of some new element is difficult to isolate from that of all other elements of the system with which it interacts. The measure of performance is the performance of the system of knowledge, not its elements in isolation. The same is true of adequate measures of the new elements or changes in social systems. It is this social systemic orientation that is so often missing from evaluation research. Further, both the thought structure and the institutional structure of project and program evaluation discourage this orientation. I regret the current domination of the allocations of research effort in Washington in the concept "evaluation research" because of its thrust toward specificity, rather than generality—toward work undertaken for a specific client on a specific project evaluated in terms of specific outputs delivered to specific individuals.

We cannot satisfactorily evaluate our own activity, scientific study, that way any more than any other form of essentially social effort. The reference count criterion, for example, ignores the fact that the most important contributions to science are ones that do not require referencing when they are used, since they become part of the universally accepted, integrated, familiar, taken-for-granted body of knowledge and thought. One need not reference (nor even know of the existence of) Napier or Kelvin each time one uses logs or absolute temperature, nor Merton every time one uses the word or idea, "serendipity."

But knowing the defects of the rationales we use does not automatically suggest superior ones. So, while I can show many ways in which the assumptions underlying the use of open competitive bidding as a means for choosing among evaluation study designs and performers are false assumptions, it is not an easy task to suggest alternative rationales that are equally easily applied, comprehended and defended.

ABT: I would just like to make a comment about the split I see developing here between Deutscher, Biderman, and Bell who are involved more or less in the process evaluation side of things, and Keith Marvin, the statisticians and engineers who are on the quantitative analysis side. I think it is a mistake for us to feel they exist as mutually exclusive points of view. I agree with Dan Bell that anecdotes are the best form of current knowledge, especially in terms of information transmissions. If we could communicate our knowledge or findings in the form of deeply memorable humorous anecdotes it would be great, but most of us do not have the art to do that. Much of the time we are unable to translate the salient issues into elegant mathematical inspiration. Most of our work is somewhere in between; I do not think we should throw out either dramatic extreme for the sake of emphasizing the ability of the other.

John Tukey made a remark about the importance of analyzing goals of studies—these are complementary views of research—and we have all kinds of history of serendipitous findings from the more synthetically oriented anecdotally inclined scientists who have had a kind of synoptic vision of a new idea and were not terribly neat about working it out, and others worked by neat analytical steps who maybe ran into something that way. The point is we should not think of these as opposites, except for dramatic illustration, but part of the whole spectrum of available evaluation research tools.

BELL: I must insist on the reality of a split. The point is that I do not believe social science is like natural science.

AVERCH: I approach this discussion as a research funder and would therefore have to agree with Joe Newhouse that we need to do more analysis and evaluation of what we are getting from our research. NSF itself has embarked on a number of experiments to evaluate both from a technical and policy point of view. That whole technology needs to be developed. On the other hand, I have to agree with Professor Bell that R&D funding, if not an irrational process, is a political or bureaucratic process and what has come to concern me especially in an era of tight budgets is the kind of justifications that were used by OMB and in the Congress for $&D. I do not think it is sufficient anymore to say that we got all these serendipitous results for all these dollars. I think in the political arena we need better justifications, better arguments—in an essentially political process. Congressmen have a sense of R&D researchers as not being of much practical use. Much more work needs to be done to demonstrate use.

AUTHOR/TITLE INDEX

Note: The following lists (in alphabetical order) the names of all authors who have contributed to this book and the titles of all the articles presented. The numbers supplied indicate the page on which each article begins.

LIST OF PARTICIPANTS

Note: The following is a list of those who participated in the conference on Social Programs Evaluation sponsored by Abt Associates Inc., from which materials for this book were prepared.

Dr. Clark C. Abt
Abt Associates Inc.

Dr. Darrell K. Adams
U.S. Bureau of Reclamation
Engineering and Research Center

Mr. Gregory J. Ahart
U.S. General Accounting Office

Dr. Rae Archibald
Rand Corporation

Professor Chris Argyris
Harvard University Graduate School of
    Education
Gutman Library

Professor Kenneth Arrow
Harvard University

Dr. Harvey Averch
National Science Foundation

Dr. Richard Barnes
National Institute for Law Enforcement and
    Criminal Justice

Dr. Norman Beckman
Congressional Research Service
Library of Congress

Professor Daniel Bell
Harvard University

Professor Ralph Berry
Harvard School of Public Health

Dr. Albert D. Biderman
Bureau of Social Science Research Inc.

Dr. Martha Blaxall
National Academy of Sciences

Professor Anthony E. Boardman
Fels Center of Government

Dr. Aaron Bodin
U.S. Department of Labor

Mr. Wilbur D. Campbell
U.S. General Accounting Office
Resources and Economic Development Division

Dr. William Capron
John F. Kennedy School of Government

Dr. Nancy Chisholm
U.S. Department of Housing and Urban
    Development
Office of Policy Development and Research

Dr. Marvin Gerry Cline
Abt Associates Inc.

Dr. Robert Coates
Harvard Law School
Center for Criminal Justice

Dr. Jerry Cromwell
Abt Associates Inc.

Dr. Joseph M. Cronin
Secretary of Educational Affairs
Commonwealth of Massachusetts

Dr. Lois-ellin Datta
National Institute of Education
Career Education Program

Dean Otto A. Davis
Carnegie-Mellon University
School of Urban and Public Affairs

Dr. Robert Dendy
National Drug Abuse Training Center

Professor Irwin Deutscher
The University of Akron

Mr. William Diepenbrock
U.S. Department of Health, Education, and
     Welfare
Office of Child Development

Dr. John W. Evans
U.S. Office of Education

Professor James Fennessey
The Johns Hopkins University

Mr. Harley Frankel
U.S. Department of Health, Education, and
     Welfare
Office of Child Development

Professor Bernard Frieden
Director, MIT-Harvard Joint Center for
     Urban Studies

Dr. Alton Frye
The Institute for Congress

Professor John P. Gilbert
Harvard University

Dr. Thomas K. Glennan
National Institute of Education

Mr. Norman Gold
National Institute of Education

Dr. Robert B. Goldmann
Ford Foundation

Mr. Quinton Gordon
U.S. Department of Housing and Urban
     Development
Office of Policy Development and Research

Dr. John Greacen
National Institute of Law Enforcement and
     Criminal Justice

Dr. Marcia Guttentag
Harvard Graduate School of Education

Dr. Stefan Halper
Office of Management and Budget

Dr. Kenneth F. Holbert
U.S. Department of Housing and Urban
    Development
Office of Economic Opportunity

Dr. Peter House
Environmental Protection Agency

Dr. Mats Hultin
International Bank for Reconstruction and
    Development

Mrs. Victoria Jaycox
National Institute for Law Enforcement and
    Criminal Justice

Mr. David Kershaw
Mathematica, Inc.

Mr. Randall Kinder
U.S. Department of Housing and Urban
    Development
Office of Policy Development and Research

Mr. Laurence Kivens
Evaluation Magazine

Professor Norman Kurtz
Brandeis University

Professor Paul Lazarsfeld
Columbia University

Professor Richard Light
Harvard University Graduate School of Education

Dr. Sylvain Lourie
UNESCO

Dr. Ira Lowry
Rand Corporation

Dr. Bette Mahoney
U.S. Department of Health, Education, and
  Welfare

Dr. Keith E. Marvin
U.S. General Accounting Office

Mr. Garry McDaniels
National Institute of Education

Mr. Keith Miles
National Institute of Law Enforcement and
  Criminal Justice

Dr. James Molitor
National Drug Abuse Training Center

Professor Alexander Mood
University of California
Public Policy Research Corporation

Dr. Frederick Mosteller
Harvard University

Dr. Delbert T. Myren
U.S. Department of State
Office of Research and Institutional Grants

Dr. George Nash
Westchester County Community Mental
  Health Services
White Plains, New York

Dr. Charles Nelson
Rand Corporation

Dr. Joseph Newhouse
Rand Corporation

Commissioner Constance B. Newman
U.S. Consumer Product Safety Commission

Dr. Helen Nowlis
U.S. Office of Education

Professor Mancur Olson
University of Maryland

Professor Arthur Solomon
MIT-Harvard Joint Center for Urban Studies

Dr. Walter Stellwagen
Abt Associates Inc.

Professor Daniel L. Stufflebeam
Western Michigan University

Dr. Michael Timpane
Rand Corporation

Ms. Alair Townsend
Research Director, U.S. House of
    Representatives Subcommittee on Fiscal Policy

Professor Edward Tufte
Princeton University

Dr. John Tukey
Bell Laboratories

Mr. Daniel Tunstall
U.S. Office of Management and Budgets

Dr. Joseph Wholey
The Urban Institute

Professor Paul Wortman
Northwestern University

Professor Adam Yarmolinsky
University of Massachusetts

Professor Norman E. Zinberg
Harvard Medical School

BIOGRAPHICAL NOTES

Note: The following provides current short biographical notations on all those who participated in the conference on Social Programs Evaluation sponsored by Abt Associates Inc., from which materials for this book were prepared.

Dr. Clark C. Abt is founder and president of Abt Associates Inc., a social science research firm located in Cambridge, Massachusetts.

Dr. Kenneth J. Arrow is James Bryant Conant University Professor of Economics at Harvard University.

Dr. Harvey A. Averch is Deputy Assistant Director for Analysis and Planning, Research Applications Directorate, National Science Foundation.

Dr. Richard T. Barnes is presently at the National Institute of Law Enforcement and Criminal Justice.

Dr. Norman Beckman is Acting Director of the Congressional Research Service of the Library of Congress.

Dr. Daniel Bell is Professor of Sociology at Harvard University.

Dr. Ralph E. Berry is Professor of Economics at Harvard University School of Public Health.

Dr. Martha Blaxall was Senior Professional Associate at the Institute of Medicine, and is currently Branch Chief, Health Insurance Research Study, HEW.

Dr. Anthony E. Boardman is Assistant Professor of Public Policy Analysis, School of Public and Urban Policy, University of Pennsylvania.

Dr. William M. Capron is Associate Dean, and Senior Lecturer on Political Economy, John F. Kennedy School of Government, Harvard University.

Dr. Marvin G. Cline is a Senior Scientist at Abt Associates Inc.

Dr. Jerry Cromwell is Senior Economist and project director at Abt Associates Inc.

Dr. Joseph M. Cronin is State Superintendent of Education of Illinois.

Dr. Lois-ellen Datta is Assistant Director for Education and Work at the National Institute of Education.

Dr. Irwin Deutscher is Professor of Sociology at The University of Akron.

Dr. John W. Evans is Assistant Commissioner of Education and Director of the Office of Planning, Budgeting, and Evaluation of the Department of Health, Education, and Welfare.

Dr. James Fennessey is Assistant Professor at the Department of Social Relations, The John Hopkins University.

Dr. John Gilbert, Senior Staff Statistician, Harvard Computing Center, Harvard University.

Norman Gold is Director of Experimental Schools at the National Institute of Education.

Dr. Mats G. Hultin is a senior advisor at the World Bank.

Dr. Paul Lazarsfeld was University Professor of Sociology at the University of Pittsburgh.

Dr. Richard Light is Professor of Education and Public Policy at Harvard University.

Dr. Sylvain Lourie is UNESCO Senior Educational Advisor based in Guatemala.

Dr. Ira S. Lowry is a senior staff member of the Management Sciences Department of the Rand Corporation.

Dr. Bette S. Mahoney is Director of the Office of Research, Evaluation and Data Systems, Office of the Assistant Secretary for Planning and Evaluation, Department of Health, Education, and Welfare.

Keith E. Marvin is Associate Director in the Financial and General Management Studies Division of the General Accounting Office.

Dr. Alexander Mood is Professor of Administration at the University of California.

Dr. Frederick Mosteller is Professor of Mathematical Statistics at Harvard University.

Dr. George Nash is Deputy Director for Evaluation and Research at Westchester County Community Mental Health Services, White Plains, New York.

Dr. Joseph P. Newhouse is a Senior Staff Economist at the Rand Corporation.

Constance B. Newman was Commissioner and Vice Chairman of the Consumer Product Safety Commission; she is currently Assistant Secretary for Consumer Affairs and Regulatory Functions, Department of Housing and Urban Development.

Dr. Helen Nowlis is Director, Division of Alcohol and Drug Education, Health and Nutrition Programs, United States Office of Education.

Dr. Mancur Olson, Jr. is Professor of Economics at the University of Maryland.

Dr. William Pollin is the Director of the Division of Research at the National Institute on Drug Abuse.

Dr. Andrew Porter is the Associate Director, Basic Skills Group, at the National Institute of Education and a Professor of Educational Psychology at Michigan State University.

Dr. Henry W. Riecken is Professor of Behavioral Sciences, School of Medicine, University of Pennsylvania.

Dr. Alice M. Rivlin, an economist, formerly a Senior Fellow at the Brookings Institute, is currently director of the Congressional Budget Office.

Dr. Mary Rowe, an economist who is Special Assistant to the President and Chancellor for Women and Work, Massachusetts Institute of Technology.

Dr. Michael Scriven is Professor in the Department of Philosophy at the University of California, Berkeley.

Dr. John C. Sessler is a Senior Program Analyst at the Drug Abuse Council, Inc.

Mildred B. Shapiro is the Director of the Bureau of Economic Analysis, New York State Department of Health and Adjunct Professor of Health Economics at Union College.

Dr. Eleanor Sheldon is the President of the Social Science Research Council.

Dr. Marshall Savidge Smith is an Acting Assistant Director, National Institute of Education and an Associate Professor at the Graduate School of Education of Harvard University.

Dr. Walter Stellwagen is a Vice President of Abt Associates Inc.

Dr. P. Michael Timpane is a Senior Researcher at the Rand Corporation and coordinates activities of the Brookings' Panel on Social Experimentation.

Alair A. Townsend is Research Director of the Subcommittee on Fiscal Policy of the Joint Economic Committee.

Dr. Edward Tufte is Professor of Public Affairs, Princeton University and Adjunct Professor of Law, New York University Law School.

Dr. John W. Tukey is Associate Executive Director, Research-

Communications Principles Division of Bell Laboratories and Professor of Statistics, Princeton University.

Dr. Joseph Wholey is Director of Program Evaluation Studies at the Urban Institute.

Dr. Paul M. Wortman is Associate Director of the Northwestern University Methodology and Evaluation Research Program and a Senior Research Associate in Psychology.

Dr. Adam Yarmolinsky is Ralph Waldo Emerson University Professor, University of Massachusetts.

Dr. Norman E. Zinberg is Associate Clinical Professor of Psychiatry, Harvard Medical School.

EPILOGUE

The materials published in this volume are really as much about the effectiveness and efficiency of *social research* applied to social policies and programs, as they are about *social programs* themselves. This book might as easily have been called "The Evaluation of Evaluations of Social Programs," were that not such an awkward title. These evaluations of evaluations were often very critical. Implicit throughout the discussions is the widely shared concern for impact and productivity, as well as the suspicion that evaluation research in particular and social research in general have not achieved their full potential. There is energetic disagreement, however, about the reasons.

Many critics of government social programs and their evaluations—social scientists, legislators, and federal executives—are skeptical about the usefulness of much of the research. Some liberals see the investment in evaluation research as a diversion of resources from the government's social action programs at best, or a termination threat to the programs evaluated at worst, particularly because the Nixon administration made substantial use of program evaluation to justify the reduction or non-expansion of some important education, health, and housing programs. Some conservative critics feel that evaluations are too positively biased and wasteful, and that social experiments may stimulate unrealistic aspirations. Critical social scientists feel that large government investment in social experiments and evaluation research could corrupt the intellectual independence of some researchers, could divert resources from basic, primarily academic research, and could be used by the government to justify limiting or reducing social reforms.

The advocates of social experiments and evaluation research within the social research community argue that it is the only rational approach to better social policy and program decisions. The roughly half billion dollars a year spent for this research and development is considered an unusually small percentage of the $200 billion a year the

U.S. government now spends on social programs. New kinds of research always have many failures, but it is argued that the small percentage of successes more than pay for them. The probability of such social research alleviating our social problems appears greater than any alternative investments to its advocates. Social problems are so complex that the typical government ad hoc legislative and administrative responses are believed to be wasteful when not informed by scientific evaluations and experiments.

This argument about the value of government social programs evaluations and social experiments in the United States is of historical importance. If the critics have their way, even though the advocates of social research are right, opportunities for social improvement will be lost. Alternatively, if the critics are correct but the advocates prevail, at best we will continue to waste the funds expended and at worst the inadequate evaluation research will have a mismanaging influence on social programs, wasting many more billions and stirring up yet more social and political dissatisfaction.

Enormous national potential benefits and costs are involved, whichever way the argument is decided. There has been a lot of argument but very little research devoted to assessing the *overall* benefits and costs of all this policy-oriented social research, evaluation research, and social experimentation. Critics and advocates have cited a few case studies and some scholars have reached tentative general conclusions on the basis of small samples of selected case studies.* These are helpful, but possibly because of the very enormity of the task, there have been no known attempts to evaluate the *overall* benefits and costs of U.S. applied social research, evaluations, and experiments on public policy issues. Without some objective data on the *overall* benefits and costs, one fears that this crucial issue will be decided on an ideological basis that will not be in the highest public interest because advocates or critics can always select a few unrepresentative examples to support their views.

The problem is of course enormously difficult. Some 500 new social programs were legislated and implemented in the U.S. during the late

---

*See, for example, Averch, 1972; Banfield, 1974; Bernstein, 1975; Campbell, 1969, 1972; Cohen, 1973, 1975; Coleman, 1972; Freeman, 1975; Glennan, 1974, 1976; Gorham, 1972; Caplan, 1975; Lazarsfeld, 1974, 1967; Levitan, 1975; Light, 1974, 1975; McLaughlin, 1975; Moynihan, 1973; Mosteller, 1975; Pelz, 1975; Plotnick, 1975; Riecken, 1975; Rossi, 1969, 1972; Simon, 1975; Skidmore, 1975; Weiss, 1972.

1960s. There are literally thousands of social programs evaluations operating in the U.S. at any particular time. The impacts of the findings of social evaluations and experiments on government policy decisions, program decisions, and program administration may be delayed from months to decades. If we do not know the lead times from when evaluations deliver their findings to when (or if) they are applied and the results of that application become discernible, then it is difficult to determine whether the quality of social programs in 1975 is the result of evaluations and experiments completed in 1974, 1972, 1965, or 1955, or some, all, or none of these. The problem of attributing policy impacts to research results, and subsequently, attributing social impacts to policies and programs, involves major theoretical and data problems. We do not yet know how to account for the relative impact of politics, the economy, and demographic changes which may totally overwhelm and obscure the effects of program evaluations.

The contributors to this book (as well as the other participants in the conference), almost all of whom are expert practitioners of policy-oriented social research and evaluation, expressed at least the following hypotheses for the less than ideal relationship between evaluations and program productivity: flawed research designs, ineffective communication and application of findings to policy audiences, inability of social researchers to meet the relevance, timeliness, and budgetary requirements of policy research, inadequate resources and inefficient resource allocation, lack of sufficient continuity and quality of research supervision in government, and inefficient or excessive (depending on one's point of view) dependence on large scale social experiments.

The conference, and this report of it, offer some unusually candid discussions in the intellectual history of that intersection of government administration, social policy, evaluation research, social science and social experimentation that we call policy-oriented social research. In the nearly two years since the conference, there is evidence of increasing attention to all of these problems of social programs evaluation, and many of us understand them better as a result of this mutual effort.

The large-scale social experiments and their evaluations for which so many of us at the conference expressed the highest hopes have encountered severe opposition in Congress. The multi-million dollar costs and five-to-ten year wait for results of the larger social experiments in education, health, housing, and income maintenance have incurred the impatience of budget-cutting legislators. Apparently not all Congresspersons share the view expressed here and shared by many of us that the potential benefits of large-scale social experiments far outweigh the costs.

There is a developing confrontation between the needs and constraints of government social policy and the needs of policy-oriented social research that was remarkably anticipated in many of the discussions in this volume. The disjunctions of time horizons, expectations for research findings, and standards of research process between many government policy audiences and social researchers, have increased in the last two years. The social research community of both producers and consumers must effectively address the issues raised here, by research on itself and by the reform of itself. Such activities are growing, and the discussions reported here may contribute impetus and information to what is likely to be a salutary self-corrective process. The emerging evaluation research community, drawn together from government, universities, and independent research organizations by a common interest in scientifically improving social programs, will take the problem from here.

Clark C. Abt

Cambridge, Massachusetts
October 1976

INDEX